The end-of-century experience is generating intense interest among contemporary critics. *Cultural politics at the fin de siècle* scrutinizes ways in which current conflicts of 'race', class and gender have their origins in the cultural politics of the last *fin de siècle*, whose influence stretched from the 1880s, when economic depression signalled the end of Britain's role as 'the workshop of the world', to 1914 when world war accelerated imperial decline. This collaborative venture by new and established scholars includes discussion of the New Woman, the reconstruction of masculinities, feminism and empire. The imperialist theme is pursued in essays on Yeats and Ireland, Gilbert and Sullivan, and the figure of the vampire. The rise of socialism and psychoanalysis, and the relationship between nascent modernism and late twentieth-century postmodernism are also addressed in this radical account.

CULTURAL POLITICS AT
THE *FIN DE SIÈCLE*

CULTURAL POLITICS AT THE *FIN DE SIÈCLE*

EDITED BY

SALLY LEDGER

University of the West of England, Bristol

AND

SCOTT McCRACKEN

University of Salford

CAMBRIDGE
UNIVERSITY PRESS

Published by the Press Syndicate of the University of Cambridge
The Pitt Building, Trumpington Street, Cambridge CB2 1RP
40 West 20th Street, New York, NY 10011-4211, USA
10 Stamford Road, Oakleigh, Melbourne 3166, Australia

First published 1995

Printed in Great Britain at the University Press, Cambridge

A catalogue record for this book is available from the British Library

Library of Congress cataloguing in publication data

Cultural politics at the fin de siècle / edited by Sally Ledger and Scott McCracken.
p.   cm.
Includes bibliographical references and index.
ISBN 0 521 44385 7 (hardback)
ISBN 0 521 48499 5 (paperback)
1. English literature – 19th century – History and criticism.   2. Literature and society –
Great Britain – History – 19th century.   3. Great Britain – History – Victoria, 1837–1901.
4. Great Britain – Civilization – 19th century.   5. Social problems in literature.
6. Psychoanalysis and literature.   I. Ledger, Sally.   II. McCracken, Scott.
PR468.S6C85   1995
820.9'355'09034–DC20   94-7064   CIP

ISBN 0 521 44385 7 hardback
ISBN 0 521 48499 5 paperback

Contents

Illustrations

Contributors

LAURA CHRISMAN is Lecturer in English at the School of African and Asian Studies, University of Sussex. She has published articles on Olive Schreiner, Rider Haggard and the early African novel, and is co-editor of *Colonial Discourse/Post-Colonial Theory: A Reader* (Harvester, 1993). She is currently writing a book on late nineteenth-century African writing and imperialist discourse.

ED COHEN is Assistant Professor in English at Rutgers University. He has published articles on gay identity and on Oscar Wilde. He is author of *Talk on the Wilde Side: Towards a Genealogy of a Discourse on Male Sexualities* (Routledge, 1993).

TERRY EAGLETON is Warton Professor of English at the University of Oxford. As well as several major works on critical theory, he is the author of a novel, *Saints and Scholars* (1987), two plays performed in London and Ireland (*Saint Oscar*, 1989, and *The White, the Gold and the Gangrene*, 1993) and is a director of the Dubbeljoint Theatre Company, Northern Ireland.

REGENIA GAGNIER is Professor of English and Director of the Programme in Modern Thought and Literature at Stanford University. Her books include *Idylls of the Marketplace: Oscar Wilde and the Victorian Public* (Stanford, 1986), *Critical Essays on Oscar Wilde* (G. K. Hall, 1991) and *Subjectivities: A History of Self-Representation in Britain, 1832–1920* (Oxford, 1991). She is currently writing a book on economics and aesthetics.

JUDITH HALBERSTAM is Assistant Professor of Literature at the University of California, San Diego. She is currently writing a book on nineteenth-century Gothic monsters.

xi

LYNNE HAPGOOD is Lecturer in English at Nottingham Trent University, where she is also the BA course leader for Broadcast Journalism. She has an article on the novelist Richard Whiteing in a collection of essays entitled *Critical Revaluations: 1890s Fiction* (forthcoming, University Press of Kentucky).

MARCIA IAN is Associate Professor of Modern British and American Literature at Rutgers University. She is author of *Remembering the Phallic Mother: Psychoanalysis, Modernism and the Fetish* (Cornell, 1992).

ANNE JANOWITZ is Associate Professor of English at Rutgers University. She has published several articles on romanticism and revolution as well as on American literature, and her book, *England's Ruins: Poetic Purpose and the National Landscape*, was published by Blackwell in 1990. She is on the editorial board of the Reconstructing Romanticism project at Harvester Wheatsheaf, and is advisory editor for MUP's *Text in Culture* series.

SALLY LEDGER is Lecturer in Literary Studies at the University of the West of England, Bristol. She has published articles on Mark Rutherford and William Morris, on the politics of English teaching, and is co-editor of *Political Gender: Texts and Contexts* (Harvester Wheatsheaf, 1994). She is currently writing a book on the New Woman at the *fin de siècle* for Manchester University Press.

SCOTT McCRACKEN is Lecturer in English at the University of Salford. He has published articles on the theory of historical criticism, Joseph Conrad, Fredric Jameson and postmodernism, Edward Carpenter and George Gissing.

STEPHEN REGAN is Tutor in English at Ruskin College, Oxford. He has published articles on Yeats, and his books include *Raymond Williams* (Harvester, 1993). He is currently teaching at the University of Warsaw.

RUTH ROBBINS is Lecturer in English at the University of Luton. She is currently finishing her thesis on *fin-de-siècle* literature. She has published on Vernon Lee in John Stokes (ed.) *Fin de Siècle/Fin du Globe* (Macmillan, 1992).

ALEXANDRA WARWICK is Lecturer in English at the University of Westminster. She has a book forthcoming from Daedalus Press on 'the fantastic building' in literature, and is currently working on a book about women writers of fantasy in the nineteenth century.

CAROLYN WILLIAMS is Associate Professor of English at Rutgers University, where she is also Associate Director of the Center for the Critical Analysis of Contemporary Culture. She is the author of *Transfigured World: Walter Pater's Aesthetic Historicism* (Cornell University Press, 1989) and of essays on various other Victorian writers. She is currently working on a cultural study of the Gilbert and Sullivan operas.

Acknowledgements

We would like to thank Jim Porteous and Georgina Waylen for their advice and support throughout this project; without them it could not have been accomplished. Thanks are also due to Terry Eagleton and John Stokes for their early encouragement and helpful suggestions, and to Kevin Taylor at Cambridge University Press, whose care and expertise have proved invaluable.

Introduction

Sally Ledger and Scott McCracken

The idea of the *fin de siècle* has been given a renewed cachet by the coming end of the twentieth century. The approach of another turn-of-the-century experience has concentrated minds. After a lapse of some seventy years, Holbrook Jackson's seminal work on the 1890s has been joined by a rash of new studies.[1] This revival of interest demands scrutiny, for within the discourse of literary and cultural criticism the end of the nineteenth century has traditionally fallen somewhere (somewhere not very interesting) between the grand narratives of Victorianism and modernism. Raymond Williams famously characterized the *fin de siècle* as an interregnum, half dismissing it as a 'working-out, rather, of unfinished lines; a tentative redirection'.[2] Such a designation of the late nineteenth century as a *transitional* period has led to its backwater status in literary and cultural criticism.

This volume testifies to the intense interest that the *fin de siècle* has for the late twentieth-century cultural critic. Current debates about the period are focused around questions of periodization and the concepts of cultural crisis and fragmentation. Both these questions are relevant to the idea of a cultural politics, by which we mean the recognition that culture is never fixed or stable and that cultural artifacts are the product of dialogue, debate and conflict.

Periodization has always been a problem for the *fin de siècle* because its position between cultural epochs disturbs traditional historiography. The problem is particularly acute in what has been called a postmodern age, when historical criticism is self-conscious about the formal or metahistorical processes that the conceptualization of periods or epochs implies. The process of cultural fragmentation that characterized the *fin de siècle* threw the norms of the Victorian age into crisis: empires were threatened, feminism was on the march, and the first socialist parties in Britain were formed. The appeal to that late twentieth-century form of postmodernism which celebrates fragmentation is clear here; but that celebration does not pay sufficient attention to the relationship between the fragmentations of the past and those of the present.

The problem facing the cultural historian is how to reread the past from the inescapable perspective of the present, without denying the specificity and difference of the past. Gillian Beer, in tackling the problem, has described the reinterpretation of the past through the critical apparatuses and cultural preoccupations of the present as 'presentism'. Beer characterizes presentism as the belief that 'now' offers the only authoritative source of meaning, and that the past is to be read for its relevance to our contemporary concerns. A rigid historicization, by contrast, is charged with ignoring the effect of the present altogether. Beer claims that in both cases the outcome is the same: the collapse of historical difference.[3]

The cultural historian's problematic position is that she or he always knows more than was known at the time, namely what followed. This sense that an 'event' includes its posterior effects is usefully reflected upon by Walter Benjamin in his 'Theses on the Philosophy of History':

Historicism contents itself with establishing a causal connection between various moments in history. But no fact that is a cause is for that very reason historical. It became historical posthumously, as it were, through events that may be separated from it by thousands of years. An historian who takes this as his point of departure stops telling the sequence of events like the beads of a rosary. Instead, he grasps the constellation which his own era has formed with a definite earlier one.[4]

Cultural critics and historians are currently grasping the 'constellation' which our own *fin de siècle* forms with the last one.

Amongst the recent studies of the period it is Elaine Showalter's *Sexual Anarchy: Gender and Culture at the Fin de Siècle* that most strikingly draws parallels between the 1890s and the 1990s. Seeking to contextualize the turn-of-the-century experience, Showalter remarks that from 'urban homelessness to imperial decline, from sexual revolution to sexual epidemics, the last decades of the twentieth century seem to be repeating the problems, themes and metaphors of the *fin de siècle*'; and she nominates Allan Bloom as the late twentieth century's 'endist' answer to Max Nordau, the late nineteenth century's prophet of doom. The parallels between the two *fin de siècles* are indeed suggestive, but, while they invite further investigation, an historiography which seems to see the problematics of the present so clearly in an earlier historical period must surely be open to question. The idea of a cyclical end-of-the-century experience should also be regarded with some suspicion. Showalter's claim that 'the crises of the *fin de siècle*... are more intensely experienced, more emotionally fraught, more weighted with symbolic and historical meaning, because we invest them with the metaphors of death and rebirth that we project onto the final decades and years of a century' constructs a circular argument which makes it difficult to engage with questions of historical difference as well as those of historical identity.[5] Showalter's failure to give an adequate theoretical account of the *fin de siècle* as a transhistorical category means she is left reiterating – somewhat glibly – the cultural similarities between the two periods.

If Showalter's cyclical conception of the *fin de siècle* experience is an example of Beer's presentism, then the alternative is a rigid historicization, a whole-hearted differentiation of the late nineteenth century as a discrete period determined by an historically specific set of cultural preoccupations, economic and social factors which can in no sense be compared with the very different circumstances of the late twentieth century. Such an alternative, though, is barely preferable to Showalter's position: whereas she fails to take adequate account of historical difference, the rigidly historicist view errs in the opposite direction by setting up a *too* rigid polarity between historical difference and identity.

From the vantage point of the late twentieth century, many of the concepts and conflicts around issues of 'race', class and gender which inform contemporary cultural criticism would seem to have emerged in the last *fin de siècle*. In fact, the *fin de siècle* proves so fertile a ground for the type of cultural history which emphasizes 'difference' and which has in latter years tended to focus on the critical 'holy trinity' of 'race', class and gender, that it is tempting to see the end of the nineteenth century and the beginning of the twentieth century as the origin or beginning of many of the debates which occupy centre stage in our own post-epochal, postmodern *fin de siècle*. However, one need only turn to Foucault in his essay 'Nietzsche, Genealogy, and History', to be reminded of the danger of origins:

What is found at the historical beginning of things is not the inviolable identity of their origin; it is the dissension of other things. It is their disparity ... the origin makes possible a field of knowledge whose function is to recover it, but always in a false recognition due to the excesses of its own speech. The origin lies at a place of inevitable loss, the point where the truth of things corresponded to a truthful discourse, the site of a fleeting articulation that discourse has obscured and finally lost.[6]

To put this more succinctly, the *fin de siècle* was only an epoch of beginnings and endings if we look for them: the cultural forms and conflicts we find there are inescapably constructed by the double-look of the 1890s and the 1990s, and can only be reconstructed via the discursive practices available to us in the 1990s, which may of course include – but will undoubtedly exceed – those available in the last *fin de siècle*. What is required, then, to make sense of the *fin de siècle*, is a sophisticated historical criticism which is capable of standing back not only from the period, but also from our own time, and then examining the dialectical relationship between the two.

The *fin de siècle* period we address in this book stretches from the 1880s, when economic depression signalled the end of Britain's reign as the 'workshop of the world', up until the onset of the First World War in 1914, an event which signifies imperial catastrophe and ultimate decline. Among the texts discussed are William Morris's *Pilgrims of Hope*, which was serialized between 1885 and 1886, and Joseph Conrad's *Chance*, which was serialized in 1912. Both texts can be seen as belonging to a distinct cultural epoch, an epoch that was particularly notable for its political ferment.

Cultural and political conflict is one of the keynotes of this essay collection, and it is the contrast between the politics of the last *fin de siècle* and our own which provides the starting point for Terry Eagleton's chapter, 'The Flight to the Real'. Eagleton reminds us that the last *fin de siècle*, even while engaged in spiritual and psychological explorations, never forgot the inextricable tangle of relations between the inner and the outer worlds. Warning us that in the 1990s we are left with the culture of the previous *fin de siècle* shorn of its politics, he calls us to reinvent the 1890s' amalgam of spiritual and material ferment, as well as its generous plurality.

Generous plurality and socio-cultural fragmentation are two sides of the same political coin; and whilst in the *fin de siècle* these fragmentations manifested themselves around the categories of 'race', class and gender, it was often gender issues which mediated the cultural politics of the day. At the same time, gender is one of the most significant critical categories to have emerged in the last twenty years in Europe and the United States. It is not then surprising that the preoccupation with gender is quite striking in this essay collection.

Nor is this a case of Gillian Beer's presentism, since the resurgence of the women's movement as a political force in the late nineteenth century is irrefutable, and began with the campaign led by Josephine Butler against the Contagious Diseases Acts. The feminism of the time was both a product of social relations and itself an agent in their transformation. Working-class women struggled for an improvement in living conditions and for the vote, whilst militant suffragism in the mill towns of the industrial north often had a conflictual relationship with the new unionism. Middle-class women found a degree of personal autonomy in the female communities that grew up around religion, social work and teaching. The new century began with a new orientation led by the Women's Social and Political Union, whose militant tactics challenged accepted notions of middle-class femininity with their protest actions on the streets and in gaol.

The relationship between the Woman Question at the last *fin de siècle* and current feminist responses to it is, then, dialectical. The emergence of a criticism that reinserts gender as an analytical category in critical discourse is a direct product of the women's movement of the 1960s and 1970s. One of several examples in this collection of how new political and social movements can create a context in which historical texts are reread is Sally Ledger's 'The New Woman and the Crisis of Victorianism'. Ledger describes how, amidst cultural anxieties about gender, 'race' and class, it was the complex figure of the New Woman who acted as a signifier for social disintegration and the break-up of the cultural boundaries that had been so carefully erected earlier in the century. She demonstrates that, for all that they carried the weight of society's fears, the New Women of the time were not ideal models for today's feminists, and that the feminist politics of the 1890s was a product of the contradictory ideologies of the day.

Continuing a similar line of argument, Laura Chrisman puts the cultural politics of the New Woman under further scrutiny in her chapter, 'Empire, "Race" and Feminism at the *Fin de Siècle*'. Chrisman traces the difficult relationship between narratives of emancipation for European women and narratives of domination of the European colonies, in the work of two of the most creative New Woman writers: George Egerton and Olive Schreiner. Here, as in Ledger's chapter, the New Woman's complicity with the ideologies of imperialism is made explicit. The chapter reminds us that the end of the nineteenth century marked the end of Britain's hegemony as a global economic power, now rivalled by Germany and the United States of America: 'Britain, we may say, was becoming a parasitic rather than a competitive world economy, living off the remains of world monopoly, the underdeveloped world, her past accumulations of wealth and the advance of her rivals.'[7] The turn towards colonial markets was accompanied by an increase in popular ideologies of imperialism, and the politics of empire is another thematic focus of this book. Racist representations were a widespread part of the new journalism and the growing advertising and consumer culture. Social conflicts were articulated within a discourse that assumed the 'racial' and imperial superiority of the British ruling class. It should come as no surprise that the imperialist politics of the last *fin de siècle* are of such interest at the close of the twentieth century, when the collapse of the Eastern Bloc has led to a global morass of competing nationalisms. Alexandra Warwick, Carolyn Williams and Judith Halberstam make manifest this critical interest in chapters which also explore the crises in imperial cultural politics at the last *fin de siècle*.

The theme of imperial oppression and resistance is continued in Stephen Regan's chapter, 'W. B. Yeats and Irish Cultural Politics in the 1890s'. Whilst arguing that the value of Yeats's *fin-de-siècle* poetry has less to do with English aestheticism than with challenging and complicating our understanding of what it means to be Irish, Regan nonetheless questions recent developments in Yeats criticism that would see him as a poet of decolonization. The 'Irish Yeats', Regan argues, is a complex writer, drawing as much upon the traditions and inheritance of the Protestant middle class as on new republican nationalism.

While Ledger, Chrisman and Regan address themselves to the question of historical reassessment (how the past is appropriated by the cultural politics of the present), the next three chapters in the book address a major current critical concern in the 1990s, that of subjectivity. Ed Cohen's chapter, 'The Double Lives of Man', concentrates on the emergence of a split subjectivity in the representation of *fin-de-siècle* masculinities. Cohen's work is another example of how the late twentieth-century political movements such as lesbian and gay liberation have shaped cultural criticism and history in a way that has enabled what he calls 'ec-centric' masculine subjects – that is, those outside the norms of Victorian middle-class society – to be relocated as part of a more complex, rich and varied historical narrative than was available (or allowable) hitherto.

Marcia Ian's chapter, 'Henry James and the Spectacle of Loss', is part of a similar process. In a discussion which includes readings of *The Ambassadors*, *What Maisie Knew*, and 'Is There a Life After Death?' she uses the critical apparatus of psychoanalysis, itself a *fin-de-siècle* phenomenon, to reassess the historical transformations of both consciousness and the representation of consciousness that were a part of the *fin-de-siècle* experience. Also addressing the question of *fin-de-siècle* subjectivities, Ruth Robbins's chapter, '"A Very Curious Construction": Masculinity and the Poetry of A. E. Housman and Oscar Wilde', describes the textual strategies deployed by these writers to explore, overtly or covertly, the new masculine selves born of aestheticism. She focuses on the real dangers risked by those who were prepared to live the new aesthetic in the public sphere. For example, by the time *The Ballad of Reading Gaol* was published Wilde's *persona* was *non grata* to the extent that even his identity was excised from the poem's title page.

It is one of most glaring contradictions of the *fin de siècle* that even as the New Woman and Wildean decadence emphasized the cultural force of the individual, the poverty wrought by the depression years of the 1880s weakened the ideological dominance of *economic* liberalism and individualism. A period which saw the gradual decline of competitive capitalism and the emergence of its monopoly successor also saw a decline in the Liberal Party and, in the 1880s, the formation of the first, tiny Marxist parties in Britain. The London Dockers' Strike of 1889 led the unionization of unskilled workers (the 'new unionism') and the Labour Party was founded in 1900. From the 1880s onwards a growing number of middle-class intellectuals found themselves more attracted to socialist than to liberal ideas. The early meetings at William Morris's London home which were attended by, amongst others, George Bernard Shaw and W. B. Yeats, established socialism as an almost respectable pursuit; but it was as yet an unstable category and, apart from its collectivist emphasis, had yet to take on a fixed meaning.

There is an uncanny sense of recognition here for the post-Stalinist 1990s. The plurality of progressive forces at the end of the nineteenth century: the Humanitarian League and the Fellowship of the New Life (both forerunners of the Fabian society), the flourishing movements for vegetarianism, campaigns for rational dress, anti-vivisectionist societies and neo-Malthusians (advocating birth-control), might well remind us of the fragmented new social movements of the late twentieth century. Again, however, the similarities can be misleading. There are few correspondences between the burgeoning utopian optimism of the early socialists and today's tired atmosphere of despondency. The term 'progressive' is equally deceptive, as, especially in sexual politics, eugenic ideas which we would now associate with the political right were mixed up with, and indeed were often part of, socialist ideology.

It is, then, in the spirit of exploring what Ernst Bloch would have called the *Erbe*, the inheritance, heritage or reservoir that is the past, that Anne Janowitz sets out to explore the potential contained within the socialist politics and culture of the period, starting from the opposition between Romantic individualism and communitarianism implicit in William Morris's *The Pilgrims of Hope*. In a chapter that sets the tone for the collection, Janowitz argues forcefully for the kind of conscious reappropriation of the *fin de siècle* that seeks to rebuild a sense of social solidarity against the cult of the individual. Lynne Hapgood approaches the same theme from a different perspective in her 'Urban Utopias: Socialism, Religion and the City, 1880–1900'. She points to the strong links, often mutually reinforcing, between socialist and Christian discourses in the period. Both were used to articulate a form of utopianism amidst the social upheaval of the new Victorian city, even though, she concludes, ultimately the two could not hold together.

One of the most significant reasons for the disorientation felt in the period was the way in which the new experience of mass culture threw all previous definitions into confusion.[8] The period initiated some of the most important popular cultural forms of the twentieth century. Detectives, like Sherlock Holmes, and monsters, like Mr Hyde and Dracula, step through the portals of the end of the century. Two chapters in the book tackle the multiple representations and interpretations of the ubiquitous vampire phenomenon, which takes its classic form in Bram Stoker's novel of 1897.

Alexandra Warwick's 'Vampires and the Empire: Fears and Fictions of the 1890s' traces representations of the vampire through the nineteenth century, arguing that as the century progressed anxieties about otherness shifted away from a threat to domestic femininity towards a threat from women themselves. These fears were inextricably bound up with fears regarding the continuation of the British Empire as the century moved towards its close. Whilst vampires also take centre stage in Judith Halberstam's 'Technologies of Monstrosity', she looks back at Bram Stoker's *Dracula* from the perspective of the late twentieth century. Her argument is that the vampire has operated as a signifier of numerous different types of monstrosity and cannot yield to any one interpretation. The plurality of readings available to the critic of popular culture is demonstrated again by Carolyn Williams in her chapter on Gilbert and Sullivan. The peculiar status of their operas in English culture is reconsidered in her discussion of a lesser-known work, *Utopia, Limited.* Returning to the theme of empire, Williams finds a subversive aspect to the opera's satire which parodies British institutions and the imperial project of 'civilization'.

The final two chapters confront directly the book's double-look at the *fin de siècle*, both from a historical and a contemporary perspective. Scott McCracken's 'Postmodernism, a *Chance* to Reread?', asks how useful the concept of postmodernism is in addressing texts like Conrad's *Chance*, which, although written by a modernist author, and in the modernist era, exhibits some of the characteristics attributed to postmodernism. In part a product of the burgeoning mass culture of the period – it was one of Conrad's few financial and popular successes – *Chance*'s problematic aesthetic status is the focus of McCracken's discussion. The book closes with Regenia Gagnier's disquieting question, 'Is Market Society the *Fin* of History?' In a chapter which provides a long perspective on the history of liberal economics, from Adam Smith through to Francis Fukuyama, Gagnier focuses in particular on the relationship between aesthetics and economics in texts such as *Salomé* and *Dorian Gray* from the last *fin de siècle*. She remains radically sceptical of the concept of posthistory, arguing that the logic of the market, whether in aesthetics or economics, always falls short of the potential and promise of any historical moment. It is on this politically challenging note that the volume closes.

There is no false optimism in Gagnier's chapter nor in the others in this book. The difficulties and conflicts in the cultural politics of the last *fin de siècle* and of our own cannot be evaded. For example, the new subjectivities represented by John Addington Symonds, Olive Schreiner or A. E. Housman demonstrate that the fragmentation that enabled the modernism of the twentieth century was neither wholly progressive, nor wholly reactionary or indeed 'decadent'. Similarly the collapse of familiar narratives in the late twentieth century cannot be categorized in simple political terms. The political optimism which remains, however, is born of the last *fin de siècle*'s defiance of the oppressive cultural boundaries constructed in the earlier Victorian period. It was such radical defiance and healthy disrespect which gave, to borrow from Morris's *Pilgrims of Hope*, 'A Glimpse of the Coming Day' – it is a glimpse which retains political value in our own disorientated *fin de siècle*.

NOTES

1 Holbrook Jackson, *The Eighteen Nineties* (1913; reprint London: The Cresset Library, 1988). Recent studies include John Stokes, *In the Nineties* (Hemel Hempstead: Harvester Wheatsheaf, 1989); Robert Colls and Philip Dodd (eds.), *Englishness: Politics and Culture 1880–1920* (London and Sydney: Croom Helm, 1987); and Elaine Showalter, *Sexual Anarchy: Gender and Culture at the Fin de Siècle* (New York: Viking, 1990, and London: Bloomsbury, 1991).

2 Raymond Williams, *Culture and Society* (Harmondsworth: Penguin, 1963), p. 165.

3 Gillian Beer, 'Representing Women: Re-Presenting the Past', in Catherine Belsey and Jane Moore (eds.), *The Feminist Reader* (London: Macmillan, 1989).

4 Walter Benjamin, *Illuminations* (1955; reprint London: Fontana, 1970), p. 265.

5 Showalter, *Sexual Anarchy*, p. 1.

6 Michel Foucault, 'Nietzsche, Genealogy, and History', in Paul Rabinow (ed.), *The Foucault Reader* (Harmondsworth: Penguin, 1984), p. 79.

7 Eric Hobsbawm, *Industry and Empire* (Harmondsworth: Penguin, 1969), p. 192.

8 Stephen Kern has written about the important impact on cultural form made by the new technologies of steam, telegraph and mass production in his book, *The Culture of Time and Space 1880–1918* (Cambridge, Mass.: Harvard University Press, 1983).

CHAPTER I

The flight to the real

Terry Eagleton

The *fin de siècle* arrived early this century. It arrived, in fact, in the 1960s, a period whose structure of feeling uncannily reproduces much of the culture of late Victorian England. Sexual experiment, pseudo-orientalism, gospels of peace and fellowship, emancipatory politics, exotic art-forms, hallucinatory states, flights from civilization: in all these ways, the sixties seemed the eighties and nineties reanimated, with Twiggy, Conran and Carnaby Street thrown in for good measure. The postmodern 1980s and nineties have, of course, some claim to this inheritance too; but they differ from the Victorian end-of-the-century in one crucial respect. For ours is not an era of revolutionary doctrines, even if it resembles its nineteenth-century forebear in being one of global capitalist recession. The capitalist system approaches this millennium, as it did the last, in grave disarray; but the political forces which mustered around the turn of the century to offer an alternative polity to this failed experiment have been temporarily scattered and diffused.

What we seem left with in the nineties, then, is something of the culture of the previous *fin de siècle* shorn of its politics. For what characterized that earlier era was an astonishing amalgam of spiritual and material ferment: the boisterous emergence of new political forces, to be sure, but also a veritable transformation of subjectivity, as the high-rationalist subject of Mill or *Middlemarch* gradually imploded into Madame Blavatsky and Dorian Gray. In this sense, the Victorian end-of-the-century poses an implicit challenge to those for whom the 'turn to the subject' has been an alternative to revolutionary politics rather than an essential correlate of them. That celebrated turn happened for us in the 1970s, as discourse, desire, semiotics and schizoanalysis rushed to occupy the space vacated by the defeated revolutionary projects of the 1960s. Discourse and desire have been at once ways of valuably extending those politics into neglected regions of subjectivity, and of displacing them; and this, indeed, is exactly the Derridean logic of the supplement, which ends up ousting what it was meant to elaborate. Somewhere around the mid-1970s, feminists, film theorists and fledgling post-structuralists were insisting that there can be no political transformation of class society without the revolution of word and body; somewhere around the late 1980s, we had a discourse of word and body and an embarrassed silence about class, state, imperialism, modes of production, all of which could now be briskly consigned to the ash-can of totality.

If the late nineteenth century has an urgent significance for us, then it is precisely because it did not make this mistake. We are speaking of the period of Aubrey Beardsley *and* the Second International; of aestheticism and anarchism; of decadence and the Dock Strike. William Morris knew about the politics of how things felt and looked, but also about theories of surplus value; Maud Gonne and Connie Markowitz moved between theatre, the women's movement, the Parisian avant-garde and Irish republicanism. The same figures can be found demonstrating for the unemployed and dabbling in occultism, linking an enthusiasm for symbolism with an interest in syndicalism. In much of this, of course, there is a good deal of modishness, eccentricity and excessive credulity; one thinks of the débutante in Evelyn Waugh who had got wind of an Independent Labour Party and was furious that she had not been invited. *Fin-de-siècle* intellectuals blend belief systems with staggering nonchalance, blithely confident of some invisible omega point at which Baudelaire and Kropotkin consort harmoniously together and Emerson lies down with Engels. But for all their naive excitement and conceptual consumerism, these men and women saw no ultimate divide between the more rational organization of industry and the dismantling of the transcendental ego; whereas today the one party glowers suspiciously at the other over some well-policed frontier of the mind, the heirs of the Second International confident that discourse and desire are mere bourgeois distractions, the exponents of the latter assured that all revolutionary organization is patriarchal. To put the point another way: the watershed of the 1970s divided sixties political utopianism from eighties postmodernism, and in doing so fissured what had been for the radicals of late Victorian England a set of compatible rather than antagonistic concerns.

What is happening from the late 1870s onwards confirms this

compatibility. For materially speaking, the era of Victorian pros-perity is now over; the oldest industrial capitalist nation in the world is being shamefully outpaced by its juvenile rivals; the mid-Victorian bonanza has bred a minatory underworld of urban lumpen-proletariat; and the unedifying spectacle of too much Western capital chasing too few colonial territories is about to lead to the conflagration of the first imperialist world war. But the spiritual correlative of this human waste and wretchedness is a cataclysmic crisis of Victorian rationality itself, on which the *fin de siècle* is no more than a set of extravagant variations. Base and superstructure are dramatically matched, in a unity which might embarrass even the most vulgar of Marxists; and though one would not wish to scandalize sophisticated theorists everywhere by claiming that Thomas Hardy's pessimism might have something to do with the steady collapse of the English countryside, and that in turn with the opening up of the American Midwest, there are, nonetheless, complex connections between international competition and the Immanent Will. What is less clear, of course, is whether this spiritually agitated epoch is the first puff or the fag-end. Are we witnessing the tumultuous dawn of some brave new world altogether (some apocalyptic crack-up which will render all of our available models of the subject quaintly antique), or the very different hectic flush of decadence, as the splintered bits and pieces of late Enlightenment slide down the chute into the abyss of 1914, giving off a little false glitter as they go? In this, too, the period contradictorily unites the exhilarated utopianism of the 1960s with the end-of-history ambience of our own more depressive age, for which – if one is to believe the tales of those American evangelical television companies already searching for the best locales from which to film the Second Coming – even apocalypse has become a media event.

When Victorian reason began to crumble, it split into two opposed directions. The *fin de siècle* cuts above it and beneath it at a stroke, fleeing its top-heavy reifications for the consolation of the real, or alternatively subliming its prosaic language into something al-together more ethereal. The epoch is, at once, more concrete and more cosmic than what came before, either searching anxiously for some sure foundation or making do with frail intimations of the infinite. On the one hand, the years from 1880 to the turn of the century are the decades of Tolstoyan *simplicitas* and the Fellowship of New Life; of the garden city and rational diet and dress, of a poetry which enacts the *quidditas* of the sensuous object and a philosophy which clings tenaciously to the contours of the real. On the other hand, the mind, so Darwin had taught his successors, was a clumsy, extraneous mechanism thrown up by senseless material process; so that from Schopenhauer to Joseph Conrad consciousness is now itself a form of alienation, and an art which posits the overcoming of this, a performative contradiction. The pragmatism of a William James seeks to dethrone the tyranny of the rational concept, stripping it to a mere function or device by which we can move as efficiently as possible from this to that bit of our experience; and the later art of his brother will spin a style which tries to capture that experience at its very point of emergence, weaving a syntax so supple and devious that not a single discursive nuance or psychological flicker can escape it. The relations between this and Paterian aestheticism are obvious enough: aestheticism is not just some anodyne cult of *l'art pour l'art*, but the considerably more subversive project of living every facet of our experience, including those conventionally thought illicit, with the passionate intensity of our most precious aesthetic investments. It might seem a far cry from all this to those gay intellectuals like Edward Carpenter, who were especially enamoured of hunky railway workers and athletic East End policemen; but this is just a rather more literal version of the symbolic embracing of the 'real', the brawny proletarian as material object with which the estranged intellect must libidinally unite. For this above all is the age of artistic slumming, in which some raw, fascinating but fearful underworld lurks beneath the paper-thin structure of civilization, and in which destructive element you must immerse in the name of authenticity. Whether this is Gissing's nether world of the metropolitan working class, the opium dens and whore houses of *Dorian Gray* or an ontological void at the heart of the Belgian Congo, it is at least preferable to a middle-class society which is now, as in the later Dickens, less vicious than vacuous – a realm which has its secret roots in crime, labour, money and material filth (*Great Expectations, Little Dorrit, Our Mutual Friend*) but which has repressed its own squalid parentage and constituted itself in that act as 'culture'.

It is no wonder, then, that the two shadowy figures who symbolically dominate the age are Jack the Ripper and Jekyll-and-Hyde. The century closes with Freud's discovery of the unconscious; but that violent, anarchic region has already been prefigured in the East End, in primitivist anthropology, in the exotically intensified sensations of the decadents; and the line which divides it from the socially respectable ego is as tenuous as that which demarcates Wilde's ebullient drawing-room presence from his furtive disporting with rent boys in cheap hotels. This fissure between private and public is also one between experience and rational doctrine; and for Walter Pater and his spiritual kin the former has now grown too delicate, impalpable and richly intricate to be funnelled into the ossified categories of the latter. This is one reason why the era is so fascinated by the various Lamarckian and Bergsonian vitalisms, all of which envisage some inexorably unfolding dynamic which shucks off creeds, conventions and institutions as so many empty shells. Every formula or social arrangement must now be provisional and self-ironizing – so much ephemeral spume on the wave of the infinite – and the resultant cultural relativism threatens in Conrad, Kipling and others to pull the rug from beneath imperialist ideology, unmasking its fictional nature at just the moment it needed to absolutize itself. The artist moves at the contradictory juncture of private and public worlds, experience and convention, as public figure in one sense and anarchist, Satanic rebel and Baudelairean outcast in another.

What marks this whole dimension of the *fin de siècle* is a kind of mystical positivism, for which, after the endless lucubrations of high Victorian reason, that which simply, brutely, self-identically is, is the most alluring mystery of all. There is much of Whitman in this reverent espousal of the actual, but also a more general neurotic hankering for the very pith and texture of things, behind which we *Nachgeborener* may glimpse that old familiar lost object, the body of the mother. Evolutionary thought has struck all hierarchy out of Nature: in the tangled skeins of material development, it is impossible to say with any certainty which obscure life forms will give birth to some later mighty flourishing and which will not; which mollusc will perish in some biological cul-de-sac and which will pave the way to monopoly capitalism. The whole of material reality may thus be indiscriminately embraced, in a daring cancellation of traditional ethical binaries. The upshot of this is a kind of evolutionary version of deism, in which even the most apparently noxious and deviant of phenomena, could we but glimpse them from a God's eye viewpoint, are stealthily contributing to the good of the material whole. Its consequence in art will be naturalism, a Zolaesque spurning of anything as bourgeois as moral judgement for a clinical portrayal of the subtly interwoven whole. The artist as scientist, then, dispassionately registering the most rebarbative of experiences; but the artist therefore as amoralist, and thus as leagued with that very different aesthetic cult in the period, the artist as demoniac and pervert, the Nietzschean Yea-sayer beyond good and evil, the social pariah who would sell his own baby daughter for the sake of an exquisitely turned phrase. The clinical naturalist artist is bound to be sensationalist, and so not clinical at all; or rather he fuses the two structures of feeling in a genre which approaches pornography. It is not for nothing that this is the age of the new 'science' of sexology, solemnly categorizing human sexual behaviour with all the sub-limated prurience of a high-toned neutrality. Naturalism and aestheticism couple in curious ways: if Nature is powered by its own grandly autonomous laws, if nothing in the great scheme of things could have happened other than it did, then this is at once powerful ideological consolation in a guilt-infested, politically turbulent age, and a license for rendering the shapes and textures of things as tenderly and meticulously as you can – not only because even the most repellent of them are intrinsically positive but also because, if determinism is true, then consciousness can now only register rather than intervene. The point is to photograph the world, not to change it. Aestheticizing the unacceptable is a common *fin-de-siècle* pastime; and one of its forms is a kind of sub-Nietzschean *amor fati*, contemplating in passive Paterian style the inexorable cosmic laws out of which your very flesh is woven, and rejoicing in them as some splendid artifact which will survive all humble particulars like oneself.

It is often enough forgotten, in fact, just how rigorously deter-ministic the period actually is, given the more familiar images of random impression and fragmentary sensation. The teleological thrust of high Victorian positivism may have faltered; but for many of the age's thinkers the human subject is still the bearer of iron historical laws, and if, like those late-Victorian positivists the Fabians, one is to intervene creatively in human arrangements, one can do so only on the basis of a scientific knowledge of their law-like structure. The *fin de siècle* is the age of the subjective and extravagant, of a complex inwardness and individual deviancy which threaten to burst the stereotyping moulds of language and convention; but it is also an era in which, as with the Shavian life-force, we are mere instruments of some ulterior, altogether impersonal evolution. It is just that this evolution is now commonly cast in spiritualized rather than Spencerian terms, powered by it as by some ineffable *élan vital* which is accessible only to intuition. Hence the age's preference for Lamarck over Darwin – though in the hands of Shaw, Samuel Butler and others it is, to be sure, a suitably caricatured version of that highly materialist thinker. Hence also, no doubt, the re-emergence in Bradley and his cohorts of an Hegelian history of *Geist*, embarrassingly close as it is to the metaphysical materialism of the later Engels. All of this slipshod vitalism will find its disreputable apotheosis in the writings of D. H. Lawrence, who was canny enough to conceal his dubious *fin-de-siècle* sources, and for whom what we articulate in our most authentic acts is absolutely not ourselves. This, too, has its affinities with some indiscriminately embracing naturalism, though now one transferred to the inward space of the self: for if the autonomous subject is an ideological fiction, if I am no more than a feeler momentarily put forth by some inscrutable spiritual evolution, then I am in no sense responsible for my own actions and am bound to express all of my impulses, however apparently base, simply by virtue of the fact that they go to make up myself. Who am I, as Lawrence remarks, to hold myself above my lowest desire? Vitalism, Nietzscheanism, ethical naturalism, scientific neutrality and the cult of anarchic spontaneity thus configurate in strange ways in the cross-currents of these decades. If all the subject's impulses demand expression, yet those impulses are mutually contradictory, then one has the phenomenon of an Oscar Wilde, for whom consistency can be left to shop-keepers, and whose epigrams are an impudent inversion or deconstruction of a conventional wisdom.

The *fin de siècle*'s flight to the real is as contradictory a project as the phrase suggests. For this stubbornly self-identical 'real', whether seen as the simple life, the garden city, South Sea islanders, the immediacy of sensation, proletarian lovers or a language brimmed to the brink with sheer thing-hood, represents a kind of collective intellectual suicide in the face of a social order apparently too abstract and elaborate for human control. But nothing resembles the immediacy of sensation as much as the transcendent, since both are accessible to us only by virtue of an intuition which is radically non-discursive. Infinity and a grain of sand are perceptible in roughly the same ways; and if to know a particular is to grasp it in its mysterious self-identity, shorn of the superfluous divisions and categorizations which an alienated human consciousness projects upon it, then no finer model for such self-referentiality can be found than the universe itself, which is by definition non-relational. So it is that the period's impatience with discursive rationality leads it to the stars as well as to the gutter – to various mysticisms and occultisms and neo-Kantianisms, to so-called cosmic consciousness and the whole spurious fascination with the Orient. If language has staled and blunted, then it can either be violently returned à la Hopkins to the freshness of the material world, or it can be cut loose from such materiality altogether and floated off into some incorporeal realm. This is the way out for the formalists and symbolists, for whom language must be purged of its alienated social meanings by being cranked up a gear to the condition of music, sublimed to a condition in which, by alluding only to itself, it will permit us a glimpse of the self-enclosed cosmos. That which is tenaciously self-identical, as logocentrically replete as a line of Whitman, and that which eludes all identity in its Mallarmean suggestiveness, are then sides of the same coin; antithetical strategies for tackling a condition in which the commodity form has struck the world abstract and mechanistic. It is a peculiarly comforting thought (one, indeed, on which *Middlemarch* closes), that by staying pretty much where you are and attending to the task to hand you are mysteriously in touch with the totality; and this is certainly one of the period's more powerful rationalizations. What else is Hopkins's theory of inscape but the claim that to taste any object in its uniqueness is to grasp the universal spirit which sustains it? And why else should Hegel's concrete universal return in this period so forcibly, just when that whole conceptual paraphernalia had been apparently discredited? The dream of the *fin de siècle* is to pass without mediation from the concrete to the cosmic, linked as the two realms are in their resistance to that analytic rationality which is the sign of social alienation.

If Victorian rationality is now suspect, it is in part because it is thought to be a mere cloak for human interests. It is in the *fin de siècle*, under the gigantic shadow of Friedrich Nietzsche, that postmodernism first germinates, even before modernism proper had got off the ground. Language is now just the reflex of power and desire, ideals are mere specious rationalizations of material interests, and if Conrad will pen a whole novel on this topic (*Nostromo*), Vilfredo Pareto is just about to spin a whole sociology from it. In one sense, of course, the doctrine is at least as old as the English Civil War: in Hobbes and Hume it forms the basis of a bourgeois individualist philosophy, which is why it is odd that the postmodernists should imagine there is anything very radical in unmasking a supposedly disinterested reason as the slave of passion. For Conrad, and in a different way for Hardy, men and women view reality perspectivally, from the standpoint of their own brooding obsessions, and the resultant clash of these multiple versions of the world is known as tragedy. If God exists, then he would figure as the metaperspective which unified all these others; but in fact he does not, which is why cultural relativism thrives. There is now an empty space which he once occupied, in which individuals collide and mutually mis-perceive, desire all the way through one another and out the other side. What has replaced the Almighty, in short, is that place of the 'other' which Lacan dubs the unconscious. And it is hard to know, in this condition, whether to remain faithful to one's desire even though it will prove tragically disruptive, or to abnegate it on the altar of selflessness. George Moore can never decide whether to let the self rip or rein it in, lurching as he does from a pagan emancipation of the senses to an austere self-disciplining which will sublime them into something rich and rare. If the Roman Catholic Church is so popular in the period, it is partly because it allows you, in this respect, to have your cake and eat it: the sensuous whiff of incense *and* self-flagellation, all those gorgeous icons and vestments along with a masochistic self-denial. It is not accidental in this respect that Hopkins was a Jesuit: the more you stress and discipline your language, subjecting it to an extreme pressure and rigour, the more lush and plump it becomes. It is a kind of poetic equivalent of sexual bondage; and if Hopkins is particularly taken with bugler boys in scarlet uniforms, it is because imperialism allows you just the same perverse fusion of discipline and exoticism. It might be, however, that the distinction between self-affirmation and self-abnegation is simply undecidable, and the name for this aporia is the later Henry James. For these novels, the highest virtue, like the finest work of art, is an intelligence rendered supremely disinterested in the service of love; and this, rather than *News From Nowhere*, is perhaps the true utopian image of the epoch. It is at this point that the ethical and the aesthetic, so rigorously distinguished by Kant, merge into unity. In the end there was nothing that Henry didn't know; but such a supremely beautiful intelligence is hardly compatible with living, which of course he knew as well. Strether wants to get out of all that fatiguing complexity with not a drop spilt and his hands clean, salvaging nothing for himself, pregnant with an enormous, useless intelligence completely bereft of exchange value. And Milly Theale will turn her face to the wall and hand over her inheritance, in a magnificent *acte gratuit*, to her predatory lover. If the price of all this for James is the empty life of an ageing celibate then he is prepared to pay it, and has, he knows, enough money to do so: enough money to live as little as possible and to practise instead that supreme mode of virtue known as writing. It is the good who will enter the kingdom, but it is the fine who make life worth living; and James found a way of synthesizing the two by producing fictions of great fineness with all the ascetic renunciation of the virtuous. In the war between the Tolstoyans and the Nietzscheans, the Tolstoyans finally have it, but only when the chips are down. The history of art is not worth the suffering of a single child, which is why Dimitri Karamazov turned in his entry ticket to eternity. James knew that we can only enter eternity empty-handed, though he also knew that such renunciation might be no more than the most monstrous egoism of all. But such a life, as Walter Benjamin might have remarked, is not one which sets the angels' bodies burning as one flame of praise before God. It is simply not fine enough; and though the fine pay tribute to the demonic, and must do so in fear and trembling, there is nevertheless much to be said for them. For the angels are in love with the crookedness and cunning of the human mind, and it is hard to believe that all that unfathomable intelligence has merely to be surrendered. It is in fiction alone that virtue and intelligence, goodness and fineness, can be united; and in this way James's novels act as a negative critique of a society in which it is the fine that have the pleasure and the good that take the blame.

It is never easy to know with James whether the splendidly self-sacrificial act is one which gives the slip to power, or figures as its most triumphal exercise. Is it the transcendence of politics, or its most devious incarnation? Here, as everywhere in the *fin de siècle*, we suspect that politics and deep subjectivity are sides of the same coin; and this, to return to where we started out, is where the period can be most instructive for us today. Annie Besant coming hotfoot from spiritual meditation to industrial struggle; Edward Carpenter in Trafalgar Square; Oscar Wilde championing socialism; Yeats veering between theosophy and Irish Republican Brotherhood: these are salutary images for an age like our own, in which the discourse of subjectivity, and the language of social transformation, no longer consort so obviously together. It is not, of course, that there is any simple way of putting them together. The paradox of all social transformation is that it requires as one of its prerequisites a changed human subject, yet that such reconstructed subjects are as much the product of social transformation as the precondition of it. This is not a conundrum which will yield to any purely theoretical resolution. Yet in the area which will no doubt dominate the left's political agenda for some years to come – the question of postcolonialism – the split between these two perspectives is painfully evident. On the one hand, an 'identity politics' of impressive sophistication, with a suggestive psychoanalytic version of post-colonial oppression, which is loftily remote from the realm of political practice; on the other hand, an ominously unreconstructed revolutionary nationalism which can at least organize effectively to achieve its goals. Much the same could be said of the friction between French and Anglo-Saxon feminisms, or of those North American feminisms which, while admirably militant on women's issues, show about as much interest in socialism as Oliver North. It is to our own divided end of the century, strung out between the 1960s and the 1980s, that the Besants and Gonnes, Wildes and Carpenters, speak most urgently. And if in the 1990s we can recapture something of the generous plurality of their project, then we will be spared the shameful admission that the late Victorians have happened again in our own epoch, this time as farce.

CHAPTER 2

The New Woman and the crisis of Victorianism

Sally Ledger

The rise of the New Woman at the *fin de siècle* was symptomatic of an ongoing challenge to the monolithic ideological certainties of mid-Victorian Britain. The New Woman, the New Journalism, the New Criticism, the New Unionism: an emergent ideological epoch is clearly announced by these coinages of the 1880s and 1890s. The collision between the old and the new that characterized the *fin de siècle* marks it as an excitingly volatile transitional period; a time when British cultural politics were caught between two ages, the Victorian and the modern; a time fraught both with anxiety and with an exhilarating sense of possibility.

The recurrent theme of the cultural politics of the *fin de siècle* was instability, and gender was arguably the most destabilizing category. It is no coincidence that the New Woman materialized alongside the decadent and the dandy. Whilst the New Woman was perceived as a direct threat to classic Victorian definitions of femininity, the decadent and the dandy undermined the Victorians' valorization of a robust, muscular brand of British masculinity deemed to be crucial to the maintenance of the British Empire. The significance of the crisis in gender relations at the close of the nineteenth century has not been understated by feminist critics. Most notably perhaps, Elaine Showalter's *Sexual Anarchy* explores the sense of imminent anarchy within gender relations which characterized the 1880s and 1890s. Illuminating and well researched as Showalter's study is, it is limited by its virtual exclusion of socio-cultural discourses adjacent to those pertaining to sexuality and gender. Whilst acknowledging that sexual difference was only one of the ideological battlegrounds of the *fin de siècle*, citing the rise of trade unionism, fears of colonial rebellion, urban poverty and homelessness as other destabilizing factors, Showalter chooses largely to ignore these and to concentrate solely on gender relations.[1]

My aim here is to open up and extend the parameters of Showalter's commentary on gender relations at the *fin de siècle* by considering the rise of the New Woman in her relationship with other social and cultural phenomena of the period in a more thorough way than Showalter's volume attempts. By examining the extent to which the emergent, radical socio-cultural phenomena of the *fin de siècle* interacted with one another, and the extent to which they lacked common ideological ground, one of the objects will be to illuminate those political factors which enabled residual elements of the dominant ideology of Victorianism to survive the crisis years at the end of the nineteenth century. The chapter will examine the nature of the relationship between, variously: the New Woman and decadence; the New Woman and the politics of empire; and the New Woman and the nascent socialisms of the late nineteenth century.

As well as exploring the aspirations and limitations of the 'new' socio-cultural phenomena of the *fin de siècle*, my purpose will also be to contribute to an understanding of the relationship between gender politics, class politics and the politics of empire at the close of the nineteenth century. The critical preoccupation of our own *fin de siècle* with the so-called 'holy trinity' of gender, 'race' and class had its origins in the cultural politics of the 1880s and 1890s. By scrutinizing these origins, and the points at which each component part of the trinity intersected, an analysis of the tensions between the cultural politics of gender, 'race' and class at the end of the nineteenth century can elucidate the current, ongoing critical debates around these issues within cultural theory.

The New Woman as a category was by no means stable: the relationship between the New Woman as a discursive construct and the New Woman as a representative of the women's movement of the *fin de siècle* was complex, and by no means free of contradictions. The gap between ideological projection and social praxis was often considerable. Even within discourse the New Woman was not a consistent category. Whilst medico-scientific discourse, for example, concentrated on the threat she apparently posed to women's role as mothers, anti-feminist fictional discourse frequently constructed her as a sexual decadent. The New Woman writers themselves did not always agree on who or what the New Woman was: whilst Sarah Grand championed sexual purity and motherhood in *The Heavenly Twins*, Mona Caird's attack on motherhood in *The Daughters of Danaus* is devastating. Grant Allen's heroine in *The Woman Who Did* is a champion of free love, in contrast to the more sexually circumspect heroines of Grand's novels.[2] The constitutional feminists of the late nineteenth century saw themselves neither as campaigners against motherhood nor as sexual radicals, but as supporters of female suffrage.

The elusive quality of the New Woman of the *fin de siècle* clearly marks her as a problem, as a challenge to the apparently self-identical culture of Victorianism which could not find a consistent language by which she could be categorized and dealt with. All that was certain was that she was dangerous, a threat to the *status quo*.

In the discursive sphere the New Woman was frequently figured alongside the decadent, and it was for this reason that the fate of the New Woman of the 1890s was inextricably linked with the public disgracing of Oscar Wilde. On 25 May 1895, Wilde was sentenced to two years hard labour for committing acts of 'gross indecency'.[3] On 21 December 1895, *Punch* triumphantly announced 'THE END OF THE NEW WOMAN – The crash has come at last': Victorian feminism, for this most misogynist of Victorian journals, was on the run.[4] An enormous number of New Woman novels had been published and widely read in the early 1890s, concomitant both with the rise of mass-market fiction and with the resurgence of interest in the Woman Question at the *fin de siècle*. But this deluge of popular New Woman fiction dwindled dramatically after 1895, confirming *Punch*'s prediction at the close of that year. The fictional New Woman was almost certainly a victim of the moral rearguard action which followed the Wilde trials.

Although ideologically they had surprisingly little in common (as Showalter has remarked, they did not perceive themselves to be natural allies[5]) the New Women and the decadents of the *fin de siècle* were repeatedly lumped together in the flourishing periodical press of the 1890s. In 1895 the *Speaker* asserted that 'For many years past Mr Wilde has been the real leader in this country of the "new school" in literature – the revolutionary and anarchist school which has forced itself into such prominence in every domain of art... The new criticism, the new poetry, even the new woman, are all, more or less, the creatures of Mr Oscar Wilde's fancy.'[6] This radical conjunction of the 'new' was seized upon by conservative writers of the period as a threat to the dominant moral, socio-sexual and aesthetic codes of the Victorian age. Eliza Lynn Linton, in an onslaught upon 'The Partisans of the Wild Woman' yoked together the New Journalism, the New Woman and decadence into an unholy trinity of radical degeneration.[7]

What most obviously linked the New Woman with the Wildean decadents of the 1890s was the fact that both overtly challenged Victorian sexual codes. The New Woman fiction is generally characterized by a sexual candour which was also a feature of literary decadence. A writer for the *Westminster Review* speculated that the dominant note of sexuality in all literature of the 1890s was 'a sign that English fiction has entered a stage of decadence'.[8] The attacks on the sexual content of New Woman fiction were of course symptomatic of the discursive explosion around the subject of sexuality in the Victorian years. The fictional New Woman was a product of, rather than a pioneering voice within, this discursive sphere. Although the Victorian age has traditionally been characterized by sexual repression, in fact, as Foucault has pointed out, never before had sex entered into discourse with such vehemence: there was a general discursive erethism surrounding sexuality from the mid-Victorian period onwards.[9] The full-scale entry of sexuality into discourse at this time partly exemplifies the Victorian obsession with taxonomy. Scientifically to classify and medically to analyze sexuality was institutionally to control it, and in this way it is possible to see how Victorian sexual repression and prohibition actually went hand in hand with the discursive explosion around the subject of sex.

The multiple medico-scientific discourses on sexuality in the 1890s were both an instrument and effect of power, the result of a desire to control: but at the same time they operated, in Foucauldian terms, as a point of resistance and a starting point for opposing discursive strategies. The series of attacks on the New Woman and the decadents in the periodical press of the 1890s effectively prised open a discursive space for both of them. How this discursive space was used by the supporters of the New Woman in particular is something which will be addressed further on.

The trials of Oscar Wilde in April and May of 1895 crystallized in the general cultural psyche the challenge to gender definitions posed by the decadents and the New Woman, and the immediate result was an attempt both to ridicule and to silence them. The second Wilde trial began on 26 April 1895, and on 27 April *Punch* published a diatribe against 'Sexomania', written 'By an Angry Old Buffer':

282   PUNCH, OR THE LONDON CHARIVARI.   [June 15, 1895.

THE NEW WOMAN.

"You 're not leaving us, Jack! Tea will be here directly!"
"Oh, I 'm going for a Cup of Tea in the Servants' Hall. I can't get on without Female Society, you know!"

Figure 1.

When Adam delved and Eve span
No one need ask which was the man.
Bicycling, footballing, scarce human,
All wonder now, 'Which is the woman?'
But a new fear my bosom vexes;
Tomorrow there may be no sexes!
Unless, as end to all the pother,
Each one in fact become the other.[10]

New Women on bicycles, garbed in bloomers – a product of the
campaign for rational dress at the *fin de siècle* – fill this Old Buffer with
fears that the counterpart of the effeminate man was the unwomanly
woman. New Women and feminists in general were often constructed
in the periodical press as mannish, over-educated, humourless bores.
The Girton Girl was much maligned and ridiculed throughout the
period. Severely dressed, wearing college ties, and smoking, the New
Women in a *Punch* cartoon from 1895 (figure 1) are presumably
discussing the books which are on the table whilst the man of the
house escapes to the servants' hall for a cup of tea and a gossip. Here,
as elsewhere, the specificity of the New Woman as a product of the

Figure 2 'The Woman Who Wouldn't Do', *Punch*, 30 March 1895.

middle and upper classes is clear (I shall return to this further on). Cartoon representations of physically masculine New Women in *Punch* were accompanied by pictures of correspondingly effeminate men: figures 2 and 3 are entirely representative of a general trend. Homophobic and misogynist discourses were by no means exclusive to *Punch*, although it is interesting to note the extent to which a satirical discourse was deployed in the attempt to attack and silence all who were perceived to have transgressed prescribed Victorian gender codes in the 1890s. Eliza Lynn Linton among many others was also quick to challenge the masculinity of those men who actually supported the New Woman, claiming that 'Their morals are the morals of women, not of men... Affiliated to the Wild Women and their cause, they are themselves like women in all essentials of mind and character... The truth is simply this – THE UNSEXED WOMAN PLEASES THE UNSEXED MAN.'[11]

Figure 3 'From the Queer and Yellow Book', *Punch*, 2 February 1895.

Although both the New Women and Wildean decadents defined themselves against the dominant sexual ideology of the Victorian period, and were connected in the journalistic writings of the time, they actually shared little ideological common ground, a fact which weakened the political clout of both. To lump together all the new movements of the *fin de siècle*, and to hold Wilde responsible for them all, was, as John Stokes has remarked, to be rather too generous to Wilde[12] (and Wilde's *Picture of Dorian Gray* – the so-called 'bible' of English decadence – is in many respects a profoundly misogynist text). This is not to deny that Wilde had one or two feminist credentials, and a sympathetic feminist reading of Wilde and his work could plausibly set him up both as the most radical inhabitant of the discursive space prised open by the erethism surrounding sexuality in the *fin de siècle*, and as a key figure in the perceived connection between late-Victorian feminism and decadence. Wilde, after all, edited *Woman's World* for two years, changing the title from *Lady's World* and insisting that the paper become less frivolous. He also commissioned articles on feminism and the women's suffrage campaign. As for his own writings, an earlier draft of *The Importance of Being Earnest* apparently cast Gwendoline as a more New Womanish figure than she is in the final version; presumably Wilde changed her because such a casting would be contradictory and inappropriate to the play as a whole, which is not sexually radical.[13] In *A Woman of No Importance*, the puritanical Hester, who believes in democracy, could be seen to be a species of New Woman.

But the possible correlations between Wilde and the New Women of the 1890s cannot be stretched too far. Altogether typical of the response of the feminist press to the trial of Oscar Wilde was an article in the *Woman's Signal* – a feminist newspaper – which welcomed 'The fall of Mr Oscar Wilde and the malodorous decadents' which, the columnist wrote, 'must hearten every mother who, in the love of God, is training her sons to habits of purity and manliness.'[14] Despite the protestations of many of the periodicals of the 1890s, the mainstream women's movement was anxious to distance itself from Oscar Wilde and his followers.

In pragmatic terms, it is easy to see why this should have been the case: to have aligned themselves with Oscar Wilde, who had been publicly disgraced as a sexual deviant, would almost certainly have damaged the feminists' demands for civic and constitutional rights. But the series of outraged denunciations of Wildean decadence which poured from the feminist press of the 1890s is also symptomatic of the absence of any fully articulated discourse on female sexuality – let alone other sexualities – within the mainstream women's movement of the late nineteenth century. Within the Victorian male medical discourse New Women were hardly constructed as sexual subjects at all. It was only towards the close of the century that sexologists such as Havelock Ellis and Richard von Krafft-Ebing associated feminism with a challenge to Victorian constructions of female sexuality.[15] Instead, women's socio-sexual deviance was generally described almost exclusively in terms of the New Woman's supposed rejection of motherhood: female reproduction rather than female sexuality was the main issue in the debate. The first generation New Women of the Victorian age seem by and large to have accepted these medico-scientific parameters of the field of discourse surrounding female sexuality, inasmuch as that they rarely, in the discursive realm at least, constructed themselves as sexual subjects. Carroll Smith-Rosenberg, in an essay in *Hidden From History*, has argued that this silence within feminist discourse of the late nineteenth century was a profoundly disabling inheritance for the second generation of New Women in the twentieth century.[16]

Despite this silence surrounding female sexuality within the mainstream feminist movement, many of the fictional writers of the time had no qualms about constructing the New Woman as a voracious sexual subject. Marie Corelli's best-selling novel of 1895, *The Sorrows of Satan*, presents the New Woman as a dangerously voluptuous sexual libertine: this is the species of New Woman most commonly associated with Wildean decadence.[17] Sybil Elton, the New Woman of the piece, is a 'harpy – a vulture of vice.' She has an enormous sexual appetite which terrifies and disgusts the man she marries, and in her suicide note she blames the New Woman fiction and decadence for her own moral corruption. Sybil is sexually decadent and vampire-like, and the vampire could be another fictional version of the New Woman. Bram Stoker's *Dracula*, published in 1897, was very much a response to the New Woman: there are a number of explicit references to her in the text. Mina Harker, a stereotypically 'good' little Victorian Miss, innocently describes in her diary the tea that she and the angelic Lucy Westenra have eaten together, reflecting that 'we should have shocked [even] the "New Woman" with our appetites.'[18] During the night following the decorous little tea party, Lucy Westenra is bitten in her sleep by Count Dracula, and thereafter develops appetites of a more wanton kind: she is transformed from a blonde-haired innocent into an oversexed vampire, who has to be massacred in the most appalling way by the brave young English men of the piece in order to be removed as a threat to the British 'race'. What this analysis reveals is that whilst the mainstream women's movement of the *fin de siècle* was busy distancing itself from the sexual excesses associated with Wildean decadence and concentrating instead on civic and constitutional rights for women, the popular fictional press often insisted on representing the New Woman as a sexual decadent.

Contemporary with these fictional attacks on the New Woman which constructed her as a sexually rampant monster, many periodical writers of a medico-scientific bent were busy depicting New Women as the mothers of a degenerate 'race', as the breeders of 'monsters'. The 1890s constituted Britain's so-called 'Age of Empire', and notions of 'race' abounded in the intellectual culture of the period. Following the death of General Gordon in Khartoum in 1885, the 1890s were characterized by a perceived threat to Britain's interests abroad, and doubts about the continuation of the British Empire often focused on the necessity of breeding a strong, pure English 'race'. If Wildean decadence threatened British masculinity of the sort represented by the heroic young saviours of Mina Harker in *Dracula*, the New Woman was also frequently presented as a danger to the continuance of the 'race', in the guise of a potential mother of physically weak and mentally feeble children. The crisis in gender definitions was accompanied by – and inextricably linked with – a crisis within the politics of empire. It was, as I've mentioned earlier, the threat to women's reproductive function – the threat to their role as mothers of the 'race' – which was used as ammunition against the New Woman in medico-scientific discourse. Charles Harper, writing in 1894, warned the New Woman that:

nature, which never contemplated the production of a learned or a muscular woman, will be revenged upon her offspring, and the New Woman, if a mother at all, will be the mother of a New Man, as different indeed, from the present race as possible, but how different, the clamorous females of today cannot expect ... [There is] the prospect of peopling the world with stunted and hydrocephalic children ... and ultimate extinction of the race.[19]

There were plenty of such arguments around at the time. Grant Allen had warned in an 1889 article called 'Plain Words on the Woman Question' that 'many of the most cultivated and able families of the English-speaking race will have become extinct, through the prime error of supposing that an education which is good for men must also be good for women'.[20] *Punch*, as usual, also had something to say on the subject, warning that the New Woman 'made further development in generations to come quite impossible'.[21] At the same time aestheticism and decadence were being attacked as 'this manhood-blighting cant of art', and 'plain sturdy Britons' were urged to rise and defeat the decadents, who were a threat to the strength and purity of the British 'race'.[22]

What emerges here is that the crisis of Victorianism at the *fin de siècle* centred not just on gender issues, but also on the inter-connections between gender roles and contemporary anxieties pertaining to the continuation of the 'race' in the best interests of the

British Empire. Laura Marholm Hansson, giving a continental perspective on the New Woman, momentously declared that:

the many honest people who think they hear in the Woman Movement the memento mori of a race, and the gnawing of the death-worm, are not so far wrong. As it manifests itself outwardly it is a sign of decay and corruption, and where it has produced conditions – or more accurately has grown out of conditions – as in the lauded lands of women's emancipation, the decline of a race is clearly shown.[23]

What is remarkable, and ironic, about the discursive constructions of the New Woman as a threat to the 'race' is that the middle-class feminists of the 1890s themselves had a considerable ideological investment in notions of empire and in the continuance of the 'race', with many of the New Woman writers championing motherhood and ardently supporting purity campaigns. Not least of these was Sarah Grand who originally coined the phrase the 'New Woman' in 1894. In an article written for the *North American Review*, Grand described the New Woman as a morally superior being who was a 'little above' men. The idea was that men should emulate the moral superiority of women, rather than that the New Woman should have the moral freedoms allowed to men. It is perhaps difficult now to see Grand's position as particularly new, in so far as it was almost entirely complicit with the medico-scientific, not to mention Ruskinian, constructions of femininity which abounded in the periodical press of the time; and it certainly has nothing in common with the sexual excesses associated with Wildean decadence. Nonetheless, it is easy to see how Grand's novels would have upset the guardians of Victorian morality, in that they speak the unspeakable, revealing the murky side of masculine sexuality in the Victorian age.

Grand's first novel, *The Heavenly Twins*, was probably the most famous and infamous of the New Woman texts written by women in the 1890s. Published after the furore surrounding the Contagious Diseases Acts, it caused a scandal through its broaching of the subject of venereal disease contracted by unsuspecting wives and their offspring from their promiscuous husbands. Evadne, one of the New Women of the novel, refuses to consummate her marriage when she discovers that her husband has a dubious sexual past. She suffers from sexual frustration and, more important, from the denial of her maternal instinct. Grand is complicit with the notion, articulated by many Victorian medical men, that 'normal' women only have sexual intercourse so as to satisfy their desire for motherhood. Yet at the same time, it *is* made clear that Evadne has to repress her sexual desire for her husband in order to take up a 'pure' position, and it is in the articulation of this repressed desire that the pleasure of the text resides.

Evadne's friend, Edith, contracts syphilis from her husband, gives birth to a syphilitic child and dies from dementia. Edith's sexual ignorance is emphasized: Evadne, by contrast, has studied anatomy and physiology, has read John Stuart Mill's *Subjection of Women*, and is able to defend herself from the dangers of masculine promiscuity. It was this desire for the sexual education of women which outraged critics and reviewers, as well as the frankness with which the subject of syphilis is treated. And yet again, alongside this radical thread in the novel there is a confirmation of Victorian ideals concerning monogamy and motherhood, which are presented as the norm in the text. Whilst this is undoubtedly a transgressive novel, residual elements of Victorian sexual ideology mark it as a transitional text, caught, like the New Woman of the 1890s herself, between the old and the new, the Victorian and the modern. Grand's own loyalty to traditional sexual codes is revealed in an article of 1896 in which she affirmed the importance of marriage and maternity.[24] More notable still is Grand's persistent emphasis on sexual purity: she was no sexual radical.

The puritanical strand in the feminist politics of the *fin de siècle* – a sexual puritanism which persists to a lesser extent even in the feminist movement of today – provided good fodder for the champions of the British Empire who repeatedly called upon women to be the breeders of a pure, strong British 'race'. Millicent Garrett Fawcett reiterated mainstream feminism's dissociation from any kind of sexual libertarianism when she reviewed Grant Allen's *The Woman Who Did*, a New Woman novel whose heroine is an advocate of free love.[25] Fawcett wrote of Allen's relationship with the women's movement that 'He is not a friend, but an enemy, and it is as an enemy that he endeavours to link together the claim of women to citizenship and social and industrial independence with attacks upon marriage and the family.'[26] It is no coincidence that Fawcett wrote this review in 1895. After the Wilde scandal she seems anxious once and for all to distance the Victorian women's movement from the challenges to the dominant sexual ideology of the time. A writer for the *Woman's Signal* made an implicit connection between sexual purity and the defence of empire. In a defence of the New Woman she declaimed:

> If lofty purpose, strength of will
> To cleanse the world of every ill
> Be just a little 'New', dear sir,
> 'Tis right that we should make a stir.
> For God and Home and Land we fight
> And God above defends the right.

A patriotic inflection is unmistakable in the stated defence of mother country here. In the same issue of the *Woman's Signal*, another writer, seemingly influenced by Sarah Grand, claimed that 'Women are fortunate in belonging to the less tainted half of the race. Dr Benjamin Ward Richardson tells us that but for this conserving fact it would deteriorate to the point of failure.'[27]

The preoccupation with sexual purity and motherhood in *The Heavenly Twins*, and the desire to re-moralize society through the extermination of disease, both suggest an eugenic subtext to Grand's novel. The eugenics movement was heavily implicated in the new imperialism of the *fin de siècle*; at the same time, eugenics appealed to many feminists because it seemed to offer a channel (and a language) through which women could influence public events. As Penny Boumelha has remarked, eugenics seemed to offer feminists an illusion of power without challenging the existing separation of male and female spheres of influence.[28] The deployment of a eugenic discourse within feminism could be seen as an attempt to appropriate and transform a dominant socio-scientific discourse for subversive feminist ends. It may seem quite reasonable for the marginal or powerless to challenge the dominant discourse by framing their challenge in a language which is meaningful within the hegemonical discourse: to this extent it is understandable that Victorian feminists should challenge the dominant sexual codes with ammunition from within the dominant ideology of the time. Moreover, to speak always within the language of the marginal frustrates those who seek to exercise power. But to inhabit the discursive space of the dominant ideology is also profoundly problematic; in the case of the New Woman writers it severely disabled the radical drift of their project.

The eugenic project is more overt in Menie Muriel Dowie's *Gallia*, a popular New Woman novel from 1895. In this novel the New Woman heroine suppresses the sexual desire she feels for the man she loves on the basis that he is a physically flawed specimen of manhood (he has heart disease), and she chooses instead to marry and mate with a fit healthy man for whom she feels nothing because, as she puts it, 'I have wanted the father of my child to be a fine, strong, manly man, full of health and strength.'[29] It is in the greater interest of the 'race' that she should marry the healthy male. Notwithstanding its complicity with eugenics, *Gallia* is a challenging, transgressive novel: Gallia's rationale for marrying the 'strong, manly man' is at once socially reactionary *and* a remarkable statement of feminine assertiveness. What she seems to be saying is: 'if I am only of value as a breeding machine, then that is what I will be, and I will not let any other considerations, like love, enter into the equation.'[30] And basing her choice of marriage partner on the logistics of eugenics might seem preferable to the more generally accepted economic factors which influenced middle-class marriages in the Victorian years.

Given the preoccupation with empire in the 1890s, it is fascinating the way in which the post-Darwinian meaning of the word 'race' time and time again becomes inflected with imperialist overtones in the writings of the period. It would thus seem that the eugenics arguments which began to gather momentum in the 1890s were connected in a complex way with Britain's ongoing imperialist project, and many of the New Woman writers showed themselves to be complicit with this. In this context it is significant that alongside the feminist interest in eugenics in the 1890s, at the level of practice there was a general suspension of suffrage activity following the onset of the Boer War at the turn of the century; Millicent Garrett Fawcett wrote later that 'Two fires cannot burn together, and the most ardent of the suffragists felt that, while the war lasted, it was not a fitting time to press their own claims and objects.'[31] Emmeline and Christabel Pankhurst similarly ceased their struggle for women's suffrage at the outbreak of World War One (another imperialist catastrophe), and dedicated themselves instead to war work and fanatical patriotism, changing the name of the Women's Social and Political Union journal from *The Suffragette* to *Britannia*.[32]

The ideology of imperialism is, of course, powerfully assimilative, its power lying in its ability to override ideological distinctions and oppositions based on class and gender. At the *fin de siècle* the ideology of imperialism succeeded to a not inconsiderable extent in incorporating large sections of the feminist and socialist movements of the day. Henry Hyndman, the leader of the Social Democratic Federation, had asserted in 1883 that he was 'quite content to bear the reproach of chauvinism'. By 1910 he went so far as to admit that

'I am a jingo'.[33] Robert Blatchford's socialist newspaper, *The Clarion*, was unabashedly patriotic. By contrast, William Morris's profound anti-imperialism (he consistently opposed Britain's imperialist policies from the 'Eastern Question' in 1876 onwards) was arguably a socialist exception rather than the rule. The assimilation of substantial parts of the late nineteenth century's feminist and socialist movements into the discourse of imperialism, which was so pervasive in the *fin-de-siècle* years, undermined the radical credentials of both.

Although feminism and socialism both showed themselves to be complicit with the politics of empire in the *fin de siècle*, in other respects they decidedly lacked a common sense of identity. A socialist-feminist novel from 1888, Jane Hume Clapperton's *Margaret Dunmore; or, A Socialist Home*, throws an interesting light on feminism's troubled relationship with the nascent socialisms of the late nineteenth century. Set two years into the future the novel takes the form of a utopia, elaborating a socialist-feminist community set up by the unmarried Margaret Dunmore. The aim of Margaret Dunmore's 'socialist home' is to provide 'a Provincial Communistic Group – ladies and gentlemen who intend to live, rather than preach, Socialism; and who hope to rear children of a purely Socialistic type'.[34] The inspiration of the communitarian Fellowship of the New Life formed by Edward Carpenter, Havelock Ellis and others at the *fin de siècle* is, of course, evident here. Although the 'socialist home' of the novel enables unmarried women such as Margaret Dunmore to fulfil themselves in roles which do not involve marriage or motherhood, the tensions in traditional bourgeois gender relations when brought up against communitarian living are not altogether resolved. Margaret Dunmore has a close intellectual relationship with Frank Ray, whose wife Rose provides for the more purely domestic and familial areas of his life; Rose becomes jealous of Margaret, and withdrawn from the marriage. There is implicit in the novel a recognition that gender relations will have to be modified under socialism; but at the same time, the fundamentals of bourgeois marriage itself are not challenged. Neither is the problematic relationship between motherhood and participation in political and intellectual life fully hammered out: Monsieur Henri Martin, a revolutionary socialist who continues his work for international socialism whilst living as a community member, believes of Margaret that 'by simple motherhood she would accomplish more for the race than by this regenerative scheme of hers' (p. 56). Again the eugenic discourse which was so powerful within both feminism and socialism at the *fin de siècle* is evident here, and the novel closes with a vague prescription for a 'conference of mothers' to decide how best to further the interests of the 'race'. The capitalistic division of labour which kept women in the domestic sphere is never fully challenged in the novel either: it is the women of the socialist home who undertake the domestic labour. In the event, Jane Hume Clapperton shows herself to have been more a socialist than a feminist.

There was a decidedly anti-feminist drift within some areas of the late nineteenth-century socialist movement. Whilst H. M. Hyndman was utterly dismissive of feminism and sexual politics, even the more sympathetic marxists and socialists such as Frederic Engels and Edward Carpenter did not ultimately challenge the sexual division of labour.[35] In his *Origin of the Family, Private Property and the State*, Engels argued that 'The predominance of the man in marriage is simply a consequence of his economic predominance and will vanish with it automatically.'[36] But Engels failed to offer an analysis of domestic labour, regarding it simply as a part of personal life, irrelevant to women's insertion into waged labour. Edward Carpenter's Fellowship of the New Life included women and was sexually radical; but the fact remained that it was the women of the communities who did most of the housework. In *Love's Coming of Age*, which went through eleven editions between 1896 and 1919, Carpenter traced women's oppression from the introduction of private property. But he, like Engels, accepted the 'naturalness' of the sexual division of labour because of the biological difference between men and women, and he accepted 'masculinity' and 'femininity' as fixed terms.[37]

Robert Blatchford, editor of the popular newspaper *The Clarion*, was one of many socialists hostile to any association between socialism and the sex question. Writing to Edward Carpenter in January 1894, he admitted that sexual relations must change, but that this must come after (rather than as part of) economic and industrial change. His fear was that 'if Socialists identify themselves with any sweeping changes in those relations, the Industrial change will be seriously retarded', and he concluded that 'the time is not ripe to meddle with the sexual question'.[38] In a general way, both the Social Democratic Federation and the Independent Labour Party regarded the sexual division of labour as natural, and conflict between the sexes was always subordinated to class conflict. Robert Blatchford's immensely popular utopian-socialist essay of 1895, *Merrie England*, shows itself

altogether complicit with the existing sexual division of labour.[39]
Whilst Blatchford recognizes the domestic misery of the artisan's wife
who is endlessly 'Cooking, cleaning, managing, mending, washing
clothes, waiting on husband and children, her work is never done' (p.
45), his solution is not to free women from the yoke of domestic
labour, but merely to reorganize it on large-scale, militaristic lines, so
that 'We set up one laundry, with all the best machinery; we set up
one big drying field; we set up one great kitchen, one general dining
hall, and one pleasant tea garden. Then we buy all the provisions and
other things in large quantities, and we appoint certain wives as cooks
and laundresses, or, as is the case with many military duties, we let
the wives take the duties in turn.' (p. 54)

Given the general attitude of the new socialist parties of the *fin de
siècle* to feminist issues, it is not surprising that evidence from the
feminist periodicals of the day would seem to suggest that there was
relatively little sympathy within the 'equal rights' bourgeois women's
movement for the various new socialist groupings. It must be added,
though, that this is as much attributable to the narrow class identity
of the New Woman as to the failure of the new socialist parties to take
on board the Woman Question. The Independent Labour Party
(ILP) was formed in 1893, and in 1895 Tom Mann gave a speech to
the feminist Pioneer Club: the report on his speech in *Shafts*, a
feminist newspaper, declared indignantly that 'Tom Mann and the
socialists were wrong in trying to drive women back into the home.'[40]
There was undeniably a degree of truth in this charge against the
ILP.

Notwithstanding the conflicts between the 'equal rights' women's
movement and the socialist parties of the 1890s, there had nonetheless
long been a sense, sometimes a fear, that the women's movement and
socialism were in some way connected. Herbert Spencer, in his
Principles of Ethics, published in 1893, had argued that women should
be denied access to political activity because their 'propensity to give
most where capacity is least' (all very well in the domestic sphere)
would 'increase the ability of public agencies to override individual
rights in pursuit of what were thought beneficent ends'.[41] As Lorna
Duffin has pointed out, this blueprint for political control by women
looks suspiciously like a blueprint for socialism. Karl Pearson, a
socialist, eugenicist, friend of Olive Schreiner and member of the
Men and Women's Club, also made a connection between feminism
and socialism by arguing that 'There has never been a Labour

Question without a Woman's Question also,' and he linked the two groups by affirming that 'Both labour and woman are seeking to throw off the slavery arising from economic dependence; both are demanding – it may be in different spheres – that education shall be free; both desire equality and opportunity.'[42]

A substantial number of women were indeed actively involved in the labour movement of the late nineteenth century, and a number of these were feminists. A growing body of research is now devoted to the work of such women. Prominent amongst them was Isabella Ford, New Woman novelist, trade unionist and pioneering member of the ILP. She was by no means alone in adding a woman's voice to the Independent Labour Party, a third of whose members were women. There were a number of feminists at grass-roots level in the Social Democratic Federation (SDF), too, as well as the more prominently placed Olive Schreiner, one of the founders of the SDF's Women's League. Schreiner was also a member, with Havelock Ellis, of the communitarian Fellowship of the New Life, as well as being a pioneering New Woman novelist. Eleanor Marx was another notable socialist feminist whose extensive political work for socialism included setting up foreign language and debating classes for the SDF, translating all the papers for the miners' international conference of 1897,[43] and helping to organize the Gas Workers' Union, one of the new unions of the *fin de siècle* in which women had equal status with men.[44] As a feminist Marx translated Ibsen and *Madame Bovary*, and her lecture on Shelley's socialism stresses the influence of Mary Wollstonecraft and Mary Shelley on the poet's 'perception of woman's real position'. In the lecture, she reflected that 'The woman is to the man as the producing class is to the possessing.'[45]

By no means a majority of the socialist women of the *fin de siècle* were feminists, though, and this is partly because of the very different social and political preoccupations out of which socialism and feminism grew. Eleanor Marx herself, whilst undoubtedly being a supporter of women's suffrage, owed her primary loyalties – unsurprisingly – to the overcoming of social inequality based on class oppressions. She had grave reservations about the class politics of the equal rights women's movement, caustically remarking that as a social reformer she saw 'no more in common between Mrs Fawcett and a laundress than … between Rothschild and one of his employees'. Her conclusion was that 'In short, there is for us only the working-class movement.'[46] When it came to the crunch, Marx's

socialism took precedence over her feminism, and she reflected in
1892 that 'If every demand raised by these women [the equal rights
feminists] were granted today, we working women would still be just
where we were before. Women workers would still work infamously
long hours, for infamously low wages, under infamously unhealthful
conditions.'[47] Beatrice Webb, another notable female socialist, was
ambivalent towards the women's movement. Webb's political
sympathies lay with the trade union movement, and she was an
ardent supporter, for example, of the 1895 Factory Act which aimed
to curb women's employment.

The separation between the feminist and socialist movements of
the *fin de siècle* is graphically illustrated, in fact, by the conflict
between the women's movement and the trade unionist labour
movement over the Factory Acts of the 1890s. Jessie Boucherett's
Women's Employment Defence League regarded the acts as a sinister
attempt to drive women out of the workforce and back into the home.
Yet from the point of view of the labour movement, and its supporters
such as Beatrice Webb, society as a whole had an interest in
improving conditions of employment. Allowing absolute freedom
of action to women whose bargaining position was either weak or
non-existent (such women were by and large willing to work however
low the wage) would have been to set into reverse the gradually
improving material and economic standards of industrial society.
Both the representatives of the women's movement, who opposed the
Factory Acts of the 1890s, and the labour movement, who supported
them, claimed to be on the side of liberty.[48] It was such heroic New
Women as Annie Besant who attempted to yoke the two movements
together by unionizing women. By and large, though, the common
ground between mainstream feminism and the nascent socialist
parties in the *fin de siècle* was relatively scarce, and the responsibility
for this has to be shared by both political groupings. Whilst the
socialist parties had very limited sympathies for the bourgeois
women's movement, the relatively narrow demands of that movement, largely based on suffrage, education and property rights,
meant that Eleanor Marx's charges contained a good deal of truth. It
is noteworthy too that at a time when novelists such as Gissing,
Walter Besant, and even Henry James, were concerning themselves
with London's slumland, the New Woman novelists tended to recast
the social question in terms of the 'pollution' of society by masculine
sexuality. This shift in focus away from the naturalistic slumland

fiction of the 1880s was largely a consequence of the specific class identity of the literary advocates of the New Woman, which was emphatically bourgeois and rarely socialist.[49]

The complex dialogue between feminist politics, socialist politics and the politics of empire which was so strongly manifested in the *fin de siècle* is ongoing at the close of the twentieth century. What emerges from an analysis of these issues in the 1880s and 1890s is that the New Woman and her advocates were, although a transgressive socio-cultural force, in many respects complicit with residual elements of the dominant Victorian ideologies concerning gender roles, sexuality, 'race', empire and social class. Although the New Women and the decadents were forced to occupy the same discursive space in the cultural politics of the 1890s, they inhabited it in radically different ways, with little consensus in the realm of sexual politics emerging between them. At the same time, the new socialist parties of the *fin de siècle* failed either to question the sexual division of labour or fully to take on board the Woman Question. The radical socio-cultural and political challenge posed respectively by the New Woman, the decadents and the socialists in the last years of the nineteenth century was ultimately too fragmented to form a coherent alternative ideological programme to that posed by the monolithic grand narrative of Victorianism. The advocates of the New Woman, the decadents and aesthetes, the New Lifers, the new socialist parties and growing trade union movement – all had their particular ideological programmes which, whilst frequently being conflated in the period-ical press, in fact shared all too little common ground. Such ideological incompatibility was disabling both for the feminist movement of the *fin de siècle* and for other radicals who were beginning to develop voices of their own at the close of the nineteenth century.

In the postmodern years of the late twentieth century when grand narratives are altogether *passé*, it is perhaps tempting to celebrate rather than to mourn the ideological fragmentations which charac-terized the radical challenges to Victorianism at the *fin de siècle*. To replace one totality with another might simply lead to a different set of oppressions. Nonetheless, at a time when cultural theory is dominated by issues pertaining to gender, class and 'race', and when the so-called 'new world order' of the late twentieth century is collapsing into a morass of competing nationalisms, with socialism apparently on its knees and feminists having to deal with 'post-feminism', it is surely instructive to scrutinize the fissures and interrelationships between gender politics, class politics and the politics of empire as they emerged in the late nineteenth century. To the extent that the fissures remain today, the crisis of Victorianism at the *fin de siècle* is a crisis which persists in the final years of our own century.

NOTES

I would like to thank Scott McCracken and Bill Greenslade for reading and commenting on a draft of this essay.

1 Elaine Showalter, *Sexual Anarchy: Gender and Culture at the Fin de Siècle* (London: Bloomsbury, 1991).

2 Sarah Grand, *The Heavenly Twins* (3 vols., London: William Heinemann, 1893); Mona Caird, *The Daughters of Danaus* (London: Bliss, Sands and Foster, 1894); Grant Allen, *The Woman Who Did* (London: John Lane, 1895).

3 For an account of the two trials see Richard Ellmann, *Oscar Wilde* (New York: Alfred Knopf, 1988), pp. 462–478.

4 *Punch*, 21 December 1895, p. 297.

5 Showalter, *Sexual Anarchy*, p. 170.

6 *Speaker*, 13 April 1895, p. 403. Quoted by John Stokes, *In the Nineties* (Hemel Hempstead: Harvester Wheatsheaf, 1989), p. 14.

7 Eliza Lynn Linton, 'The Partisans of the Wild Woman', *Nineteenth Century*, 31 (1892), 463.

8 Thomas Bradfield, 'A Dominant Note of Some Recent Fiction', *Westminster Review*, 142 (1894), 543.

9 Michel Foucault, *History of Sexuality*, vol. 1, tr. Robert Hurley (New York: Vintage, 1978).

10 *Punch*, 27 April 1895, p. 203.

11 Linton, 'The Partisans', pp. 458–461.

12 Stokes, *In the Nineties*, pp. 14–15.

13 I owe this piece of information to Alan Sinfield, who gave a paper on '"Effeminacy" – Wilde and the Emergence of a Homosexual Identity', at History Workshop 25, Ruskin College, Oxford, November 1991.

14 'Death of a Decadent', *Woman's Signal*, 3 (May 1895), 289.

15 Havelock Ellis, *Man and Woman: A Study of Human Secondary Sexual Characteristics* (London: Walter Scott, 1904); R. von Krafft-Ebing, *Psychopathia Sexualis with Especial Reference to Contrary Sexual Instinct: A Medico-Legal Study*, tr. Charles Chaddock (Philadelphia: F. A. Davis and Co., 1893).

16 Caroll Smith-Rosenberg, 'Discourses of Sexuality and Subjectivity: the New Woman 1870–1936', in Martin Duberman, Martha Vicinus and George Chauncey (eds.) *Hidden From History: Reclaiming the Gay and Lesbian Past* (Harmondsworth: Penguin 1991).

17 Marie Corelli, *The Sorrows of Satan* (London: Methuen, 1895), p. 301, pp. 405–406.
18 Bram Stoker, *Dracula* (1897; reprint Oxford: Oxford University Press, 1989), p. 88. See also Carol A. Senf, '*Dracula*; Stoker's response to the New Woman', *Victorian Studies*, 26 (1982).
19 Charles G. Harper, *Revolted Woman: Past, Present and to Come* (London: Elkin Matthews, 1894), p. 27.
20 Grant Allen, 'Plain Words on the Woman Question', *Fortnightly Review*, 46 (1889), 455–456.
21 *Punch*, 24 November 1894, p. 249.
22 *Punch*, 13 April 1895, p. 177.
23 Laura Marholm Hansson, *Studies in the Psychology of Woman*, tr. Georgia A. Etchinson (Chicago and New York: Herbert S. Stone, 1899), p. 301. Quoted by Linda Dowling, 'The Decadent and the New Woman in the 1890s', *Nineteenth-Century Fiction*, 33 (1979), 447.
24 Sarah Grand, 'The Woman's Question', *Humanitarian*, 8 (1896), 160–169. The article in which the term the 'New Woman' was coined was 'The New aspect of the Woman Question', *North American Review*, 158 (1894), 271–273.
25 For a longer discussion of the campaign for Free Love in the 1890s see David Rubinstein, *Before the Suffragettes* (Brighton: Harvester Press, 1986), pp. 45–47.
26 Millicent Garrett Fawcett, review of *The Woman Who Did*, *Contemporary Review*, 47 (1895), 630.
27 *Woman's Signal*, 3 (January 1895), 26, 27.
28 Penny Boumelha, *Thomas Hardy and Women* (Brighton: Harvester Press, 1982), p. 21.
29 Menie Muriel Dowie, *Gallia* (London: Methuen, 1895), p. 321.
30 I am indebted to Scott McCracken for this reading of Gallia's actions in the novel.
31 Millicent Garrett Fawcett, *Woman's Suffrage* (London: T. C. and E. C. Jack, 1912), p. 58.
32 Bonnie S. Anderson and Judith P. Zinsser, *A History of Their Own*, vol. 2 (Harmondsworth: Penguin, 1990), p. 366.
33 H. M. Hyndman, *The Historical Basis of Socialism in England* (London: Kegan Paul, 1883), p. 194n; and *Justice*, 3 September 1910, quoted by C. Tsuki, *H. M. Hyndman and British Socialism* (Oxford: Oxford University Press, 1961), p. 211.
34 Jane Hume Clapperton, *Margaret Dunmore: or, A Socialist Home* (London: Swan, Sonnenschein and Lowrey, 1888), p. 23.
35 Sheila Rowbotham and Jeffrey Weeks, *Socialism and the New Life* (London: Pluto Press, 1977), p. 116.
36 Ibid., p. 20.
37 Edward Carpenter, *Love's Coming of Age* (1896; reprint New York and London: Mitchell Kennerley, 1911).

38 Robert Blatchford, letter to Edward Carpenter, 11 January 1894; quoted in Rowbotham and Weeks, *Socialism and the New Life*, p. 116.
39 Robert Blatchford, *Merrie England* (1895; reprint London: Clarion Press, 1908).
40 *Shafts*, 3 (June 1895), 35.
41 Herbert Spencer, *Principles of Ethics* (2 vols.; London: Williams and Norgate, 1892–1893), vol. 2, pp. 196–97.
42 Karl Pearson, 'Woman and Labour', *Fortnightly Review*, 29 (May 1894), 563–564.
43 Ruth Brandon, *The New Women and the Old Men* (London: Secker and Warburg, 1990), p. 134.
44 Rowbotham and Weeks, *Socialism and the New Life*, p. 18.
45 Edward Aveling and Eleanor Marx, *Shelley's Socialism: Two Lectures* (Manchester: Lesley Preger, 1947).
46 Cited in Hal Draper and Anne G. Lipow, 'Marxist Women Versus Bourgeois Feminism', *The Socialist Register* (1976), 224.
47 Ibid., p. 224.
48 For a more detailed discussion of the feminist movement's quarrels with the advocates of the factory acts of the 1890s, see Rubinstein, *Before the Suffragettes*, chapter 8.
49 One remarkable exception is Margaret Harkness, a novelist who used the pseudonym 'John Law'. For a discussion of her writing see John Goode, 'Margaret Harkness and the Socialist Novel', in Gustave Klaus (ed.) *The Socialist Novel in Britain* (Brighton: Harvester Press, 1982), and John Goode, 'Feminism, Class and Literary Criticism', in Kate Campbell (ed.) *Critical Feminism* (Buckingham and Philadelphia: Open University Press, 1992).

CHAPTER 3

Empire, 'race' and feminism at the fin de siècle: the work of George Egerton and Olive Schreiner

Laura Chrisman

That nineteenth-century British feminist literary identity was inextricable from contemporary ideologies of 'race', empire and colonialism, was pointed out as long ago as 1985 by Gayatri Spivak, in her essay 'Three Women's Texts and a Critique of Imperialism.'[1] Nonetheless, recent critics of New Woman fiction have persisted in ignoring the connections, as does Gerd Bjorhovde, or alternatively have acknowledged them only to claim, as does Ann Ardis, that the writers constantly challenge 'the pattern of thinking in hierarchically organized binary opposites that pits men against women, "good" women against "fallen" ones, the middle class against the working class, and *European against non-European cultures*' (emphasis added).[2] Against this I want to argue that for many nineteenth-century white English women writers, it was precisely through collusion with, and not in opposition to, hierarchical notions of ethnic and cultural difference, that feminist identity was articulated. Following Spivak, I will argue that this writing articulated female individuation in relation to 'two registers: childbearing and soul making. The first is domestic-society-through-sexual reproduction cathected as "companionate love"; the second is the imperialist project cathected as civil-society-through-social-mission'.[3] The first register translates into a highly maternalized imperial feminism, definable as the making of racial bodies (a eugenically inspired concept), while the second translates into an equally, though metaphorically, maternal and missionary notion of feminism as the making and saving of souls. The two writers I will examine – George Egerton and Olive Schreiner – utilize these notions, among others, to rather different ends. I focus on Egerton's two most celebrated collections, *Keynotes* (1893) and *Discords* (1894).[4] Of Schreiner's diverse writings, I focus on short stories sporadically written between 1887 and 1892, during the period in which Schreiner returned to South Africa from Europe.[5]

45

Perhaps the most quoted passage of George Egerton is the woman's speech from the opening story of *Keynotes*: 'They [men] have all overlooked the eternal wildness, the untamed primitive savage temperament that lurks in the mildest, best woman. Deep in through ages of convention this primeval trait burns, an untameable quantity that may be concealed but is never eradicated by culture – the keynote of woman's witchcraft and woman's strength.'[6] The linkage of European femininity with an (implicitly racialized) ideology of savage primitivism is unavoidable here. Equally striking, though often overlooked, is the specifically sexual and reproductive rationale for this speech: the woman is explaining what it is that prompts women to select seemingly inappropriate and brutish partners to mate with. Sexual preference and sexual reproduction are not separable concerns in Egerton's work, and underlying both is a broadly eugenic ideology. Later in the same conversation the woman remarks that:

if it were not for that [affection], we women would master the world. I tell you men would be no match for us. At heart we care nothing for laws, nothing for systems... It is a wise disposition of providence that this untameableness of ours is corrected by our affections. We forge our own chains in a moment of softness... the qualities that go to make a Napoleon-superstition, want of honour, disregard of opinion and the eternal I – are oftener to be found in a woman.[7]

The potential imperial superwoman, held back from full global realization of her powers by her susceptibility to the bonds of love and affection, is a figure which also features in popular culture, as for instance in Rider Haggard's *She* (1887).[8] Both the figure, and the chains which restrain her, testify to Egerton's essentially romantic conception of femininity, a romanticism overlaid and complicated by Nietzschean anti-idealism and eugenicism.[9] Egerton's analysis of European women's oppression attends mostly to the sphere of ideology, and in particular, to what she sees as the artificial social conventions which prohibit women's natural expression of sexual and maternal desire. Her solution lies in a course of ideological demystification, spiritual regeneration and assertion of natural instinct in defiance of conventionality. The short story medium serves her romanticism well: she uses it as a vehicle for dramatic epiphanies, life-changing sudden encounters, and melodrama.

Schreiner's short stories do not share the ideological coherence of Egerton's *œuvre*, nor their optimism about feminist self-realizability.

They combine what were two separate, but overlapping, concerns of her theoretical writing of that period: feminism and contemporary South African politics and economics. Schreiner, in contrast to Egerton, constantly dramatizes and interrogates the antinomies of rationalist and romantic, materialist and idealist, approaches to white female oppression and emancipation. In these stories, she pushes such antinomies, arguably, either into open mutual conflict or deconstruction; what emerges is none of Egerton's political optimism, but instead, an exposure of the obstacles to such affirmative thought. Compared to Egerton, Schreiner uses the short story to equally powerful, very different, effect. These stories represent an aesthetic experiment which falls somewhere in between the abstract short allegories of Schreiner's 1890 *Dreams* and the prose of her novels.[10] Combining realism and symbolism, the stories centre upon conversational exchanges, but use these to present an essentially monologic and isolationist perspective, in which the speech patterns expose the impossibility of social communication and an integrated feminist identity and collectivity.

For Egerton, Scandinavian or English countryside provides the pastoral corrective to urban reification.[11] Femininity is foregrounded: the country facilitates, or mirrors, the romantic and spiritual regeneration of British white women, and it personifies the forces of untamed nature with which Egerton associates women. In the open air, women engage in traditionally masculine pursuits: the women of 'A Cross-Line' and 'The Grey Glove' go fishing and in so doing, appropriately enough, meet their soulmates. The woman of 'The Grey Glove' literally hooks her man, accidentally throwing her hook into his earlobe. Nor is pastoralism restricted to leisure activities such as fishing: the woman of 'The Regeneration of Two' meets her future mate in a Scandinavian wood. She ends up inhabiting a country manor house in which she and the 'fallen' women she collects experience a kind of spiritual salvation, practising the pre-industrial labour of spinning and weaving. The women are so successful that they are able to become economically self-sufficient.

Crucially, however, this allegory of pastoral self-sufficiency, in which an independent livelihood is constructed from scratch, is no more authentic than that of Robinson Crusoe, who commences his island sojourn with the advantage of many technological aids from the metropolis. In 'The Regeneration of Two', for instance, the woman is enabled to develop her colony of women only because she has inherited property and wealth from her dead husband. The achievement of self-sufficiency through 'honest' cottage labour, in other words, is possible only through the unearned wealth of an inheritance which precedes it. This is a recurrent feature of Egerton's stories: her protagonists are often released from economic dependency by virtue of an inheritance. Financial inheritance operates rather like the genetic inheritance of racial or temperamental traits, in Egerton: it is structurally just as 'natural' and as 'inevitable'. What this means is that the world of nature as expressed in the pastoralism of Scandinavia and Britain, is a merely symbolic alternative to the world of social organization and convention. Pastoralism's attendant virtues of pre-capitalist labour and self-sufficiency constitute an escapism from a modernity associated with constrictive urban industrialism and the pursuit of capital accumulation. The material of modernity remains intact while these women absent themselves from it.

The pastoral scene contains explicitly colonial and imperial elements in Egerton. Where the setting is Scandinavia, an alien British settler constitutes the narrative's central protagonist, and where the setting is Britain, the narrative focuses on upper-class women transplanted from the city. These settlers bring with them and enact what is at times an overtly missionary ideology, in which the object of missionary concern becomes the white European instead of the black overseas subject. A colonial settler ideology of self-rejuvenation, that is, combines with an imperialist ideology in which the superior conquering race rescues the native population from its own degeneration, as occurs in 'The Regeneration of Two'. This is a crucial element of Egerton's textual ideology which is at times directly critical of actual European overseas colonialism, imperialism, and missionary philanthropy. Egerton's criticism stems from separatist convictions of an essential racial/cultural difference, and from vaguely populist and eugenic principles of domestic social reformism, in which overseas imperialism is seen as incurring a cost to the domestic working population, and charitable energies currently invested abroad are seen as having a more important object of investment in the needy home population.[12] The poet's outburst against empire-building, in 'The Regeneration of Two' (pp. 191–192), loosely links imperial war-mongering with the exploitation and destruction of honest working men (such as carpenters) and with the degeneration of working people through manufacturing industries.

In 'The Regeneration of Two' the protagonist's final redemption of 'fallen' women is anticipated by her opening dialogue with her maid. She laments her general *ennui*, and her maid suggests that she engage in philanthropic missionary activity like other British women. Her response illustrates Egerton's notion of racial and cultural difference, and her aestheticism. The woman replies:

What on earth's the good of sewing flannel petticoats for poor little niggers in Zanzibar? I am sure it's much nicer for them to roll their little brown bodies in the warm sand ... It's ... an aesthetic sin to send them out Christian fig-leaves.[13]

However the woman immediately continues: 'they [British women] go in for suffrage, social reformation, politics, all sorts of fatiguing things. I thought of doing something of that kind myself, of *having a mission*; but it would last just as long as it was a new sensation' (emphases added).[14] Subsequently, herself liberated into a full social conscience by her encounter with a poet, she eventually fulfils her missionary urges. It is important to Egerton's deterministic belief in the recoverability of an essential character or nature, be it sexual, racial or individual, that the narrative establish the woman as being in possession of innate missionary tendencies. She cannot be converted by the poet if that social tendency is not a fundamental if dormant part of her nature. The same applies to the women she rescues. Missionary colonization, then, can only succeed if the native subject already shares some of the characteristics of the missionary agent.

A typical figure in Egerton is a woman, strongly endowed with instinctive clairvoyance, intellectual gifts, moral sensitivity and compassion for the suffering and weaker people of Europe, upon whom she wishes a subject-making salvation. One of the most striking, and complex, examples of this can be found in 'A Psychological Moment' (*Discords*), which narrates the sexual exploitation of one such dominant specimen, who surrenders to this exploitation because she is blackmailed by her abuser who possesses (it is implied) incriminating information about the woman's family. The text commences with her childhood, establishing the early foundations of the intellectual and moral supremacy which marks her adulthood. The middle section charts her adolescence, and focuses on an agonizing scene in which the girl accompanies (in protective maternal style) a slow-witted girl on the merry-go-round. The

carousel is furnished with music from a hurdy-gurdy inside the ring.
Importantly, the music which accompanies them is a South African
polka 'Polly Witfoet' ('Polly Whitefoot'). The protagonist has the
misfortune to glimpse the person who plays the hurdy-gurdy, an
'idiot lad', fastened to the pole. The offensiveness of the scene is
featured as being aesthetic as much as it is moral: 'His head is
abnormally large, the heavy eyelids lie half folded on the prominent
eyeballs so that only the whites show, his damp hair clings to his
temples and about his outstanding ears. His mouth gapes, and his
long tongue lolls from side to side, the saliva forming little bubbles as
the great head wags heavily as he grinds – indeed every part of his
stunted, sweat-dripping body sways mechanically to the lively air of
white-footed Polly.'[15]

The girl is sent into a spiritual crisis over this vision of deformity
and oppressive labour, exclaiming:

Oh, that poor thing!... *You needn't have made him*; God, I tell you, you needn't
have made him! You knew from all time he'd be there, and why should he
be?... I love all those poor things of your creation far more, and how I hate
to live! I don't want to – always I see the pain, the sorrow, underneath the
music – and I tell you... if I were a great queen I would build a new tower
of Babel with a monster search-light to show up all the dark places of your
monstrous creation. *I would raise a crusade for the service of the suffering*, the
liberation of the idiots who grind the music for the world to dance –
(emphases added).[16]

The missionary ideology receives a clear articulation here. It is
inspired by the girl's vision of suffering humanity; the psychological
and social crisis belongs not to the idiot boy (whose idiocy presumably
robs him of the capacity to have existential or indeed political crises),
nor to exploited labour in general, but solely to the exceptionally
gifted female who alone is cursed with insight into the wretched of the
earth.

It is no accident that the refrain is a South African one, evoking
that scene of 'monstrous' economic and racial exploitation, epito-
mized in (for example) the inhumane systems of gold and diamond
mining endured by black miners. In keeping with her domestic
social-reformism, and her textual metaphorics of empire, Egerton
effectively transposes the colonial scene into a domestic/European
one. At the same time, economic materialism gives way to aestheticism, fatalism and existentialism. The idiot boy is a pathologized
and therefore naturalized image of labour; Egerton's answer to such

exploitation is a mixture of eugenic fatalism (ideally, the deformed would not exist in the first place) and missionary philanthropy (they are to be liberated in an unspecified way through a crusade).

There is then a fatalism at work here, which suggests that physical pain and exploitation is the natural corollary of biologically 'weaker' groups of people or races; their liberation may or may not result from the crusades of the dominant peoples, but at the least such crusades, and the pity which feeds them, morally aggrandize the subjectivity of the dominant. The South African song recurs in the scene when the girl, now a young woman, is forced to submit to the blackmail of her oppressor who produces evidence of her family's receipt of illicit money. Fatalism is conveyed by the very structural repetition of the song, as well as its thematic message.

Olive Schreiner's writing connects white femininity with colonialism and missionary ideology in very different ways, and draws rather different conclusions. Notably absent from Schreiner's work is any sense of contemporary colonial space, be it nature or small town settlement, as a site of potential regeneration for white women. This does not prevent Schreiner from venerating a notion of intensive cultivation of the land, as an example of the kind of socially useful toil women once participated in. The colonies, as in Egerton, become identified with positive values of pre-industrial labour, self-sufficiency and self-determination, and as such are also associated with notions of sexual and familial interdependency and harmony, exemplified in the Boer or at times in the black African people.[17] But unlike Egerton, for Schreiner this version of the pastoral is available only as history; it is romanticized and subjected to a nostalgic treatment by Schreiner as part of an irreversible earlier stage of social development. As things stood in contemporary South African rural and small town life, however, when viewed by Schreiner in the major novels *Story of an African Farm, From Man to Man*, in the non-fiction of *Thoughts on South Africa*, or in the short stories of this essay's discussion, the colonial space provides no opportunity for women's spiritual or social liberation, but rather, their suffocation.

In 'The Woman's Rose' and 'The Policy in Favour of Protection', the sexual economy of white women is explicitly connected to the political economy of colonies, albeit in complex and ambiguous ways. This reflects Schreiner's great interest in political economy and in a materialist analysis of women's oppression. Schreiner throughout her writing is concerned with what she calls 'sex-parasitism', women's economic dependency on men, their removal from the sphere of socially useful labour; Egerton, as has already been pointed out, is unperturbed by women's removal from that sphere and is happy to endow her protagonists with the benefits of legacies which prevent them from having to labour at all.[18]

In 'The Woman's Rose', the narrator tells of how she once visited a small colonial town and found herself in structural rivalry with the resident belle as a sexual commodity. The men forsake the belle and convert the import into a measure of feminine value: 'I knew she knew that at the hotel men had made a bet as to which was the prettier, she or I, and had asked each man who came in, and that the one who had staked on me won' (p. 57).[19] The narrator has no sexual interest in any of the men; it is implied that the resident young woman does, at least insofar as she resents the narrator's usurpation of her role. She is presumably dependent upon the male-pool, as the source of a future spouse, in a way that the narrator, a visitor, is not. At the visitor's farewell party, the two women temporarily overcome their reserve and rivalry when the belle fastens a rose on to the other woman's hair. Far from the colony being a place where female sexual desire, and self-realization, can be expressed, and sisterhood flourish, as in Egerton, the colony is a space of restriction, where sexuality itself is reduced to merely economic processes, and women's status in relation to men is reduced, or exposed, as that of mere commodity. The women cannot freely express sexual desire (for men or for one another), nor sisterhood.

In 'The Policy in Favour of Protection', a professional woman journalist, in love with and loved by a professional man, gives up her relationship when a younger, 'parasitical' woman, also in love with the man and ignorant of the older woman's involvement with him, implores her to help in her suit. The man goes on to marry someone else, another young woman, the parasite goes on to marry someone else and writes an ecstatic letter to the journalist about her new husband and the superficiality of her previous passion. The journalist violently tears up and burns the letter and resumes her article on 'the causes which in differing peoples lead to the adoption of Free Trade or Protectionist principles'. The ending of the story witholds her conclusion: 'She took up her pen – "the policy of the Australian Colonies in favour of Protection is easily understood" – she waited – "when one considers the fact – the fact"; then she finished the article' (pp. 90-91).

While the text invites an interpretation of the women's behaviours as corresponding to either a free trade or 'protectionist' model, neither behaviour neatly and exclusively corresponds with either model. If free trade is seen as the principle of open economic competition by different countries, or firms, without interference from government, then the older woman has violated this by interfering with the sexual competition between her and the other woman for the man. In the open free trade market, it seems, the older woman would have won. This then seems to imply that she has practised protectionism by her artificial intervention. This interpretation equates the young woman as the domestic market of the colony, and the older woman as the government. Seen this way, white femininity becomes a single unit; the superior woman has voluntarily abdicated her selfish claim on the man, to protect the interests of femininity in general, aiding the weaker of the sex. But the older woman, and the man also, is the loser of the transaction; not only is she, structurally, the woman's protective government, she is also a competing country. Seen this way, the woman has failed to protect her own 'country's' interests and emotions, her economic development, and one conclusion is that a policy of self-protectionism is indeed advisable.

The women are more than countries or governments: they are also commodities. A sexual economy, that is, converts both sexes into commodities and consumers simultaneously; what it does not do is give both sexes equal powers to declare their desires and therefore compete openly. The younger woman first appeals to the older woman to help on the grounds that she cannot herself directly express her love to the man; nor does she want the older woman to: 'Don't tell him that I love him...Just say something to him. Oh, it's so terrible to be a woman; I can't do anything. You won't tell him exactly that I love him? That's the thing that makes a man hate a woman, if you tell it him plainly.'[20] In this sense, one can read Schreiner, like Egerton, to be criticizing the double standards of sexual etiquette, which preclude women from being active suitors; by extension, the text can be read as a plea for lifting the restrictions which prevent a truly free trade of sexual desire from operating. Schreiner then suggests, ambiguously, that neither self-interested open competition nor maternal/sisterly altruism, nurture and self-sacrifice by women for other women is desirable as a policy within the existing white heterosexual economy. The domestic maternal model

as advocated by Egerton is here subjected to a sharp interrogation. At
one point, reeling with the pain of the man's marriage to a third
party, the older woman asks the young woman to adopt her ethics of
sisterly solidarity:

If ... something you have killed out in your heart for long years wakes up and
cries, 'Let each man play his own game, and care nothing for the hand of
his fellow! Each man for himself. *So* the game must be played!' and you
doubt all you have lived for, and the ground seems washing out under your
feet – . She paused. Such a time has come to me now. If you would promise
me that if ever another woman comes to seek your help, you will give it to
her, and try to love her for my sake, I think it will help me.[21]

The attempt here to inculcate, missionary style, values of love,
charity and sisterhood, signally fails, as the young woman's consciousness throughout the story shows no sign of being raised. And
no-one – the young woman, the professional woman, the loved man
– benefits from the older woman's voluntary sacrifice. In Egerton's
writing, by contrast, no such conflict is presented: missionary self-
sacrificing superior women are always vindicated in their actions
with other women. They help save the souls – raise the consciousness
of other women – though sometimes they are helpless to save them
from material decline, as in 'Gone Under' and 'Wedlock', of
Discords. And Egerton's superior woman can achieve permanent
romantic union with an intellectual or professional equal, something
Schreiner's texts cannot contemplate, caught up as they are with
dramatizing the obstacles to such a union. Schreiner's texts, indeed,
present yet another complication: the possibility that sexual fulfilment is itself a threat to the sovereignty and self-realization of the
superior professional woman, and that, concomitantly, the pairing of
such a woman with a mate is not necessarily in the eugenic interests
of the imperial society as a whole.

In Egerton's work, white women are partially associated with the
identities and cultural resources of blackness and the Orient; and
Egerton is prepared to posit equivalences between non-European
and European cultures. The woman writer of 'White Elf' has been
researching 'esquimaux marriage songs, and the analogy between
them and the Song of Solomon' (p. 84). One of the characters in 'A
Psychological Moment', commenting on the patriarchal basis of her
Irish arranged marriage, suggests that 'no Zulu strikes a harder
bargain for cows with his prospective father-in-law than the average

Irishman for the girl's dowry. They are huckstered and traded for, and matches made up for them, just the same as they bargain for heifers at a fair' (p. 57). Significantly, both of these parallels pertain to sexual love and marriage, and function more to affirm Egerton's romanticism (by definition, opposed to any notions of social or cultural evolution) than as a progressive critique of European claims to racial and cultural supremacy.

The subjectivity of the European woman is dependent upon non-European cultural space in many ways. In one of the most celebrated passages of *Keynotes*, the protagonist fantasizes herself performing, Salomé style, in front of an audience of erotically charged Eastern men. The Orient becomes quite literally a stage for the performance and production of Occidental identity. In this scene, the woman herself takes on the accoutrements of Orientalism:

> She fancies herself in Arabia on the back of a swift steed ... Then she fancies she is on the stage of an ancient theatre out in the open air, with hundreds of faces upturned towards her. She is gauze-clad in a cobweb garment of wondrous tissue. Her arms are clasped by jewelled snakes, and one with quivering diamond fangs coils round her hips.[22]

What this scene plays out is the prospect, more reassuring than it is discomfiting to contemporary patriarchy, of white women's identity being founded on an eroticism, and intense potential for social, professional and aesthetic power, that will in reality always be contained (by its restriction to fantasy) or cancelled out (by maternal and affectionate drives, as happens in the story's conclusion). The scene illustrates Egerton's collusion with an imperialistic orientalism. Far from seeing the scene as a proof of the radical oppositionality of Egerton's sexual, cultural and racial ideology to dominant ideologies, and her political affinity with racial/cultural others of Europe, as Ann Ardis might argue, I see it as an illustration of Egerton's instrumental and essentialist approach to cultural/racial othernesss. The Orient serves as a signifier and repository of aestheticized eroticism.

Egerton's aestheticization of non-white scenes and symbols corresponds to a particular kind of racism: it is only in the form, and as a resource, of aesthetic culture, that racial others can be legitimately admitted to, and valorized by, European subjectivity. This is borne out by the ideology of physical racial separation which underpins Egerton's writings.

Egerton's modern white femininity gets caught between conflicting judgements of empire in 'Virgin Soil', a story of a young woman who has been raised by her mother in sexual ignorance, and has consequently made an unhappy marriage. She returns to indict marriage as a form of legalized prostitution, and to indict her mother for selling her into marriage. Before she launches her attack she stares at a portrait on the mantelpiece:

It is her father, the father who was killed in India in a hill skirmish when she was a little lint-locked maid barely up to his knee. She studies it with new eyes, trying to read what man he was, what soul he had, what part of him is in her, tries to find herself by reading him. Something in his face touches her, strikes some underlying chord in her, and she grinds her teeth at a thought it rouses.[23]

Insofar as the father has neglected home duties in favour of overseas duties, leaving what is presented as a self-centred materialistic mother in charge of the girl's upbringing, the ideology here supports Egerton's general distaste for imperial action as one which is negligent of domestic needs and desires. On the other hand, the father here supplies a spiritual ally, an image of military aggression to fortify her in the forthcoming battle against her mother. And in keeping with Egerton's biological determinism, it is the girl's inheritance of her father's pugnacity, as expressed in his colonial venture, which causes and helps her to rebel.

For Schreiner, the Orient, black Africa and empire perform very different roles in the play of white femininity from those they have in Egerton's play. The differences between their utilization of the trope of the Orient is well illustrated in the contrast between Schreiner's short story 'The Buddhist Priest's Wife' and Egerton's 'A Cross Line'. Both feature a strong and magnetic woman, of superior intellectual endowments, who loves a man her intellectual equal. In both stories, the Orient features as a place of refuge for European femininity's contradictions and frustrations.

But the similarities end there. In Schreiner's text, the East is real, not located in Egerton's fantasy of antiquity, and serves rationalist rather than romantic ends. Insofar as the woman's conscious intentions in travelling there are indicated at all, they have to do with her pursuit of life-enhancing experience and anthropological knowledge of the 'complex, interesting' life of the other. This involves a removal of self from centre stage (which is where self literally is in

Egerton's Orient) to the wings or stalls, observing the play of others. Self-aggrandizement it is, but the sovereignty of the self is to be achieved by its severance from, not its fusion with, the cultural other. Most crucially, perhaps, white female personal fulfilment in Schreiner's Oriental scene is officially to occur within the realm of the intellect, not sexuality, as in Egerton; Schreiner's heroine is presented as being motivated to flee the demands of her sexuality, rather than finding a public expression for those demands (as Egerton's heroine does) in her construction of the Orient.

In the Egerton piece, the setting for the woman's fantasy is the clash between her desire for romantic union with her lover, and her desire for domestic union with her forthcoming child. What the fantasy reveals is a further desire, for professional fulfilment – the dancer on stage is identifiable as professional in her artistry, who satisfies her own eroticism in an autonomous fashion, by catering to the erotic desires of her male audience. In Schreiner's piece, by contrast, the woman's professional identity, and individual auton-omy, constitutes the setting of the narrative, rather than being, as with Egerton, the object of fantasy. Instead of a conflict between two types of bonding, romantic and maternal, Schreiner presents a conflict between the woman's desire for independence and her desire for union with a man.

For Schreiner, then, there is the possibility that sexual fulfilment is as much a threat to women's self-development as it is an expression of it; for Egerton, it is the social repression of women's sexuality that is, unequivocally, the obstacle to self-determination. (She does not seem too concerned with foregrounding the realization of women's professional urges; in general they do not feature strongly except as a backdrop or as a fantasy in relation to the more central stuff of personal fulfilment.) But this is only one aspect of Schreiner's ideology. The story, typically for her, effects an interrogation which leaves both explanations of femininity's discontents – rationalist and romantic – equally valid or problematic. The woman is clearly in love with the man; the drama of the story hinges on the reader's intuition, and the man's ignorance, of this fact, until her final revelation through a kiss. All of their intellectual discoursing on the nature of love develops this irony, together with the irony of the gap between intellectual and emotional expression. The woman seems compelled to withold communication of her own love.

This leads the reader to read the woman's pronouncements with some suspicion; they are as likely to be rationalizations as statements whose truth value is endorsed by Schreiner. The woman argues:

Nature ordains that she [woman] should never show what she feels; the woman who had told a man she loved him would have put between them a barrier once and for ever that could not be crossed ... Therefore she must always go with her arms folded sexually; only the love which lays itself down at her feet and implores of her to accept it is love she can ever rightly take up. That is the true difference between a man and a woman. You may seek for love because you can do it openly; we cannot because we must do it subtly.[24]

This argument for the natural basis of sexual difference, then, has at best a relative truth. One can read the woman's exit to India, finally, in a number of divergent ways. Taking the 'Schreiner as rationalist' approach, the trip to India, and the woman's imaginary marriage to a Buddhist priest, signify the impossibility for 'superior' professional/ intellectual women of marrying the antinomies of reason and sexuality; the trip is a vindication of reason's paramountcy for feminism. Or one can argue the woman to be taking Oriental and rationalist refuge from the very possibility that her antinomies are not, in fact, necessary at all except in social ideology and in her own defensive consciousness. If one takes Schreiner to be pursuing a more deconstructive approach, India becomes an empty site of possibility, a space outside of the antinomies, in which femininity, like masculinity, becomes unimaginable. To the rationalist interpretation can be added a eugenic twist: India serves Schreiner, arguably, as as a repository for evolutionarily overdeveloped women, who are marked out as being unsuitable wifely and maternal material. Sexual and familial activity is to be denied them as a wastage of their resources; they can make the greatest social contribution through their intellect. Or by simply removing themselves or graciously dying out, like Lyndall and Waldo in Schreiner's *Story of an African Farm*.

In 'The Buddhist Priest's Wife', India remains the point at which narrative ends and speculation begins. In 'The Child's Day', by contrast, India is a condition which is fully agreeable to narration, supplying the fantasy of female moral self-consolidation through European missionary maternity. The story narrates one day in the life of a white South African five-year-old girl Rebekah, whose mother gives birth to twins on that day, one dead, one alive. The girl plays a number of games and tells a number of stories to an imaginary infant of her own, The piece suggests the inextricability of emergent femininity from fantasies of mothering, on the one hand, and empire, on the other. As with other texts of Schreiner, however, the ideology is nothing if not ambiguous and contradictory.

The child tells her imaginary baby two stories of empire, in quick succession. The first is a story of the 'Indian mutiny'. An unhappy English woman, Hester Durham, whose son has died, is encouraged to go to India by a clergyman, to find something to live for. She finds her vocation ministering comfort and moral if not physical support to a household of women and children, surrounded by 'the black soldiers (they call them Sepoys)' who 'wanted to kill them'(p. 42):

> They were only women and children there; and all of them were very frightened; even the old black Ayah. But Hester Durham was not afraid … it says in the Book: – '*Alone, like a rock in a raging sea: Hester Durham stood there.*' They hadn't been *so* afraid, because she was there to comfort them. And at last the Sepoys did come in, and killed them all.[25]

At first this seems a clear enough repetition of missionary maternity. It also recounts the official mythology of the Indian mutiny, in which helpless white women and children were represented as being the innocent victims of rape and murder by violent natives. Apart from its general vindication of empire as a civilizing mission, this mythology served to justify counter-insurgent imperial violence as necessary to the protection of vulnerable women. But this official version is offset by quirks of the child Rebekah's rendition. The mythology relies upon the essential *whiteness* of the vulnerable women and children; this essentialism is broken by the child's inclusion of 'the old black Ayah' as one of the number. Then there is the fatalism: Hester Durham's spiritual succour makes the collective death a little more tolerable, but cannot prevent it. The inevitability of the death of the Empire does, arguably, become a challenge to imperial authority and identity. This is suggested by the next story the child narrates, a truncated Gibbon-style narrative of the Roman Empire's invasion of Boadicea's Britain:

> But the nicest of all is about a woman. The Romans came and they took away her country and they beat her till the blood ran off her back on to the ground, and they were cruel to her daughters. The Romans were people who took other peoples' countries; and she got into a chariot with her two daughters and her long hair flying in the wind.[26]

In the first story, England features as empire; in the second, as nation oppressed by empire. In both instances, England is feminized and maternalized, by (respectively) Hester Durham's maternal ministrations and Boadicea's salient motherhood, while those who threaten England, Indians and Romans, are masculinized. In both stories, the fate of the imperial country is death. One can read Schreiner as testifying to, and supporting, the ideology of the English Empire, in representing it as playing a formative role in the acquisition of colonial feminine subjectivity. As the child's primary matrix of cultural identity and moral value, the English Empire is synonymous with the 'mother', Hester Durham, it features. Alternatively, one can read Schreiner to suggest the child's psyche as effecting a critical subversion or deformation of English imperial syntax, divesting it of its sovereignty, exposing it as futile and impermanent.

By constructing Boadicea as mother, the child divests the idea of empire of its monopoly on maternity, thereby offering a qualification of empire's legitimation process. At the same time, however, the common denominator of both stories remains England itself, whose status as nurturing if ineffective mother is upheld. To break down the distinction between England as empire and England as colonized nation in this way is, arguably, both to vindicate and to weaken English imperial self-identity.

England-as-Empire is subjected to the ambiguities of the child's fantasy, and as such, emerges as an ambiguous signifier. The child's black Ayah, on the other hand, is located firmly by the child as the anti-fantasy principle, the oppressive super-ego who, throughout 'The Child's Day', spares no opportunity to chastize the child; the child is forthright in her hatred for the woman. Old Ayah is associated with chief responsibility for performing and organizing the household's domestic labour of cooking and cleaning. It is she who has the primary responsibility, too, for looking after the child Rebekah.

It is Ayah who rudely informs the child that the baby she has claimed and is mothering is dead. The child goes on to associate Ayah with responsibility for the death she mediates: in the story's final scene, she hears the live baby cry out and fights her way into the room, against Ayah's wishes, accusing the woman of killing this baby as she did the first one. This is consistent with the text as a whole, in which black African people are identified with the very (destructive) forces of mortality, physical brutality, and systematic domestic subjugation by which they are themselves victimized and controlled under settler colonialism. Within this system of transference and reversal old Ayah plays a particularly prominent role. She regularly represents the child as savage, uncouth and undomesticated, a threat to domestic order:

If she were my child, I wouldn't let her come into the house at all, where respectable people live who like to be indoors. I'd just tie her fast with a chain to a monkey post outside, and let her go round and round there. Then she could eat Kaffir beans like a baboon, and climb, and scream as much as she liked![27]

This is in response to the child's 'strange' habits of wandering about outside in the fierce sun, talking to herself, and generally not conforming to conventional standards of domestic femininity. Ayah opposes the child's attempts to look after her newly born baby sister, claiming that she will instruct the baby to become a tomboy and acquire her wild ways (p. 58).

Ayah is set up by Schreiner as being hateful for the power she does possess, and simultaneously contemptible for her lack of power. Schreiner's representation is an undeniably racist, and unpleasant, one. It is also complex, and this stems, arguably, from an ambivalence towards the project of settler colonialism as much as an ambivalence towards black ethnicity. As refracted through Ayah's malicious consciousness, colonialism is interrogated and upheld to an equal degree. Ayah castigates the child for her undomesticated ways; she is constantly termed 'a strange child'. Schreiner seems caught between a desire to endorse and to discredit this judgement of the child's unconventionality.

Schreiner seems to want to establish the child as being unorthodox in her individuality, standing outside accepted colonial norms of femininity, whilst at the same time desiring to invent her own domestic scene. This is the corollary of Schreiner's ambivalence towards Ayah: she needs to represent her as both superego and as id. She serves as an impartial adult who embodies and mouths the oppressive but inevitable realities of colonial life and its attendant social ideology, and as a juvenile who distorts and misuses those realities for petty and personal ends, those ends being cruelty to the child, and demonization, misreading Rebekah's very precociousness as its anti-social opposite.

In these texts of Olive Schreiner, black Africa is the point at which identification, for white female subjectivity, stops; it also marks the point where the possibility of metaphor ends, and ideological anxieties about inexorable repressive laws of social and physical determinism receive their most intense expression. As the Ayah's example suggests, black Africa functions as emergent white femininity's antagonist, the structural opponent of white female self-expansion through fantasy and imagination. The Ayah also functions as the container as well as the supplement of colonial domestic ideology; she is what enables the white nuclear family, including Rebekah, to operate as an ambiguous entity, the figure onto which the negative aspects of both domestic power and powerlessness are projected. This reflects Schreiner's ambivalence about how to locate her white feminism in relation to imperial and colonial social structures.

Similarly, Schreiner is not sure whether to locate feminism's means and end in the concept of the individual or in the concept of white women as a collectivity and entity, and this is played out in her representation of the conflicts between white women, in which neither missionary/maternal nor individualist ideologies appear appropriate. It is significant that (in 'The Policy', for instance) the very terms Schreiner uses to represent these ideologies are those of the colonial and imperial economic models of free trade and protectionism: what this suggests is that white femininity is, for Schreiner, simultaneously inextricable from, and irreducible to, conceptions of colonies and empires. The Orient, in contrast to black Africa or indeed white colonial space, is available to Schreiner as an enabling and metaphorical space for white female subjectivity.

For George Egerton, racial and cultural othernesses of both black/'savage' and Oriental kinds are (unlike Schreiner) open to metaphorical appropriation and identification in the mapping of white female subjectivity. But these othernesses are admissible only as part of an essentialist ideology which advocates actual social separatism of ethnicities. The metaphorization of blackness indeed can be seen as part of a general policy of Eurocentric domestification, in which the assimilation of blackness into the discourse of white female subjectivity is mirrored by a social missionary ideology which consciously advocates a disinvestment from the overseas empire in the interests of the home population, and translates those overseas dynamics into relations between superior women and domestic others. The metaphorization of blackness also belongs to Egerton's overall aestheticism, in which black culture is converted into blackness-*as*-aesthetic culture.

The notion of women's subjectivity as containing a repressed 'savage wildness', associated with lawlessness, amorality, individualist will-to-power and unfettered sexual appetite is itself subjected by Egerton to an ideological containment which leaves it as a largely rhetorical gesture. The potentially anti-social, and self-serving, thrust of this notion is seen to give way to a feminism which instead emphasizes women's subjectivity as more truly driven, and fulfilled, by reproductive and romantic drives, at times in conflict with each other. The more systematic conflict, however, is between social convention and legal systems, on the one hand, and the fulfilment of those urges, on the other. Egerton's valorization of these urges posits no fundamental opposition between women and the 'race', or European society in general: indeed, the jettisoning of social conventions in the interests of women's development is ultimately all to the good of the imperial/colonial people. This underlying premise of racial and social unity applies also to Egerton's vision of domestic 'imperial'/missionary relations, in which missionaries and their subjects share common interests and values.

NOTES

1 Gayatri Chakavorty Spivak, 'Three Women's Texts and a Critique of Imperialism', in Henry Louis Gates, Jr. (ed.), *Race, Writing and Difference* (London: University of Chicago Press, 1986). See also Vron Ware's *Beyond the Pale: White Women, Racism and History* (London: Verso, 1992), for a discussion of nineteenth-century cultural and political feminism in relation to empire.

2 Gerd Bjorhovde, *Rebellious Structures: Women Writers and the Crisis of the Novel* (Oslo: Norwegian University Press, 1987). Ann L. Ardis, *New Women, New Novels: Feminism and Early Modernism* (London: Rutgers University Press, 1990), p. 27. Ardis's convictions are shared by Sandra Gilbert and Susan Gubar in their *No Man's Land. The Place of the Woman Writer in the Twentieth Century* (London: Yale University Press, 1989).

3 Spivak, 'Three Women's Texts', p. 263. For a useful general history of this period of imperialism, see Eric Hobsbawm's *The Age of Empire, 1875–1914* (London: Weidenfeld and Nicolson, 1987). For a discussion of imperialist idealism, see Richard Faber's *The Vision and the Need: Late Victorian Imperialist Aims* (London: Faber and Faber, 1966). For a discussion of social Darwinian and eugenic thought, see Greta Jones's *Social Darwinism and English Thought* (Brighton: Harvester Press, 1980).

Karl Pearson's *The Ethic of Freethought* (London: T. Fisher Unwin, 1888) provides a good example of eugenic ideology.

4 George Egerton, *Keynotes and Discords* (1893 and 1894), introduced by Martha Vicinus (London: Virago, 1983). For a historical discussion of the social and institutional relations between imperialism and maternity during this period, see Anna Davin's important article 'Imperialism and Motherhood', *History Workshop*, 5 (Spring 1978).

5 These stories are 'The Woman's Rose', *Dream Life and Real Life* (1892) (Chicago: Academy Chicago, 1981); 'The Policy in Favour of Protection', *Dream Life and Real Life* (1892) (Chicago: Academy Chicago, 1981); 'The Buddhist Priest's Wife' (1892), *An Olive Schreiner Reader*, ed. Carol Barash (London: Pandora Press, 1987); 'The Child's Day' (1887), *An Olive Schreiner Reader*, ed. Carol Barash (London: Pandora Press, 1987).

6 Egerton, 'A Cross Line', *Discords*, p. 22.

7 *Ibid.*, pp. 27–28.

8 H. Rider Haggard, *She* (London: Longman, Green and Co., 1887).

9 Another Nietzsche-influenced, pro-imperialist *fin-de-siècle* British writer, was the poet John Davidson. See, for example, his *The Testament of an Empire Builder* (London: Grant Richards, 1901).

10 Olive Schreiner's theoretical and political writings include *Woman and Labour* (London: T. Fisher Unwin, 1911) and *Thoughts on South Africa* (London: T. Fisher Unwin, 1923). The 1899 essay 'The Woman Question' in *An Olive Schreiner Reader*, ed. Carol Barash (London: Pandora Press, 1987), contains the origins of the feminist argument that were to culminate in *Woman and Labour*. Her shorter allegorical fiction includes *Dreams* (London: T. Fisher Unwin, 1890). Published novels by Schreiner include *The Story of an African Farm* (London: Chapman and Hall, 1883) and *From Man to Man: or Perhaps Only…* (London: T. Fisher Unwin, 1926). Her novella *Trooper Peter Halket of Mashonaland* (London: T. Fisher Unwin, 1897), like the stories under discussion here, represents something of a synthesis of the allegorical and novelistic methods. For a discussion of Schreiner's 1890s allegories, see Laura Chrisman, 'Allegory, Feminist Thought and the *Dreams* of Olive Schreiner', *Edward Carpenter and Late Victorian Radicalism*, ed. Tony Brown (London: Frank Cass, 1990).

11 H. Rider Haggard's *King Solomon's Mines* (London: Longman Green and Co., 1885) articulates a similar colonial pastoralism. For a contemporary expression of urban degeneration/reification anxiety, see James Cantlie, *Degeneration Amongst Londoners* (London: Field and Tuer, the Leadenhall Press, 1885). Egerton's construction of Scandinavian ruralism is indebted to Knut Hamsun's writings. Leo Lownthal's essay 'Knut Hamsun', in *The Essential Frankfurt School Reader*, eds. Andrew Arato and Eike Gebhardt, introduced by Paul Piccone (New York: Continuum, 1982), contains political insights applicable to Egerton's work.

12 See Bernard Semmel's *Imperialism and Social Reform: English Social-Imperial Thought, 1895–1914* (London: Allen and Unwin, 1960), for a thorough discussion of the complex relations between imperialist and domestic social-reformist ideology of this period.

13 Egerton, 'The Regeneration of Two', *Discords*, p. 166.

14 *Ibid.*, p. 166.

15 Egerton, 'A Psychological Moment', *Discords*, pp. 18–19.

16 *Ibid.*, p. 19.

17 See Schreiner's *Thoughts on South Africa* for examples of her nostalgic constructions of Boer settlement colonialism.

18 See Schreiner's 'The Woman Question' and *Woman and Labour* for discussions of sex-parasitism.

19 For a fuller discussion of this text, and 'The Policy', see Laura Chrisman, 'Colonialism and Feminism in Olive Schreiner's 1890s fiction', *English in Africa*, 20: 1 (May 1993).

20 Schreiner, 'The Policy', p. 71.

21 *Ibid.*, pp. 85–86.

22 Egerton, 'A Cross Line', *Keynotes*, p. 19.

23 Egerton, 'Virgin Soil', *Discords*, p. 152.

24 Schreiner, 'Buddhist Priest's Wife', pp. 116–117.

25 Schreiner, 'The Child's Day', p. 42. On the gender ideology of the Indian Mutiny, see Jenny Sharpe's 'The Unspeakable Limits of Rape: Colonial Violence and Counter-Insurgency', in Patrick Williams and Laura Chrisman (eds.), *Colonial Discourse/Post-Colonial Theory: A Reader* (Hemel Hempstead: Harvester Wheatsheaf, 1993).

26 Schreiner, 'The Child's Day', p. 43.

27 *Ibid.*, p. 56.

CHAPTER 4

W. B. Yeats and Irish cultural politics in the 1890s

Stephen Regan

It is tempting to linger over the early lyrics of W. B. Yeats and find in their yearning for ideal beauty the consummate expression of *fin de siècle* aestheticism and decadence. The poems of the 1890s, especially those which appeared in *The Rose* (1893) and *The Wind Among the Reeds* (1899), are everywhere infused with what Yeats himself recognized as 'those faint lights and faint colours and faint outlines and faint energies which many call "the decadence"'. Yeats, having a more progressive and dynamic view of cultural history than many of his contemporaries, preferred to think of the *fin de siècle* as 'the autumn of the body' because the arts were but sleeping and 'dreaming of things to come'.[1] This idea of decadence giving birth to new life is in keeping with the legendary account Yeats gives of his fellow 'Rhymers' – Ernest Dowson, Lionel Johnson, Arthur Symons and others – and his careful staging of 'The Tragic Generation' is designed, in part, to present his own work as a distinctive and emergent 'new poetic'. In the modernist twenties, however, Yeats was still composing decadent lyrics like 'Oil and Blood', and happily proclaiming 'We have returned of late to the mood of the nineties.'[2] Notwithstanding this surge of *fin-de-siècle* fervour, it is commonly accepted that the 1890s were essentially a time of transition for Yeats, a dabbling with the palette in preparation for the big canvases to come.

One familiar explanation of Yeats's poetic development has to do with Ireland. Yeats, it would seem, moved on from late Victorian aestheticism and decadence into a more robust and heroic mode of writing based on Irish national ideals. By bringing the example of French symbolism to bear on the myths and legends of his native Ireland, Yeats was able to make a formidable contribution to the ideas and techniques of European modernism. The major problem with this account of Yeats's transition from English aestheticism to

66

Irish nationalism is that England and Ireland are frequently subjected to the kind of mythologizing that Yeats himself was fond of. If late-Victorian England is redolent of wine and roses, then Ireland at the turn of the century is a place of fairytale and folklore. What is needed is a more exact analysis of the early poetry of W. B. Yeats, not in terms of some imagined transformation from *fin-de-siècle* romanticism to the 'Celtic Twilight', but in terms of how the writing gathers momentum and power from the intense political and cultural friction between two nations at a critical turning point in modern history. To look back on the Literary Revival or 'Celtic Twilight' of the 1890s from our own *fin de siècle* is to see the extent to which Yeats designed and willed a particular version of Ireland and of Irish history. That version of history has often been construed very loosely as nationalist and even, more recently, as revolutionary. It has become increasingly clear, however, especially in the work of Irish historians and critics, that what generated Yeats's nationalist ideals was the disaffection of the Irish Protestant rather than the ardour of the revolutionary patriot. Yeats's own mythologizing of history is apt to overstate the national importance and political consequences of the Irish 'renaissance', but the 1890s is nevertheless one of the most significant decades in modern Irish culture.

Aestheticism and decadence might well be prominent signposts on the map of late Victorian culture, but the map looks very different when viewed from Dublin rather than London. The sense Yeats had of the arts 'dreaming of things to come' finds some verification in the energetic activities of the so-called Literary Revival: the Irish Literary Society was founded in London in 1891, the National Literary Society in Dublin in 1892, the Gaelic League in 1893, and the Irish Literary Theatre in 1897. Yeats was a tireless and committed agitator on behalf of such organizations, and the image of Yeats the committee man sits uneasily alongside the more popular image of Yeats the unworldly aesthete. The most significant event of the decade in Yeats's estimation, though, was undoubtedly the fall from power and subsequent death of Charles Stewart Parnell in 1891. On the day Parnell died, Yeats seized the opportunity to make a public statement with his elegiac 'Mourn – and then Onward', a hastily written piece which was never reprinted in his lifetime. Looking back on the event from 1923, however, Yeats saw the death of Parnell as the starting point of modern cultural politics in Ireland:

The modern literature of Ireland, and indeed all that stir of thought which prepared for the Anglo-Irish war, began when Parnell fell from power in 1891. A disillusioned and embittered Ireland turned from parliamentary politics; an event was conceived; and the race began, as I think, to be troubled by that event's long gestation.[3]

Yeats acknowledges here a turning point from political nationalism to cultural nationalism, and yet he wishes to believe that poetry *can* make things happen, including, perhaps, the Easter Rising of 1916. This stirring account of the dawn of modern Irish culture has been seriously questioned by both historians and literary critics.[4] The most recent investigation, by R. F. Foster, claims that 'the supposed "lull" in politics should not be taken as read', since the Irish Parliamentary Party and the United Irish League continued to make an energetic and productive contribution to nationalist politics, especially in such areas as local government and agrarian ex-perimentation.[5] Foster disputes the idea that the cultural revival of the 1890s fed the hearts and minds of 1916, and is inclined to see that particular 'event' taking shape in the early years of the twentieth century.

There is no doubt, however, that the 1890s witnessed the most powerful burst of cultural nationalism in Irish history, even though the ground had been well prepared by Thomas Davis and the Young Ireland Movement some fifty years earlier. The disputes are likely to arise over the aims and methods of that nationalism, and over its possible political consequences. If, as George Watson points out, there is still a tendency in English literary criticism 'to underplay the Irish cultural and political context, or to treat it as peripheral', there is also now a tendency to regard that context as unambiguously 'colonial'.[6] At a time when post-colonial discourse is the subject of intense theorizing, the early work of Yeats is likely to be labelled 'anti-colonialist' or 'anti-imperialist', without proper consideration of the complexities and contradictions inherent in the version of nationalism that Yeats espoused. It is all too easy to envisage some single, uniform nationalism being pitted against an equally general-ized and global colonialism.

One of the most striking and engaging studies of Yeats as an anti-imperialist writer is Edward Said's essay 'Yeats and decolonization', which first appeared in the Field Day series of pamphlets on 'Nationalism, Colonialism and Literature' in 1988. Said places Yeats's early poetry in a phase of anti-imperialist resistance (generated mainly by poets and visionaries) which preceded the more openly liberationist movements of the mid-twentieth century. He rests his claim on those poems, such as 'The Lake Isle of Innisfree', which are concerned with the recovery and repossession of colonized land through the act of imagination. Yeats, in Said's estimation, belongs with 'the great nationalist artists of decolonization and revolutionary nationalism, like Tagore, Senghor, Neruda, Vallejo, Césaire, Faiz, Darwish'.[7] In the revised version of this essay which appears in his monumental *Culture and Imperialism*, Said offers two important qualifications which serve to complicate any assessment of Yeats's nationalism. As well as writing in English, not Irish, Yeats was also a descendant of the Anglo-Irish or Protestant 'ascendancy' and therefore an unlikely militant. Said chooses not to explore these seeming contradictions in Yeats's nationalism, and instead repeats his original claim that the early poetry embodies 'liberationist and Utopian revolutionism'. In a powerful and provocative way, Said enables a reconsideration of both the alleged 'wilful mysticism' of Yeats's poetry and its later drift into reactionary politics. When Yeats's nationalism is measured against other forms of nationalist sentiment and activity in the 1890s, however, the word 'revolutionary' is likely to appear exaggerated and unjustified. It is then necessary to question the extent to which Yeats did, in fact, 'lift the burdens of Ireland's colonial afflictions'.[8]

Some indication of the brusque and uncompromising nationalism which Yeats sometimes affected in the 1890s can be found in a series of fourteen articles written for the Boston *Pilot* and titled 'The Celt in London'. The repeated theme of these pieces is succinctly conveyed in a review dated 22 February 1890: 'There is no great literature without nationality, no great nationality without literature.' Elsewhere, Yeats insists that 'Ireland is the true subject for the Irish' and that 'an Irish magazine should give us Irish subjects'. In his column for 19 November 1892 he refers to London as 'the capital of the enemy'.[9] It is equally surprising to discover that the *Pilot* was an Irish Catholic weekly newspaper (formerly the *Jesuit*), under the management of a well-known Fenian, John Boyle O'Reilly, to whom Yeats had been introduced by John O'Leary. It needs to be observed, however, that the opportunity of playing 'The Celt in London' to an American audience appears to have encouraged Yeats to adopt an outspoken manner that he might otherwise have avoided. There is a good deal of style and rhetoric but relatively little substance in his nationalist proclamations. In 1932 Yeats was to comment on his 'Letters to the New Island': 'I was a propagandist and hated being one.'[10] Even the Fenian connection is liable to prove disappointing, since it appears to have been a matter of pragmatism rather than revolutionary commitment. O'Leary himself had told Yeats: 'In this country a man must have upon his side the Church or the Fenians, and you will never have the Church.'[11]

O'Leary had enjoyed some notoriety after serving a prison sentence, but at the time Yeats knew him it would seem that his colleagues in the Irish Republican Brotherhood regarded him as a spent force and treated him with some amusement. Yeats could commune with his mentor without fearing any actual revolutionary involvement. Michael North even doubts whether O'Leary could be called a republican, since he nourished 'an aristocratic dream' that Ireland would one day have its own king.[12] If R. F. Foster is correct, the Fenian label was not as dangerous as it retrospectively sounded, since Fenianism in the 1890s could imply a public and recreational activity as much as a revolutionary, separatist force.[13]

In August 1891 – that critical year – Yeats adopted a new title, 'The Celt in Ireland', explaining to his readers that he was 'back in Ireland for the time being, writing out on the lawn of an old Irish thatched farmhouse'. The lyrical sentences that follow are hardly Irish, though, since they emulate the florid English prose style of Walter Pater, whose potent influence is repeatedly acknowledged by Yeats in his *Autobiographies*: 'An apple tree covered with red apples shakes softly before me in the sunlight, and the paper on which I write rests on the top of a sundial.' Yeats was reading *Marius the Epicurean* at the time, and has to affect a severe dismissal of Pater's novel in the interests of an exclusivist nationalism: '*Marius the Epicurean* is not writ in my bond. With Irish literature and Irish thought alone have I to do.' The uncompromising stance soon wavers, however, and on reflection Yeats wonders if his own search for 'stories of the fairies and the phantoms' in Ireland might not resemble Pater's search for the 'spiritual beings of Plato'. He is finally persuaded to 'go away and dream among the green shadows and the red apples'.[14] The essay provides a valuable and revealing illustration of the extent to which Yeats was drawn *simultaneously* to English aestheticism and Irish nationalism in the early 1890s.

How revolutionary, then, was the nationalism Yeats espoused, and what possible relationships existed between the nationalist Literary

Revival and the aestheticism and decadence of the 1890s? At a superficial glance it might seem as if there is little possibility of any collaboration between these distinctive tendencies in Yeats's early writings, hence the common assumption that aestheticism was supplanted or displaced by a growing commitment to specifically Irish themes and images. The aesthete in this respect is one who openly spurns political actualities, being too wrapped up in dreams to suffer the real world for very long. As Seamus Deane has pointed out, however, the Celtic Twilight can in other respects be regarded as a regional variation of aestheticism and decadence. The overt 'balladeering nationalism' of the Young Ireland movement is subtly modified so that 'harps and wolfhounds' give way to 'roses and moonlight'.[15] R. K. R. Thornton complies with such a view when he points out that 'One of the most specifically Decadent poems – "Into the Twilight" – first appeared in the National Observer on 29 July 1893 with the title "The Celtic Twilight"':[16]

> Out-worn heart, in a time out-worn,
> Come clear of the nets of wrong and right;
> Laugh, heart, again in the grey twilight,
> Sigh, heart, again in the dew of the morn.
>
> Your mother Eire is always young,
> Dew ever shining and twilight grey;
> Though hope fall from you and love decay,
> Burning in fires of a slanderous tongue.
>
> Come, heart, where hill is heaped upon hill:
> For there the mystical brotherhood
> Of sun and moon and hollow and wood
> And river and stream work out their will;
>
> And God stands winding His lonely horn,
> And time and the world are ever in flight;
> And love is less kind than the grey twilight,
> And hope is less dear than the dew of the moon.

Many of the images and devices of *fin-de-siècle* English poetry were clearly compatible with those of the Irish Literary Revival, and there is no reason to suppose that Yeats's commitment to a revitalized Irish cultural identity should have been fundamentally at odds with his involvement in the aestheticism and decadence of the 1890s.

There is, however, a more compelling explanation of the close relationship between aestheticism and nationalism in Yeats's early work. What the aesthete and the nationalist shared was a deep

hostility to English industrial and utilitarian society. The Ireland
Yeats imagined in the 1890s was conceived in opposition to a
philistine, commercial, urban England. While England was 'a place
where there are great wheels turning and great chimneys vomiting
smoke', Ireland would always be 'a place where men plow and sow
and reap'. Yeats, like many of his fellow 'Rhymers', firmly adheres
to a tradition of cultural criticism exemplified by Matthew Arnold,
John Ruskin, Walter Pater, William Morris and Oscar Wilde. The
attachment is immediately evident in Yeats's remark that 'I had
dreamed of enlarging Irish hate, till we had come to hate with a
passion of patriotism what Morris and Ruskin hated.'[17] Ironically,
then, Yeats draws upon a mode of criticism already at work within
English culture, and one that was directed at reforming England
rather than ensuring its divorce from Ireland. We might be forgiven
for identifying such a tendency as 'literary unionism'[18] rather than
revolutionary nationalism. At the very least we need to recognize the
deep ambivalence in Yeats's nationalist ideals. If the cultural
nationalism of the Literary Revival served to justify and support the
more overt political struggle for freedom, it could in other instances
serve as a diversion and a distraction from that political struggle.
Literature might inspire and inflame its listeners, but it might also
soften and ennoble them in precisely the way that Matthew Arnold
had recommended in *Culture and Anarchy*. There was, then, a
possibility that cultural nationalism could both endorse and undermine the more strident political nationalism of the 1890s, and to
apply the word 'revolutionary' to Yeats is to adopt a limited and
one-sided view of his work.

What facilitated the unusual convergence of *fin-de-siècle* aestheticism and Irish nationalism in the writings of Yeats was an abiding
interest in spiritualism and the occult. To espouse a belief in esoteric
forms of knowledge was an implicit criticism of English materialism
and utilitarianism. Yeats did not need to emulate the Catholic
mysticism of Ernest Dowson and Lionel Johnson, since he was able to
draw on a long tradition of occultism and supernaturalism inherent
in his own specifically Protestant background. As Terence Brown has
argued, there were significant areas of compatibility between Yeats's
Irish Protestantism and Victorian evangelicalism. The very term
'revival' has obvious evangelical associations and gives to literary
endeavour a seemingly religious sanction. At a more fundamental
level, cultural nationalism was able to 'satisfy minds hungry for

mystery in an increasingly unmysterious and materialist world'. John Millington Synge was among those writers for whom cultural nationalism offered some compensation for a lost religious belief: 'Soon after I relinquished the Kingdom of God I began to take a real interest in the Kingdom of Ireland.' In its search for 'a sustainable and imaginatively satisfying spirituality', the Irish Literary Revival found common ground with a form of dissent already manifest in late-Victorian England.[19] It was here, among other places, that Yeats was able to reconcile the claims of art with the claims of nationhood.

R. F. Foster has written forcefully and convincingly of 'the supernatural dimension of the Protestant subculture', stressing the extent to which Yeats's lifetime interest in the occult was an essential part of his social and cultural identity. Equally striking is his contention that occultism and magic provided a refuge for a Protestant class that was becoming increasingly marginalized in modern Ireland. Yeats, in this context, belongs to a line of writers 'whose occult preoccupations surely mirror a sense of displacement, a loss of social and psychological integration, and an escapism motivated by the threat of a takeover by the Catholic middle classes.'[20] The kind of nationalism Yeats espouses in the 1890s is the product of a complex set of allegiances and identities; it emerges from a deep sense of colonial insecurity and a deep sense of anxiety about the future of his own embattled class. Yeats's concern about the increasing dislocation of his class – the so-called 'Anglo-Irish Ascendancy' – provides the psychological impulse and motivation behind such early works as 'The Crucifixion of the Outcast' and 'The Wanderings of Oisin'.

What Yeats was seeking in the 1890s was a way of re-establishing his own cultural identity – and that of his class – in a country which was witnessing a strongly emerging Catholic nationalism. Behind the changing balance of power lay the Catholic Emancipation Act of 1829, the Disestablishment of the Church of Ireland in 1869, the Land Wars in the 1880s and the Home Rule Crisis in 1886. Given this historical context, it is difficult to ignore Seamus Deane's opinion that the story of the Literary Revival is 'the story of the spiritual heroics of a fading class – the Ascendancy – in the face of a transformed Catholic "nation"'. Put more bluntly, 'Irish culture became the new property of those who were losing their grip on Irish land... It was in essence a strategic retreat from political to cultural supremacy.'[21] It is hardly surprising that Yeats's esoteric references to a new universal order and a new state of being should coincide with the perceived decline of the Anglo-Irish Ascendancy.

We cannot begin to understand the complex nature of Yeats's nationalism until we first acknowledge and then begin to dismantle the various strategic defences through which he concealed and protected his own vulnerability as a member of a marginalized and displaced Protestant middle class. To do so is to encounter again those seeming contradictions in Yeats's nationalist endeavours. It is necessary, in the first place, to observe that in a predominantly Catholic country it was primarily Irish Protestants who were involved in the Literary Revival: not just Yeats, but Standish O'Grady, George Russell (A. E.), Lady Augusta Gregory and others. It is equally important, though, to observe that the cultural nationalism Yeats and many of his associates espoused was founded not on Gaelic but on the English language. It is only when a contrast is made with the exclusively Catholic and Gaelic ideals of more militant Irish writers and political thinkers that the peculiar and particular form of Yeats's nationalism comes into focus. To make an obvious point, there was more than one kind of nationalism at work in late nineteenth-century Ireland, and the relations between nationalism, socialism and cosmopolitanism are, in themselves, complex enough to merit a separate study. One immediate source of disagreement was the extent to which Irish literature might be specifically national *and* broadly universal, and this was to become a major point of discussion in the debate which Yeats conducted with John Eglinton and George Russell (A. E.) in the pages of the Dublin *Daily Express* in 1898.

It was the question of language, however, which heightened and dramatized the differences between one version of nationalism and another. The question was a critical one because it was in language, above all else, that the essence of Irishness was thought to be preserved and transmitted. To what extent, it was asked, could a strong and distinctive Irish identity be conveyed through the English language, and to what extent did the survival of a uniquely Irish spirit depend on the survival of the Irish language? Some editors of Irish ballads in the 1840s had claimed that it was, indeed, possible to reproduce the Irish spirit in English words. Charles Gavan Duffy described his *Ballad Poetry of Ireland* (1845) as 'the production of educated men, with English tongues but Irish hearts', while D. F. MacCarthy introduced his *Book of Irish Ballads* (1846) with the assertion that 'we can be thoroughly Irish in our writings without ceasing to be English'.[22] Not surprisingly, a good deal of attention was given to the act of translation. Samuel Ferguson was among those who believed that a desirable union might be effected between two cultures and two languages through careful translation, and Yeats was to acknowledge his debt to Ferguson on numerous occasions. In the early years of his career, however, Yeats also encountered the uncompromising linguistic ideals of associates like Douglas Hyde, a Protestant who conceded 'the necessity for de-Anglicising Ireland'. Hyde's lecture on the subject was delivered to the National Literary Society in November 1892 and was meant to appeal to nationalists and unionists alike. Yeats's response to Hyde's lecture was to ask: 'Can we not build up a national tradition, a national literature, which shall be none the less Irish in spirit from being English in language?'[23] Yeats's position was a familiar and oft-repeated one: that it was possible through an act of translation or 'retelling' to create a modern literature in English that would possess a rhythm and style characteristic or reminiscent of a much older Irish literature.

Even if we accept the proposition that a strong and distinctive Irish identity might be realized in the English language, there are likely to be disagreements over the extent to which such writing can be regarded as nationalist. How does the literary critic or cultural historian begin to assess the nationalist content or commitment in such writing? What weight or value should be given to this nationalist dimension, especially in relation to formal or stylistic considerations? What are the most valid and appropriate critical procedures to adopt when reading Irish poetry in the English language? One of the earliest and most persuasive arguments, as far as the poetry of W. B. Yeats is concerned, was advanced by Thomas MacDonagh in his *Literature in Ireland: Studies Irish and Anglo-Irish* in 1916.[24] By examining the metrical effects in the poems and plays, MacDonagh was able to show how Yeats reproduced in English the peculiar syllabic measure or stress tendency of Irish speech. Edward Said rests his defence of Yeats's early nationalist writings largely on the poet's imaginative recovery of the land:

One of the first tasks of the culture of resistance was to reclaim, rename, and reinhabit the land ... The search for authenticity, for a more congenial national origin than that provided by colonial history, for a new pantheon of heroes and (occasionally) heroines, myths, and religions – these too are made possible by a sense of land reappropriated by its people.[25]

The geographic or cartographic impulse that Said identifies is powerfully at play in Yeats's early poetry, the most celebrated instance being the opening stanza of 'The Lake Isle of Innisfree', written and published in 1890:

> I will arise and go now, and go to Innisfree,
> And a small cabin build there, of clay and wattles made:
> Nine bean-rows will I have there, a hive for the honey-bee,
> And live alone in the bee-loud glade.

W. J. McCormack, however, regards Yeats's poetic landscapes with a degree of scepticism and warns against 'a too easy acceptance of him as a local celebrant'. There is, at first reading, a profound sense of intimacy with the landscape of Sligo, underpinned with concrete references to the names of mountains, lakes and villages. But, as McCormack points out, 'we underestimate the subtle reservations of Yeats's poetic perception if we mistake the *possibility* of intimacy for the thing itself, if we mistake the accessibility of those place-names on the map for the integration of a poet in a known and comprehensive culture'.[26] Michael North agrees with McCormack that the poem's linguistic, as well as geographical, contours require careful scrutiny, and that what they reveal has more to do with separation than with intimacy. The title of the poem, based on 'Inis Fraoigh' (meaning 'heather island'), conveniently embodies for Yeats the English word 'free', but at the same time betrays a deep anxiety about the poet's relationship to the place: 'The only remnant of Irish in the otherwise thoroughly English speech of the poem, the place name acts to connect the poem linguistically to its subject, but just by virtue of its difference, the name also advertises the distance of that subject.'[27] In some respects, then, Yeats's relationship to the land is more complex and ambiguous than Said's anti-colonial label would suggest. Some critics would go so far as to claim that Yeats's longing for the landscape of his youth and his preoccupation with childhood in such poems as 'The Stolen Child' are evidence of 'infantile regression' rather than progressive nationalism.[28]

The same critical problems attend Yeats's treatment of the people who inhabit the land. There are many early poems, such as 'The Meditation of the Old Fisherman', in which Yeats dramatizes the voice of the Irish peasantry ('When I was a boy with never a crack in my heart'). At one level it seems valid enough to claim that 'Yeats's unique contribution to Irish thought [was] the proposition that Ireland's purest essence was located in the peasant's primitive belief in holy wells and fairy thorns.'[29] Such a view of Ireland's spiritual wealth is in keeping with the anti-philistine and anti-materialist ideals of the Literary Revival alluded to already. In addition, the stereotype of the savage, ignorant peasant is replaced with a more dignified and appealing image. At another level, however, it might be claimed that Yeats's rehabilitation of the peasantry as the source of Irish wisdom and value is so idealistic and exclusive as to hinder rather than promote the cause of national identity and national unity. Once again it seems significant that many of the virtues Yeats attributes to the Irish peasant, including depth of feeling and strength of imagination, are adopted from Matthew Arnold's series of lectures 'On the Study of Celtic Literature' (1867). Arnold, of course, insisted that Ireland should be 'a nation poetically only, not politically'.[30] Yeats often seems content to follow suit, permitting his nationalist ideals to be aestheticized in a way that renders the peasant politically inert and picturesque. As Seamus Heaney has pointed out, Yeats succeeds in creating a version of Irish life untouched by contemporary political realities such as Home Rule: 'the very elements of this life are impeccably aesthetic'.[31] It is also, as Heaney suggests, a version of Irish life that effectively predates contemporary sectarian conflict. What the peasant appears to practise is not Catholicism but a form of occult spirituality close to Yeats's own. The more prosaic features of modern Irish democracy are singularly lacking in the nation that Yeats conceives in the 1890s. The response Yeats makes to the land and the people cannot, then, be considered as a direct act of 'decolonization', since the account of English-Irish relations on which it is based is both ambivalent and evasive. Such a response issues from the insecurity and marginalization of the Anglo-Irish Ascendancy in the face of growing Catholic nationalist aspiration, and not simply from some shared or unified resistance to English colonial power.

'To Ireland in the Coming Times' (1892) is perhaps the most revealing statement of Yeats's uncertain nationalist sentiments. As

Seamus Heaney has argued, the poem is 'full of imperatives and peremptory claims' which create a sense of authority and control.[32] The poem's declarative mood, however, conceals an anxiety about the writer's relationship with Irish national culture:

> Know, that I would accounted be
> True brother of a company
> That sang, to sweeten Ireland's wrong,
> Ballad and story, rann and song.

The pursuit of the red rose of spiritual beauty is measured, as it is elsewhere in the rose poems, with a desire to 'Sing of old Eire and the ancient ways'. Each stanza involves both a commitment to an established national tradition and a declaration of difference:

> Nor may I less be counted one
> With Davis, Mangan, Ferguson,
> Because, to him who ponders well,
> My rhymes more than their rhyming tell
> Of things discovered in the deep,
> Where only body's laid asleep.

At the time of composing this poem, Yeats had already signalled his departure from Thomas Davis and James Clarence Mangan and his growing preference for the work of the Unionist, Sir Samuel Ferguson. If Davis was too dogmatic, Mangan was too melancholic; Ferguson, however, was 'the greatest poet Ireland has produced' and 'the most Celtic'. Yeats was to make the point repeatedly in an article published in the *Dublin University Review* in 1886: 'The nation has found in Davis a battle call, as in Mangan its cry of despair; but he only, the one Homeric poet of our time, could give us immortal companions still wet with the dew of their primal world.'[33] Ferguson's rewriting of Celtic legends in English showed Yeats a way of remaining true to the Protestant middle class while helping to shape and inform a new sense of nationhood in Ireland. Ferguson's Celtic virtues, though, are precisely those which Matthew Arnold hoped would temper philistinism and promote political unity. To read Ferguson's books of Celtic legend is, in Yeats's estimation, to be saved from 'that leprosy of the modern – tepid emotions and many aims'.[34] Once again, the kind of nationalism Yeats espouses seems uncomfortably close to nineteenth-century liberal reform.

This is not to deny that there are images and gestures in Yeats's early work that might aptly be described as 'revolutionary', but these are relatively few and require careful qualification. There are those poems like 'The Valley of the Black Pig' (1896) which anticipate a violent, apocalyptic transformation of Ireland:

> The dews drop slowly and dreams gather: unknown spears
> Suddenly hurtle before my dream-awakened eyes,
> And then the clash of fallen horsemen and the cries
> Of unknown perishing armies beat about my ears.
> We who still labour by the cromlech on the shore,
> The grey cairn on the hill, when day sinks drowned in dew,
> Being weary of the world's empires, bow down to you,
> Master of the still stars and of the flaming door.

As George Watson points out, Yeats had absorbed this prophetic heralding of a new epoch from Madame Blavatsky's *Secret Doctrine*, but 'the messianic belief, the sense of imminent upheaval, the eager anticipation of apocalypse, was also a part of the emotional make-up of the revolutionary patriots in the Fenian movement'.[35] Yeats himself comments on the poem that 'All over Ireland there are prophecies of the coming rout of the enemies of Ireland, in a certain Valley of the Black Pig, and these prophecies are, no doubt, now, as they were in the Fenian days, a political force.'[36] The insertion of 'no doubt' has a distancing effect which ironically casts doubt on Yeats's own commitment to the 'political force' of the prophecy. Much of his commentary on the poem is concerned with the Celtic origin of the legend, and with pointing out that the battle is a mythological one in which the pig serves as an emblem of winter battling with summer or death battling with life.

George Watson believes that 'the very cloudiness and imprecision of the poem may be one of its strengths, from a nationalist angle'.[37] While anticipating a dramatic transformation of Ireland, the poem avoids any narrow, dogmatic line. It could also be construed as a weakness, however, that Yeats continually mystifies the processes of political change and gives only a vague impression of the Ireland that might emerge from revolutionary upheaval. R. F. Foster doubts whether there was any serious political commitment behind the violent metaphors of the Literary Revival: 'the amateur poets and antiquarians who shortly began recycling the most bloodthirsty pieces of ancient mythology in order to draw apparent parallels for contemporary separatist heroics do not themselves appear to have adhered to anything like revolutionary beliefs'.[38] In private correspondence Yeats likewise appears to pursue a much more moderate nationalist line than poems like 'The Valley of the Black Pig' might suggest.

The nationalist stirrings which Yeats experienced in the 1890s found their most powerful embodiment in *Cathleen Ni Houlihan*. The play was first performed in 1902 and was dedicated to the memory of William Rooney, a proto-Sinn Feiner. The Old Woman who persuades Michael Gillane to serve his country rather than be married speaks eloquently of her suffering and dispossession. The dialogue functions naturalistically and yet acquires a tremendous mythological and allegorical charge. The Old Woman, later transformed into a young girl with 'the walk of a queen', inspires her listeners with 'the hope of getting my beautiful fields back again; the hope of putting the strangers out of my house'. The sacrifice she calls for is the blood sacrifice of militant republicanism: 'It is a hard service they take that help me. Many that are red-cheeked now will be pale-cheeked; many that have been free to walk the hills and the bogs and the rushes will be sent to walk hard streets in far countries …' At the same time it is significant that Yeats sets the play in 1798, at the time of the French landings at Killala. In doing so, Yeats appeals to the spirit of United Ireland – to a broad-based secular republicanism – and cautiously distances himself from the specifically Catholic republicanism of his own day. As George Watson argues, the play is very much 'an attempt to assert a sense of identity with an uncompromised "Irishness"'.[39] It is also a work that identifies with a strong romantic element in republican nationalism, and even if *Cathleen Ni Houlihan* appears to promote a Fenian view of Ireland there remain severe doubts about the extent to which the early writings can be considered 'revolutionary'. In asking 'Did that play of mine send out / Certain men the English shot?' Yeats was not congratulating himself but regarding with some misgiving and surprise the idea that *Cathleen Ni Houlihan* might have contributed to the mobilization of revolutionary patriots in the Easter Rising of 1916.[40]

In what remains one of the most provocative and influential accounts of Yeats's politics, Conor Cruise O'Brien claims that after the impact of *Cathleen Ni Houlihan* in 1902 Yeats 'turned aside from Irish politics'. His contention is not that Yeats ceased to be an Irish nationalist but that his nationalism became conservative and aristocratic rather than populist and active. He believes that throughout the 1890s Yeats had been emphasizing his 'Irishness' while minimizing the Protestant tradition to which he belonged. After 1902, Yeats was no longer able to disguise his contempt for the rising Catholic middle class and 'the Protestant now re-emerged with an audible sigh of relief'.[41] A similar line of thinking is adopted by Edward Said, who believes that the 'revolutionism' of Yeats's early poetry is 'belied and even cancelled out by his later reactionary politics'.[42] Both arguments emphasize a sharp distinction between the youthful radical and the elder statesman. There is a good deal of evidence, however, to suggest that Yeats's nationalism in the 1890s was not as advanced or as radical as is sometimes implied.

Any serious assessment of Yeats's nationalist commitment ought to consider the critical reception of his writings both in England and in Ireland. If, as Seamus Deane asserts, Yeats's nationalist compositions were regarded by an English audience as 'essentially picturesque manifestations of the Irish sensibility', then the term 'revolutionary' seems hardly applicable.[43] It is worth remembering, perhaps, that in 1899 Yeats was considered by Padraic Pearse to be 'a mere English poet of the third or fourth rank'.[44] Not enough attention has been given to the diverse forms that nationalism took in the 1890s, ranging from constitutional reform to physical force. The non-Catholic nationalism to which Yeats gave his allegiance should not be confused with revolutionary separatism. According to R. F. Foster, Yeats had little enthusiasm for separation from England: 'at his most committed there was always the congenital ambivalence of the Protestant bourgeois. For all his identification with the Gaelic ethos, a wistful hope remained for leadership from a regenerated landlord class.'[45] Foster reminds us that Coole Park, where Yeats was a frequent visitor after 1897, was 'an imperial house memorializing generations of service to the Empire'.[46] In the complex Protestant consciousness of the late nineteenth century it was possible to reject the worst excesses of English administration in Ireland and at the same time remain committed to the British Empire. To regard Irish nationalism in the 1890s as wholeheartedly 'anti-colonial' is to overlook many of the cultural and political complexities of the decade.

Aestheticism does not in itself provide an adequate account of the cultural shifts and transformations of the 1890s, but we ought to be wary of dismissing the 'charm' and 'delicacy' of Yeats's early work in favour of more overtly political poems such as 'Easter 1916' and 'Meditations in Time of Civil War'. For all his talk of dispelling rhetoric from his early poetry, Yeats endeavoured to create a number of powerful and enduring myths of 'Irishness' that might shape and inform a new national consciousness. The Ireland that Yeats envisaged was a nation with a distinctive cultural and spiritual identity, an imagined community free of sectarian differences and conflicts. That vision was not as revolutionary as some critics have supposed and it hardly outlasted the 1890s. The nationalism on which it was founded did not seriously entertain the idea of political separation from Britain; nor did it contemplate an idea of community that would admit the most prosaic and unromantic aspects of modern democracy. In that respect, it was a nationalism conditioned by aestheticism. A century later, however, those early writings continue to attract an unusual amount of interest and fascination. It might well be that the value of Yeats's *fin-de-siècle* poetry has less to do with illustrating aestheticism than with challenging and complicating our understanding of what it means to be Irish.

NOTES

1 W. B. Yeats, *Essays and Introductions* (London: Macmillan, 1974), p. 191.
2 See Stephen Regan, '"Oil and Blood": Yeats's Return to the Nineties', *Yeats Annual* 7 (London: Macmillan, 1990), pp. 194–99.
3 W. B. Yeats, *Autobiographies* (London: Macmillan, 1955), p. 559.
4 The seminal article on this topic is John Kelly's 'The Fall of Parnell and the Rise of Irish Literature: An Investigation', *Anglo-Irish Studies* 11 (1976), 1–23.
5 R. F. Foster, 'Anglo-Irish Literature, Gaelic Nationalism and Irish Politics in the 1890s', in *Ireland After the Union: Proceedings of the second joint meeting of the Royal Irish Academy and the British Academy, London, 1986* (Oxford: Oxford University Press, 1989), p. 63.
6 G. J. Watson, *Irish Identity and the Literary Revival* (London: Croom Helm, 1978), p. 14.
7 Edward W. Said, *Yeats and Decolonization* (Derry: Field Day, 1988), p. 8.
8 Edward W. Said, *Culture and Imperialism* (London: Chatto and Windus, 1993), p. 283, p. 287.
9 W. B. Yeats, *Letters to the New Island* (London: Macmillan, 1989), p. 30, p. 21, p. 163, p. 64.
10 Yeats, *Letters to the New Island*, p. xviii.
11 Yeats, *Autobiographies*, p. 209.
12 Michael North, *The Political Aesthetic of Yeats, Eliot, and Pound* (Cambridge: Cambridge University Press, 1991), p. 28.
13 Foster, 'Anglo-Irish Literature, Gaelic Nationalism and Irish Politics in the 1890s', p. 70.
14 Yeats, *Letters to the New Island*, p. 42.

15 Seamus Deane (ed.), *The Field Day Anthology of Irish Writing* (Derry: Field Day, 1991), vol. 2, p. 720.
16 R. K. R. Thornton, *The Decadent Dilemma* (London: Edward Arnold, 1983), p. 169.
17 Both quotations are from Foster, 'Anglo-Irish Literature, Gaelic Nationalism and Irish Politics in the 1890s', p. 73.
18 The phrase is Seamus Deane's.
19 Terence Brown, 'Cultural Nationalism 1880–1930', in Deane, *The Field Day Anthology of Irish Writing*, vol. 2, pp. 518–19.
20 R. F. Foster, 'Protestant Magic: W. B. Yeats and the Spell of Irish History', *Proceedings of the British Academy*, LXXV (1989), 254, 251.
21 Seamus Deane, 'Heroic Styles: The Tradition of an Idea', in *Ireland's Field Day* (London: Hutchinson, 1985), pp. 47–8.
22 Deane, *The Field Day Anthology of Irish Literature*, vol. 2, p. 5.
23 John Kelly and Eric Domville (eds.), *The Collected Letters of W. B. Yeats*, vol. 1: 1865–1895 (Oxford: Oxford University Press, 1986), p. 338.
24 Thomas MacDonagh, *Literature in Ireland: Studies Irish and Anglo-Irish* (Dublin: The Talbot Press, 1916).
25 Said, *Culture and Imperialism*, p. 273.
26 W. J. McCormack, *Ascendancy and Tradition in Anglo-Irish Literary History from 1789 to 1939* (Oxford: Clarendon, 1985), p. 295.
27 North, *The Political Aesthetic of Yeats, Eliot, and Pound*, p. 25.
28 Declan Kiberd, 'Yeats, Childhood and Exile', in Paul Hyland and Neil Sammells (eds.), *Irish Writing: Exile and Subversion* (London: Macmillan, 1991), pp. 126–45.
29 Malcolm Brown, *The Politics of Irish Literature from Thomas Davis to W. B. Yeats* (London: George Allen and Unwin Ltd., 1972), p. 317.
30 Matthew Arnold, 'From Easter to August', *Nineteenth Century*, 22 (1887), 321.
31 Seamus Heaney, 'A Tale of Two Islands: Reflections on the Irish Literary Revival', *Irish Studies*, 1 (1980), 8.
32 *Ibid.*, p. 4.
33 W. B. Yeats and Thomas Kinsella, *Davis, Mangan, Ferguson? Tradition and the Irish Writer* (Dublin: Dolmen Press, 1970), p. 46, p. 31.
34 *Ibid.*, p.47. Compare with Matthew Arnold's 'strange disease of modern life, / With its sick hurry, its divided aims.' ('The Scholar-Gipsy')
35 Watson, *Irish Identity and the Literary Revival*, p. 92.
36 W. B. Yeats, *Collected Poems* (London: Macmillan, 1981), pp. 526–7.
37 Watson, *Irish Identity and the Literary Revival*, p. 93.
38 Foster, 'Anglo-Irish Literature, Gaelic Nationalism and Irish Politics in the 1890s', p. 68.
39 Watson, *Irish Identity and the Literary Revival*, p. 89.
40 In 'The Man and the Echo', written in 1938.
41 Conor Cruise O'Brien, 'Passion and Cunning: An Essay on the Politics of W. B. Yeats', in A. Norman Jeffares and K. G. W. Cross (eds.), *In*

Excited Reverie: A Centenary Tribute to William Butler Yeats 1865–1939 (London: Macmillan, 1965), p. 222.

42 Said, *Culture and Imperialism*, p. 283.

43 Deane, 'Heroic Styles', p. 49.

44 Quoted by Foster, 'Anglo-Irish Literature, Gaelic Nationalism and Irish Politics in the 1890s', p. 77.

45 *Ibid.*, p. 66, p. 74.

46 Foster, 'Protestant Magic', p. 257.

CHAPTER 5

The double lives of man: narration and identification in late nineteenth-century representations of ec-centric masculinities

Ed Cohen

'Men had to do fearful things to themselves before the self, the identical, the purposive and virile nature of man was formed.'
(Horkheimer and Adorno, *Dialectic of the Enlightenment*)

CITINGS/SITINGS

For the last decade or so, one project that has delimited the emerging field of lesbian and gay studies has sought to specify the conditions of possibility within which the category of the 'homosexual' emerged into Euro-American cultures and to explore the effects of this emergence. Whether its origins are situated somewhere in the early modern period, the sixteenth, eighteenth, or nineteenth centuries, the search for an ur-form of homosexuality has constituted a critical part of a contemporary effort to destabilize the 'naturalness' – if not the 'normalness' – of what we might now call procreative hetero-sexuality as the unmarked position from which all other forms of sexual practice can be understood as (at best) detours or deviations. Elaborating the crucial disarticulations of sex and gender undertaken by feminist critics and historians on the one hand, and genealogists of sexuality on the other, writings within lesbian and gay studies (including my own) have attempted to examine the multiple determinants which crystallized in and as 'homosexuality' in order to illuminate the complex historical processes whereby such cat-egorical denominations are fixed as attributes of persons, acts, and/or bodies. Through such intellectual work not only has the con-temporary 'commonsense' understanding of human sexuality as readily locatable somewhere between the poles of 'hetero' and 'homo' been assiduously challenged, but the perception that sexuality is a separable aspect of post-Enlightenment social for-mations has been demonstrated to be analytically insufficient.

Perhaps nowhere has this analytic effort had more impact than in the recent writings in Victorian studies, where scholars influenced by sex and gender critiques have augmented their earlier considerations of social determinants like class and status to shift both the domains and methodologies encompassed by this periodizing rubric. Not coincidentally, lesbian and gay studies have flourished among those working on the nineteenth century precisely because the hegemonic constellations of economic, familial, social, and political relations that were articulated by and as the emerging dominance of the British bourgeoisie pivoted so centrally around what Michel Foucault has labelled the 'truth' of sexuality.[1] Unfortunately, following Foucault, most of us working on 'queer' topics in the Victorian period have focused our analyses at the level of what we might call 'governmental' discourses (in the broadest possible sense) such as law, medicine, education, religion, literature, and the arts, as well as those nineteenth-century discourses designated as the 'human sciences' (biology, sociology, anthropology, criminology, sexology, psychology, etc.). As a consequence, while we have begun to develop a relatively comprehensive sense of the ways in which a privileged range of sexualized meanings and practices systematically coalesced within these discourses, offering subject positions that legitimated the asymmetrical distribution of power and resources, we have a much more rudimentary notion of how what I would call sexually 'eccentric' subjects lived out their dis-positions, let alone how they made sense of them.[2] Moreover, we have not sufficiently considered the complex forms of narrativization that emerged at the end of the nineteenth century to articulate the possibility of identifying as one who might affirm one's positioning as a subject whose desire is not directed across the putative oppositions of sex and gender – for example, as what we currently denominate as lesbian, gay, or queer. In particular, I am now interested in exploring the dynamic between narration and identification as it crystallized in a number of late nineteenth-century contexts because it gestures towards these contemporary personal and political 'identities' *in as much as they are explicitly reproduced by the process of narrativization colloquially known as 'coming out'.* Hence, I would like to consider here two autobiographical texts written in the 1880s that open 'out' onto this contemporary narrative possibility, along with the first psychoanalytic theorization of male homosexuality in Freud's *Three Essays on the Theory of Sexuality* (1905). The purpose is to begin to explore the contrapuntal play between governmentality and creativity through which new possibilities for sexual pleasures and sexual meanings coalesced into the stories that we now use to signify what it means to desire affective and erotic intimacies with people of the 'same' sex.

Before moving on to this historically situated analysis, however, allow me to make a few anachronistic remarks about 'coming out'. Since the 1960s, 'coming out' has served as a rubric for the processes of self-affirmation and self-definition through which men and women begin to denominate themselves as 'gay men' and 'lesbians' in their relations with themselves, their families, friends, loved ones, and communities – processes which have been central to the creation of both gay and lesbian identities and collectivities. But more than just a process of emergence and nomination, 'coming out' is also a way of telling a life story. Indeed, to some extent the 'coming out story' becomes the basis for both the production *and* reproduction of an identity to which the narrating individual lays claim precisely by pronouncing this story to be his or her own. We might even say that the conventional understanding of 'coming out' as an event precipitated by an emergent sexual identity, is a metaleptic representation of such transitional moments: that the 'event' of 'coming out' *per se* is only cognizable within a story which retrospectively fixes a narrative identification, reproducing what I would call an 'identity effect' by constituting it as the position from which the story both makes sense and gives pleasure.

Schematically, the coming out tale is often described as depicting a passage from the darkness, ignorance and repression of the non-self affirming 'closet' to the colourful, illuminated, self-affirming freedom of gay/lesbian/queer identity. A recent Keith Haring graphic designed to advertise National Coming Out Day makes the implications of this movement clear. In the centre of the drawing is a large black rectangle (which symbolically doubles as both the closet and the grave) from which a typically dynamic Haring figure emerges into the boldly coloured, vividly alive world of queer identity: in the same way that when Dorothy lands in Oz, suddenly the movie goes into Technicolour. The significance of this imaginary movement from darkness into colour, however, is not simply one of 'conversion', 'enlightenment', or 'liberation', for the transformative force of the coming out story is not just prospective but also *retrospective*. That is, the effective dynamic of the narrative structure gives shape not just to the landscape into which the figure steps but just as prominently to the black box from which the figure has emerged, now retroactively defined both as having a (safe) regular shape and as being (safely) confined to the past. The combination of these temporal shapings, then, is articulated through the subject position of the 'I' who tells the coming out tale such that this 'telling I' can assume his or her 'sexual identity' precisely by offering the imaginary (somatic) space within and across which this story is inscribed.[3]

Coming out was clearly not a possibility available to late-Victorian men. Nevertheless, a number of men in the period attempted to signify their sense of ec-centricity with respect to the prevailing understanding that 'sexual instinct' naturally *and* normally directed desire towards the 'opposite sex', by retrospectively narrativizing what they described as a 'doubleness' within themselves. In other words, as these men sought to represent their heretofore unrepresentable affective and erotic experiences, they articulated stories within which their manifest maleness was overwritten by another narrative trajectory that sought to circumvent the binary logistics of sex and gender. In order to do so, however, it was necessary for them to interrupt those earlier definitions of self-consistent, self-identified 'character', inscribed as both a sociological and a narratological category, which established the standard for 'proper' male subjectivity in the period. Hence, these late-Victorian men engendered new possibilities for articulating – if not embodying – sexual and emotional relations outside the naturalized opposition of sex by imagining new narrative modes that encompassed non-unitary forms of male subjectivity. Moreover, when Freud took up these complex narratives as he found them in the sexological literature to which he turned for his earliest accounts of male homosexuality, he used them as a point of departure for his psychoanalytic project precisely because they emplotted the (temporal) dynamic we now recognize as a 'splitting' within the psyche – a splitting which he believed to be the generalized condition of human subjectivity. Freud's seminal theorization of sexuality, then, is predicated upon a set of narrative strategies that were emerging during the last decades of the nineteenth century in texts written by European men who were struggling to articulate, in the stories they called their own, their own experiences, affects, meanings, desires, sensations, and pleasure that their cultures defined not only as non-normative or 'unnatural', but quite literally as 'unrepresentable'. By focusing on these various narrative strategies and locating my inquiry at the level of story, I hope to suggest that those late nineteenth-century representations which rendered male subjectivity as split may also have contributed to the development of those narrative possibilities through which eccentric sexualities continue to be affirmed, even today.

'DIPSYCHIA', OR REPRESENTING 'THE EVOLUTION OF A CHARACTER SOMEWHAT STRANGELY CONSTITUTED'

When, in 1889, at the age of fifty, the nineteenth-century littérateur and critic John Addington Symonds sat down to write an account of his life, he believed that he was engaged in a 'foolish' project that was destined to remain unpublished. Yet having previously translated the autobiographies of the sixteenth-century Italian sculptor Benvenuto Cellini and the eighteenth-century Venetian nobleman and playwright Carlo Gozzi, Symonds felt 'it [would be] a pity, after acquiring the art of the autobiographer through the translation of two masterpieces, not to employ my skill upon a rich mine of psychological curiosities as I am conscious of possessing'.[4] Describing his self-reflective undertaking in a letter to his friend Graham Dakyns, Symonds foregrounded what he believed to be both the utility and the anomalousness of his endeavour:

I have begun scribbling my own reminiscences. This is a foolish thing to do, because I do not think they will ever be fit to publish. I have nothing to relate except the evolution of a character somewhat strangely constituted in its moral and aesthetic qualities. The study of this evolution, written with the candor and precision I feel capable of using, would I am sure be of interest to psychologists and not without its utility. There does not exist anything like it in print; and I am certain that 999 men out of a thousand do not believe in the existence of a personality like mine. Still it would be hardly fair to my posterity if I were to yield up my vile soul to the psychopathological investigators.[5]

To those of us who read Symonds's *Memoirs* at the end of the twentieth century, a little more than 100 years after it was first written and less than fifty years since it was made accessible to 'bona fide scholars' by the London Library (to which it was ultimately bequeathed), his circumspection might seem quaintly anachronistic. Today the unmentionable aspects of Symonds's 'somewhat strangely constituted' personality, in other words his erotic and affective intimacies with other men, have long since passed from the pages of

obscure medico-forensic texts to become the subjects of one of the
fastest growing sectors in the mass-market publishing industry.[6]
Indeed, even in the few remaining years of own his life, as he began
to gather case histories for a collaborative project with Havelock Ellis
– which appeared in English under Ellis's name as *Sexual Inversion*
(1897) after Symonds's death in 1893[7] – Symonds came to realize
that his experiences were not quite as unique as he might have once
thought. Nevertheless, Symonds was right in his assertion about his
Memoirs that 'there does not exist anything in print like it', since until
the last decade of the nineteenth century, the possibility of conceiving
– let alone disseminating – a life story that included experiences of
sexual pleasure and emotional connection with members of ones own
sex certainly exceeded the representational limits which defined male
'character' simultaneously as a narratological and as a gendered
social category.

By taking up his pen to produce what (in the preface to the
manuscript) he tellingly calls 'this piece of sterile self-delineation',[8]
then, Symonds was quite consciously engaging in an activity of self
characterization that moved athwart the historical *and* narrative
constraints which had heretofore circumscribed the possibilities for
(his) autobiography. The preface itself, written in May 1889 and
ambiguously addressed to an unforeseen future reader, underscores
the problem embedded in Symonds's his-story:

Carlo Gozzi called his memoirs 'useless', and published them (as he
professes) from motives of 'humility'. Mine are sure to be more useless than
his; for *I* shall not publish them; and it is only too probable that they will
never be published – nobody's humility or pride or pecuniary interests
being likely to gain any benefit from the printing of what I have veraciously
written concerning myself.[9]

Here the discrepancy between the italicized '*I*' who 'shall not
publish' and the unmarked 'I' who has 'veraciously written
concerning myself' marks out the dichotomy which Symonds's
account of 'a life without action' will attempt both to reconcile and
to represent. Inscribing a disjunction between the realms of public
'value' (here aligned with utility, morality, pecuniary interest) and
private 'truth', the text mediates between these *loci classici* of the
Victorian middle class(es), but in a problematic and hence unprintable way. For, rather than private truth bearing witness to – or
at least shoring up – the ideological legitimacy of public value, in
Symonds's case the division within his awareness implicitly calls into

question the nominal self-consistency of (male) character *per se*. To understand the context for Symonds's interrogatory – if not profoundly ec-centric[10] – disposition we need to recall the extent to which the imbrication of gender and sexuality as natural manifestations of male character were central to the reproduction of middle-class (male) subjectivity. As the nineteenth-century articulations of class and gender increasingly sought to reproduce normative (middle-class) masculinity by figuring it as that which was antithetical to and necessarily exclusive of sexual desires for other men, they made this exclusionary criteria the (psychological) basis for possessing appropriate forms of male subjectivity. Hence, the 'veracity' which impelled Symonds's autobiographical project also necessitated his interrupting the prevailing (discursive) standards that constituted the unitary male subject as the quintessential political, economic, and sexual agent in order to encompass Symonds's 'propensities', 'sensibilities', and 'audacities'[11] within his 'own' story.

In a chapter notably entitled 'Containing material which none but students of psychology and ethics need peruse', Symonds introduces the terms within which he will 'describe the evolution of a somewhat abnormally constituted individual' (p. 54). As this phrase suggests, Symonds implicitly evokes the biologistic naturalization of ideological categories endemic to late nineteenth-century bourgeois culture in order to gesture beyond them towards '[his] inborn craving after persons of [his] own sex' (p. 63). Indeed, the invocation of evolution both here and in the letter to Graham Dakyns cited above ('the evolution of a character somewhat strangely constituted in its moral and aesthetic qualities') indicates how crucial this biological conceptualization of 'the natural' was for Symonds's personal/developmental account, precisely because it foregrounded the narrative dimension embedded in Darwin's increasingly popular 'scientific' explanation – as its catachrestic deployment in the phrase 'evolution of a character' illustrates.[12] When he moves beyond this largely rhetorical usage of scientific discourse, however, Symonds explicitly juxtaposes the biologically inscribed writings of the early sexologists ('in short I exhibited many of the symptoms which Krafft-Ebing and his school recognize as hereditary neuroticism predisposing its subject to sexual inversion' (p. 64)) to the theory of inborn gender inversion developed by Karl Heinrich Ulrichs, one of the earliest apologists for sexual relations between men,[13] and decides

that both are insufficient to represent the (narrative) complexity of
his own example. On the one hand he asserts that his self-evident
literary productivity and his success as an intellectual belie the
nosological characterization derived from Krafft-Ebing which would
cast him as 'a victim of conceptional neurotic malady'. On the other
hand, his affirmation that 'morally and intellectually, in character
and taste and habits, I am more masculine than many men I know
who adore women' (p. 65) contradicts Ulrichs's famous claim that
'urnings' possess a woman's soul trapped in a man's body (*anima
muliebris virile corpore inclusa*). Hence Symonds concludes:

[I]t appears to me the abnormality in question is not to be explained either
by Ulrich's theory, or by the presumptions of the psychological pathologists.
Its solution must be sought far deeper in the mystery of sex, and in the
variety of type exhibited by nature. For this reason, a detailed study of one
subject, such as I mean to attempt, may be valuable. (p. 65)

Positioning himself in relation to Krafft-Ebing's classifications and
Ulrichs's apologies, Symonds indicates that the particularities
evinced through his 'study' will serve as a necessary supplement to
the categorizations developed by those who would invoke the nature
embedded in biology either to pathologize or to normalize sexual and
emotional intimacies between men. Thus, it is the life history itself as
an evolutionary narrative representing 'the variety of type exhibited
by nature' that becomes the occasion for explicating the 'abnormality in question' insofar as this textualization provides the
possibility for a deeper inquiry beyond and behind the limitations of
biologically derived theories and presumptions.

In the chapter devoted to the 'First Period of Boyhood, 1851–4',
Symonds tries to elucidate the complexities of his own personality by
offering examples of early fantasies that retrospectively confirm the
trajectory of his desire for other men as he now 'knows' it (in other
words, at the point when he undertakes his autobiography). However
it is, of course, only through this kind of metaleptic manœuvre that
Symonds can produce the effect of making such self-knowledge his
'own' in the first place. For it is only by conferring an 'originary'
legitimacy on these anecdotes as part of a developmental narrative
that he confirms the integrity of the narrative's 'telling I' as an effect
of these anterior causes. Recalling, among other instances, a recurrent
dream about 'the beautiful face of a young man, with large blue eyes
and waving yellow hair which emitted a halo of misty light', a

waking obsession with a photograph of the Praxitelean Cupid, 'the impressions made by Shakespeare's Adonis and Homeric Hermes', and a rather explicit sexual wish that 'some honest youth or comrade, a sailor or groom or a labourer ... would have introduced me to the masculine existence I craved in a dim shrinking way' (pp. 77–8),[14] he asserts:

The love of a robust and manly lad, even if it had not been wholly pure, must have been beneficial to a boy like me. As it was, I lived into emotion through the brooding imagination; and nothing is more dangerous and unhealthy than this. (p. 78)

Appealing implicitly to the prevailing bourgeois ideology which readily and unambiguously equated social propriety – of both the class and gendered varieties – with somatic and economic wellbeing, Symonds here inverts this cultural logic on his own behalf. Whereas contemporary medical and moral literature would have universally condemned the 'love' Symonds desired, whether 'wholly pure' or not, as a pernicious embodiment of all that threatened 'healthy' middle-class masculinity, Symonds locates the 'lived' danger in the imbrication of 'emotion' and 'imagination' where the latter becomes the displaced site of the former. Through this chiasmus, a space of self-contradiction was produced 'in' *and as* Symonds's 'character' so that he found himself simultaneously conforming with and yet deviating from the class and gender proprieties which ideologically and materially circumscribed his behaviour – if not his subsequent story:

The result of my habitual reserve was that I now dissembled my deepest feelings, and only revealed those sentiments which I knew would pass muster. Without meaning to do so, I came to act a part, and no one knew what was going on inside me ... I allowed an outer self of commonplace cheerfulness and easy-going pliability to settle like crust upon *my inner and real character* ... Congenital qualities and external circumstance acted together to determine *a mental duality* – or shall I call it duplicity – of which I became aware when it had taken hold upon my nature. (pp. 81–82; emphases added)

Structurally, the possibility of Symonds's rendering his life *as a story* necessitates that he constitute his character as a divided one, positing the notion of mental duality in order to explain a mediation between 'inner' and 'outer', 'real' and 'artificial', that not only makes sense to the 'telling I' but quite literally produces it. In order to constitute a subject position from which the (inner) truth he ascribes to his 'deepest feelings' can be made to coincide both spatially and temporally with the (outer) values that not only abhorred them but in fact mandated their criminalization,[15] Symonds must rend the consistency of subjectivity as it has been socially constituted. Hence, somewhat later in *Memoirs*, Symonds reiterates the necessity for this conceptual bifurcation even more explicitly:

> The distinction in my character between an inner and real self and an outer and artificial self, to which I have already alluded, emphasized itself during this period [his last years at Harrow]. So separate were the two selves, so deep was my dipsychia, that my most intimate friends there ... have each and all emphatically told me they thought I passed through school without being affected by, almost without being aware of, its peculiar vices. And yet those vices furnished a perpetual subject of contemplation and casuistical reflection to my inner life. (pp. 95–96)

Coining the word 'dipsychia' to describe the subjective experience induced by the all male world of the public school – an institution which was specifically designed as a factory for producing consistent (bourgeois) male character[16] – Symonds indicates that it was the discrepancy between his real, inner obsession with the schoolboys' 'peculiar vices' and his outer, artificial, and *yet thoroughly 'proper'* denial of them that gave rise to the painful 'distinction in [his] character'.[17] What is at stake in Symonds's unprintable *Memoirs* is how to represent a 'man of no mean talents, of no abnormal depravity, whose life has been perplexed from first to last by passion – natural, instinctive, healthy in his own particular case – but morbid and abominable from the point of view of the society in which he lives – persistent passion for the male sex' (p. 182). The effective solution Symonds offers to the representational crisis engendered by his passionate dilemma seems to be: *only as a double life.*

By the end of the 1880s, John Addington Symonds had already distinguished himself as a man of letters who was more than successful enough to support himself, his wife and his children through his profession. Hence, when he took up his *Memoirs* he was thoroughly aware as both a scholar and a professional author that his text transgressed the conventional boundaries of representability. Nevertheless, he took time away from writing other works which could have been published and remunerated, as he himself notes, in order to complete the manuscript, and then directed those responsible for his estate to ensure its existence after his demise. What was of central concern to him in making these decisions was to provide a veracious account of sexual desires for and sexual acts with members of his own sex – desires and acts which had heretofore been unarticulable as part of a life history.

From our vantage point, however, it appears that Symonds was rather circumspect about the very issues which would seem to make his autobiography historically remarkable. There is, in fact, little if any of what we would today consider 'explicit' discussion or description of 'sexuality', as we can find it almost any weekday afternoon on Oprah Winfrey or Phil Donahue. Hence, what now appears most salient about Symonds's text is not so much its detailed depiction of 'homosexual' (or even 'homotextual') acts as the representational strategies it utilizes in order to address them at all. In this regard, it is Symonds's notion of dipsychia that seems most critical, since it is with this neologism and the concept it seeks to specify that he foregrounds the necessity for splitting open the dominant characterization of (bourgeois male) subjectivity in order to engender a narrative affirmation of sexual and emotional intimacies between members of the same sex. Indeed, we could perhaps anachronistically nominate Symonds's *Memoirs* as the first 'coming out story', precisely because it inscribes what in the rhetorics of Lacan and Derrida we might call a 'dehiscence' of the (male) subject which is metaleptically sutured by a narrative that retro-spectively attributes meaning and value to what had earlier appeared only as unrepresentable.[18] Moreover, it simultaneously engenders the narrator's 'subjectivity' – or the text's 'telling I' – as an effect of this narrative practice and thereby creates the possibility for representing this divided 'masculinity' to others, even if only in the distant future.

THE CASE OF THE IMAGINARY VULVA

Just about the same time that Symonds was working on his unpublishable *Memoirs*, another less famous late Victorian was at work writing his own tale of two selves. The autobiography of this anonymous Hungarian physician appears as Case 99 in the first English edition of Krafft-Ebing's *Psychopathia Sexualis* under the heading 'Acquired Homosexuality': 'Degree III: Stage of Tran-sition to *Metamorphosis Sexualis Paranoia*'.[19] There it provides a painful yet compelling account of an 'imaginary' splitting within a bourgeois male subject – a splitting that effects the complete transvaluation, if not transformation, of the subject's 'own' body: 'When a respectable man who enjoys an unusual degree of public confidence, and possesses authority, must go about with his vulva – imaginary though it be … what must all this be?'[20] Presenting the self-description of a middle-aged man, who was married, had fathered five children, had been a decorated military officer, was a well-established physician, and 'fe[lt] like a woman in a man's form', (p. 209) the poignant text develops a set of discursive strategies through which it seeks to represent '*in' the author's own person* an experience of sexual dissonance which had hitherto been both unimaginable and unrepresentable. While today the designation 'transsexual' seeks to convey an experience of gender dysphoria which Case 99's unnamed author can only gesture towards, situating this contemporary notion of sexual 'ambiguity' in proximity to (at least the possibility for) psychological counselling, support groups, newsletters, hormone treatments, speciality clothing stores and gender reassignment surgery, neither this designation nor any of these options were even remotely available to this late nineteenth-century man.[21] Indeed, so overwhelming is the pathos of his isolated condition – which even Krafft-Ebing, the sexual typologer *par excellence*, has to admit is, in his considered opinion, 'unique' – that it is truly remarkable he was able to record 'his' story at all. Yet having read an earlier edition of *Psychopathia Sexualis*, the case's unnamed author finds that the presence of the numerous other 'pathological' narratives in Krafft-Ebing's 'Medico-Legal Study', coupled with the absence of any depiction comparable to his experience of what he terms 'extinguished' masculinity, inspires him to transcribe his own.

Sir: I must next beg your indulgence for troubling you with my communication. I lost all control, and thought of myself only as a monster, before which I myself shuddered. Then your work gave me courage again; and I determined to go to the bottom of the matter, and examine my past life, let the results be what they might. It seemed a duty of gratitude to you to tell you the result of my recollection and observation, since I had not seen any description by you of an analogous case; and, finally, I thought it might perhaps interest you to learn, from the pen of a physician, how such a worthless human, or masculine, being thinks and feels under the weight of the imperative idea of being a woman. (p. 215)

This passage from the cover letter addressed to Krafft-Ebing, which the writer appends to his autobiographical study and which Krafft-Ebing in turn appends to his representation of the case, illuminates the effects reproduced by the anonymous doctor's ability to narrativize – or, at least, to textualize – his dubiously gendered 'self'. In it, the author suggests that having had no frame of reference within which he could make sense of the 'imperative idea of being a woman', he considered himself a 'monster' in his own mind, a characterization he apposes to the loss of that most 'masculine' of attributes, the 'lo[ss] of self control'. However, after reading an earlier edition of *Psychopathia Sexualis*, he discovers both a discourse (medico-forensic pathology) and a genre (the sexual case-study) that enable him to recast his self-reflection such that he comes to imagine himself, at least insofar as his story constitutes a 'case', as occupying a gap within Krafft-Ebing's text. Not surprisingly, then, the autobiography conforms quite strictly to the format that Krafft-Ebing has developed throughout his compendious book. Moreover, it seems crucial that the author's 'examination' – in both the self-reflexive and medical senses – is specifically situated as being inscribed 'from the pen of the physician'. For it is his identification with the mental (con)text, and its interpellating analytic gaze, that provides the author with the critical vantage point from which he can evaluate and thereby articulate the significance (if not the meaning) of his own experience. The act of textualization, then, is also a practice of transvaluation whereby the delineated self-representation recoups the author's transgressive ('monstrous') gender ideation on the side of the masculine norm: 'After reading your work [and writing an addendum to it], I hope that, if I fulfill my duties as physician, citizen, father, and husband, I may still count myself among human beings who do not deserve merely to be despised.' (p. 215) Thus, by retrospectively considering his 'past life' and then inscribing his 'recollection[s] and observation[s]' in the shape of a case that serves to supplement the text from which it formally derives, the unnamed 'physician, citizen, father and husband' narratively induces the effects of a gender(ed) coherence that simultaneously acknowledges and seeks to remediate the profound dehiscence in 'his' (male) subjectivity from which the germ of his 'female' self grows.

Like Symonds's narrative, Case 99 offers a historical perspective on the development of the text's 'telling I' that inscribes its putative 'identity' in or as the source of the account which purports to describe its unfolding. Yet the work of discursive production here is much more pronounced than in the other text, since the author of this text also seeks to provide a credible portrayal of the trajectory which leads across the sexual divide to 'his' (fantasmatic) incarnation as a 'woman'. In order to perform this 'unnatural' explanatory labour, the author not surprisingly begins by foregrounding the material consequences of his imaginary activities: 'With a very active imagination – my enemy throughout life – my talents developed rapidly.' (p. 203) This sentence, the case's fourth, introduces a paragraph in which the author explains that despite his attempts to play the boy, 'I must have already been on the road to become just like a girl.' (p. 203) Using a metaphor of spatial displacement to gloss the temporal distance between his birth as a male child and his subsequent 'female' incarnation, this formulation embeds the origin of the narrator's story of gender transformation in the rhetorical guise of a simile, 'to become just *like* a girl', through which he constitutes an 'imaginary' semblance that will subsequently signify an earlier stage in 'his' development. What the ensuing narrative then seeks to stabilize, through its articulation of precisely such a teleological movement, is the slippage between 'becom[ing] *like* a girl' or 'feeling *like* a girl', and 'fe[eling] that I *was* a woman in a man's form'. (p. 207) In order to mark this shift from cross-sex similarity to equivalence, and eventually even 'identity', the author has recourse to that most famous of nineteenth-century threats to adolescent masculinity:

My friends loved me dearly; I hated only one, who seduced me into onanism. Shame on those days, which injured me for life! I practised it quite frequently, but *in it seemed to my self like a double man*. I cannot describe the feeling; I think it was masculine, but mixed with feminine elements. I could not approach girls; I feared them, but they were not strange to me. They impressed me as being more like myself; I envied them. I would have denied myself all pleasures if, after my classes, at home I could have been a girl and thus gone out. Crinoline and a smooth-fitting glove were my ideals. With every lady's gown I saw I fancied how I should feel in it – i.e., as a lady. I had no inclination towards men. (p. 205; my emphasis)

By constituting the author's autoerotic relation to himself as the narrative site of self-transformation, the case foregrounds the overdetermined dynamic between somatic and imaginary processes. Retrospectively, the author considers his 'frequent' masturbatory 'practice' as the source of an irremediable 'injury' which produces such a wound to his sense of self that it renders impossible a unitary male identification. Since his autoerotic relation to his body – and especially to that 'part' which (psychoanalytically) purports to cover the (w)hole[22] – stands out as the decisive moment in this story, as the moment in which for the first time the narrator 'seemed to myself like a double man', it foregrounds the disparate dimensions of self (representation) that must be made to cohere in order to reproduce 'masculinity' as a stable subject position. Here the text's very first use of the signifier 'man' is modified by the qualifier 'double', not to evoke a 'hyper' or 'redoubled' masculinity, but on the contrary to suggest that in its 'doubling' (unitary) masculinity is, in fact, lessened if not negated. While the author professes that the 'feeling' of this ambiguous, 'double' masculinity exceeds his ability to represent it, he gestures towards it by indicating that it mediates between what would or should otherwise appear as a mutually exclusive gender binary, masculine/feminine ('masculine, but mixed with feminine elements'). Having offered this boundary-crossing interpretation, the text then immediately moves to describe the author's relations with/to 'girls', apparently using these interactions with the 'opposite sex' as another index to further clarify the otherwise indescribable experience of male 'doubleness'. Although he claims to have isolated himself from 'girls' whom he feared, the writer nevertheless professes to have experienced them as 'not strange' since he perceived them as 'being more like myself'. The rhetorical force of the negation 'not strange' thus interrupts the exclusivity of the male/female binary that would 'normally' make each side of the opposition 'strange' to the 'other' – or, given that this was written within a sex/gender system that reproduced male privilege, that would make women 'strange' and 'other' to men. Yet it is important to note that the 'likeness' asserted by the text is a 'likeness' which inheres in the habits that signify not just 'generic' femaleness but the femaleness of a particular class and culture ('crinoline and a smoothly-fitting glove were my ideals'). Using women's clothing – and as we shall see, women's anatomy – as a metonym for socially inscribed forms of femininity, the writer collapses the historically determined dimensions of gendered representation with 'sex' in order to reproduce for himself a position within the very binary that his narrative seemingly subverts. Hence, his disavowal of any erotic attraction towards other men, which might otherwise seem a *non sequitur*, follows from a cultural logic that necessarily situates all forms of (male) eroticism in relation to this sexual opposition – a logic which is more than a little reproduced by the (con)text in which this case appears, namely the section on 'Acquired Homosexuality' in *Psychopathia Sexualis*.

As the writer continues to examine his life for further evidence that would explain his anomalousness, he describes his first sexual experiences ('the girl had to treat me as a girl'), his continuing desires to appear in female attire, his suicide attempts ('on account of unhappy circumstances, I twice attempted suicide'), his success as a military officer ('decorations were not wanting, but I was indifferent to them'), his marriage ('I married an energetic, amiable lady, of a family in which female government was rampant'), the births of his five children, and his subsequent submission to various painful neurasthenic ailments. Throughout all this, he asserts his ongoing, if increasingly problematic, identifications as a man:

I was wanting in only one respect: I could not understand my own condition. I knew I had feminine inclinations, but believed I was a man. (p. 206)

Still, I always thought I was a man with obscure masculine feeling; and whenever I associated with ladies, I was still soon treated as an inexperienced lady. (p. 206)

[F]or I still believed that I was a depressed man, who would come to himself, and find himself out by marriage. (p. 207)

However, three years prior to the writing of his case, the writer succumbed to his intensifying (perhaps hysterical?) physical disabilities, 'which impressed [him] as being female or effeminate', breaking down entirely. The recollected portrayal of this crisis of (male) subjectivity is so incredible that it requires quoting here at length:

But before this terrible attack of gout occurred, in despair, to lessen the pain of gout, I had taken hot baths, as near the temperature of the body as possible. On one of these occasions it happened that I suddenly changed, and seemed to be near death. I sprang with all my remaining strength out of the bath: *I had felt exactly like a woman with libido.* Too, at the time when the extract of Indian hemp came into vogue, and was highly prized, in a state of fear of a threatened attack of gout (feeling perfectly indifferent about life), I took three or four times the usual dose of it, and almost died with haschisch poisoning. *Convulsive laughter, a feeling of unheard of strength and swiftness, a peculiar feeling in the brain and eyes, millions of sparks streaming from the brain through the skin – all these feelings occurred. But I could not force myself to speak. All at once I saw myself a woman from my toes to my breast;* I felt, as before while in the bath, that the genitals had shrunken, the pelvis broadened, the breasts swollen out; *a feeling of unspeakable delight came over me.* I closed my eyes, so that at least I did not see the face changed. My physician looked as if he had a gigantic potato instead of a head; my wife had the full moon on her nates. And yet I was strong enough to briefly record my will in my note-book when both left the room for a short time.

But who could describe my fright, when, on the next morning, *I awoke and found myself feeling as if completely changed into a woman; and when, on standing and walking, I felt vulva and mammae*! When at last I raised myself out of bed, I felt that a complete transformation had taken place in me... During the last sickness I had many visual and auditory hallucinations – spoke with the dead, etc.; saw and heard familiar spirits; *felt like a double person*; but, while lying ill, I did not notice that *the man in me had been extinguished*. The change in my disposition was a piece of good fortune which came over me like lightening, and which, had it come with me feeling as I formerly did, would have killed me; but now I gave myself up to it, and no longer recognized myself. (pp. 207–8; emphases added)

While it would be possible to read this narrative of self-transformation either as a display of an underlying psychogenic disorder, as Freud does in his famous interpretation of Schreber's *Memoirs of My Nervous Illness*, or perhaps as a hallucinogenically induced conversion experience, I would like to focus instead on the narrative strategies the text employs in order to give (temporal) shape to the cognitive and somatic processes that induce the effects of 'femaleness' for the unnamed (male) subject. Initially, the passage foregrounds the narrator's body as the site of an intense affective investment, which the previous paragraph had already glossed as connoting a cross-gender identification, even possibly a form of ('hysterical'?) pregnancy: 'For about three years I had a feeling as if the prostate were enlarged – a bearing-down feeling, as if giving birth to something; and, also, pain in the hips, constant pain in the back, and the like.' (p. 207) Moving from this associative, gendered nexus, the writer indicates that he underwent hydrotherapy sessions in order to ameliorate his physical distress and during one of these sessions 'it happened that I suddenly changed, and seemed to be near death'. Locating this critical moment of transition during an experience of immersion, which also becomes a moment 'near death', the story of transformation conforms structurally to the paradigm of Christian baptism (transubstantiation?) in which the secular subject 'dies' in order to be reborn in 'the body of Christ' thereby recognizing that these transformations are at once profoundly material and meta-physical. Indeed, in order to narrativize the kind of bodily meta-morphoses which this text seeks to inscribe, it is necessary that it put into abeyance the ontological and epistemological assumptions that ground post-Enlightenment concepts of personhood – and concomitantly of gendered sex – in the presumption of somatic stability.

Not surprisingly, then, in representing his second and ultimate experience of gender transformation, an experience that radically reorganizes the (gendered) qualities he attributes to both his feelings and his anatomy, the author first describes the physiological effects induced by an overdose of hashish as interrupting his 'proper' (proprietary) identification with and as 'his' body: 'Convulsive laughter, a feeling of unheard of strength and swiftness, a peculiar feeling in brain and eyes, millions of sparks streaming from the brain through the skin – all these occurred.' Abjuring the genitive case to modify bodily parts and attributes, the text depersonalizes physical experience, constituting it instead as a constellation of processes, intensities, affects and images. Moreover, as the syntax of the description suggests, the usual attribution of agency to the linguistic subject is disrupted here, such that the narrator's body becomes simply the locus of inscription within which 'all these feelings occurred'. Concomitantly, 'he' surrenders his linguistic ability altogether: 'But I could not force myself to speak.' The 'I' who loses the capacity to 'force' speech here is the subject unmoored from the linguistic determinants of 'gender' and 'person' that appear to naturalize his 'identity' as a male subject. Hence, this inability to speak, which is significantly not a regression to the infant's 'without speech', but rather the performative failure of articulation, constitutes the narrative *segue* into the 'male' subject's 'female' self-reflection: 'All at once I saw myself a woman from my toes to my breast; I felt, as before while in the bath, that the genitals had shrunken, the pelvis broadened, the breasts swollen out; a feeling of unspeakable delight came over me.' As if inventorying his new properties, the writer surveys and reterritorializes 'his' body parts, seeing in them the anatomical features which he as a doctor 'knows' to belong to the mappings of female anatomy. This practice, which brings him 'unspeakable delight', and which (excepting the face) he elaborates further to include 'vulva and mammae', provides the paradigm for his ongoing 'female' self-representation. By mobilizing a highly developed, highly idealized, medical knowledge of women's bodies, the writer effects a part by part substitution in order to refashion the gendered signifieds he ascribes to 'his' somatic signifiers, as the following passage illustrates:

I feel like a woman in a man's form; and even though I often am sensible of the man's form, yet it is always in a feminine sense. Thus, for example, I feel the penis as a clitoris; the urethra as urethra and vaginal orifice, which always feels a little wet, even when it is actually dry; the scrotum as labia majora; in short, I always feel the vulva. And all that means one alone can know who feels or has felt so. But the skin all over my body feels feminine; it receives all impressions, whether of touch, of warmth, or whether unfriendly, as feminine, and I have the sensations of a woman. (p. 209)

Here, the writer's 'female' self-representation derives from a one-to-one mapping between 'analogous' elements of male and female anatomy. While recognizing that no morphological change has occurred, the anonymous doctor implicitly asserts that the 'visible' facts do not sufficiently account for what (s)he 'feels'. Moreover, (s)he asserts that these 'feelings' are only 'knowable' experientially, positing a counter-empiricism that supersedes a purely medical gaze and constitutes authority on the side of one 'who feels or has felt so'. In affirming his sense of 'fe[eling] like a double person', the writer necessarily moves athwart the representational conventions which seek to situate the 'singularities' of gender and person in an 'identical' grammatical, narrative, somatic, spatial, temporal, and historical locus, thereby fictioning a 'different' configuration of (male) subjectivity that marks out the 'double man'.

Unlike Robert Louis Stevenson's novel, *The Strange Case of Dr Jekyll and Mr Hyde*, however, where the eponymous character's 'somatic' transformation can 'occur' in the folds of the plot,[23] the success of this narrative endeavour is necessarily more limited, though not so limited as to prevent its author from 'go[ing] about with his vulva – imaginary though it be'. Given both the relative anatomical immutability of his male form and the historical intransigence of 'his' language, the narrating subject is forced to recognize that he embodies a painful contradiction which he cannot reconcile 'in' himself. Whereas his initial sense of being a double person had been received as 'a piece of good fortune' precisely because it marked the moment in which 'he' no longer coincided with his earlier representations of 'himself' ('I gave my self up to it, and no longer recognized myself'), his subsequent need to re-cognize his 'self' reinscribes 'him' within the culture's dominant sex/gender codes. Thus although he is able to conceive of his sexual relations with his wife as 'lesbian' ('Contact with a woman seems homogeneous to me; coitus with my wife seems possible to me because she is somewhat masculine, and has a firm skin; and yet it is more an *amor lesbicus'* (p. 213)), his understanding that he might also desire sexual relations with a man leads him to fantasize about self-mutilation:

Since the anus feels feminine, it would not be hard to become a passive pederast; only positive religious command prevents it, as all other deterrent ideas would be overcome. Since such conditions are repugnant, as they would be to any one, I have the desire to be sexless, or to make myself sexless. If I had been single, I should long ago have taken leave of testes, scrotum, and penis. (pp. 209–210)

This one reference to what could be construed as desire for someone of the 'same' sex foregrounds the limit up against which the writer's autobiographical narrative butts. So long as (s)he is able to circumscribe his/her 'imaginary' identification as a woman within the (con)text of reproductive, monogamous, marital intercourse, the possibilities engendered by this positioning can be experienced as 'blissful', 'powerful', or 'delight[ful]'. However, as soon as these desires lead in the direction of acts that are culturally and religiously inscribed as 'repugnant', they interrupt the author's ability to sustain his affirmation of female subjectivity and foreground its incompatibility with the anatomical signifiers of sex. Hence an earlier declaration that 'the man in me had been extinguished' now takes on the active force of a wish to expunge the somatic metonyms of (male) 'sex' – testes, scrotum and penis – in order to induce, or indeed, produce a null condition: 'to make myself sexless'.

Given such a poignant articulation of the anonymous doctor's desire to take leave of sex, it is probably a bit banal at this point to note that Case 99 demonstrates the intense degree of linguistic, grammatical, and narrative work that must be brought to bear in order to produce a story that can articulate the experience of being – or *feeling* – a 'double man'. It is perhaps even a bit trite to suggest that if we bracket psychopathological evaluations and attend to this discursive labour itself, we can begin to discern how the reproduction of our 'normal' (binary) gender categories is predicated on the suppression of this (historical) activity. However, what the self-reflexive 'evaluation' of the unnamed doctor (who 'must go about with his vulva – imaginary though it may be') can teach us is the extent to which, in the last decades of the nineteenth century, the desire to render such an ambiguously gendered self-representation *as a story* necessitated rending the singular-ness of 'person' which 'is' its 'subject'. Now it may be the case that ontologically speaking the 'subject' was split even prior to engaging in this narrative endeavour – that the psychopathology which engendered his 'female' identifications were symptoms of subtending endopsychic conflicts, even of an 'irreducible lack of being', that could be retrospectively 'explained' by interpretation, including psychoanalytic. Nevertheless, it seems helpful to consider that the act of narration itself was needed in order to produce the transvaluation which shifted the writer's sense of 'monstrousness' and 'worthlessness' so that he was capable of articulating the painfulness of 'his' experience. Indeed, it may even suggest that our contemporary notions of split subjectivity presuppose a narrative situation which can reproduce the spatial and temporal, not to mention 'somatic', coherence of this 'imaginary' mapping of the self. For, to the extent that this 'respectable' late Victorian 'man', who 'enjoy[ed] an unusual degree of public confidence and possesse[d] authority', transposes the grid of meaning ascribed to 'his' bodily coordinates, a grid which 'naturally' ought to have located his 'identity' securely on the terrain of bourgeois masculinity, he demonstrates the possibilities for fictioning new historical configurations for 'male' self-representation: possibilities that now appear so 'normal' that we have perhaps begun to take them too much for granted.

QUIT AIMING AT MY OBJECT

In the four brief paragraphs that introduce the first of his *Three Essays on the Theory of Sexuality*, Sigmund Freud deftly prises apart the 'biological' notion of 'sexual instinct' which had heretofore circumscribed both the discourses on human sexuality and the mappings of human anatomy.[24] Succinctly describing the 'popular' interpretation of sexual instinct as 'the manifestations of an irresistible attraction exercised by one sex upon the other; [whose] aim is presumed to be sexual union, or at all events actions leading in that direction', Freud archly comments: 'We have every reason to believe, however, that these views give a very false picture of the true situation.' (p. 1) It is in order to parse out the 'false' from the 'true', then, that Freud introduces his famous distinction between 'sexual object' and 'sexual aim', thereby distinguishing between 'the person from whom the sexual attraction proceeds' and 'the act towards which the instinct tends'. With this seemingly simple distinction, the founding father of psychoanalysis effectively rends the conceptual fabric that had enmeshed the human body in the circuits of 'reproductive' desire throughout most of the nineteenth century – a desire whose effects were so powerful that the anonymous author of Krafft-Ebing's Case 99 even 'felt' them with his imaginary vulva. Moreover, Freud lays out his own 'scientific' project by way of making this distinction, since it allows him to imagine alternative mappings both of 'deviations' with respect to 'object' and 'aim' and of 'the relation between these deviations and what is assumed to be normal'. In other words, by resolving the concept of 'sexual instinct' into the components 'sexual object' and 'sexual aim', Freud summarily cleaves the 'natural' from the 'normal' and hence problematizes the very slippage that reproduced the previous century's dominant gender ideologies.

It seems hardly coincidental, then, that by way of demonstrating this theoretical premise, the first example Freud uses in order to debunk 'the popular view of the sexual instinct... beautifully reflected in the poetic fable which tells how the original human beings were cut up into two halves – man and woman – and how these are always striving to unite again in love' (p. 2) is the example of sexual desire between men. Taking up 'inversion' as the initial and most significant example of 'deviations in respect of the sexual object', Freud seeks to establish a critical vantage that will enable him to interrupt the 'opposition' of sex which grounds the normative nineteenth-century understandings of gender. However, rather than beginning to articulate the terms of his own interpretation directly, the first psychoanalyst immediately regresses into the very binary logic that he would otherwise abjure. Thus, of what he calls 'absolute inverts', Freud states:

In that case their sexual objects are exclusively of their own sex. Persons of the opposite sex are never objects of their sexual desire, but leave them cold, or even arouse sexual aversion in them. As a consequence of this aversion, they are incapable, if they are men, of carrying out the sexual act, or else they derive no enjoyment from it. (p. 2)

Here Freud adapts the sexological notion of 'homosexuality', derived from the works of Krafft-Ebing among others, which views it as displacing/replacing the 'sexual instinct' that should direct 'desire' across the 'opposition' between male and female.[25] Moreover, as the syntax of the last sentence quoted suggests, the linkage between 'aversion' and 'incapacity' not only interrupts function with respect to 'the sexual act' – the indefinite article qualifying this phrase to mean heterosexual intercourse exclusively – but also disrupts the assignments of gender. For while the clause 'if they are men' nominally refers to the indices of anatomical sex, it also works in this context to call into question the unproblematized correspondence between what we now distinguish as sex and gender. Freud however is not concerned to pursue this distinction; instead he proceeds to explicate the prevailing explanations of and for sexual relations between men.[26] The essay goes on to recapitulate theories that ascribe 'the nature of inversion' to 'degeneracy' or 'innate character' only to reject them both as inadequate explanations for the data available. Hence, Freud's consideration of inversion can be seen not only (or even primarily) as an attempt to explore the specificity of sexual desires between and among men, but also as a challenge to the sexological discourse to which he is indebted for his understanding of it.[27] It is only when he subsequently turns to adumbrate the theory of 'bisexuality' – a theory that seemingly finesses the biological/developmental divide – that Freud finds something more congenial to his model.

Freud's introduction of bisexuality into his discussion of male homosexuality is itself not unproblematic, since it simultaneously relies on the negation of what he takes to be its conceptual sibling 'hermaphroditism'. Although he (thinks he) finally casts aside the dualism inherent in the physiological theories of hermaphroditism as too crude for his purposes, scorning the analogy between 'the hypothetical psychical hermaphroditism [Krafft-Ebing (pp. 230–255)] and the established anatomical one', nevertheless Freud is clearly indebted to the conceptual bifurcation that underlies this isomorphism for his understanding of 'bisexuality'. Whilst foreclosing the possibility of positing an isomorphism between 'physical' and 'psychical' hermaphroditism and hence bisexuality, at the same time he nonetheless relies on this very possibility in order to explicate his theory of male homosexuality. He argues that the theory of 'psychical hermaphroditism' or 'bisexuality' – terms he uses interchangeably with little distinction – might be true if it could be shown that 'the inversion of the sexual object were at least accompanied by a parallel change-over of the subject's other mental qualities, instincts and character traits into those marking the opposite sex. But it is only in inverted women that character-inversion of this kind can be looked for with any regularity. In men the most complete mental masculinity can be combined with inversion.' (p. 8) This statement sits uneasily alongside Freud's claim apropos of anatomical difference a page earlier that 'In every male or female individual, traces are found of the apparatus of the opposite sex.' (p. 7) That he then proceeds unselfconsciously to contradict the very distinctions he has drawn with respect to anatomical difference when he comes to consider 'mental qualities, instincts and character traits' illustrates the relative intransigence of gender as compared to the seemingly more immutable corporeality of (male) sex. Of course, it is not exactly surprising that with the embedded example of 'inverted women', for whom *as women* the dominant sexual ideology reproduces a stronger correspondence between sex and gender, the paradigm should be inverted. Thus, even as Freud seeks to destabilize one set of gendered oppositions *for men* he invokes their sexed corollary *for women* in order to stabilize his analysis. It is a striking feature of Freud's essay that the 'female invert' is largely obscured throughout his discussion. Instead, he highlights what he perceives as the problems with earlier sexological discussions of male inversion produced by Ulrichs and Krafft-Ebing which (like Symonds) he lumps together as roughly asserting that 'male inverts [possess] a feminine brain in a masculine body' to which he summarily responds: 'But we are ignorant of what characterizes a feminine brain.'[28] With this disavowal of knowledge, Freud believes he has cast aside the remaining vestiges of anatomical determinism inherent in the elision of hermaphroditism with bisexuality, so that he now can take up the latter for his own purposes: 'Nevertheless, two things emerge from these discussions. In the first place, a bisexual disposition is somehow concerned in inversion, though we do not know in what that disposition consists, beyond anatomical structure. And secondly, we have to deal with disturbances that affect the sexual instinct in the course of its development.' (pp. 9–10) From these two premises Freud elaborates his famous – albeit brief – consideration of the 'sexual object of inverts'.

Having meticulously worked his way through earlier theories of inversion in order to distance himself from them, Freud somewhat surprisingly returns to them yet again, apparently in order to make this distinction absolutely clear:

The theory of psychical hermaphroditism presupposes that the sexual object of an invert is the opposite of that of a normal person. An inverted man, it holds, is like a woman in being subject to the charm that proceeds from masculine attributes both physical and mental: he feels he is a woman in search of a man. But however well this applies to quite a number of inverts, it is, nevertheless, far from revealing a universal characteristic of inversion. There can be no doubt that a large proportion of male inverts retain the mental quality of masculinity, that they possess relatively few of the secondary characters of the opposite sex and what they look for in their sexual object are in fact feminine mental traits. (p. 10)

This passage illustrates the series of contradictions through which the logic of sexual normality must pass in order to represent the case of the inverted 'normal' (masculine) male. If inversion is not just a reversion to the 'opposite' sexual position (where again the un-questioned 'opposition' between male and female guarantees that this does not become an infinite regress), then the male invert who seeks 'feminine mental traits' in another man appropriately conforms to the gendered pairing masculine/feminine even while disregarding the sexed pairing male/female. In other words, by parsing out gendered 'mental traits' from sexed physical attributes in order to explain what he takes to be the exemplary case of inversion – a case he glosses by reference to 'Greece, where the most masculine men were numbered among the inverts' (p. 10) – Freud uses his discussion to demonstrate that there is no natural or even normal coincidence between the two. The masculine male invert who desires a man with feminine mental traits, then, deconstructs for Freud the assumption that there is a necessary identity within male subjectivity that aligns anatomy, disposition, and desire. Thus Freud concludes in a sentence added in 1915: 'the sexual object [of the masculine male invert] is a kind of reflection of the subject's own bisexual nature.' (p. 10)

By now it probably comes as no surprise that Freud's imputation of a 'bisexual nature' to the masculine male invert echoes the 'doubleness' that I have located in a number of representations of late nineteenth-century masculinity. Indeed, the structural similarity between these accounts illustrates the extent to which these depictions of non-normative forms of masculinity necessarily challenged the dominant sex/gender ideologies which portrayed male 'character' as unitary and self-consistent and therefore fomented the reconceptu-alization of male subjectivity in these cases as inherently – or at least locally – divided or split. Yet Freud's contribution was precisely to have moved beyond this localization, for in elucidating the con-tradictory dynamic that subtends the desire of otherwise 'masculine' men for other men, Freud detects a psychic organization that he generalizes as being the same as the structure of normality itself. Hence in the famous footnote which Freud revised many times through the various editions of the *Essays* and that is quoted in almost every psychoanalytic discussion of male homosexuality, he concludes:

Psycho-analytic research is most decidedly opposed to any attempt at separating off homosexuals from the rest of mankind as a group of a special character. By studying sexual excitations other than those manifestly displayed, it has found that all human beings are capable of making a homosexual object-choice and have in fact made one in the unconscious. Indeed, libidinal attachments to persons of the same sex play no less a part as factors in normal mental life, and a greater part as a motive force for illness, than do similar attachments to the opposite sex.

On the contrary, psycho-analysis considers that a choice of an object independently of its sex – freedom to range equally over male and female objects – as it is found in childhood, in primitive states of society and early periods of history, is the original basis from which as a result of restriction in one direction or the other, both the normal and the inverted types develop. Thus from the point of view of psycho-analysis the exclusive sexual interest felt by men for women is also a problem that needs elucidating and is not a self evident fact based upon an attraction that is ultimately of a chemical nature. (pp. 11–12)

With this statement, Freud uses the structural contradictions that he recognizes as embedded in the sexological accounts of male homosexuality in order to problematize the entire field of sexual relations. Rather than taking the example of male inverts as anomalous, he defines it as paradigmatic, thereby establishing the doubleness that he finds 'reflected' in their sexual object choices as a constituent bifurcation of all subjects who 'are capable of making a homosexual object-choice and have in fact made one in their unconscious'. In other words, Freud uses the splitting between 'mental traits' and anatomical structure that he perceives so self-evidently in 'masculine' male inverts as a structural analogue for the condition of all (sexual) subjects for whom the notion of 'sexual instinct' obscures the constructedness of their pleasures and desires:

Experience of the cases that are considered abnormal has shown us that in them the sexual instinct and the sexual object are merely soldered together – a fact which we have been in danger of overlooking in consequence of the uniformity of the normal picture, where the object appears to form part and parcel of the instinct. We are thus warned to loosen the bond that exists in our thoughts between instinct and object. It seems probable that the sexual instinct is in the first instance independent of its object; nor is its origin likely to be due to its object's attractions. (p. 14)

Freud's determination that 'the normal picture' of sexual relations presents an optical illusion which represents as 'uniform' that which is but 'soldered together', opens the possibility for his further examination of the separate components that constitute the dynamics of human sexuality. Indeed, we might consider that it is only insofar as he is able to 'loosen the bond that exists in our thoughts' that his psychoanalytic project becomes tenable at all. Thus, the appearance of male inversion as the example which Freud employs to make evident the fiction of 'normal' undifferentiated sexual identification seems critical to the establishment of his undertaking. If, as I have been trying to suggest throughout this piece, the representation of a constituent doubleness 'within' male subjects opened the possibility for signifying non-normative or even transgressive forms of male sexuality in the late nineteenth century, then Freud's rearticulation of this strategy in introducing one of his foundational texts illustrates not just its recuperation as the generic mapping for counter-normative male behaviours, but also its ability to disrupt normative mappings of masculinity as well. For to the extent that Freud opposes male inversion to the unproblematic assertions of a unitary 'sexual instinct', he conversely normalizes a dehiscence within and as the precondition for (male) subjectivity. That is to say, Freud deconstructs the earlier delineations of a unitary male sexuality in order to establish in their stead what I have been calling the 'double lives of man'. And perhaps it is in part from this historically inscribed transposition that we post-Freudians derive the notion that 'our' masculinity is always already, necessarily, split.

NOTES

1 Needless to say, Michel Foucault's writings (especially the *History of Sexuality*, vol. 1, tr. Robert Hurley (New York: Vintage, 1978)) have been 'seminal' for both Victorian studies and lesbian and gay studies. For a discussion of the implications that Foucault's work presents to gay studies, see my 'Foucauldian Necrologies' in *Textual Practice*, 2: 1 (Spring 1988).

2 I use the adjective 'ec-centric' here to gesture towards the sexual positionings of those individuals who are circumscribed by and yet profoundly out of alignment with the historical 'centrings' of their cultures. For a theoretical elaboration of this concept see my, 'Are We

(Not) What We Are Becoming?' in J. Boone and M. Caden (eds.), *Engendering Masculinity: The Question of Male Feminist Criticism* (London: Routledge, 1990).

3 I use the phrase 'telling I' throughout this essay to gesture towards the historical imbrication of narration and identification. In particular, I would like to suggest that the 'imaginary formation' which Lacan 'identifies' as the 'I' in his famous 'Mirror Stage' essay is always already inscribed in narrative, as the developmental aspects of that essay itself illustrate. Moreover, I would like to suggest by this formulation, that the positioning of the 'I' as the location from which and within which the (narrative) 'subject' coheres conversely foreground this 'I' as effect of narrative itself. Hence, the dynamic between forms of narrative and forms of subjectivity becomes 'telling' insofar as it crystallizes those 'subjective' representations through which we come to 'know' ourselves.

4 Phyllis Grosskurth, *John Addington Symonds* (London: Longmans, 1964), p. 16.

5 *Ibid.*, p. 16.

6 Esther Fein, 'Big Publishers Profit as Gay Literature Thrives' in *The New York Times*, 6 July 1992, D1.

7 After having first been published in German, *Sexual Inversion* (Havelock Ellis and John Addington Symonds (London: Wilson and Macmillan, 1897)) appeared in English under the joint authorship of Ellis and Symonds. Symonds, who along with Edward Carpenter was largely responsible for collecting the male case histories that constitute much of the book and whose privately printed *A Problem of Greek Ethics* (1883) and *A Problem in Modern Ethics* (1891) presented literary and historical precedents for such relations, was instrumental in crystallizing Ellis's approach to sexual inversion.

8 Grosskurth, *John Addington Symonds*, p. 29.

9 *Ibid.*, p. 29.

10 Symonds himself uses the qualifier 'eccentric' to denominate his situation in a letter to Edward Carpenter, 29 December 1892. (I thank Scott McCracken for bringing this to my attention.)

11 John Addington Symonds, *The Memoirs of John Addington Symonds*, ed. Phyllis Grosskurth (New York: Random, 1984), p. 54. All further references to this text will be cited in the main body of the text.

12 On the increasing popularity of evolutionary explanations and rhetoric see: Greta Jones, *Social Darwinism and English Thought: The Interaction Between Biological and Social Theory* (Brighton: Harvester, 1980); Walter Houghton, *The Victorian Frame of Mind, 1830–1870* (New Haven: Yale UP, 1957); R. J. Halliday, 'Social Darwinism: A Definition', *Victorian Studies*, 14 (1971).

13 On Ulrichs's place among the early apologists for sexual relations between men see Hurbert Kennedy, *Ulrichs* (Boston: Alyson, 1988); Manfred Herzer, 'Kertbeny and the Nameless Love', *Journal of*

Homosexuality, 12: 1 (1985), 1–26; Jean Claude Féray and Manfred Herzer, 'Homosexual Studies and Politics in the 19th Century: Karl Maria Kertbeny', *Journal of Homosexuality*, 19: 1 (1990), 23–47.

14 In the case history written by Symonds himself which appears in *Sexual Inversion* as Case XVII, Symonds presents a much clearer version of this craving: 'About the age of eight, if not before, he became subject to singular half-waking dreams. He fancied himself seated on the floor among several adult and naked sailors, whose genitals and buttocks he contemplated and handled with relish. He called himself the "dirty pig" of these men, and felt that they were in some way his masters, ordering him to do unclean service to their bodies.' (p. 284)

15 On the transformations in the legal and moral classifications of sexual relations between men, see Ed Cohen, 'Legislating the Norm', *South Atlantic Quarterly*, 88: 1 (Winter 1989), 181–218.

16 On the public schools, see Regenia Gagnier, *Idylls of the Marketplace: Oscar Wilde and the Victorian Public* (Stanford: Stanford University Press, 1986).

17 For a discussion of the institutional effects of the public schools along with (the attempts to control) their 'Peculiar vices,' see Ed Cohen, *Talk on the Wilde Side* (London and New York: Routledge, 1993), pp. 35–86.

18 See for example Jacques Lacan's assertion: 'In man, however, th[e] relationship to nature is altered by a certain dehiscence at the heart of the organism, a primordial discord' or his reference to a 'vital dehiscence that is constituitive of man'. *Écrits: A Selection*, tr. Alan Sheridan (New York: Norton, 1977), p. 4, p. 21.

19 The first English edition, which appeared in 1892, was a translation by Charles Chaddock of the seventh German edition. Since I neither read German nor have access to the earlier German language editions, I haven't yet ascertained in which edition this case first appears. However, the first German edition appeared in 1886 and the second in 1887, so this case must have been written between then and 1892.

20 R. von Krafft-Ebing, *Psychopathia Sexualis with Especial Reference to Contrary Sexual Instinct: A Medico-Legal Study*, trans. Charles Chaddock (Philadelphia: F. A. Davis and Co., 1893), p. 212. All further references to this text will be cited in the main body of the text.

21 Marjorie Garber, in her provocative book *Vested Interests: Cross-Dressing and Cultural Anxiety* (New York: Routledge, 1992), considers 'the cultural discourse of transvestitism and transsexualism as limit cases for "male subjectivities"' (p. 94). For a very interesting, highly psychoanalytic account of transsexuality, see Catherine Millot, *Horesexe: Essay on Transsexuality*, tr. Kenneth Hylton (New York: Autonomedia, 1990).

22 For a recent example of the polemics engendered within and/or around psychoanalysis by the 'is the penis the phallus' controversy, see 'The Phallus Issue', *Differences* 4: 1 (Spring 1992).

23 Robert Louis Stevenson, *The Strange Case of Doctor Jekyll and Mr Hyde* (New York: Bantam, 1985).

24 Sigmund Freud, *Three Essays On The Theory of Sexuality*, trans. James Strachey (New York: Basic Books, 1962). All further references to this text will be cited in the main body of the text.

25 For a more extended analysis of Krafft-Ebing's distinctions, see my *Talk on the Wilde Side*, pp. 9–10, as well as David Halperin, *One Hundred Years of Homosexuality* (London and New York: Routledge, 1990).

26 While Freud does occasionally invoke a homology between relations between men and relations between women, the latter remains significantly undeveloped in this piece. A more comprehensive reading of this essay would undoubtedly force open the way that Freud's theory of male homosexuality is founded on the necessary disappearance of the 'female invert.'

27 In the first footnote Freud notes that 'the information contained in this first essay is derived from the well-known writings of Krafft-Ebing, Moll, Moebius, Havelock Ellis, Schrenck-Notzing, Löwenfeld, Eulenburg, Block and Hirschfeld, and from the *Jahrbuch für sexualle Zwischenstufen*, published under the direction of the last-named author' (p. 1). It seems clear that Freud's experience with 'inversion' himself at the time the first edition of the *Essays* appeared was quite limited. Not coincidentally, then, Symonds's narrative (collected in *Sexual Inversion* – of which he was the unnamed collaborator) and Case 99 would both have been part of the material Freud drew upon for his account.

28 Actually Ulrich's famous maxim quoted in part 1 above is best translated as a 'woman's soul/spirit [anima] in a man's body'. Freud's collapse of 'soul' into 'brain' translates the imagery of Ulrich's account of his own self-understanding as a man who desired other men into the (pseudo) materialism of biology. Hence, he discounts its force as an affirmation, rather than a description.

CHAPTER 6

Henry James and the spectacle of loss: psychoanalytic metaphysics

Marcia Ian

Me, I exist – suspended in a realized void – suspended from my own dread ...

(Georges Bataille, 'Sacrifices')

'Art is the apotheosis of solitude', wrote Samuel Beckett while on the subject of Marcel Proust.[1] In the case of Henry James the jury is still hung (up) on the question of whether his art is the apotheosis of solitude or of sociality: whether he harboured the most exquisite social sensibility ever, or the most exquisitely antisocial; whether his fictional characters learn to separate and individuate in order to become psychologically whole, hale, and hearty, or rather remain agglutinated in one vainglorious metaphorical psychomachy; and whether we are to understand James's narrative and aesthetic 'mastery' in terms imperial, colonial, or psychosexual. It seems to me that how we answer each of these questions, whether we think of them as primarily political, psychological, ethical or aesthetical, hinges on how we interpret the construction of 'interiority' in James; whether indeed we think there is such a thing as interiority, and where, if anywhere, we might locate 'exteriority', or whatever might represent the 'world' (that which is not 'just' language or reflexive subjectivity).

In this chapter I shall argue that one reason why it is so difficult to locate what is not 'interior' in Henry James is that in his fiction the topography of knowledge is, as it were, backward; or, better, it constitutes the rejection *avant la lettre* of interiority as Freud will define it. If we are commonsensical post-Freudians, and not thoroughly postmodernized, we probably think of the unconscious as 'inside' the head, as the deepest recess of mind or personality, closer than consciousness to instinct, to species, to autonomic physiological process, to the pre- or non-verbal. We probably think of consciousness as something analogous to Freud's description of the ego, that is, as a kind of rationalizing mediator between the opposing irrationalities of instinctual desire and of lived reality, while reality remains 'out there' to be experienced as it comes in to us through the portals of the senses. But James represents consciousness as if it were our deepest, darkest secret, the sign of ineluctable desire, the inner sanctum where we fondle our favourite wishes. What is unconscious is that which is outside (not interior or anterior to) consciousness, alien even, including the body (as *res extensa*), or anything else we might rather not know about, but which nevertheless may demand attention – for example, the vulgarity of cupidity, the comedy of sex, or the waste of death. At such times consciousness must defend, in order to affirm, itself against 'the things we can not possibly *not* know, sooner or later, in one way or another',[2] either by negating ('sacrificing' oneself to) them, appropriating them, or mystifying them as 'uncanny'.

According to Sharon Cameron, 'for Henry James consciousness exists in a realm that cannot be touched by a materialist account'.[3] On the other hand, as long as a character in James – take John Marcher in 'The Beast in the Jungle', for example, or the governess in *The Turn of the Screw* – mistakenly believes he (or she) is actually *having* real material relations with others, he can be read as un-conscious, a mere subject questing deludedly after objects. Christopher Newman also falls into this category. Even Isabel Archer in *A Portrait of a Lady* (1880–81) becomes 'conscious' only after she realizes that the relationship she thought she had with her husband was a sham. The 'mere still lucidity' that marks the penetration of this realization to the centre of Isabel's 'being' constitutes the novel's climax, a climax James later says he finds as exciting as 'the surprise of a caravan or the identification of a pirate' would be to the reader of a romance novel. Occurring during her night of meditation alone by the fire, 'without her being approached by another person and without her leaving her chair', this climax is the 'representation simply of her motionlessly *seeing*'.[4]

At such times consciousness in James introverts and sequesters itself, contracting to a lamp-like point of view that can illumine and examine its objects in private. At other times, in its quest for knowledge and experience, it seems to give up its unique point of view to become more like a boundless tapestry pierced by innumerable such points or peep-holes, to expand from a 'safe paradise of self-criticism' into what he called 'the great extension'. (The narrator of *The Ambassadors*, because of its disinterested spectatorial relation to the tragicomedy it describes, offers an example of such extended consciousness.) On the other hand what is unconscious in James might be comparable to the darkness between points of light, the abyss, whether internal or external (to whatever topography is in question), between consciousness and its subjects, its objects. Whether this abyss is fatal to, or constitutive of, consciousness at first may not be clear (as it was not at first in *The Wings of the Dove* to Milly Theale, who came to London to 'see abysses' (p. 175) and would have fallen into them if she had not risen above them instead). Rising above them required that she 'evolve' from subjectivity to selfhood, and from selfhood to consciousness; to that transcendent point of view from which she could at last see that, all along, the fatal and the constitutive were distinct in fact, but not in mind, that she had 'lived' only as long as the distinction between living and dying remained ambiguous (that is, as long as Densher's perception of her as dying remained unreal to her). While she lived, however, she could never be certain 'if, in the general connexion, it were of bridges or of intervals that the spirit not locally disciplined would find itself most conscious'.[5]

Presumably 'the spirit … locally disciplined' knows its bridges from its intervals. Or perhaps consciousness constructs itself merely by distinguishing itself from the darkness 'between'. As long as something, bridge or interval, lies between consciousness and whatever else there might be, subjects and objects appear as such. For James there can be no object unless it is an object for consciousness (the self is one such object); otherwise what would one know of it? Ditto for the subject. Consciousness in James, then, recognizes itself in – can know itself only through its (safe?) distance from – both subject and object, but does not identify itself with either. Although we tend to think of consciousness as defined by the polarity of subject and object, both are objects for the Jamesian consciousness which triangulates itself in relation to them via what Lacan has called 'the inexhaustible quadrature of the ego's verifications'.[6] One could even say that here subject and object are roles acted in a drama or spectacle performed for consciousness. But if consciousness in James is necessarily consciousness of (formal, spatial, sexual, political) relations (between and among subjects and objects), they are relations from which, by virtue of the same 'quadrature', consciousness is necessarily excluded, even as it is located and 'fixed' (a word James frequently uses in just this way) by them. For these reasons, Kaja Silverman's use of Freud's 'primal scene' to theorize Jamesian subjectivity is richly suggestive and moving, if narrowly psychoanalytic.[7]

It seems to me that the loss James's primal scene stages and defends against with greatest urgency is not the loss of gender, sex, or agency, phallic activity or sodomitical connection, but of relation. To stage this loss requires that one view relations as other people have, while what belongs to (is proper to) the self is loss. For example, consider Lambert Strether, the protagonist in *The Ambassadors*, who 'before' the novel begins has already lost a wife and son and who goes on to lose, abandon, or be abandoned by, dear friends almost as fast as he makes them.

I would say of Strether that he is obliged to witness a primal scene in reverse, that is, one that shows him not his origin, but his end (and I don't mean his posterior). What Strether is to learn in the course of this long, dense, ironic novel is the full extent to which he has not lived. He knows from the start, James tells us in his preface to the novel, that he has made a 'mistake': 'He has accordingly missed too much, though perhaps after all constitutionally qualified for a better part, and he wakes up to it in conditions that press the spring of a terrible question. *Would* there yet perhaps be time for reparation?'[8] It is readily apparent to the reader, however, that Strether has plenty of *time* for reparation – in fact the fruit of reparation is more than ripe and all but stuffs itself into his mouth. But reparation is not what he wants. He wants, rather, the contrary: 'not, out of the whole affair, to have got anything for myself'.[9]

Twin questions remain: why doesn't Strether seize the opportunity to live now that he has it; and why does James pretend that the 'terrible question' here concerns reparation? (Unless not 'to have got' would be reparation of the unpleasant fact that he almost got something; indeed he could have had his choice of several some-things.) James's view of this case, as of Isabel Archer's, is that what matters most is not what he gets, but that Strether 'now at all events sees; so that the business of my tale and the march of my action, not to say the precious moral of everything is just my demonstration of this process of vision'.[10] Strether accepts his dual role as spectator and spectacle, specifically as the spectator at the spectacle of his own negativity, while others enact what he will not, namely, intimacy. When at last he '*sees*', he sees himself seeing them, and being seen by them as not having seen. Like Milly in relation to Densher and Kate, as long as he did not know what Chad and Mme de Vionnet were doing together (having real material relations), he thought that perhaps he was living at last. Now that he sees, that he is conscious of what he did and did not know, have, and do, he knows he wasn't 'living' after all. Ultimately he walks out on the tragicomic drama of his own subjectivity just as it belatedly and farcically comes into relation with the panorama of the real (having seen Chad and Mme de Vionnet together in their little boat), taking home nothing for himself except the memory of himself making a spectacle of himself.

The Ambassadors is the novel James considered 'quite the best, "all round", of [his] productions',[11] and many readers would agree as well that it is the most Jamesian, in part because of the elaborate way Strether is set up 'not, out of the whole affair, to have got anything for [him]self'. It is also a perfect example of what I am calling 'the spectacle of loss' in Henry James, the spectacle of the loss of relation. Considering how important 'not getting' is in James, perhaps it would be more accurate to say that the loss feared most in James is not so much the loss of relation, but rather, the loss of the bittersweet *sense of lost relation*. The sense of lost relation is precious because it seems to support the notion that consciousness still at least has itself (and that that's all it ever really needed anyway); when all else is gone, and one is aware of that fact, one still has that ache to identify as 'I', as identity, as that which remains constant. One can be all 'motionlessly seeing' without seeing anything in particular. The drama of this loss is both highly erotic, saturated with the anxiety of dependency and nostalgic melancholy, and highly ironic, precisely because of the absurdity of this eros. Consciousness cannot exist without something to have seen, something to have loved, something or someone whose loss leaves the clinging scent of self-presence. James repeatedly stages the spectacle of its near deprivation in order repeatedly to resurrect consciousness from its own detritus.

The beginning of Book XL of *The Ambassadors* stages just such a moment. At the end of Book X, Sarah Pocock, acting as Mrs Newsome's 'ambassador', cruelly and officially severs all diplomatic and connubial links between her mother and the dilatory Strether. Strether now has nothing and no one waiting for him back in the United States. Sarah had 'let fly at him as from a stretched cord' and 'pierced' him with her 'sharp shaft', so that now 'it probably *was* all at an end'. In a sense, then, at this point Strether is like the walking dead. When Book XL opens it is 'late that evening'. Strether goes to

Chad's place, but Chad is not there. Chad is in the country with his lover (a fact as yet unknown to Strether), and his absence allows Strether to enjoy Chad's rooms and his things, to feel 'in possession as he never yet had been'. He feels 'in possession' precisely because he is not; as he wanders about Chad's rooms, he 'tried to recover the impression that they made on him three months ago', but he cannot. The voice he had once heard there 'failed audibly to sound'. Instead he hears a multitude of voices that 'had grown thicker and meant more things', voices that 'crowded on him as he moved about' to reveal to him his own missed life as a keenly palpable presence:

the main truth of the actual appeal of everything was none the less that everything represented the substance of his loss, put it within reach, within touch, made it, to a degree it had never been, an affair of the senses. That was what it became for him at this singular time, the youth he had long ago missed – a queer concrete presence, full of mystery, yet full of reality, which he could handle, taste, smell, the deep breathing of which he could positively hear.[12]

Strether's missed youth stands before him as if embodied and alive; it breathes. Chad's absence bodies forth as presence Strether's own absence; at this moment, indeed, 'everything represented the substance of his loss'. Further, that he can perceive this multiplied representation as substantial signals the freedom, the peculiar 'possession' that loss makes possible: 'He felt, strangely, as sad as if he had come for some wrong, and yet as excited as if he had come for some freedom. But the freedom was what was most in the place and the hour; it was the freedom that most brought him round again'.

Characters in James's stories and novels tend to wander about in a wilderness of 'relation', often, as I said above, not realizing they are lost, until perforce they either attain the kind of spiritualized consciousness Isabel Archer achieves, or else go home, collapse, die, or otherwise fail to make the leap. Sometimes it seems to be the narrator who is put to this test; in the prefaces, James magisterially narrates as 'the story of the story' the successes and failures of these narrators. (The narrator of *The American Scene*, I would argue, is one narrator whose peril James neither fully understands nor enjoys.) For 'James' (by which I almost always mean the implied author of what we read rather than the person who implied him), to feel that consciousness is intransitively 'in possession' is to come as close as possible to absolute being, while loss of control is near perdition. Martha Banta describes the post-religious paradox inherent in this predicament in the introduction to her book *Henry James and The Occult* when she writes about 'the non-credo of Henry James': he 'was a secular man who felt no shame, anxiety or doubt about his secularism', at the same time that his 'full faith in the powers of the human consciousness sufficed as the only religion he knew or needed'.[13] He did not believe in 'those tenets of the Christian orthodoxy that speak of other beings, other worlds, or other lives than those discernible by the human heart', but on the other hand, the words 'supernatural, occult, psychical, and transcendent' in James apply solely to hidden powers of the human mind. James's non-credo, in other words, is tantamount to a credo.

In an essay entitled 'Sacrifices', Georges Bataille describes as an existential predicament the paradox of a consciousness that believes in itself, in a 'me' that is at once the validation of a credo and its negation. Bataille defines the 'me' as a unique improbability compounded of contingency, dread, and violence, suspended over a void: '*Me*, I exist – suspended in a realized void – suspended from my own dread – different from all other being and such that the various events that can reach all other being and not *me* cruelly throw this me out of a total existence' (p. 130). (To throw 'me' *into* existence, 'various events' must *reach* 'my' being – and, perhaps not reach that of others.) This version of consciousness is made meaningful primarily by the loneliness of its own absurd uniqueness, a uniqueness at bottom random and meaningless:

There exists, in fact, a unique moment in relation to the possibility of me – and thus the infinite improbability of this coming into the world appears. For if the tiniest difference had occurred in the course of the successive events of which I am the result, in the place of this *me*, integrally avid to be *me*, there would have been "an *other*". (p. 130)

The meaninglessness of the 'me's' uniqueness generates its despotic avidity to be itself, an avidity that 'is comparable to the exercise of a dominion, as if the void in whose midst I am demands that I be *me* and the dread of this *me*'. 'I' am therefore the double or mirror-image of an 'immense realized void' which in turn 'impl[ies]' not undifferen-tiated being but the painful improbability of the unique *me*'. 'Across [this void] I, as imperative existence, play'.[14]

To play 'across' this void or interval, 'I' must build the bridge that is the illusion of 'my' existence.

For Henry James representation, in particular prose fiction, is that bridge. The rest of this chapter will focus on the construction of that bridge, and the near unthinkability of its collapse. I will begin by discussing the newly anti-theological suspicion of interiority (as opposed to the traditional religious castigation of selfhood) gathering force at the end of the nineteenth, and beginning of the twentieth, century. Then I will look briefly at two of Henry James's works, a novel, *What Maisie Knew* (1897), and an essay, 'Is There a Life After Death?' (1910), to suggest how James constructs consciousness as a form of resistance to, but also enjoyment of, the spectacle of loss, that is, as a negation which functions, as Freud says about the fetish, as both a denial and an asseveration. Each of these works offers a slightly different view of the Jamesian psycho-spiritual topography; a topography marked by the history of its own variety of ethnic, racial, and national 'cleansings' (subjects I am addressing elsewhere).

Clearly, although James may have given up the idea of a god, he has not given up on hierarchical metaphysics. What he proposes could be thought of as a psychoanalytic metaphysics. Explaining what I mean by this will, no doubt, require raising (if not answering) existential or ontological questions. Even though fully aware of the extent to which 'we' have learned to reject transcendental accounts of consciousness, and to avoid speaking of obvious 'things we cannot possibly *not* know, sooner or later', I confess that I find James's insistence upon the significance of consciousness (an insistence nearly megalomaniac in 'Is There a Life After Death?') fascinating, even while I define the problematic of its interiorization, its privatization, as a *fin-de-siècle* problem, and therefore as anything but a private matter.

*   *   *

I, say I. Unbelieving.

(Samuel Beckett, *The Unnamable*)

The question of just what constitutes or represents interiority or exteriority in fiction, or discourse generally, has become inseparable from the more fundamental question of the validity of the distinction between them; the suspicion that these terms should interest us only as artifacts of the period prior to the postmodern. This uncertainty attests to the crisis of interiority (which psychoanalysis tried to solve but instead complicated) that marked *fin-de-siècle* epistemology, or perhaps rather its demise, and that persists a century later as we debate questions of subjectivity, agency, historiography, politics, and popular culture. For example, according to Nietzsche, by the time he came to write *The Genealogy of Morals* in 1887, man had become as interiorized as he could get. Just as man's belief in a Christian god had reached its peak and headed into 'steady decline' toward the 'complete and definitive victory of atheism', Nietzsche hoped that what he called 'man's interiorization' had also reached its limit.[15] For Nietzsche, belief in something absolute and transcendent (God, for example) and the development of a subjective interiority which mirrored that something (such as reason or the soul), were complementary phenomena. Or, as Georges Bataille put it in 'Materialism': 'Dead matter, the pure idea, and God in fact answer a question in the same way', because they all answer 'the question of the essence of things, precisely of the *idea* by which things become intelligible'.[16] Nietzsche saw man's interiorization as the result of the guilt consciousness Judaism and Christianity had cultivated in him for centuries at the expense of his primitive innocence and unconscious instinctual nature. Modern man had declared 'war against the old instincts that had hitherto been the foundation of his power, his joy, and his awesomeness', and instead 'began rending, persecuting, terrifying himself, like a wild beast hurling itself against the bars of its cage'. In ancient days men had been 'happily adapted to the wilderness, to war, free roaming, and adventure'. But then 'of a sudden they found all their instincts devalued', and 'they felt inapt', unable to 'count on the guidance of their unconscious drives', or to find any but 'covert satisfactions'. Worst of all, 'they were forced to think, deduce, calculate, weigh cause and effect', pathetically 'reduced to their weakest, most fallible organ, their consciousness!'[17]

Both Nietzsche and Bataille identify reason not with man's divine nature, but with his morbid fear of being alive. They see man's persistent idealism not as his link with eternity, but rather as his love of inert vacuous forms, and attribute his willing sublimation not to *eros* but *thanatos*. Man had (tragically or comically) lost touch with his 'true nature', defined as the ability to act and to interact unfettered by consciousness or conscience. His interiorization marked, was equivalent to, a loss of nature, and his consciousness nothing but a fetish, a memorial that denied and attested to this loss. Like Nietzsche, at the end of the nineteenth century Freud also saw his task as deflating the ideas and ideals man had substituted for repressed physiological and psychological feeling, for the ability to be in 'touch' with himself and others. He thought psychoanalysis could knock consciousness off the throne it had occupied at least since Descartes. As Freud put it near the end of *The Interpretation of Dreams* (1900), in his theory consciousness, 'which was once so omnipotent and hid all else from view', had been reduced to a mere 'sense-organ for the perception of psychical qualities'.[18]

Meanwhile, on the other side of the Atlantic, psychologist and philosopher William James had been deconstructing consciousness in ways arguably analogous to those of Nietzsche and Freud. In 'Does "Consciousness" Exist?'(1904), for example, as Sharon Cameron explains, William James suggests that consciousness is a false abstraction from breath, which is material. According to Cameron, James argues that '[c]onsciousness has been gratuitously introduced as an unreal, second entity which divides and interiorizes what is essentially concrete, external, and *whole*'.[19] William rejects the notion of a real, interior consciousness. For him 'consciousness does not exist because the stuff of which it is made is outside the self... He is scientifically attacking the conditions of a psychology that isolates consciousness, allies it with a self, and falsely conceives it as anterior and interior.'(p. 80) Cameron argues that Henry also often represents consciousness as outside the self but that it is not thereby 'made to disappear. Rather it is freed up' (p. 80). For Henry 'consciousness *does* exist, and commands attention, because the stuff of which it is made is outside the self' (p. 80). She finds that, unlike the prefaces, Henry James's novels represent consciousness as 'disseminated', 'extrinsic, made to take shape – indeed, to become social – as an *inter*subjective phenomenon' (p. 77).

Regarding Henry, I am arguing a somewhat opposite case, namely that for him consciousness is 'interior' in quite the Cartesian way. James does not want to regard consciousness as made of stuff from 'outside'. On the contrary, the notion that consciousness might be intersubjective is the unpleasant premise of ghost stories such as *The Turn of the Screw*, the object of satire in others, for instance 'The Altar of the Dead', and in still others the threat that must be neutralized by the will-to-consciousness of characters such as Merton Densher in *The Wings of the Dove*. For him what Freudians would define as the unconscious is the stuff 'outside'. In *Beyond the Pleasure Principle* (1920), Freud presents a kind of biological fairytale (he calls it 'speculation, often far-fetched speculation' (p. 24)) about the origins of consciousness in simple living organisms that in its way explains this theory. Freud's tale reveals two different dualisms: that of consciousness versus the 'outside' world, and that of consciousness versus its own dark 'interior'.[20] Because it will help clarify the problematic I am describing, I shall discuss this tale of two dualisms briefly. Freud wrote *Beyond the Pleasure Principle* to counter the total dominance he had earlier ascribed to the pleasure principle, most notably in *The Interpretation of Dreams* (1900), where he had asserted that dreams are always wish fulfilments. It had become obvious to him that some dreams, feelings and behaviours contradicted this assertion, especially certain repetition compulsions and the anguish we would now call 'post-traumatic stress syndrome'. Accordingly, he thought about this contradiction until he came up with the 'death instinct' and reported his findings in *Beyond the Pleasure Principle*. As Freud saw it, it is the stuff on the inside and not the stuff on the outside that is the problem. Given 'that everything living dies for *internal* reasons', he wrote in one of the grimmest locutions extant: 'the aim of all life is death' (p. 38). The instincts – that nature which Nietzsche worried that we had learned to ignore – simply 'assure that the organism shall follow its own path to death', albeit 'through ever more complicated *détours*' (p. 39). Ultimately it is the role of consciousness to trick or entice the organism into taking these detours. Freud wrote that consciousness is 'not the most universal attribute of mental processes, but only a particular function of them', namely 'perceptions of excitations coming from the external world and of feelings of pleasure and unpleasure which can only arise from within the mental apparatus'. Logically, then, he could 'assign to the system *Pcpt.-Cs.* [perception-consciousness] a position in space. It must lie on the borderline between outside and inside; it must be turned towards the external world and must envelop the other psychical systems.' This topography is in accordance, Freud explains, with 'cerebral anatomy, which locates the "seat" of consciousness in the cerebral cortex – the outermost, enveloping layer of the central organ'. Consciousness, in other words, is 'lodged on the surface of the brain instead of being safely housed somewhere in its inmost interior' (p. 24). Cerebral anatomy, however, offered no explanation of how this came to be, so Freud came up with a 'just so story' about how 'a living organism in its most simplified possible form as an undifferentiated vesicle of a substance that is susceptible to stimulation' learned to protect and preserve itself (p. 26).

The 'surface [of the primitive organism] turned towards the external world' constitutes its only differentiated feature; yet this

differentiation is highly significant, comprising 'an organ for receiving stimuli' (p. 26). Embryology provides a basis for this inference
by showing 'that the central nervous system originates from the
ectoderm; the grey matter of the cortex remains a derivative of the
primitive superficial layer' (p. 26). In line with this one can 'suppose,
then, that as a result of the ceaseless impact of external stimuli on the
surface of the vesicle, its substance to a certain depth may have
become permanently modified ... A crust would thus be formed
which would at last have been so thoroughly "baked through" by
stimulation that it would present the most favourable possible
conditions for the reception of stimuli and become incapable of any
further modification.' (p. 26) This would explain why consciousness
'is characterized by the peculiarity that in it (in contrast to what
happens in the other psychical systems) excitatory processes do not
leave behind any permanent change ... but expire, as it were, in the
phenomenon of becoming conscious' (p. 25).

   This crust both exposes the organism to horrific amounts of
stimulation and protects it from overload. This 'little fragment of
living substance' which exists 'suspended in the middle of an external
world charged with the most powerful energies' would be 'killed by
the stimulation emanating from these if it were not provided with a
protective shield against stimuli' (p. 27). Such *protection against
stimuli* is therefore 'an almost more important function for the living
organism than the *reception of* stimuli' (p. 27). To protect itself the
organism partly shuts itself off from the outside world and creates a
more active inner world. As a result the 'outermost surface [of the
organism] ceases to have the structure proper to living matter,
becomes to some degree inorganic and thenceforward functions as a
special envelope or membrane resistant to stimuli' (p. 27). This
envelope, this barrier against the world, then has sacrificed its
livingness so that 'the next underlying layers' might survive and
'"devote themselves" to the reception of the amounts of stimulus
which have been allowed through' (p. 27). As the organism evolves,
these more sensitive layers, continually sampling the 'outside world',
develop, Freud thinks, into the 'system *Cs*.', eventually receiving
stimuli from deeper within as well, stimuli against which system *Cs*.
has no defence (p. 27).

   The sensitive cortical layer which shields the interior and 'which is
later to become the system *Cs*., also receives excitations from *within*'
(p. 29). But, although the system *Cs*. is protected by its outermost

'crust' from stimulations from outside, 'towards the inside there can be no such shield'. According to Freud, the organism does, however, develop 'a particular way ... of dealing with any internal excitations which produce too great an increase of unpleasure':

> there is a tendency to treat them as though they were acting, not from the inside, but from the outside, so that it may be possible to bring the shield against stimuli into operation as a means of defence against them. This is the origin of *projection*, which is destined to play such a large part in the causation of pathological processes. (p. 29)

Evidently, just as we are to understand the cortical layer of the organism to be the forerunner of consciousness, so are we to see this interior against which the organism has no 'shield' as the ancestor of the unconscious. Freud suggests 'projection' as the primal defence mechanism: the tendency to, as it were, misread internal excitations and perceive them as if they were acting, not from the inside, but from the outside. To protect the organism from its own interior, then, consciousness must not recognize as its own the threat it senses. The unconscious, on the contrary, becomes a kind of spectacle whose 'audience' must diffuse, resist, misconstrue, or deny its effect. This insight into the essential surrealism of the unconscious is fundamental to psychoanalysis, including Lacan's uncanny 'return' to Freud.

But it is also at the core of Henry James's literary project, if often in the form of psychological satire. The story 'The Altar of the Dead', for example, satirizes the wilful *méconnaissance* of 'projection', and the all-round stupidity of the unconscious. Unlike Nietzsche, William James and Freud, he unambivalently celebrates the ability of human consciousness to differentiate itself from the hurly-burly of the real as well as from its own personal desires. If Jamesian consciousness can do all this, can objectively '*see*' what it is about, while knowing always where its interest lies, what then would be unconscious in James? How should the (psychoanalytically inclined) literary critic perform her job of work on James, how find the secret subtexts that escaped the author but which clever hermeneutic sleuths can detect? Does it make sense to claim we discern the Jamesian unconscious in the host of scopophilic, fetishistic, sodomitic, and epistemophilic pathologies we attribute to his characters and narrators? Probably not, since James took clear conscious delight in representing their every vicissitude, and doubtless was acquainted with their names, etiologies and teleologies as well. In other words, such pathologies in

James are not symptoms, unless, rather, they are the symptoms of consciousness itself.

*   *   *

> I say 'I', and I am not 'I'. 'I' means you, and you are going to
> die.   (Edmond Jabès, *The Book of Questions*)

The child hero of James's novel *What Maisie Knew* (1897) in certain ways resembles the primitive organism of *Beyond the Pleasure Principle*. Her consciousness forms in response to the need to preserve herself in the face of a barrage of stimuli assaulting her from 'outside' (thanks to her dysfunctional family) and 'inside' (as her pubescent sexuality awakens her to loneliness and desire). Accordingly she learns to cultivate, to protect, to consecrate 'her personal relation to her knowledge' in order not to be swallowed up by the desires of others, and to begin to know what she wants, as opposed to what others expect of her.[21] When Maisie was three, the novel begins by telling us, her parents, Ida and Beale, began those separation proceedings which ended three years later with 'the little girl...divided in two and the portions tossed impartially to the disputants' (p. 35). She was to spend half the year with each. But the former *sposi* hate each other so passionately that during each such period, in the early years, the parent in charge spent considerable energy vilifying the other, thus keeping the other always 'before [Maisie] by perpetually abusing him' in his absence, and at the end of each visit virtually hurling the child together with a barrage of heated insults at the hated ex-spouse.

In this situation Ida and Beale are clearly sadistic players of 'fort/da' ('gone/there!') – that symbolic game of 'disappearance and return' Freud observed his grandson playing with a wooden spool and then elaborated into a famous theory of how children use play to substitute a sense of mastery (presence) for the loss of mother (absence). In a footnote Freud adds that on another occasion the child used his own image in a mirror to play fort/da, happily greeting his mother with the words 'Baby O–O–O–!' or 'Baby gone!' which turned out to refer to the child's new diversion of making himself disappear and reappear by crouching beneath an almost full-length mirror, and then popping up in front of it.[22] (Lacan's theory of the mirror stage, though descriptive of a younger child, no doubt owes itself to this footnote in Freud.) But with so many playing a game which ought clearly to have been kept more private, Maisie finds it hard to gain mastery or pleasure from the chaotic comings and goings, comings-back and goings-away again, of the adults surrounding her. She *does* know what it is to feel loss and longing, desire and need. She is less sure of what or whom she is missing, where it might have gone, or whether she ever had it, let alone whether, perchance, it might miss her too. But, just as Freud's grandson masters his loss by making himself disappear, Maisie will triumph by making her 'self' invisible to those around her, while projecting the spectacle of her loss outward where she can both see it better and disavow it.

Maisie, meanwhile, becomes prey to 'the complete vision, private but final, of the strange office she filled' as a receptacle for and transmitter of hatred, and begins to seal her face against her parents. At the same time she feels a new 'feeling, the feeling of danger', in response to which she discovers the 'remedy' afforded by 'the idea of an inner self or, in other words, of concealment' (p. 43). On the surface, the narrator tells us, she will gladly appear to her parents an idiot, an imbecile, by pretending not to register what they are saying and doing. This way, although all the sordid details do register upon and within her fully and deeply, at least she will not be used, she thinks, by the parents she never stops loving and wanting, to communicate to each other through her the badness with which she has been taught to identify herself. But strangely, surreally, at about this very same time, her dolls seem to come to life: 'The stiff dolls on the dusky shelves began to move their arms and legs' (p. 43). And the more things go on about her which she is 'never to ask about', the more lively her dolls become, especially the French doll Lisette. Much goes on about which she is never to ask, but about which she knows nevertheless. Her father hires a governess for Maisie, and then marries her and betrays her, repeatedly; while her mother marries a kind young man whom *she* then betrays, repeatedly. Subsequently the stepmother and the stepfather get involved with each other, during which time Maisie is batted about like a shuttlecock, landing occasionally in the ample lap of an ugly, ignorant, sentimental, moralistic but affectionate woman named Mrs Wix, who seizes upon her as a handy substitute for her own long-dead daughter.

The sexual and filial permutations implicit in this tangle are multiple, and James exploits them all. Meanwhile Maisie tries to know what is going on without seeming to know too much, and get a little something for herself in the process. Family psychology being what it is, Maisie, not surprisingly, reproduces and acts out some of the behaviour of the adults she sees coming and going. In the passage which follows, she forces herself on her doll Lisette as an incomprehensible spectacle, the very embodiment of the fort/da game, and mocks Lisette for being unable to escape the role of passive spectator. In a life which resembles 'a long, long corridor with rows of closed doors', Maisie has herself learned not to knock, since the desire expressed by her knock has been, in her experience, always met with derision. But then, 'it was far from new to her that the questions of the small are the peculiar diversion of the great':

Little by little, however, [Maisie] understood more, for it befell that she was enlightened by Lisette's questions, which reproduced the effect of her own upon those for whom she sat in the very darkness of Lisette. Was she not herself convulsed by such innocence? ... There were at any rate things she really couldn't tell even a French doll. She could only pass on her lessons and study to produce on Lisette the impression of having mysteries in her life, wondering the while whether she succeeded in the air of shading off, like her mother, into the unknowable ... Yes, there were matters one couldn't 'go into' with a pupil. There were, for instance, days when, after prolonged absence, Lisette, watching her take off her things, tried hard to discover where she had been. Well, she discovered a little, but never discovered all. There was an occasion when, on her being particularly indiscreet, Maisie replied to her – and precisely about the motive of a disappearance – as she, Maisie, had once been replied to by [her mother]: 'Find out for yourself!' (p. 55)

Here, by taking Maisie's play seriously as an inquiry and a lament, James brilliantly and tenderly dramatizes that painful convergence, in the symbolic, of psychic and social reality thanks to which we often cannot help reproducing the forms and contents of the 'knowledge' and 'action' into which we are born. It does not matter whether or to what degree Maisie is conscious of how she is treating Lisette. Although, as it happens, she *is* conscious, and ashamed, of her cruelty to Lisette, that awareness does not make it possible for her to stop needing to play the game or to step outside the system it represents.

Like so many Jamesian heroes, Maisie ends up not having 'got' anything for herself except 'her personal relation to her knowledge', but in James this counts for something. Indeed, for James the 'treasure itself of consciousness' is cumulative. Many of his works could attest to this, but the essay 'Is There a Life after Death?' – which Henry contributed to a symposium on immortality earlier the same year his 'ideal, elder brother' William died, leaving him so desolate that he sought help and solace from the eminent American

Freudian James Jackson Putnam[23] – comprises his consummate apology for consciousness.[24] In it he asserts that the consciousness of the artist will live forever, surviving the death of what he disparagingly calls the 'laboratory brain', because of the artist's 'accumulation of the very treasure itself of consciousness'.[25]

James remarks that over the years he became increasingly troubled by the prospect of the disappearance from the world of his personal self. The question, for him, about life after death, 'is of the *personal* experience … of another existence; of its being I my very self, and you, definitely, and he and she, who resume and go on, and not of unthinkable substitutes or metamorphoses. The whole interest of the matter is that it is my or your sensibility that is involved and at stake.' (p. 604) Admittedly, séances and trances notwithstanding, no one reliable has come back to tell us whether 'the personal experience' continues after death; 'we [merely] watch the relentless ebb of the tide on which the vessel of experience carries us, and which to our earthly eyes never flows again.' (p. 605) Even the most vigorous 'who could have been backed, as we call it, not to fail, on occasion, of somehow reaching us' from beyond, don't. Jeepers – '"Talk of triumphant identity if they, wanting to triumph, haven't done it."'(p. 607) Yet, despite the lack of evidence that identity as such can triumph over death, James chooses to believe that it can, both in the cases of those for whom 'the mere acquired momentum of intelligence, of perception, of vibration, of experience in a word, would have carried them on … to something' (p. 608) and in his own case. He found that, in growing older, 'a process takes place which I can only describe as the accumulation of the very treasure itself of consciousness' (p. 610). James carefully husbanded this treasure over the course of his lifetime, 'trying to take the measure of [his] consciousness' to see if it really were 'so finite'. In the process:

I had learned, as I may say, to live in it more, and with the consequence of thereby not a little undermining the conclusion most unfavourable to it [of its finitude]. I had doubtless taken thus to increased living in it by reaction against so grossly finite a world – for it at least contained the world, and could handle and criticize it, could play with it and deride it; it had that superiority: which meant, all the while, such successful living that the abode itself grew more and more interesting to me. (p. 609)

In this passage we can see the consistency of what James learns about psychic life with the lessons his fictional characters learn, from Rowland Mallet to Isabel Archer to Merton Densher to Maggie

Verver: when the world proves gross and finite, go and live inside your head. There you can 'contain' the world, handle and criticize it – play with it and deride it. You will gain *that* superiority, *that* success.

Within the house of fiction he calls consciousness James develops inwardly, much like little Nora in *Watch and Ward* whose own consciousness expands into a 'throbbing immensity' capable of 'floating through the whole circle of emotion and the full realization of being'.[26] 'Above all, as an artist' James feels himself peculiarly capable of appreciating and enjoying this 'independence of thought'. 'I deal with being, I invoke and evoke, I figure and represent, I seize and fix, as many phases and aspects and conceptions of it as my infirm hand allows me strength for; and in so doing I find myself – I can't express it otherwise – in communication with *sources*' he says (p. 611). Those of us who are not artists, or who may belong to that 'class' to whom 'dreadful things have happened', James speculates, may well face extinction, if we are not among those 'whose life is to work and work their inner spirit to a productive or illustrative end' (p. 612). Such people cannot afford to invest in the treasure of consciousness: 'It is, in a word [only] the artistic consciousness and privilege in itself that thus shines as from immersion in the fountain of being.' (p. 613) While we live, James writes, we do so encased in personality which is – and here follows a metaphor that pre-empts Lacan's '*trotte-bébé*' in 'The Mirror Stage' –

not unlike the sustaining frame on little wheels that often encases growing infants, so that, dangling and shaking about in it, they may feel their assurance of walking increase and teach their small toes to know the ground. I like to think that we here, as to soul, dangle from the infinite and shake about in the universe; that this world and this conformation and these senses are our helpful and ingenious frame, amply provided with wheels and replete with the lesson for us of how to plant, spiritually, our feet. (p. 613)

This image of the individual – specifically, of the artist – as being like a mind seated in a wheeled baby-walker, dangling briefly from the universe, soon to be snapped up when the gizmo wears out – compares the artist, the flower of creation, immersed in being and in touch with sources, to an infant dependent on and indeed from heaven and specially equipped with bumpers and immortality.

With his metaphor of the 'mind in a baby-walker', James describes an embattled consciousness profiting by hardening itself to the world outside its precincts and freeing itself within its prison for some form of further conscious evolution. The authority James claims for his vision of immortality is the same 'I' which for Freud is a by-product of its own evolutionary history; that 'I' which desires its own survival and to hell with species; that 'I' which (for example) in Samuel Beckett inadvertently dreams itself into being by speaking itself. How, James asks rhetorically, can he know that immortality will prove to be at once 'personal' and dissociated? This is his answer: 'I practically know what I am talking about when I say, "I", hypothetically, for my full experience of another term of being, just as I know it when I say "I" for my experience of this one.' Because he *can* say 'I', he can count on his continuance and does not have 'to reckon, that is, with a failure of the signs by which I know myself' (p. 607).

Henry James's body of work, like the discourse of psychoanalysis taken as a whole, participates in the construction of the modern 'self' as both the sovereign creator of its world and a product of language. Many readers find James's version of subjectivity forbidding, even repellent. The house of fiction inhabited by the Jamesian self may seem to be, in Donna Przybylowicz's words, a suspiciously 'homogeneous world' maintained as such by 'the logocentric impulses of a central consciousness who through his or her aestheticization of the world deforms it in order to have it conform to the dictates of his or her imagination.'[27] This world is homogeneous only because it is, in Paul Zweig's phrase, 'ego-morphic',[28] constituted by, for and about the 'me', and thus constitutionally closed to others and even to otherness *per se*. From the point of view of a postmodern, semiotized poetics, such ego-morphic plenitude must fall short because the 'failure of the signs by which I know myself' – what Lacan has called our 'ever-growing dispossession of... being' – is precisely what we must reckon with.[29] And from the point of view of a postmodern, multicultural politics, it must fall short because of its unapologetic elitism.

But from the point of view of (my) postmodern, post-psycho-analytic constructivism, James's work raises important theoretical and political questions about the different kinds of so-called 'materiality' we attribute to persons, language, and culture. His work also stands out as a unique literary link between and among the wilful and paradoxical immaterialisms of, for example, Pater and Lacan, Emerson and Beckett. James thought that his lifelong investment in consciousness might conceivably pay off in the form of a transcendent equilibrium thanks to which his consciousness could eternally 'function immanently' within carefully determined bounds. This 'I' would require no 'signs' to know itself by; it could embody, without a body, pure presence, the unity of source with source; it would enact the pure performance of relationless being. James's affirmation presents us with the frightening spectacle of a 'narcissism [that] is *never* abandoned',[30] that knows itself to be pure desire yet refuses the annihilation of self that desire demands. For James, this was a non-consummation devoutly to be wished. In *Death and Sensuality*, Georges Bataille wrote: 'Two things are inevitable; we cannot avoid dying nor can we avoid bursting through our barriers, and they are one and the same.'[31] Disproving that these two 'are one and the same' was very much Henry James's 'project', a project he planned to continue in the great beyond. 'It has long been known', Leon Edel informs us at the end of the last volume of James's letters, that 'after his first and second strokes in December 1915, [James] called for his typist and told her to take dictation'.[32] He was in bed and 'semi-delirious', but over the next ten days or so he soothed himself by dictating six fragmentary texts, two of which were from 'Napoléone' (one signed as such), one to one of his married sisters, and one to William James and his sister-in-law. But in the text dated 11 December 1915, James comments, seemingly in his own voice, that it was 'wondrous' to feel like himself again and 'in such a concert' that he could touch 'the large old phrase into the right amplitude'. He had thought his sources might have at last dried up, withered and shrunk, he says, like an emptied breast. But then, lo and behold, he could 'simply shift the sweet nursling of genius from one maternal breast to the other' to avert 'the false note'. 'Astounding little stepchild of God's astounding young stepmother!' he cries (pp. 809–10).

These words fairly boggle the mind with the images they suggest of James in bed conceiving of, even birthing, his own genius for the 'large phrase' in the form of a sweet cosmic nursling, now, at the end, being shifted comfortably from one maternal breast to the other. Are these 'breasts' by turns this world, and then the next? Is this little stepchild of God's young stepmother God, or God's brother, and does either correspond to Henry and/or William? And who might be 'God's astounding young stepmother'? On his deathbed a semi-delirious but contented James seems to be playing a thoroughly satisfying game of fort/da in which disappearance and return happen simultaneously to confirm a divinely step-maternal plenitude of consciousness in which the tiresome dualisms of self and other, self and mother, self and brother, lose themselves in a blissful dialectic of God-like breasts.

NOTES

1 Samuel Beckett, *Proust* (New York: Grove Press, 1957), p. 47.
2 Henry James, 'Preface to *The American*', in *The Art of the Novel* (New York: Charles Scribner's Sons, 1934), p. 31. All emphases in material quoted from James are his.
3 Sharon Cameron, *Thinking in Henry James* (Chicago: University of Chicago Press, 1989), p. 81.
4 James, 'Preface to *A Portrait of a Lady*', in *The Art of the Novel*, p. 57.
5 Henry James, *The Wings of the Dove* (1902), (Harmondsworth: Penguin, 1986), p. 178.
6 Jacques Lacan, 'The Mirror Stage' (1949), in *Écrits: A Selection*, tr. Alan Sheridan (New York: Norton, 1977), pp. 1–7, especially p. 4.
7 Kaja Silverman, *Male Subjectivity at the Margins* (New York and London: Routledge, 1992), pp. 157–81.
8 James, 'Preface to *The Ambassadors*', p. 308.
9 Henry James, *The Ambassadors* (1903) (New York: Norton, 1964), p. 344.
10 James, 'Preface to *The Ambassadors*', p. 308. For what remains a peerless discussion of the significance of 'seeing' in James, see Laurence Bedwell Holland, *The Expense of Vision: Essays in the Craft of Henry James* (Princeton: Princeton University Press, 1964).
11 *Ibid.*, p. 309.
12 James, *The Ambassadors*, pp. 281–2.
13 Martha Banta, *Henry James and The Occult: The Great Extension* (Bloomington: Indiana University Press, 1972), pp. 3–4.
14 Georges Bataille, *Visions of Excess: Selected Writings 1927–1939*, tr. Allan Stoekl (Minneapolis: University of Minnesota Press, 1985), p. 130.
15 Friedrich Nietzsche, *The Birth of Tragedy* and *The Genealogy of Morals*, tr. Francis Golffing (New York: Anchor Books, 1956), p. 224.
16 Bataille, *Visions of Excess*, p. 15.
17 Nietzsche, *The Birth of Tragedy*, pp. 217–19.
18 Sigmund Freud, *The Interpretation of Dreams* in *The Standard Edition of the Complete Psychological Works of Sigmund Freud* (London: Hogarth Press, 1953), vol. 5, p. 615.
19 Sharon Cameron, *Thinking in Henry James* (Chicago: University of Chicago Press, 1989), p. 80.
20 Sigmund Freud, *Beyond the Pleasure Principle* (1920), in *The Standard Edition*, vol. 18, pp. 1–64 (see especially pp. 24–33). All emphases in quoted materials are Freud's.
21 Henry James, *What Maisie Knew* (1897) (Middlesex: Penguin, 1966), p. 204.

22 Freud, *Beyond the Pleasure Principle*, p. 16, n.

23 Leon Edel (ed.), *Henry James: Letters*, vol. 4: 1895–1916 (Cambridge: Harvard University Press, 1984). See James's letter to Putnam, dated 4 January, 1912.

24 W. D. Howells *et al.*, *In After Days: Thoughts on the Future Life* (New York and London: Harper and Brothers, 1910). These are the published proceedings of the symposium. James's paper stands out as the only one that is not an exercise in religious piety.

25 Henry James, 'Is There a Life After Death?' (1910). Included, slightly excerpted, in *The James Family*, ed. F. O. Matthiessen (New York: Vintage, 1980), p. 610. Citations are from this more readily available edition.

26 Henry James, *Watch and Ward* (1878), (New York: Grove Press, 1960), p. 236.

27 Donna Przybylowicz, 'Review of Paul B. Armstrong, *The Phenomenology of Henry James*', *Henry James Review*, 7: 1 (Autumn 1985), 49.

28 Paul Zweig, *The Heresy of Self-Love: A Study of Subversive Individualism* (Princeton: Princeton University Press, 1968), p. 165.

29 Jacques Lacan, 'The Function and Field of Speech and Language in Psychoanalysis' (1953), in *Écrits*, p. 42.

30 Mikkel Borch-Jacobsen, *The Freudian Subject*, tr. Catherine Porter (Stanford: Stanford University Press, 1988), p. 95 (his emphasis).

31 Georges Bataille, *Death and Sensuality: A Study of Eroticism and the Taboo* (New York: Walker and Company, 1962), p. 140.

32 Edel, *Letters*, pp. 809–10.

CHAPTER 7

'A very curious construction': masculinity and the poetry of A. E. Housman and Oscar Wilde

Ruth Robbins

In its widest possible sense ... a man's Self is the sum-total of what he can call his; not only his body and his psychic powers, but his clothes and his house, his wife and his children, his ancestors and friends, his reputation and works, his lands and horses, and yacht and bank account.

(William James, *Principles of Psychology*, 1890)

Do you know why poetry and philosophy are nothing but dead letter these days? It is because they have severed themselves from life. In Greece, ideas went hand in hand with life; so that the artist's life was already a poetic realization, the philosopher's life a putting into action of his philosophy; in this way, both philosophy and poetry took part in life, instead of remaining unacquainted with each other, philosophy provided food for poetry – and the result was admirably persuasive. Nowadays, beauty no longer acts; action no longer desires to be beautiful; and wisdom works in a sphere apart.

(André Gide, *The Immoralist*, 1902)

This chapter is concerned with cultural boundaries and their enforcement as binary oppositions in the lives and work of two *fin-de-siècle* poets.[1] It takes masculinity as its focus, because masculinity's dominant ideological position means that the boundaries which define it are most in need of policing. At the end of the nineteenth century masculinity had become an unstable entity. Its dominance was under threat from both a *fin-de-siècle* sense of ending, and from the anxieties of definition which are the result of what Foucault calls 'the multiplicity of discursive elements'.[2] The chapter looks at two exemplary texts: Wilde's *The Sphynx* (1894) and A. E. Housman's *Shropshire Lad* collection (1896). These two poems fall either side of a temporal boundary: April and May 1895, the dates of the trials and imprisonment of Oscar Wilde. Wilde's trial may be understood as the end of an era,[3] and in that sense the dates of the two poems may be said to have a particular cultural significance. I conclude with a discussion of Wilde's poetic response both to his own disgrace, and to Housman's poetry, *The Ballad of Reading Gaol* (1897).

The hypothesis which these examples will be used to test is one based on Foucault's view of unstable relationships between discursive strategies in the 'world of discourse'.[4] The fear of an ending aroused by the term *fin de siècle* is intimately related to notions of multiplicity: above all the fear that the anarchy of multiple interpretations will replace the safety of one view of the world. The events of 1895 were of crucial importance here. Wilde's downfall dramatized the conflict between those who were prepared to live at the margins, to live simultaneously several different versions of life, and those who wished to use the full ideological weight of church and state to enforce nineteenth-century sexual norms. It is part of the bizarre effects of this enforcement that it was for some preferable to have prostitutes dancing triumphantly outside, than to entertain inside the courtroom the thought that it might be acceptable for men to love each other.

In the trial, it was the discourse of poetry which provided the index of a 'criminal' sexuality. The poetry of Wilde and Housman may be seen as different but comparable models for the construction of masculinity in the run up to and aftermath of the events of April and May 1895. Both were trying to articulate same-sex love, the love that dare not speak its name, via the strategy of a poetic code. An example of how the classification of discourse was used in the proceedings is the way that a letter written by Wilde to Lord Alfred Douglas was used as one of the key pieces of evidence. The letter had been used in an attempt to blackmail Wilde by the renters patronized by himself and Douglas.

My Own Boy, Your sonnet is quite lovely, and it is a marvel that those red rose-leaf lips of yours should have been made no less for music of song than for madness of kisses. Your slim gilt soul walks between passion and poetry. I know Hyacinthus, whom Apollo loved so madly, was you in Greek days.

Wilde signed off, 'Always, with undying love, yours, Oscar'.[5] At the trial, Wilde described how this letter was open to more than one interpretation. Carelessly left in the pocket of an old suit of clothes by Douglas, it had been used to try to extort money from Wilde. The blackmailer, William Allen, had commented to Wilde that 'a very curious construction can be put on that letter'; but in his account of this affair at the first trial, Wilde told how he had replied that 'The letter, which is a prose poem, will shortly be published in sonnet form in a delightful magazine, and I will send you a copy of it.'[6] The response was a typical Wildean move. Allen clearly meant the letter could be constructed as evidence of criminal congress between Wilde and Douglas; at best it represented an example of linguistic effeminacy; at worst, it 'proved' homosexual activity. Wilde's response was intended to turn the tables on his interlocutor. Poetry, after all, is an art which encourages curious constructions to be put on it, and in terms of Wilde's own theories of art, that meant that the responsibility for meaning was finally to be located with the recipient rather than the originator: 'Those who find ugly meanings in beautiful places are corrupt without being charming. This is a fault.'[7] Here, it was the blackmailer/reader rather than the victim/writer who was at fault because in order to find the 'ugly meaning', he had to know such meanings are possible. Thus, the recognition of the ugly meaning points to the reader's – not the writer's – guilt.

In the context of the court proceedings, however, this attempted strategy of shifting the 'blame' was turned back against Wilde. As Ed Cohen has argued, the questions which Wilde was asked at the trial 'were not intended to elicit the explicitly sexual aspects of his interactions with the various men named in the plea. Instead, they sought to reiterate *the parallel between the sexual and the textual* by foregrounding precisely those aspects of Wilde's life that seemed to corroborate the "immorality" of his texts.'[8] For the court, the connection between signifier and signified was absolute; the very connection which Wilde had consistently sought to undermine in his works.[9]

Wilde was not, of course, only convicted on the basis of the letter. But its appearance at the trial is nonetheless significant, as is his defence of it to Allen that it was a poem. Part of Wilde's 'guilt' resided in the fact that he refused to take seriously the threat that a curious construction could be put on the letter. 'There is no use in trying to "rent" you', said another of the blackmailers, 'as you only laugh at us'.[10] More importantly, the letter represents the ways in which Wilde habitually broke down boundaries and called into question the certainties by which late nineteenth-century England wanted to live. The letter, which had been private property, had become public property; it was prose but it was also a poem. It walked, in its own words, the line 'between passion and poetry', the boundary between life and art, and as such was a fitting emblem of

Wilde's own position. It is therefore symptomatic of the breakdown of the certainties of the binary thought in which art is defined in terms of contemplation, and life, in direct opposition, is defined by action.[11] Life, in this formulation, is excluded from art by the policing of its margins, in what Derrida calls the 'discourse of the frame'.[12] A love-letter from one man to another is bad enough in 1895. Add to that Wilde's claim for its legitimacy – it is a work of art, a poem – and it is clear that the binary terminology is being subverted in order to validate, not one or other of the binary terms, the certainties, but the space between them.

The end of a century is symbolically a time in which certainties are under stress; the term 'an age of transition' when applied to the 1890s may be, as Helmut Gerber has argued,[13] inaccurate, but it is suggestive of the anxieties attendant upon the fear that known values will break down in the unknowable and imminent future. In the 1890s, this stress was further compounded by the fact that the categories in which certainty was defined were themselves transitional. Alison Hennegan has described for example, how the descriptions of gender, masculinity and femininity, had come to be defined in opposition to each other. Earlier in the century,

the opposite of 'manliness' was deemed to be 'childishness' and it was a man's adult qualities rather than his masculine ones which made him manly. By the end of the century, 'manliness' is constantly defined in opposition to 'womanliness': to be a 'real man' is to avoid the appalling stigma of effeminacy.[14]

She goes on to suggest that these new definitions were vulnerable precisely because they were new. In a matter of a generation, a form of behaviour which had once been acceptable, for example, the writing of passionate letters between same-sex friends, could now, as we have seen, provide evidence in a criminal prosecution. Only weak boundaries need to be policed, and Wilde's letter, harmless in itself so long as it remained private, in its publication at his trial exposed both the weakness of the boundary and the methods by which it was enforced.

The very description of the end of the nineteenth century as the *fin de siècle* articulates a fear of what lies beyond the end. There is no exactly equivalent term in English, and its enunciation in the French language linguistically implies a fear of some 'other', the unknown quantity of the future which opposes the comparative safety of the present. It is a fear which cannot be spoken in English. A century's ending may only be an ending in a psychological sense – the naming of centuries and years is, after all, arbitrary. Nonetheless, the anxiety about crossing the temporal boundary at the end of the nineteenth century was real enough. What Kermode has called 'the sense of an ending' often contains within it the fear that this might be *the* ending. In his ennui at a dinner party, Lord Henry Wootton murmurs '*fin de siècle*'; his hostess caps this remark with a more apocalyptic version: '*Fin du globe*'.[15]

This concern with limits and endings is a twentieth century one as well. Both Derrida and Foucault have concluded that limits, frames, boundaries and margins are, as it were, at the 'centre' of any analysis of the world. Derrida, by positing the 'discourse of the frame', makes the importance of the boundary explicit. The frame separates disparate spaces and defines them in opposition to each other. Without it, there can be no definition. And Foucault, in 'A Preface to Transgression', has argued that 'transgression is an action which involves the limit ...; it is likely that transgression has its entire space in the line that it crosses.'[16] At the same time, the tension between transgression and limit must not be seen as a simple binary opposition, related as 'black to white, the prohibited to the lawful, the outside to the inside ... Rather their relation takes the form of a spiral which no infraction can exhaust.' He develops the point further in *The History of Sexuality*:

We must not imagine a world of discourse divided between accepted discourse and excluded discourse, or between dominant discourse and the dominated one; but as a multiplicity of discursive elements that can come into play in various strategies ... There is not on one side a discourse of power, and opposite it, another discourse that runs counter to it ... There can exist different and even contradictory discourses within the same strategy.[17]

What Foucault does is to problematize the idea that clear distinctions between binary oppositions are possible. The line between the spoken and the unspeakable is not fixed, though we may like to pretend that it is.

* * *

How does a man write in such a way as to ensure that his audience is in no doubt about his 'manliness'? There is no precise formula, but the choices of form and matter, the how and the what in writing, and the context in which the writing takes place, provide some clues. They must be chosen in order to reflect the expected virtues of masculinity, now being defined not as adult qualities, but in opposition to femininity. Two examples from the 1880s show the distinction between the masculine and the effeminate mode. Allan Quatermain, the narrator of Rider Haggard's 1885 adventure story, *King Solomon's Mines*, has the following to say about style:

And now it only remains for me to offer my apologies for my blunt way of writing. I can only say in excuse for it that I am more accustomed to handle a rifle than a pen, and cannot make any pretence to the grand literary flights and flourishes which I see in novels – for I sometimes read novels. I suppose they – the flights and flourishes – are desirable, and I regret not being able to supply them; but at the same time I cannot help thinking that simple things are always most impressive, and books are easier to understand when they are written in plain language, though I have perhaps no right to set up an opinion on such a matter. 'A sharp spear', runs the Kukuana saying, 'needs no polish'; and so on the same principle I venture to hope that a true story, however strange it may be, does not require to be decked out in fine words.[18]

The admission that flights and flourishes might be desirable is made very grudgingly here by a man who only 'sometimes' reads novels, presumably because he is too busy having adventures and being active and virile to have the time or inclination to read them more often. He insists on the functionality of a language such as his own; it is efficient in the same way that a sharp spear is. If he writes clumsily, it is because he is a real man, whose sphere is action rather than contemplation – a man more used to the masculine pursuits of empire and rifles than to the sedentary ones of writing. The efficiency of his style more than makes up for its plainness: truth does not 'require to be decked out in fine words'. The analogy is clear. For this writer the pen is not mightier than the sword. As a reviewer of Wilde's early poems commented, the true test of manhood is in action, not in art.[19] Quatermain's language conforms to an unwritten code of acceptably masculine linguistic behaviour. He makes it clear that he would prefer to be the 'strong silent type'. He does not rely on language as his medium of expression; he uses violence instead.

The quality which most clearly defines masculine language practices therefore is the quality of restraint. And as Ed Cohen has also argued, restraint is also a class signifier, a virtue which belongs to the middle class.[20] The manly man 'talks straight', tells it only as it is, and is keen to produce an art which has no ostensible aesthetic purpose. He curtails 'flights and fancies' in the interests of efficiency. His linguistic restraint mirrors the other forms of restraint by which he might equally be expected to live his life. The control he exerts on his language is an index of his moral character. Cohen has also shown how Wilde's letter to Douglas was seen as being precisely such a marker.

The newspapers establish a homology between textual interpretation and characterological assessment. For as Wilde's words are subjected to rigorous scrutiny by both the prosecution and the defense, they form the basis for a slippage between textual meaning and authorial intention so that the imputations made against the latter (in the courtroom) will become (in the press) evidence against the latter. (p. 151)

It was not a practical letter – the newspapers reported Sir Edward Clarke's remark that it would seem extravagant to those who were more used to commercial correspondence.[21] It gave no information and exhorted no action. By those measures, it was purely phatic, but its very lack of ostensible purpose (and for Wilde, 'all art is essentially useless') is suggestive of the quality of the writer. Wilde may well have been right in his own terms to argue that the letter was art; but he forgot that his audience did not necessarily agree with his maxims on the concealment of the artist. The jury may very well have considered that the letter's linguistic exuberance evidenced the writer's lack of moral restraint.

In contrast, an effeminate use of language would be one which preferred the phatic to the functional. A George du Maurier cartoon in *Punch* (13 March 1880) shows an aesthetic art critic, Prigsby (Oscar Wilde in a *pince-nez*), in full flow at an exhibition, with an attentive audience of neo-pre-Raphaelite women along with an upright, top-hatted colonel. Prigsby comments:

The head of Alexis is distinctly divine! Nor can *I*, in the whole range of ancient, medieval, or modern art, recall anything quite so fair and precious; unless it be, perhaps, the head of that supremest masterpiece of Greek sculptchah [sic], the ILYSSUS, whereof indeed, in a certain gracious modelling of the lovely neck, and in the subtly delicate curves of the cheek and chin, it faintly, yet most exquisitely reminds me![22]

A second picture shows the bemused colonel contemplating the (of course) headless statue. The message is clear. A man whose words are so misformed, who uses too many emotional adjectives and adverbs, is using a language which has no substance. The contrast between Prigsby and the listening colonel, whose very career marks him out as the type of masculinity, immediately suggests the effeminacy of such a speaker.

*   *   *

In 1894, Oscar Wilde published in book form a poem which he had probably begun as early as 1874: the poem was illustrated by Charles Ricketts and dedicated 'To Marcel Schwob in Friendship and Admiration'. Its title was *The Sphynx*. Wilde was at this point reaching the height of his powers and his fame, and although the conception of the poem was twenty years old – the prentice work of a young student – he must nonetheless have believed that it was still relevant to his more mature aesthetic concerns.

The poem narrates the variety of moods and associations evoked by a statuette (or paperweight) in the mind of its impressionable student owner. The sphynx's perverse shape – a form which is *between* woman and beast – inspires a massive range of ideas; historical, geographical, philosophical and sensual. It permits the poetic persona to travel as far as possible from the exigencies of the here and now. It is a poem about contrasts and opposites, in which the persona's relative youth ('I have scarcely seen some twenty summers') is placed in opposition to the sphynx's ancient wisdoms and experience: 'A thousand weary centuries are thine.' His sensual proximity to this mythological creature will enable him to gain a privileged access to her past. Through her he will see the affairs of Antony and Cleopatra and of Venus and Adonis; he will see the flight of the Holy Family, and the love of Hadrian and Antinous. Touching her ('put your head upon my knee! / And let me stroke your throat') will put him in touch with the wealth of sexual experiences, both bizarre and perverse, which may have been hers:

> Did giant lizards come and crouch before you on the reedy banks?
> Did Gryphons with great metal flanks leap on you in your trampled couch?
> Did monstrous hippopotami come sidling towards you in the mist?
> Did gilt-scale dragons writhe and twist with passion as you passed them by?

These speculations continue to include lovers in more human and then in godly shapes, until he decides that the only worthy lover for her must have been Ammon, or the Libyan Jupiter.

The pleasure of speculation is eventually worn out. The poetic persona first finds himself subject to a decadent ennui, a weariness with the products of his own imagination. Then ennui becomes disgust and fear. The sphinx's major quality is her durability, but the poet becomes bored with her 'thousand weary centuries', and begins to seek closure through death. As far as he can remember, 'only one God has ever died. / Only one god has let His side be wounded by a soldier's spear.' He returns from the pagan to the Christian, and begs to be left to his crucifix.

The Sphynx is a poem about and of deferral. The arcane vocabulary defers the reader's extraction of meaning: the inordinately long, internally rhymed lines dramatize deferral, putting off closure. The poem enacts a contradiction – it shows the frenzy which the poet's imagination has engendered, whilst at the same time demonstrating that the frenzy cannot be resolved. There are no limits left to transgress. Whilst the form of the poem exemplifies excess (it overspills its meter), the content crosses boundaries of decency, to the extent that a pagan sensual experience becomes enmeshed with a spiritual one with the entrance of Christ into the poem. But Christ does not bring the release of satisfied desire since the poet only calls on him out of exhaustion. The arousal is never resolved; it can only, in this context, lead to increased arousal. As Regenia Gagnier suggests, *The Sphynx* 'is a textbook-complete catalogue ... of polymorphous perversity. The poem is a poem of excess in the sense that the object of desire is technically absent; the desire compulsively flows from the subject's brain.'[23] The absence of the object of desire means of course that the only outlet for that desire is linguistic. The poet only talks himself to a standstill, using words to replace the actions which they describe, and which he would like presumably to enact. Instead of having adventures like Allan Quatermain, the poet merely talks about them. And since language is his only outlet, and since the actions which he wants to perform are in a sense 'unspeakable' and excessive, then so too are the words in which he expresses himself. This language has nothing to do with efficiency of communication; in the substitution of words for deeds, the poem is insisting only on the pleasure of words, to which extent, the poem is, like the courtroom letter, phatic.

The poem however, unlike the letter and indeed much of Wilde's other literary work, did not form part of the evidence against him at his trials. On the other hand, it does share many of the features of the

texts which were used as evidence of his guilt. Like the letter, and like
Dorian Gray, it gives voice to actions which should be neither spoken
nor performed. And in a context in which, as Frank Mort has argued,
all sexual pleasure was referenced as '*sexual immorality*',[24] the 'love
that dares not speak its name' was the most immoral of possible
forms. Wilde did dare to speak the name of sexual pleasure, and got
away with it until the point where the word and the deed were
'proved' by a court of law to be intimately connected. Revenge was
exacted not only on his person, but also on his plays, which were
swiftly withdrawn from the theatres. The linguistic pleasure which he
took in his creations, and which he invited his audience to share, was
harmless whilst ever it was not understood. Whilst he could rely on
the ignorance of an audience who could not find 'ugly meanings in
beautiful things', the literature was more or less safe; the link
between sexual and textual significance could be ignored. But once
prove the relationship between the two and not only is the writer
implicated, but so is the reader. Reading Wilde meant that one had
shared his transgression of the limits of decency.

On 25 May 1895 Oscar Wilde was found guilty under 'the 11th
section of the Criminal Law Amendment Act [1885], and sentenced
to two years penal servitude'.[25] Wilde served his sentence, relieved
only by one or two special privileges (he was, for example, eventually
allowed to read and write in his cell) and by the visits of his very few
remaining friends, including the most faithful of them all, Robert
Ross. It is said that during these visits, Ross recited to Wilde some of
the poems from A. E. Housman's *A Shropshire Lad*, which had been
published in March 1896, and which Ross had learned by heart to
offer to his friend.[26] As visits were both rare and short, and closely
policed, Ross must have felt very strongly about these poems.

It is difficult to think of a greater contrast than that of the poetry
of Wilde and Housman. Where Wilde is verbose, pleasure-seeking,
list-making and adventurous in form and substance, Housman is
restrained, restricted, seemingly loyal to the landscape and the
Romantic poetic traditions of England. *A Shropshire Lad*, though not
an immediate success, received a range of favourable responses in the
press; the reviewer for *The Times*, 27 March 1896, commented that
Housman had struck 'a decidedly original note', and that he had a
gift for 'melodious expression'. R. P. Graves quotes at length the
review which apparently gave Housman the most pleasure, in which
Hubert Bland praised Housman's achievement of an 'essentially and

distinctively new poetry' where the 'individual voice rings out true and clear'. *A Shropshire Lad* represented the 'direct expression of elemental emotions, of heart-thoughts', and was only at fault inasmuch as the poems lacked 'gladness'.[27]

The beauty of the verse was, however, only one of Ross's likely motives for introducing it to Wilde. For the poems not only have a lyric beauty, but they also contain a strategy, which Ross may have hoped that Wilde would be able to use as well, for negotiating between the sincere expression of emotion and the public's sense of decorum. Thus, though Housman shares Wilde's fascination with youth and male beauty, his poems are so tightly controlled that any message is only just stated, and is never expanded. In *The Sphynx* Wilde had contrasted his own youth with the sphinx's wealth of experience, but his youth was not an index of his own innocence. His poem feels extravagant and exuberant. In utter contrast, Housman narrows the field. In the second of the collection's poems, he too claims to be only twenty: 'Now of my threescore years and ten, / Twenty will not come again.' But the urgency of the sense of time passing is not expressed by the need to have and to write many experiences; rather, Housman's persona only wants to have the same emotion over and over again:

> And take from seventy springs a score,
> It only leaves me fifty more.
>
> And since to look at things in bloom
> Fifty springs is little room,
> About the woodlands I will go,
> To seek the cherry hung with snow.

Housman limits his scope for emotion in a poetic form whose very vocabulary and structure is pared to the minimum. Where Wilde's lines spilled over in the excitement of what they were saying, Housman's are quite rigorously end-stopped by the strength of mostly monosyllabic rhymes. The effect is that of the seeming simplicity of verse written for children. It conveys an impression of innocence which is in complete opposition to Wilde's 'experience' and 'guilt'. The poem is also conceptually limited. The urgency of passing time is expressed in a vocabulary which is both small and 'ordinary'. It is rooted in the solidity of its woodland surroundings by the words which describe them: trees, cherry, bloom, bough and woodland. The second stanza does take us away from the wood into a more abstract concept of time, but the return to the landscape is immediate and complete, so that the first and last stanzas are virtually mirror-images of each other, where the poet returns to the 'cherry hung with snow' which in the first stanza had been the 'loveliest of trees ... Wearing white for Eastertide'.

The argument continues as to whether Housman was technically as guilty as Wilde under section 11 of the Criminal Law Amendment Act, but his 'emotional guilt' can scarcely be doubted. 'As everyone knows, Housman's thing had more to do with slaughtered soldiers, Shropshire rough trade and luxuriant misery' than with 'the heart of man', comments Francis Spufford. At Oxford he had met the athletic and brilliant Moses Jackson, 'who went off to become a rather ordinary married headmaster in India, while Housman spent the rest of his days carving "AEH 4 MJ" into every poetic tree-trunk he came across.'[28] Spufford is, of course, wrong. Not everybody knew. Some suspected and others, probably including Ross, guessed: not even Housman's homosexual brother, Laurence, was made the repository of a positive disclosure, though 'he would certainly have received a sympathetic hearing' in that quarter.[29] It was really only after Housman's death (in 1936) that his sexual preferences became widely 'known'.

What is clear from a reading of *A Shropshire Lad* is that even if Housman had stood trial as Wilde did, it is most unlikely that his poetry could ever have formed part of the evidence against him. As Neil Bartlett has pointed out, *The Oxford English Dictionary* defines love as being 'that feeling of attachment which is based upon difference of sex ... used specifically with reference to love between the sexes.' Bartlett wonders if the editor had known what he was doing 'when he cited a quotation from ... *A Shropshire Lad* as one of his authorities on the subject: "*Oh when I was in love with you, then was I clean and brave.*"'[30] It is a rhetorical question, but the answer must surely be 'no', given that the L-section was completed between 1901 and 1903, too soon after the Wilde trials for open sympathy with same-sex love to be expressed in a work which literally defined English(ness).

The keyword which defines Housman's poetry is restraint, and this may be one reason why his poetry would not have landed him in court. It never overtly transgresses any limits. The judge at Wilde's trials spoke of sexuality periphrastically ('the crime of which you stand convicted') and impersonally. He used the impersonal pronoun 'one' to represent his withdrawal from the arena of possible corruption. Housman's poetry shares that circumspection. Wilde, we might say, was convicted at least in part on a premise of his own making. If he argues, following Pater, that life reaches its highest achievement when it is lived as art, he should not have been surprised when his own art was used against him as evidence of his life. In crossing the boundary between separate spheres, he found that the interpretations of the one were the same as the interpretations of the other. Housman on the other hand, maintained what Christopher Ricks has called a *cordon sanitaire* between his poetry and the rest of his life.[31] In his lecture, 'The Name and Nature of Poetry', delivered towards the end of his life in 1933, Housman was very clear on the dangers involved in mixing up life with art: 'Experience has taught me, when I am shaving of a morning, to keep watch over my thoughts, because, if a line of poetry strays into my memory, my skin bristles so that the razor ceases to act.' He goes on to suggest that poetry 'goes through me like a spear'.[32] Mixing poetry with practicality for Housman seems to have involved endangering the physical wellbeing of his person. He therefore took the decision to police his own boundaries and to enact a radical separation of the different aspects of his life.

This decision does find its way into the poetry in that *A Shropshire Lad* is informed largely by a fear of emotional commitment. Love is consistently lost or sacrificed. The innocent enthusiasm of 'Loveliest of Trees' is repeatedly betrayed; only the love of nature is a love without risk – all other forms of attachment will be disappointed. There is, however, a price to be paid for the refusal to engage in life, and it is better to live a little than to die entirely without experience into the night where 'the bridegroom…never turns him to the bride'. The poems cannot decide whether the risk is worth it. And in poem XV the fear of involvement is explicitly the fear of same-sex love. The poem warns against love, but not the love of opposites, man and woman; the danger is to be found in the love of the same by the same, imaged as the love of one's own reflection:

> Look not in my eyes, for fear
> They mirror true the sight I see,
> And there you find your face too clear
> And love it and be lost like me.
> One the long nights through must lie
> Spent in star-defeated sights,

> But why should you as well as I
>   Perish? gaze not in my eyes.
> A Grecian lad, as I hear tell,
>   One that many loved in vain,
> Looked into a forest well
>   And never looked away again.
> There, when the turf in springtime flowers
>   With downward eye and gazes sad,
> Stands amid the glancing showers
>   A jonquil, not a Grecian lad.

For Housman there is always a choice between action and contemplation, between life and art. But whatever decision is taken, it is
not final or universal. Each solution is limited only to the context in
which it appears. Sometimes the speakers attempt to evade the choice
altogether, as in Poem xxx: 'Others, I am not the first, / Have willed
more mischief than they durst'; but this option is illusory since the
speaking subject is tortured even in the grave by the fire and ice
which represent the choice that he has not made:

> But from my grave, across my brow
> Plays no wind of healing now,
> And fire and ice within me fight
> Beneath the suffocating light.

At other times, it is the suicide's choice which is praised:

> Shot? so quick, so clean an ending?
>   Oh that was right, lad, that was brave:
> Yours was not an ill for mending,
>   'Twas best to take it to the grave.

The suicide has the speaker's envy for having made a decision which
is so final, and for having found a method for achieving utter
unconsciousness: 'Turn safe to rest, no dreams, no waking.' Another
variant is the choice of an unthinking life where unconsciousness is
achieved through camaraderie – 'jesting, dancing, drinking' (XLIX)
– favoured because it is thought which is dangerous to a man's
wellbeing: ''tis only thinking / Lays lads underground.'
   Housman shared with Wilde the theme of world-weariness.
Sometimes he spoke it directly, sometimes he dramatized it in poems
which evince a sympathetic identification with the alienated – the
enlisted soldier, the criminal, the betrayed lover and the suicide. He,
like Wilde, uses their alienation to speak of his own, but unlike Wilde,
this is a heavily coded message which does not immediately invite a

'curious construction' to be placed upon it. As Julia Kristeva has argued 'poetic language is a "double"' in which it is impossible to arrive at absolute definitions of the meaning of truth. Poetry is double in its division of the writing subject into a subject of enunciation and a subject of utterance, which may be rewritten as the 'real' source of the narrative – the writer – and its ostensible source within the text, the character constructed out of, or by, the writer to speak his or her words.[33] But there are degrees of doubleness, degrees of difficulty in sorting out the relationships between the real and the ostensible speakers of a poem's words. Housman's poems appear to invite only the simplest forms of poetic pleasure, those of familiar stanza forms, unpretentious rhythms and easy rhymes. A reader would have to work at being shocked or dazzled by *A Shropshire Lad* – unless, that is, (s)he was 'in the know' about the code which Housman was using. There is evidence of the collection's homoerotic content. There is the succession of young male speakers and more particularly, the prevalence of soldiers amongst them: and soldiers were well-documented as having semi-professional careers as prostitutes along-side their more 'manly' duties. The soldier is a particularly double image and represents the claims of both an acceptable and dominant code, and the subversive potential of counter-cultural voices.[34] For those with access to the code, the insistent reference to young male persons as 'lads' might have been evidence too: it emphasizes both maleness and youth, the twin reference points of the homoerotic. (Wilde's equivalent term was 'boy', as it is used in the letter to Douglas, and on which the prosecution commented unfavourably at his trial.[35]) Housman's insistent combination of pleasure for the moment with his overwhelming sense of the possibly fatal conse-quences of pleasurable actions is another indicator. (The majority of the poems were, after all, written in the first five months of 1895, including the period of the Wilde trials: 'From Wenlock Edge he could see as far as Reading Gaol', wrote Desmond MacCarthy.[36]) But Housman's poetry allows all these things to be read 'straight'; it invites the readings acceptable to dominant cultures at least as much as it invites counter-cultural readings. And in the context of the immediate aftermath of the Wilde trials, it would have been a brave reviewer indeed who would insist on the doubleness of possible readings of *A Shropshire Lad*. To do so would be to admit that the reader had himself access to the code, knew how to speak 'the love that dare not speak its name'. Housman had found a way of not calling a spade a spade, whilst still leaving sufficient clues for the initiated to follow his alternative meanings.

On his release, Wilde received evidence that Housman had at least sympathized with his plight when he received from the author a copy of *A Shropshire Lad*. The gift was gratefully received by Wilde who wrote to Laurence Housman (on 9 August 1897) that 'I have lately been reading your brother's lovely lyrical poems'; and in a slightly later letter he continued to praise Housman's 'light lyrical beauty ... and delicate felicity of mood and music'. He went on to announce to Laurence his own latest literary project:

> with regard to what you ask me about myself – well, I am occupied in finishing a poem, terribly realistic for me, and drawn from actual experience, a sort of denial of my own philosophy of art in many ways. I hope it is good, but every night I hear cocks crowing in Berneval, so I am afraid I have denied myself, and would weep bitterly, if I had not wept away all my tears. I will send it to you, if you allow me, when it appears.[37]

The poem to which Wilde refers was *The Ballad of Reading Gaol*, his last literary production, published in February, 1898.

Wilde hoped that his ballad would go some way towards rehabilitating his reputation both as an artist and as a man. He wanted to show that the years in prison had not destroyed him. And in these aims, the poem was not successful. He was not able to throw off public opprobrium for his crimes, knew that he would never be able to walk the streets of England again, and even the volume's relative financial success was not enough to remake the man. It was first published under the pseudonym C.3.3. (his prison number), and his own name was not appended to it until its success was absolutely assured, for the seventh printing of June 1899.

The reviews were generally favourable though many found things to blame in the poem. Reviewers noted the range of influences on *The Ballad*, including Thomas Hood's 'The Dream of Eugene Aram, the Murderer', Kipling's *Barrack Room Ballads* and Coleridge's 'Rime of the Ancient Mariner'. In 1916, Wilde's notorious friend and eventual (unreliable) biographer, Frank Harris, added Housman's *A Shropshire Lad* to the list of sources.[38] Harris's grounds for the assertion, apart from the fact that he knew Wilde had at least read the other man's poems, was the similarity between *A Shropshire Lad* IX, 'On moonlit heath and lonesome bank' and *The Ballad*. Housman's poem tells of the feeling of an outside observer on the night before the hanging of a young man:

> They hang us now in Shrewsbury jail:
> And whistles blow forlorn,
> And trains all night groan on the rail
> To men that die at morn.
>
> There sleeps in Shrewsbury jail to-night,
> Or wakes, as may betide,
> A better lad, if things went right,
> Than most that sleep outside.

Like Wilde's poem, Housman's implicitly connects the guilt of the condemned man to the guilt of mankind as a whole. The injustice of killing one man for a crime which, metaphorically or literally, everyone commits, is at the heart of Wilde's *Ballad*:

> For each man kills the thing he loves,
> By each let this be heard,
> Some do it with a bitter look,
> Some with a flattering word,
> The coward does it with a kiss,
> The brave man with a sword!

The guilt of the particular case is symptomatic of a general guilt. Housman, too, feels the force of the connection between the condemned and the free: 'They hang us now in Shrewsbury jail.' And both poems dwell on the horror of execution to demonstrate that this fate is escaped more by luck than good judgement:

> And naked to the hangman's noose
> The morning clocks will ring
> A neck God made for other use
> Than strangling on a string.
>
> And sharp the link of life will snap,
> And dead on air will stand
> Heels that held up as straight a chap
> As treads upon the land.

The comparison between these lines and Wilde's needs little comment:

> It is sweet to dance to violins
> When Love and Life are fair:
> To dance to flutes, to dance to lutes
> Is delicate and fair:
> But it is not sweet with nimble feet
> To dance upon the air!

Wilde also dwells on the 'swollen purple throat, / And stark and staring eyes' three times over in the poem.

Nonetheless, Wilde is not entirely successful in his adoption of Housman's poetic technique; he finds it impossible to capture the other man's restraint in his own poem. Housman is never 'guilty' of what Arthur Symons called Wilde's 'poetic diction'[39] (for example, the flutes and lutes quoted above), and he does not use the kinds of rhetorical effects on which *The Ballad* is predicated. So, for instance, Housman leaves unstated any precise description of what his condemned man has left behind – to him such a commentary would be superfluous. The world outside the jail, the pastoral landscape where 'the careless shepherd once would keep / The flocks by moonlight' is simultaneously an evocation of innocence and a grim metaphor for hanging: 'Hanging in chains was called keeping sheep by moonlight' was Housman's own note to the poem. The associations of the shepherd, the innocent victim conflated with the caring keeper, need no elaboration in this aesthetic.

For Wilde in contrast, there is a need to express, albeit in negative terms, precisely what has been sacrificed. The rhetorical repeated refrains of the poem refer us both to the general and the particular cases. What the soldier 'did not' do ('he did not wear his scarlet coat') is linked to what 'does not' happen to the rest of mankind, despite the universality of guilt: though each man kills the thing he loves, 'Yet each man does not die.'

> He does not die a death of shame
>   On a day of dark disgrace,
> Nor have a noose about his neck,
>   Nor a cloth upon his face,
> Nor drop feet foremost through the floor
>   Into an empty space.

The repeated negatives emphasize the contrast between the expectations of innocent and guilty men. Where the prisoner's horizons have been limited to 'the little tent of blue', those of the free man are unbounded; where the condemned man waits only for the macabre simplicity of death as expressed in the above stanza (dramatized in the quietly violent monosyllabic language), the free man has unlimited possibilities. By dwelling on the brutality of one life and death, Wilde points the contrast between this and the pleasures available to other equally guilty men.

Housman wants only to *recognize* his fellowship with the man in Shrewsbury jail. For him, the link between innocent and guilty is limited to the single pronoun 'us'. Wilde, on the other hand wants to explore his own paradoxical relationship with the condemned soldier. He recognizes that he shares guilt ('for each man kills the thing he loves'), but feels at the same time alienated from it, and it is this loss of certainty, the opposition between innocence and guilt, that he wants his readers to share:

> And I and all the other souls in pain
> Who tramped the other ring,
> Forgot if we ourselves had done
> A great or little thing,
> And watched with dull amaze
> The man who had to swing.
>
> And strange it was to see him pass
> With a step so light and gay,
> And strange it was to see him look
> So wistfully at the day,
> And strange it was to think that he
> Had such a debt to pay.

Face to face with both the opposition and with the figure of a man in utter jeopardy, the poetic persona becomes unimportant even to himself. His own experience of the world is made strange, or is forgotten entirely.

To some extent, of course, *The Ballad* is both a betrayal and a failure, in that for the first time in his professional writing career, Wilde wrote a poem with an explicit social purpose as well as an aesthetic one. As Arthur Symons commented, it was 'a plea on behalf of prison reform, and so far as it is written with that aim, it is not art'.[40] The subject of enunciation – the real man who had experienced appalling prison conditions – is no longer seamlessly conflated with the subject of utterance, the construction of a poetic persona. Consequently, the poem is not 'art' since it does not aim to be 'essentially useless', phatic as his earlier work had been. It aims to persuade its audience that the prison system is brutal, that the audience is itself implicated in that brutality, and that things ought to change:

> For they starve the little frightened child
> Till it weeps both night and day:
> And they scourge the weak, and flog the fool
> And gibe the old and grey,
> And some grow mad, and all grow bad,
> And none a word may say.

That last line refers firstly to a prison regulation which literally imposed silence on the inmates, but it also refers to the project of the poem itself, in which Wilde tries to speak the unspeakable, using his articulate art to attack a *status quo* where 'none a word may say'.

Housman, on the other hand, had a personality which, says Bevis Hillier, was 'half-military, half academic' and he accepted the constraints of silence. Discussing his diary entries on the subject of Moses Jackson, another commentator says: 'Poignant, indeed they are; but it is the poignancy of iron reticence; everything has to be read between the lines.'[41] Housman's poetry represents an arena where public perceptions of masculinity meet poetry; where the stiff upper lip comes into quiet contact with the emotions which it is supposed to conceal. The poetry both speaks and restrains the emotions, speaks 'quietly'. Wilde never learned this art of understatement. Despite Housman's lesson, *The Ballad of Reading Gaol* has a certain stridency and lack of reserve, and even the friendly critics felt that it said too much. 'From 109 stanzas', wrote one reviewer, 'we should like to remove some fifty', and when Yeats included it in the *Oxford Book of Modern Verse*, he did cut it.[42] Nobody ever accused Wilde of an iron reticence, and his last poem does not reassert the values of the masculine world of cause and effect, which is, after all, the world which also builds and maintains prisons to prove its commitment to a certain view of the world.

Wilde hoped (and feared) that his poem had 'out-Kiplinged Henley' (the nationalistic editor of *Blackwoods Magazine*), meaning that it would present the brutal realities of the masculine world for criticism. At least one critic believed that he had utterly failed in this aim:

The most remarkable poem that has appeared this year is, of course, *The Ballad of Reading Gaol*. It has been much written about, but no-one has commented ... on the curious parallel between it and Mr. Kipling's 'Danny Deever', the grim lyric which stands first in Barrack Room Ballads. The difference is just this: 'Danny Deever' – ugly, if you like, but a real poem – is a conspicuously manly piece of work; *The Ballad of Reading Gaol*, with all its feverish energy is unmanly. The central emotion is the physical horror of death, when death comes, not as a relief or in a whirl of excitement, but as an abrupt shock to be dreaded. That the emotion is genuine admits of no doubt; but it is one very fit to be concealed.[43]

Housman's poetic version of masculinity has often been dismissed as adolescent. George Orwell comments on his 'unvarying sexual pessimism (the girl always dies or marries someone else) [which] seemed like wisdom to boys who were herded together in public schools and were half-inclined to think of women as something unattainable. Whether Housman ever had the same appeal for girls I rather doubt.'[44] It is, however, possible to read sexual pessimism as a form of restraint so that the passions in general, and the homoerotic in particular, are held inside boundaries both metrically and emotionally; there is no possibility of its expression becoming a threat to either the poet or the man. The boundaries are held in place, finally unquestioned and unthreatened, and there is no need for external policing. The sympathies evinced by Housman's poetry for the outcast are left as generalized expressions of sympathy for the world at large. Wilde in contrast makes his sympathies explicit and local. His outcast has a past, an identifiable existence and his poetic alignment is therefore not only based on a principle of brotherhood or connection between all men; it is localized and permits a reading based on a personal commitment to a specific person. Moreover, linguistically speaking *The Ballad* maintains a language which is unconnected with action. Its 'poetic diction' and its length are not indicative of a lesson learned in restraint. In the discourse of the frame, Wilde is excluded geographically (he never returned to England), socially, financially, and, in 1897 at least, culturally. His persona was *non grata* to the extent that even his identity was excised from the poem's title page. The margins literally were policed in Wilde's case to the point where there was no space for him to create any curious construction of masculinity.

NOTES

1 References to Oscar Wilde's poetry are taken from *The Poems of Oscar Wilde*, in *The First Collected Edition of the Works of Oscar Wilde, 1908–1922*, ed. Robert Ross (London: Methuen and Co., 1908; and London: Dawsons of Pall Mall, 1969). References to A. E. Housman's poetry are taken from *A. E. Housman, Collected Poems and Selected Prose*, ed. Christopher Ricks (Harmondsworth: Penguin, 1988).

2 Michel Foucault, *The History of Sexuality*, vol. 1, tr. Robert Hurley (Harmondsworth: Penguin, 1979), p. 100.

3 See the introduction to *Fin de Siècle/Fin du Globe: Fears and Fantasies of the Late Nineteenth Century*, ed. John Stokes (Macmillan: Basingstoke, 1992), p. 1, and John Stokes, *In the Nineties* (Hemel Hempstead: Harvester Wheatsheaf, 1989).

4 Foucault, *The History of Sexuality*, p. 100.

5 *The Selected Letters of Oscar Wilde*, ed. Rupert Hart-Davis (Oxford and New York: Oxford University Press, 1979), p. 107.

6 Richard Ellmann, *Oscar Wilde* (Harmondsworth: Penguin, 1988), pp. 419–20.

7 Oscar Wilde, Preface to *The Picture of Dorian Gray* (1891), ed. Peter Ackroyd (Harmondsworth: Penguin, 1985), p. 21.

8 Ed Cohen, *Talk on the Wilde Side* (London and New York: Routledge, 1993), pp. 165–6. (My emphasis.)

9 For example, one of the jokes at the centre of *The Importance of Being Earnest* is that lies and truth are not necessarily different from each other. Jack Worthing discovers that he has unwittingly been telling the truth all his life, but as he has had no intention of doing so, he cannot strictly speaking be described as truthful.

10 Ellmann, *Oscar Wilde*, p. 420.

11 Lynda Nead, in her book *The Female Nude, Art, Obscenity and Sexuality* (London and New York: Routledge, 1992), quotes the art critic Kenneth Clark to this effect. For him the distinction between pornography and art is that art is neither predicated on, nor invokes action; it is purely contemplative. (See p. 27.)

12 Jacques Derrida, *Truth in Painting*, tr. Geoff Bennington and Ian MacCleod (Chicago and London: Chicago UP, 1987), p. 45.

13 Helmut Gerber, 'The Nineties: Beginning, End or Transition?', in *Edwardians and Late Victorians*, ed. Richard Ellmann (Columbia University Press, 1960), pp. 50–79.

14 Alison Hennegan, 'Personalities and Principles: Aspects of Life and Literature in *Fin-de-Siècle* England', in *Fin de Siècle and its Legacy*, eds. Mikulas Teich and Roy Porter (Cambridge: Cambridge University Press, 1990), pp. 190–1.

15 Wilde, *Dorian Gray*, p. 214.

16 Michel Foucault, 'A Preface to Transgression', in *Language, Counter-Memory, Practice: Selected Essays and Interviews*, ed. Donald F. Bouchard, tr. Donald F. Bouchard and Sherry Simon (Oxford: Basil Blackwell, 1977).

17 Michel Foucault, *The History of Sexuality*, pp. 100–101.

18 H. Rider Haggard, *King Solomon's Mines* (London: Longman, Green and Co., 1885).

19 Thomas Wentworth Higginson, 'Unmanly Manhood', *Women's Journal* (Boston) (February 1882), quoted in Karl Beckson ed. *Oscar Wilde: The Critical Heritage* (London and New York: Oxford University Press, 1970), p. 51.

20 Cohen, *Talk on the Wilde Side*, p. 30.

21 *Ibid.*, p. 152.

22 *Punch*, 13 March, 1880.

23 Regenia Gagnier, *Idylls of the Marketplace: Oscar Wilde and the Victorian Public* (Stanford: Stanford University Press, 1986), p. 45.

24 Frank Mort, *Dangerous Sexualities: Medico-Moral Politics in England since 1830* (London and New York: Routledge, 1987), p. 37.

25 Holbrook Jackson, *The Eighteen Nineties* (1913) (London: The Cresset Library, 1988), pp. 95–6. Eighteen years or so after the event, Jackson seems to have accounted it prudent not to name in so many words what Wilde had done.

26 See Richard Perceval Graves, *A. E. Housman, The Scholar-Poet* (Oxford: Oxford University Press, 1981), p. 113; and John Stokes, *In the Nineties* (New York and London: Harvester Wheatsheaf, 1989), p. 109.

27 Graves, *A. E. Housman, The Scholar-Poet*, pp. 112–13.

28 Francis Spufford, 'Those ruthless rhymes and rotten lads', review of Housman's poems by John Bayley, *The Guardian*, 6 July 1992, p. 25.

29 Norman Page, *A. E. Housman, A Critical Biography* (Basingstoke: Macmillan, 1983), p. 2.

30 Neil Bartlett, *Who Was That Man? A Present for Mr Oscar Wilde*, (London: Serpent's Tail, 1988), p. 76.

31 Ricks, *Introduction to Housman's Collected Poems and Selected Prose*, p. 7.

32 'The Name and Nature of Poetry' in Ricks, *Introduction to Housman's Collected Poems and Selected Prose*, pp. 369–70.

33 Julia Kristeva, *The Kristeva Reader*, ed. Toril Moi (Oxford: Oxford University Press, 1986), p. 40.

34 Graves quotes Marcel Proust on the subject: 'A homosexual is not a man who loves homosexuals, but merely a man who, seeing a soldier immediately wants to have him for a friend.' (*A. E. Housman, The Scholar-Poet*, p. 108.) This is quite apart from the semi-professional prostitute status which at least one soldier (Charles Parker) in the Wilde trial appeared to hold (see Ellmann, *Oscar Wilde*, p. 447.) See also Steven Marcus, *The Other Victorians, a Study of Pornography and Sexuality in Mid-Nineteenth Century England* (London: Corgi Books, 1969).

35 Cohen, *Talk on the Wilde Side*, p. 203.

36 Quoted in Page, *A. E. Housman, A Critical Biography*, p. 3.

37 *More Letters of Oscar Wilde*, ed. Rupert Hart-Davis (Oxford: Oxford University Press, 1987), pp. 152–3.

38 Frank Harris, *Oscar Wilde* (1916) (New York: Dorset Press, 1989), pp. 227 ff.

39 Review of *The Ballad of Reading Gaol*, in Beckson, *Oscar Wilde: The Critical Heritage*, p. 219.

40 Beckson, *Oscar Wilde: The Critical Heritage*, p. 219.

41 Both remarks are quoted in Bevis Hillier, 'New Found Papers throw a Light on Two Literary Giants', *The Times*, 17 June 1968, p. 8.

42 Stokes, *In the Nineties*, p. 109.

43 Beckson, *Oscar Wilde: The Critical Heritage*, pp. 221–2.

44 George Orwell, *Inside the Whale and Other Essays* (Harmondsworth: Penguin, 1957), p. 23.

CHAPTER 8

The Pilgrims of Hope: *William Morris and the dialectic of romanticism*

Anne Janowitz

This chapter makes a place for William Morris's striking verse narrative sequence, *The Pilgrims of Hope*, at the latter end of the nineteenth-century dialectic of romanticism.[1] The thirteen poems which make up *The Pilgrims of Hope* trace out the complex emotional designs discernible within political, sexual, and comradely entanglements in the setting of the British socialist and labour movement and the Paris Commune of 1871, setting against one another the individualist claims of feeling and the collective ones of social change. By commemorating a recent historical event and invoking it as an aspiration as well as a memory, Morris's poem (serialized between 1885 and 1886 in the Socialist League journal, *Commonweal*), offers a 'glimpse of the coming day' made visible through the power of 'hope' – a category of practical value for Morris and one capable of redeeming the past in a revolutionary future. In this way, Morris appropriates the romance genre for contemporary use: 'I have heard people mis-called for being a romantic' he wrote, 'but what romance means is the capacity for a true conception of history, a power of making the past part of the present.'[2]

The Pilgrims of Hope interweaves a personal dialectic of identity and a public one of history. The hero and heroine, Richard and his wife, move from the agricultural plebeian culture of the countryside to an artisanal life in London, where they become socialists. Though Richard is appalled by the poverty and exploitation that he finds in the 'grim net of London' (II), he does not create a false memory of the rural life left behind, for 'enough and to spare had I seen / Of hard and pinching want midst our quiet fields and green' (III). The contrast he makes is between the capitalism that pervades both city and country and a socialist alternative, not a nostalgic contrast between city and country. At an open-air propaganda meeting, Richard gets into a scuffle with a heckler, and ends up in prison. He is then taken up by Arthur, an activist from a bourgeois background, and while the two men develop a good political relationship, Arthur falls in love with Richard's wife. This precipitates a crisis amongst the three of them, setting at odds the claims of their personal and their political lives.[3] Narratively, the crisis is resolved by the three going off to participate in the Paris Commune, where Arthur and Richard's wife are both killed. Richard then returns to England to raise his son and organize for the socialist future. Though he settles in the countryside of his youth, the gap that has opened between Richard and his past life makes him more aware of himself as a self cut adrift from that world: 'Strange are they grown unto me; yea I to myself am strange' (VIII). But his experience has made him more aware of himself as potentially powerful within the activity of a collective, which is now decisively linked to the city. For it is in the city, in Paris, that Richard sees, albeit briefly, the materialization of his socialist yearning: 'Such joy and peace and pleasure!' In the Paris Commune Richard sees 'what few have beheld, a folk with all hearts gay ... / I say that I saw it now, real solid, and at hand' (XI). In these lines we hear a late nineteenth-century romantic voice answer Wordsworth's recollection of 1791, when he too sought in French revolutionary possibility a place for a grounded transformation of the world, 'Not in Utopia ... / But in the very world which is the world / Of all of us, the place in which, in the end, / We find our happiness or not at all.'[4]

To stake a revolutionary claim for the specifically romantic aspect of Morris's socialism, is to follow in the path set out by E. P. Thompson in 1955 in *William Morris: Romantic to Revolutionary*.[5] In the two editions of that biography, Thompson offered readings of nineteenth-century romanticism which aimed to recover within it a revolutionary tradition consistent with revolutionary practice.[6] Thompson's history of romanticism begins with the movement as 'a passionate protest against an intolerable social reality', which atrophies during the course of the century into 'little more than a yearning nostalgia or a sweet complaint'.[7]

Thompson argued strongly in his 1976 revision of the work that if the original indigenous tradition of revolutionary 'desire' had been listened to by British Marxists, the crisis-ridden history of 'scientific' English Marxism might have had quite a different outcome. But whether in his earlier discussion, in which Morris moves from being a romantic to being a revolutionary, or in the revised version, in which Morris's romanticism is understood as a significant gesture towards an English Marxism that 'failed to reciprocate' (p. 786), unquestionably the terms of the discussion of revolution and romanticism generally, and particularly the case of William Morris, were set by Thompson in the 1950s and came to be taken as assumptions by the 1980s.[8] In the revised version of the biography, Thompson specifies Keats as the chief poetic influence on Morris's own 'youthful revolt'. Thompson views Keats's late romantic achievement as 'the acute tension between the richness of the life of the senses and the imagination and the poverty of everyday experience' and applauds 'Keats's struggle to reconcile the two'. The Victorian appropriation of the medieval romance, via Keats, as a template for mid-century romanticism expressed the mid-century revolt against the industrial age.[9] However, this revolt, much enervated from Wordsworth's and Coleridge's first burst of Jacobin romanticism, as well as from the republican internationalism of the second generation romantics, Byron and Shelley, resulted in the aestheticization of the central poetic movement of the century.

Thompson's argument is developed in a sequential logic. Whereby Keats comes after Shelley, inward-turning comes after social engagement: 'Art was no longer conceived, as by Shelley, as an agent in man's struggle to master nature and discover himself. Art (if we set aside a lingering faith in its refining moral influence) was conceived as a compensation for the poverty of life.'[10] Morris enters the scene as a defender and builder of the medieval revolt and is then, through his engagement with the socialist movement, himself transmuted: 'Morris, the Romantic in revolt, became a realist and a revolutionary.'[11] But as John Goode has pointed out in 'E. P. Thompson and the Significance of Literature', Thompson's 1976 revision of the Morris biography included a reduction in his analysis of romanticism; most importantly, the excision of the extended discussion of Shelley.[12] The authority for this deletion is Thompson's remark that 'while in the 1880s Morris was to carry forward all that was most positive in the Republican and internationalist traditions of Byron and Shelley, in the 1850s these seem to have exercised only a passing influence on his conscious mind.'[13] This 1880s return to the 'positive' presents something of a problem for Thompson, since although he organizes his biography around the vindication of the romantic lineage for an understanding of the genius and contribution of Morris's work, he does not actually think that Morris's explicitly socialist verse is very good, preferring to focus on the importance of *A*

Dream of John Ball and *News From Nowhere* as the significant productions of this later period of Morris's work.

For Thompson the deficiency of the 1880s poems is precisely how much they 'rely upon words, images, rhythms coined in the romantic movement' and therefore 'cannot be said to lay the foundations of a poetry of "revolutionary realism"'.[14] Thus, even though he admires Morris's political ambitions and local motives in *The Pilgrims of Hope*, Thompson observes that it is marked by 'weakness in construction [and] technical slackness bred of haste and lack of concentration'.[15]

In this assessment, Thompson participates in a fairly long tradition of criticism of *The Pilgrims of Hope*, which begins with a letter from Morris himself to his daughter Jenny. On 29 October 1886, he wrote to her that 'It would be rather convenient for me to have a little gout in order to do some literary work. I am going to start getting my pilgrims of Hope in order, so as to make a book of it: *I shall add and alter a good deal though.*'[16] In his 1897 account of Morris's books, H. Buxton-Forman writes that he was not able to persuade Morris to undertake his own edition of the poem: '[Morris] considered it wanted more revision than he could give it at the time'.[17] So it was Buxton-Forman himself who collected and reprinted the text of the thirteen episodes which had originally appeared between March 1885 and July 1886 in *Commonweal*. In 1899, in the first major biography of Morris, J. W. Mackail wrote that a few of the sections of the poem would 'stand high among [Morris's] finest work', but that 'the narrative of which they form parts has much of the same weakness and unreality as his prose novel of fifteen years earlier'.[18] More recently, the editor of Morris's letters, Norman Kelvin, has argued that in *The Pilgrims of Hope*, Morris 'failed to create in poetry a language that would describe, express, and idealize – transform into an epic of modern time – a social-political event that had captured his imagination', and therefore Kelvin has 'ranked it decidedly below his earlier major poems'.[19] Even in one of the very few extended discussions of the poem, Michael Holzman writes from the assumption that the poem is a failure: 'We can also account for its failure as a work of art, a failure of the form to contain the conflict between the topical subject matter of the poem and the personal emotions that flowed into it when Morris began to write about the period around 1870.'[20]

There is, however, another tradition of appreciation of the poem; one which precisely does attribute to it the virtue of that 'rev-

olutionary realism' which Thompson invokes. In 1897, describing
the socialist materials written and printed between 1878 and 1890,
Buxton-Forman notices first the pamphlets and Morris's activist
songs, the *Chants for Socialists*, and goes on:

> but a far higher effort than these is the poem of modern life called *The
> Pilgrims of Hope*, which lies buried in the first two volumes of *Commonweal*...
> Although this was privately reprinted [by Buxton-Forman], the poet has
> kept it by him to render it more perfect in form; but whether he has left any
> revision or not, the poem will ultimately rank among his leading works, and
> is likely to remain, for another generation of English readers, the most
> remarkable thing in the distinctly militant literature of the Socialist
> movement among us.[21]

It was Morris's friend and comrade, Bruce Glasier, a leader of the
Socialist League in Scotland and a resolute believer in the political
efficacy of poetry, who was the first to devote full critical attention to
the text, calling *The Pilgrims of Hope* a 'proletarian epic'. Glasier
argued: 'Of all his poetical writings [*The Pilgrims of Hope*] is the most
objective or realistic, and it might be said to be of all modern poems
the most modern in ethical feeling.'[22] The most significant recent
reading of the poem, Florence Boos's 'Narrative Design in *The
Pilgrims of Hope*', has begun the recovery of the poem by showing its
interweaving of internal and external problems: '[the] balance of
interior vision and historical reality provides evidence that struggle
and resistance within these cycles may yet achieve some of our
deepest human purposes.'[23] Boos makes the case that an apparent
lack of integration between the private and public themes of the
poem in fact respects the complexity of Morris's understanding of
revolutionary struggle and personal identity.

Glasier's point was to establish the poem within the realist, not the
romantic, modality, and in its evocation of the conflicts between
personal and political commitments, it does indeed in part belong to
the traditions of English realism. Furthermore, as a poetic undertaking within realism, it has affinities with, though it also constitutes
a riposte to, George Meredith's 1862 *Modern Love*. When Richard, the
protagonist of *The Pilgrims of Hope*, realizes that his wife and Arthur
have fallen in love, he visualizes 'the sharp and bitter pain / As the
sword 'twixt the lovers bewildered in the fruitless marriage' (x).
We feel that we are very close here to Meredith's image, in *Modern
Love*, of the loveless married couple lying together like medieval
effigies, wishing for the 'sword that severs all'.[24]

But though *The Pilgrims of Hope* belongs to and investigates what Glasier calls 'the deeper moral vicissitudes of modern human existence', it does so within a framework which suggests larger and more social sources and solutions to existential problems.[25] The deep pessimism of Meredith's sonnet sequence is assuaged in *The Pilgrims of Hope* by Morris's appeal to a social good, and the possibilities of a socially redemptive 'hope'. The poem is not sacrificial or transcendent; rather it suggests an alternative understanding of love relations within a larger network of social relations. It is because of their revolutionary commitment that, unlike the estranged couple in Meredith's sonnet sequence, the feeling which wraps together Richard and his wife 'was not wrath or reproaching, or the chill of love-born hate' (x).

Here we can return to the issue of romanticism, because it is through the romantic traditions which the poem draws upon that it is able to suggest the non-transcendent, social solution to the problems it poses. If this sounds paradoxical, it is because the aspect within romanticism that Morris is most indebted to here is what we can call the *communitarian, interventionist* strain, whose genealogy moves through first and second generation romantics, into the interventionist poetic of the Chartist movement, and on to the poetic within the revival of socialism in the 1880s and 1890s. Its history, however, has been obscured by the triumph of romanticism's other, individualist, aesthetic strain.

Thompson's complaint that in returning to Shelley's 'Ode to the West Wind' in 'The Message of the March Wind', the opening poem of *The Pilgrims of Hope*, Morris was trying to recover an outmoded poetic is not adequate to the aspect of the tradition of which Morris was a part. The debt to Shelley is not antiquarian, but vital: it demonstrates the continuity of a communitarian, romantic poetic, which in the hands of the late nineteenth-century socialist movement, no longer presents itself as a complaint against industrialism or a nostalgia for the past, but as a strategy for a material, not a transcendent future. Furthermore, the rurality which Morris evokes belongs less to what Thompson calls an 'idealized pastoral scene', than to the vernacular agrarian, the tradition of popular 'agrarianism', that early nineteenth-century working-class and artisanal tradition, whose sources can be located in Thomas Spence and whose heritage can be followed in part through Shelley himself into not only the Chartist Land Plan later in the century, but the 'back to the land'

movements of both the *fin de siècle* and the 1960s.[26] Morris himself
thought very highly of the poem: he wrote to Jane Morris that it was
'not bad I think'; two weeks later he called it 'the best short poem I
have written'.[27]

In addition to Shelley's influence, we also find in Morris's socialist
poetry evidence of the even earlier revolutionary romanticism of
Blake. In 'The Bridge and the Street', the second poem in *The
Pilgrims of Hope*, the city portrayed is Blake's London, with the
trammelled and 'charter'd' river running through it as the sign of
both constraint and possibility: 'On each side lay the City, and
Thames ran between it / Dark, struggling, unheard 'neath the wheels
and the feet' (II). The war machine which the bourgeoisie has
outfitted to destroy the barricades of the Paris Commune is a
machine of those 'wheels within wheels' of Blake's fallen Jerusalem
when she is called London. And the bitter speech of Richard when he
is released from prison reverberates against Enion's lament at the end
of the second 'night' of Blake's *The Four Zoas*, where 'wisdom' can be
bought only 'in the desolate marketplace', and 'experience' with the
price 'Of all that a man hath.'[28]

Blake's righteous indignation leads the poet to attempt to intervene
in the world, and not only represent it. In his commitment to an
interventionist poetic, Morris learns from Blake and as well, from the
Chartist-communitarian reading of romanticism, which drew upon
the romantic poets to theorize the centrality of poetry to making
social and political change.

The dialectic of romanticism is, in other words, characterized
throughout its history by a *double trajectory*. Rather than observing
organic rules of growth and decay, according to which model the
revolutionary impulse within romanticism blossoms and then deteri-
orates, in truth romanticism proposes radically distinct paths at the
same historical moments. In places romanticism offers what we have
come to call the aesthetic ideology, a poetic of transcendence, solitude
and privacy, that is often associated with an explicit separating out of
poetical from political intentions in the decades at the end of the
eighteenth and the opening of the nineteenth centuries. Wordsworth's 'Tintern Abbey' breathes freely in the countryside, providing
an aesthetic location within which to cultivate an individual private
poetic of transcendence; later versions of this carry into the
aestheticism of the Victorian poetry of authenticity. Yet at the same
moments, but in other places, romanticism presents a poetic of

engagement and transpersonal voicing, as in the *Lyrical Ballads* when they enter into a discourse of community, or a poem such as Blake's *Jerusalem*, which offers a communitarian voice originating in collective desire and seeking to intervene in the world as collective agency. Similarly, Shelley's 'The Mask of Anarchy' taken literally as his attempt to intercede in political affairs, with songs 'wholly political, & destined to awaken & direct the imagination of the reformers',[29] belongs to this interventionist strain, whose direct inheritors were the Chartist poets and poetic theorists of the 1830s and 1840s.

In 'The Mask of Anarchy,' the 'selves' of political upheaval are generated from and come to know themselves through their collective experience of oppression: that is, they are what some contemporary critics of liberalism would call communitarian selves, whose identities are made through a set of traditions, goals, and social meanings. In the individualist mode within romantic poetry, by contrast, most often the self is pre-given and extremely vulnerable: the possibility of development, though inherent in each self, is understood in Wordsworth's poetry after 'Salisbury Plain', to be 'in most abated and suppressed' by society.

As soon as we observe the links between romanticism and individualism, we see more clearly the complicity between, on the one hand, that aspect of romanticism and liberalism as it developed in the nineteenth century, and on the other, between the collective aspect of romanticism and socialism as it developed out of plebeian communitarianism also in the nineteenth century. Enmeshed in those moments when liberalism, as Anthony Arblaster argues, moved from being a dream into a 'dominant, dynamic political force', individualist romanticism provides a poetic of the 'unencumbered self', nourishing liberalism's valuation of the individual as separate, autonomous in will and reason, and, crucially, private.[30] Liberalism's own contradiction is its presentation of a democratic sense of the individual, theorizing society as an aggregate of autonomous selves, but suggesting at the same time that an élite layer of selves need rise to the surface to direct the mass. This self is, like Wordsworth's poet, a 'man speaking to men' but a bit more politically astute. Romanticism in this sense depends upon liberalism, which sanctions and, importantly, protects the inner space of subjectivity. The liberal subject is at once entirely private and yet in social and political control in bourgeois society.[31] We need think only of the exemplary liberal, John Stuart Mill, who attributed his very being to the power of romantic identity formation, as he learned it from Wordsworth.[32]

But romanticism also offers a poetic grounded in a communitarian selfhood – one conscious of its social origins and aims, and committed to fulfilling itself in function of its social responsibilities. If we look at the double intention with romanticism as a literary-historical dialectic, we can see that the engagement between bourgeois liberalism (based on natural rights) and a plebeian communitarianism (grounded in community-derived notions of the customary rights of the labouring poor) yields, in the course of the nineteenth century, to both the triumph and the crisis of liberal individualism, and the permutation of plebeian into socialist communitarianism. This permutation takes place, however, in the context of the historical defeat of communitarian values at the hands of the now authorized bourgeoisie between 1848 and the 1880s.

Our ability to critically elicit the double intention within romantic poetry has been deeply hampered by the outcome of the contest in the larger regions of intellectual and political life. Because individualism won the larger debate, it has shaped the history of literary criticism, which for the most part either approvingly reads the romantic period backwards as the poetic which marks the separating out of poetry and politics, or disapprovingly exposes a 'romantic ideology' which claims it is without ideology, but which in practice enacts the individualist ideology of bourgeois universalism.[33]

The more convincing model of romanticism proposed by Thompson has recently been interestingly complemented by a pan-European theory proposed by Michael Lowy and Robert Sayre, who share Thompson's premises: 'Capitalism calls forth the independent individual to fulfil certain socio-economic functions; but when this individual transforms itself into a full-fledged subjectivity and begins to explore the internal universe of its particular constellation of feeling', it comes into conflict with its parentage. Romanticism, therefore, 'represents the revolt of the repressed, manipulated and deformed subjectivity, and of the "magic" of imagination banished from the capitalist world'.[34]

My intention here is to modify this model by arguing that there is another kind of subjectivity present in romanticism, a pre-capitalist, communitarian, plebeian subjectivity, and that this kind of subjectivity occupies romanticism throughout its life, and undergoes its own transmutation from a plebeian communitarianism into a socialist collectivity, in a movement distinct from that suggested through a growth-decay model of romanticism. The difficulty in locating this other strain arises from the fact that socialists looking for a domestic genealogy get nervous about categories such as 'tradition' and 'organic', (categories associated with Burkean conservatism) and so they turn to the same sources as those that underlie liberalism. For socialism and liberalism did arise, in part, from the same matrix. So Paine, as Anthony Arblaster argues, is both an exemplary liberal and also an incipient socialist.[35]

As an economic, social, and political ideology, liberalism, though it had not coalesced into a political party until the late 1860s, linked enlightenment rationalism to capitalism as the most congenial soil in which to develop the growth of liberty as non-interference. On the other hand, what came to be called socialism, and was dispersed across many sects and factions, and politically split into the reformist strategy of Labourism and the anti-reformist revolutionary tradition, was, from its origins, bifurcated by contradictory sources and goals, one in the direction of republicanism (the Painite thread), the other deeply anti-political, even millenarian in its goals.[36] This anti-political strain is the link to traditional, customary practice, and to a communitarian impulse which can be read through early nineteenth-century romanticism and followed to the end of the century.

What Morris drew upon in the 1880s was not only the influence of the republicanism and internationalism that Thompson associates with the rationalist individualist traditions of Byron and Shelley (that which is associated with liberalism) but also the communitarian tradition. Communitarianism in the atmosphere of socialism in the 1880s represented an important advance upon the plebeian communitarianism which had fuelled, as well, the ideology of the radical Tories and the conservative Burkeans. The difference is the historical dialectic whereby plebeian communitarianism itself was transmuted into a socialist view of the community as the collective.

The term 'romantic', then, ought to be used to describe neither (1) a set of literary functions (paradigmatically debated in discussions by Arthur J. Lovejoy and René Wellek about the reducibility or irreducibility of structures and preoccupations such as imagination, nature, myth and symbol) nor (2) a set of ideological mystifications (the literary method derived from the work of Althusser).[37] Rather, we should consider romanticism to be the literary form of a struggle taking place on many levels of society between the claims of individualism and the claims of communitarianism. Romanticism is the cultural theatre of contest between the poetic languages of traditional society and capitalist society earlier in the century, and between those of liberalism and socialism later in the century. So it is that romanticism offers itself to us as both an aesthetic and an intervention, a refusal of capitalism and the lieutenant of its purposes.

What we can call this communitarian moment within romanticism can be historically linked to aspects of the various and overlapping cultures of plebeian democracy, customary culture, radical enthusiasm, and agrarianism.[38] In order to see clearly the place of Morris's evocation of the rural, we need recall that this plebeian culture did not take place out in the country, while liberal republicanism was growing in the city. Malcolm Chase, the historian of popular radical agrarianism, makes the point that the movement was not primarily about agricultural labour at all, but about the developing industrial working class. Agrarianism is about their response 'to economic, social, and political dislocation which sought solutions in and on the land.'[39] He insists that 'for such people "nature" retained a profound meaning, not sentimental or Arcadian in character, but ingrained, realistic and born of continuing proximity (spatial and psychological) to the land.'[40] The aesthetic linked to this version of nature would be very unlike that idealized landscape of the picturesque, in other words, unlike the aesthetic ideology.

The single most significant vehicle for urbanized agrarian radicalism was the ideology of the followers of Thomas Spence. In his analysis of the vicissitudes of Spenceanism in London radical circles between the 1790s and 1820, the cultural historian Iain McCalman has demonstrated the links between Spence's agrarianism and Paine's rationalism, providing one salient instance of the communitarian-individualist debate in action within the radical world. So, a ballad links the two discourses together: 'The Rights of Man are in the Land / ... A Nation is the People's Farm / They build, they plant, 'tis their strong arm / That till the clod, defend the clan.'[41] He argues that Spence was an intellectual *bricoleur*: 'He was heir to the strange blend of social prophecy, popular materialism and scepticism which had surfaced in the writings and utterances of plebeian sectarians like the Ranters and Seekers. And he had ingested elements of enlightenment rationalism through his reading of philosophes like Volney.'[42] As its title suggests, Spence's revolutionary journal *Pig's Meat*, confronted

Burke head-on, but significantly, did not relinquish to Burke the affective themes of organicism and tradition. McCalman argues that revolutionaries in late eighteenth-century and early nineteenth-century London often yoked together the languages of rationalism and of enthusiasm: the class borders were crossed between middle-class intellectual rationalism and plebeian popular religious forms.[43] The literary historian Jon Mee has developed McCalman's work in analyzing what he, too, calls the *bricolage* of William Blake's romantic poetic which, he argues, was also such a mix of rationalism and enthusiasm, and which partially explains Blake's own ambiguous reputation amongst the rationalist intellectuals of the Joseph Johnson circle.[44]

Amongst the second generation of romantics, Shelley was most influenced by the communitarian impulse in urban plebeianism. Kenneth Cameron noted Spence's influence upon Shelley in the 1970s, but more recently William St Clair and David Worrall, in addition to McCalman, have investigated Shelley's intellectual relationship with the Spencean movement. *Queen Mab* was first published in a journal run by 'Erasmus Perkins', the pseudonym of George Cannon, an important second-generation Spencean.[45] 'The Mask of Anarchy' bears the impress of plebeianism.[46] This is the matrix of romanticism, and the familiar oppositions in romantic studies – Burke to Paine, tradition to natural rights, reaction to progress – are upset when we consider how plebeian radicalism was part of its shape.

In his discussion of eighteenth-century customary culture, Thompson stresses the intertwining of plebeian and rationalist culture by the end of that century: 'When the ideological break with paternalism came, in the 1790s, it came in the first place less from plebeian culture than from the intellectual culture of the dissenting middle class, and from thence was carried to the urban artisans. But Painite ideas, carried through by such artisans to an ever wider plebeian culture, instantly struck root there.'[47] These Painite ideas were, however, themselves influenced by the communitarian culture in which they took root, and by the continued pressure of a search for a transpersonal, collective identity. So the residual element of community from pre-capitalism was able to become the emergent element of collective identity.

In the 1830s and 1840s, it is in the Chartist movement that we see this at work vigorously. What is of interest for tracing the movement of the nineteenth-century romantic dialectic is the great extent to which activist Chartist poets and poetical theorists were particularly interested in, even preoccupied with, their inheritance from romantic poetry. Chartism fully engaged itself to the interventionist aspect of romantic poetics, and so provides a literary link between the communitarian strain evinced in the first and second generation romantic poets, and the socialist poetics of the end of the century.[48] For if the aesthetic, 'Tintern Abbey', ideology marks a moment when, in bourgeois literature, politics and poetry appear to be separating out their explicit spheres of influence, Chartist poetry refuses such a separation and asserts itself *as* action, while explicitly claiming and analytically revealing an equally romantic inheritance. An article in the *Chartist Circular* declares with an earthbound Shelleyan voice: 'Poetry is a lever of commanding influence... It penetrates to every nerve and fibre of society, stirring into ir- resistibility its innermost current, and spiriting into life and activity the obscurest dweller of the valley.'[49]

The rhetorical scaffolding within which the Chartist poetic intervention was built was the notion of a repressed 'people's' national literary heritage, which Chartist poets and poetic theorists both excavated and invented, in order to claim the name of 'the people' for the labouring classes. Chartist poetry and literary culture took on the task of wresting away the middle class's own new claim to universality by providing its own alternate, though equally purposive genealogy. For the Chartist movement, the building of the working-class movement and the naming of a national culture were identified. And importantly, popular sovereignty would define the nation not from Painite and rationalist first principles, but out of and in relation to an inherited tradition; a tradition linked to the land. The nationalism of Chartism awkwardly but affectively intertwined the nationalism that we associate with the French revolutionary-democratic movement which invented the nation-state in its modern form, and the earlier radical patriotism of community as well as the tradition of radical agrarianism.[50] This intertwining of older with contemporary ideas is itself linked to the disorder of human elements within Chartism itself: a movement made up of artisans, with their local traditions and customary practices, radical reformers, and new industrial workers, naming themselves as something new – the working class – but just as eager to give themselves an historical ground. So, Chartist poets and literary theorists tried to define working-class identity by yoking it to a national poetic tradition in which, they asserted, the history of the labouring poor had always been woven into poetic purpose. In aid of that intention, the *Chartist Circular* ran a year-long series of articles in 1839 on 'Politics of Poets'.

The explicit thrust of that inheritance, as the Chartists saw it, was associated with what they read as the democratic impulse of both Shelley and Byron. *Queen Mab* and 'The Mask of Anarchy' were the poems most often reprinted in the *Northern Star*, the chief Chartist newspaper, which ran a weekly poetry column throughout its life.[51] An article in the *Chartist Circular* tells us that Byron was able to trace 'through its ramified complications the development of the democratic principle'.[52] The liberal republicanism of Shelley and Byron is invoked; but so is the sense of a collective democratic identity grounded in a poetic tradition, in which 'The Mask of Anarchy' appears as a consummate poem of both the agricultural and industrial proletariat.

The decline of Chartism by the 1850s defeated, for a period, this tradition within romanticism as well. From the success of the ruling class came a thorough campaign of ruining the autonomous institutions of working-class culture, and of universalizing both politics and literature as middle class and liberal.

William Morris occupies a late and significant moment in the dialectic I have asserted here, when an explicit and revived discourse of socialism is jammed, as a wedge, into the emergency within hegemonic bourgeois liberalism, and offers a communitarian vision which, though carrying traces of plebeian custom, has mutated into something quite distinct through its encounter with, and pressure on, that aspect of enlightenment liberalism which moved in an increasingly popularly democratic direction. Liberalism itself became increasingly scared of its theorization of democracy, 'when the prospect of a second enlargement of the male electorate brought many fears and misgivings into the open'.[53]

Morris's own movement from Gladstone's liberalism to Marxist socialism offered to him from within the dialectic of romanticism, an alternative set of poetic resources from which to draw. In the 1880s, when the old Chartists rallied round the new socialist movement, Morris found open to him that version of romanticism which foregrounded the interventionist, not the meditative turn within romanticism, and the voice of the collective, not the solitary. (As Chris Waters has pointed out, Morris's own *Chants for Socialists* had much in common with Chartist songs.[54]) It is his recovery of this aspect of the romantic tradition that allows the poetic sequence to be written. In the 'Message of the March Wind', the speaker laments the irrelevance of most art to those who work in what Richard later calls 'city squalor and country stupor' (v):

> The singers have sung and the builders have builded;
> The painters have fashioned their tales of delight;
> For what and for whom hath the world's book been gilded,
> When all is for these but the blackness of night? (i)

Richard then vows that 'from henceforth no fair words shall be hiding / The night of the wretched, the days of the poor' (ii). *The Pilgrims of Hope* then goes on to recover a possible poetic: one which will harness the truth of the past to build for 'the day to be' (xiii).

In the autumn before he began composition of *The Pilgrims of Hope*, Morris wrote in the dialect of the interventionist poetic to James Frederick Henderson, an aspiring poet and political activist. Henderson had found himself, Morris wrote,

confronted by the rising hope of the people, and have been able to declare yourself a soldier of the Cause ... believe me this is better than mere poetry-writing, for you will find something to do in the movement & doubtless will fill your place worthily ... you will find you will add such backbone to your poetry by your work in the Cause as will make it indeed worthwhile to write poetry.[55]

As in the Chartist history of the literature of the 'people', Morris was concerned with the transindividual aspect of creation, both in craft, and in poetry. Epic poems are the greatest, Morris writes: 'They are in no sense the work of individuals, but have grown up from the very heart of the people.'[56]

Morris comes at a late moment in the dialectic of romanticism, and *The Pilgrims of Hope* appears at a late stage in Morris's own poetic history, when he had begun to devote himself full-time to the Socialist League, and had immersed himself in the urban political milieu of socialist London. The poem belongs to the urbanism of socialist London; it stands out amongst English poems in its presentation of this world of street-level politics, with its 'Radical spouting-places' (v) and outdoor meetings.

It has been argued that in *The Pilgrims of Hope* the contrast created between the city and country is rather facile, 'practically the equivalent of that between capitalist oppression and revolutionary freedom'.[57] If that were true, then the poem might well be viewed as simply a recapitulation of the 'romanticism as criticism of industrialism' theme. Yet rurality is never posited as a revolutionary goal in the poem, always as the first moment in a spiralling dialectic, and the political possibilities that are seen in the city mean that it is not simply a repository of negative value. Again, it is not city versus country so much as it is capitalism – agricultural or industrial – that Morris attacks in this poem.

At its thematic centre stands the complex image of the Paris Commune – an image of a revolutionary fusion of the values of communitarianism with the assets of urban life. Because of his own access to the communitarian tradition, Morris is able to make palpable not only the contemporary political links between the Commune and the struggle for socialism in Britain, but also the connections between the values of the Commune and a set of values already deep in a British communitarian tradition. Morris is, able, in other words, to 'English' the Paris Commune, make it congruent with a nativist tradition.

The image and memory of the Paris Commune was an important screen onto which the revival of British socialism in the 1880s and 1890s came to project its own representations and fantasies. In this sense Morris's *Pilgrims of Hope* belongs very much to its socialist milieu. The end of the century as a political episode was a period of crisis within liberalism, its privileges under pressure from, on the one hand, the new trade unions of gasworkers and railway workers, unmoored from the compromises made by the trade union leaders of craft unions in the mid-century; and, on the other, from the politicization of socialism. The theorizing of collectivization gave a new turn to the deeper tradition of community. Within the London milieu, the scramble amongst socialists and liberals for the support of the working class was compounded by the difficult relationship between trade unionists and socialists.[58] Because both the Social Democratic Federation and Morris's wing of the movement, the Socialist League, were busier formulating their political positions than linking up with the newly forming unions, the Liberals for a period managed to resolve their crisis by evolving what was called 'the new liberalism', attempting to bridge the gap between working class and middle class, by channelling the push for labour representation through its own party forms, and thereby both hastening its own decline, and also weakening the autonomy of the labour movement by dosing it with liberal ideology. For the socialist movement, the Paris Commune survived as an image of purity.

The Commune, moreover, would have a particular meaning for poetics in the dialectic of romanticism as I have been describing it in this essay. For if one aspect of the 'long' nineteenth-century romantic dialectic was the persistence of a communitarian motive within urban popular poetics and politics, then this element was made explicit in the Commune, offering an image of not only a people's self-government, but one which, while resembling the practices of the medieval and rural communes, was contemporary, urban, and suffused by a new sense of power amongst the labouring poor.

Within the Leninist tradition, the Commune occupies the position of fulcrum for the narrative of revolution from 1789 to 1917. For Marx himself, one of the most crucial aspects of the Commune was the way in which it demonstrated the dialectical *reconstruction* of the form of the primitive commune as the communal structure of the future. In *The Civil War in France*, he writes: 'It is generally the fate of completely new historical creations to be mistaken for the counterpart of older and even defunct forms of social life, to which they may bear a certain likeness. Thus, this new Commune which breaks the modern State power, has been mistaken for a reproduction of the medieval communes.'[59] Just as agrarianism as an element in an urban plebeian politics was not a simple desire to 'return to the land', so the Commune bore traces of medievalism but transformed in the context of an urban heterogeneity of artisanal, industrial, and newly displaced rural workers.[60] In a first draft of the pamphlet, Marx wrote that the Commune, 'was a revolution against the State itself, of this supernaturalist abortion of society, a resumption by the people for the people of its own social life'.[61] So, the anti-hierarchical aspect of the Commune, whose meaning for workers' real lives bore absolutely no resemblance to the oppressive hierarchy of the feudal commune, nonetheless did bear a genealogical relationship to continuous plebeian traditions. These are what Victor Shanin, discussing Marx's pamphlet, calls 'vernacular traditions':

To all those steeped in Hegelian dialectics, children resembled their grandparents more than their parents. The 'primary' commune, dialectically restored on a new and higher level of material wealth and global interaction, entered Marx's images of the future communist society, one in which once more the 'individuals behave not as labourers but as owners – as members of a community which also labours'.[62]

The heterogeneous elements within the Commune were ideologically represented by and through languages of class as well as languages of custom, and enlightenment rationality. And these elements show a kinship with the same uncertain mix which had peopled London from the 1790s through the defeat of Chartism in 1848.

The Commune, then, offered itself to Morris as a representation both external to England, and yet by virtue of the same vernacular structure, internal as well. While both socialists and liberals in Britain called upon the memory of the French Revolution throughout the nineteenth century, the Commune was an image that belonged entirely to the socialist movement by the 1880s and 1890s. Though British radicals and liberals had supported the city of Paris and the republic against the Prussian invasion, they soon rallied around the bourgeois Thiers government in Versailles, which was the instrument of the brutal repression of the artisan and working-class Commune in April of 1871.[63] Central intellectuals were straightforwardly in support of the Thiers government, including Carlyle, Eliot, Browning, and Tennyson, who deplored the 'red fool-fury of the Seine'.[64] It was only the International and the Positivists who came out in support of the Commune itself. That the General Council of the International Working Men's Association would issue a pamphlet as incendiary as 'The Civil War in France', suggested to the liberals that this group, hardly heard of before, might be a grave threat to Britain. The Commune and the International were thus linked in the liberal and conservative mind, and were the objects of hundreds of attacks in the press, thus putting Karl Marx on the intellectual map in Britain for the first time. In 1871 and 1872 British politicians and establishment intellectuals argued first, that the International had been at the heart of the Paris events, and secondly, that it was planning, from its offices in High Holborn, to organize a similar insurrection in Britain.[65] Eleanor Marx recalled near the end of her life that in 1871 there had been a prevalent 'condition of perfectly frantic fury of the whole middle class against the Commune ... It was proposed – quite seriously – [that] the Communards who had taken refuge in England should be handed over to the doctors and the hospitals for purposes of vivisection.'[66]

The influx of Communard refugees did have the immediate effect of introducing a more international element into the London radical scene, and a tradition was initiated of a yearly commemoration of the aspirations of the Commune.[67] These anniversaries served a practical purpose in the political excitement of the 1880s and 1890s, providing a rallying point and a platform for the often warring factions within the socialist movement. These meetings often included exiles from the Commune itself, including famous French revolutionaries, such as the pétroleuse Louise Michel.[68] With the arrival in London of Russian anarchist exiles such as Kropotkin and Stepniak, and their inclusion on the platforms, these events gave evidence of an international movement.

Morris's own participation in the Commune anniversary began in 1884, on the first anniversary of Marx's death, and the thirteenth of the Commune, when the socialist community in London sponsored a march and rally at Highgate cemetery. Morris wrote to Jane Morris that he had been 'loath to go, but did not dislike it when I did go'. The marchers were refused entry into the cemetery, 'so we adjourned to an uncomfortable piece of waste ground near by and the song was sung and the speeches made'.[69] Over the course of the next seven years, Morris was to continue to participate in Paris Commune celebrations, and to use *Commonweal* as a site for returning to the history of the Commune and bringing its lessons out to readers. And it was in the month following the 1886 commemorative meeting that he introduced the topic of the Commune into *The Pilgrims of Hope*. In fact, though scholars and commentators write about *The Pilgrims of Hope* as if the poem were 'about' the Paris Commune, the subject of the Commune is only introduced into the sequence close to the end, in poem XI, 'A Glimpse of the Coming Day'. As one reads through the successive numbers of *Commonweal*, it seems likely that Morris, preoccupied with the anniversary celebrations being held in London for the Commune, realized that in drawing on this historical event he might locate exactly the dramatic turning point that the sequence needed, a way of demonstrating a potential material and social solution to the poem. The inability of the three friends to resolve their emotional relationships is subsumed into the more pressing problem of producing the revolutionary conditions under which a resolution might even be dreamt of. We are not left with a certain knowledge that Richard himself has resolved the question, but rather that individual issues must be answered within the scope of collective ones. The Paris Commune offers Richard the vision of a new geography in which a rational collective urban life might emerge from the communitarian impulse.

Morris finished his verse sequence by reminding his readers of the purpose of the romance, to make the past a part of the present, and so available for the future. To his child, and other children, Richard affirms the power of hope to draw from the past to build the future: 'Year after year shall men meet the red flag overhead, / And shall call on the help of the vanquished and kindness of the dead' (xiii).

In the 1880s and 1890s, the pressure of the 'new unionism' within the working class pushed liberalism to accommodate aspects of a community vision of society; the hegemony of capitalist liberalism however, was greater and it again deformed the union movement into labourism. The revival of Liberalism from the period of the Cold War and on into the neo-Liberalism in the 1980s and 1990s, no longer under that extreme pressure, has reverted to the laissez-faire principles that characterized its moment of triumph after 1848. But now it is unable to summon either material resources or moral authority, having replaced its historically contradictory vision with the pastiche of 'a return to Victorian values'. In this context, the re-emergence of socialist communitarian values within the communitarian critique of liberalism continues the persistent tradition of hope.

NOTES

I wish to thank Patrick Sikorski for discussing a draft of this essay with me.

1 William Morris, *The Pilgrims of Hope* (London: 1886). All quotations from the sequence will be made parenthetically in the text of the chapter, by reference to the poem number. For a good modern edition of the poem I would recommend *Three Works by William Morris*, introduced by A. L. Morton (London: Lawrence and Wishart, 1968).

2 William Morris, 'Address at the Twelfth Annual Meeting of the Society for the Protection of Ancient Buildings', 3 July 1889, in May Morris, *William Morris, Artist, Writer, Socialist*, 2 vols. (Oxford: Basil Blackwell, 1936), 1:148.

3 Michael Holzman makes a good case for the poem referring to the triangular relationship between Jane Morris, William Morris, and Dante Gabriel Rossetti, which was taking place during the period of the Paris Commune. See Michael Holzman, 'Propaganda, Passion, and Literary Art in William Morris's *The Pilgrims of Hope*', *Texas Studies in Literature and Language*, 24 (1982), 372–393.

4 William Wordsworth, *The Prelude* (1805), edited by Ernest de Selincourt (Oxford: Oxford University Press, 1926), 1805, Book x, lines 724–728.

5 E. P. Thompson, *William Morris: Romantic to Revolutionary* (London: Lawrence and Wishart, 1955; 2nd edn., London: Merlin Press, 1976).

6 In his 1976 revision of the 1955 text of *William Morris: Romantic to Revolutionary*, Thompson invited a consideration of his book on Morris with a view to its presentation of the issue of romanticism: 'But I would hope that one part of [the volume's] structure – the part least noted by its critics – might receive a little attention before it is pulled down: that is, the analysis of Romanticism and of its trajectory in Morris's life.' (pp. 807–808)

7 Thompson, *William Morris*, p. 1.

8 Thompson, *William Morris*, p. 786; See John Goode's excellent consideration of 'E. P. Thompson and "The Significance of Literature"', in Harvey J. Kaye and Keith McClelland (eds.), *E. P. Thompson: Critical Perspectives* (Cambridge: Polity Press, 1990), pp. 183–203; and see also Perry Anderson, *Arguments Within English Marxism* (London: Verso Press, 1980).

9 Thompson, *William Morris*, p. 2, p. 11.

10 *Ibid.*, pp. 19–20.

11 *Ibid.*, p. 2.

12 Goode, 'E. P. Thompson', pp. 183–203.

13 Thompson, *William Morris*, 1955, p. 31.

14 *Ibid.*, p. 669.

15 *Ibid.*, p. 671.

16 William Morris, *The Collected Letters*, edited by Norman Kelvin, 3 vols. (Princeton, New Jersey: Princeton University Press, 1984), 2:587. Emphasis added.

17 H. Buxton-Forman, *The Books of William Morris Described...* (London: Frank Hollings, 1897), p. 125.

18 J. W. Mackail, *The Life of William Morris* (London: Longman's, 1932), p. 148.

19 Morris, *Letters*, p. xxv, p. xxix.

20 Holzman, 'Propaganda, Passion, and Literary Art', p. 377.

21 Buxton-Forman, *The Books of William Morris*, p. 111.

22 Bruce Glasier, 'A Proletarian Epic', *The Socialist Review: A Quarterly Review of Modern Thought*, 17 (1920), 322.

23 Florence S. Boos, 'Narrative design in *The Pilgrims of Hope*', in Florence S. Boos and Carole G. Silver (eds.), *Socialism and the Literary Artistry of William Morris* (Columbia and Missouri: University of Missouri Press, 1990), p. 166.

24 George Meredith, *Modern Love* (London: Rupert Hart-Davis, 1948), Sonnet 1.

25 Glasier, 'A Proletarian Epic', p. 325.

26 Thompson, *William Morris*, p. 670; Malcolm Chase, '*The People's Farm*': *English Radical Agrarianism 1775–1840* (Oxford: Clarendon Press, 1988);

Jan Marsh, *Back to the Land: The Pastoral Impulse in England, from* 1880 *to* 1914 (London: Quartet, 1982), p. 16.

27 Morris, *Letters*, II, p. 386, p. 391.

28 William Blake, *The Complete Writings*, edited by Geoffrey Keynes (London: Nonesuch Press, 1957), p. 290.

29 Percy Bysshe Shelley, *The Letters*, edited by Frederick L. Jones (Oxford: Clarendon Press, 1964) II, p. 191.

30 For a discussion of the contemporary communitarian critique of liberalism, see the work of, among others, Alasdair MacIntyre, Michael Sandel and Charles Taylor. See MacIntyre, *After Virtue* (London: Duckworth, 1981); Sandel, *Liberalism and the Limits of Justice* (Cambridge: Cambridge University Press, 1982); Taylor, *Sources of the Self* (Cambridge:Cambridge University Press, 1990). For a useful redaction of the debates, see Stephen Mulhall and Adam Swift, *Liberals and Communitarians* (Oxford: Blackwell, 1992).

31 See Guy Oakes's introduction to Carl Schmitt, *Political Romanticism* (Cambridge, Mass.: Massachusetts Institute of Technology, 1986), p. xxxii.

32 John Stuart Mill, *Autobiography* (Harmondsworth: Penguin, 1989), p. 121.

33 For examples of discussions of the 'romantic ideology', see Jerome McGann, *The Romantic Ideology* (Chicago: University of Chicago Press, 1980); Marjorie Levinson, *Wordsworth's Great Period Poems* (Cambridge: Cambridge University Press, 1986).

34 Robert Sayre and Michael Lowy, 'Figures of Romantic Anti-Capitalism', *New German Critique*, 32 (1984), 58.

35 Anthony Arblaster, *The Rise and Decline of Western Liberalism* (Oxford: Basil Blackwell, 1984), p. 227.

36 This is the argument advanced by Gregory Claeys, *Citizens and Saints: Politics and Anti-Politics in Early British Socialism* (Cambridge: Cambridge University Press, 1989), p. 1.

37 For the orthodox statement of this debate see Arthur J. Lovejoy, 'On the Discrimination of Romanticisms', *Essays on the History of Ideas* (Baltimore: Johns Hopkins University Press, 1948), pp. 228–253; reprinted in *English Romantic Poets: Modern Essays in Criticism*, edited by M. H. Abrams (New York: Oxford University Press, 1960), pp. 3–24; and Rene Wellek, 'The Concept of Romanticism', in *Concepts of Criticism* (New Haven: Yale University Press, 1963).

38 See Jack Lindsay, 'The Commune of Paris and English Literature', *Marxist Quarterly*, 1 (1954), 169; E. P. Thompson, *Customs in Common* (London: Merlin Press, 1992); and Jon Mee, *Dangerous Enthusiasm: William Blake and the Culture of Radicalism in the 1790s* (Oxford: Clarendon Press, 1992).

39 Chase, *The People's Farm*, p. 3.

40 *Ibid.*, p. 15.

41 *Ibid.*, p. 2.
42 Iain McCalman, *Radical Underworld: Prophets, Revolutionaries and Porno-graphers in London, 1795–1840* (Cambridge: Cambridge University Press, 1988), p. 92
43 *Ibid.*, chapter 1.
44 Mee, *Dangerous Enthusiasm*, p. 51.
45 Kenneth Neill Cameron, *Shelley: The Golden Years* (Cambridge, Mass.: Harvard University Press, 1974), pp. 116–117; William St Clair, *The Godwins and the Shelleys: The Biography of a Family* (London: Faber and Faber, 1989), p. 394; McCalman, *Radical Underworld*, chapter 4: 'Cannon and Rationalist Philosophy'; David Worrall, *Radical Culture: Discourse, Resistance and Surveillance, 1790–1820* (Sussex: Harvester Press, 1992).
46 See my '"A Voice from Over the Sea": Shelley at the Limits of Romanticism', in *The Limits of Romanticism*, edited by Nicola Watson and Mary Favret (Bloomington: Indiana University Press, 1993).
47 Thompson, *Customs in Common*, p. 86.
48 For a discussion of the relationship between romanticism and Chartism, see my 'Class and Literature: The Case of Romantic Chartism', in *Class and Literature*, edited by Michael T. Gilmore and Wy-Chee Dimmock (New York: Columbia University Press, 1994).
49 *The Chartist Circular*, 24 October 1840.
50 E. J. Hobsbawm, *Nations and Nationalism Since 1790* (Cambridge: Cambridge University Press, 1990) for discussion of the meeting up of traditional and revolutionary democratic nationalisms; Raphael Samuel (ed.), *Patriotism: The Making and Unmaking of British National Identity*, 3 vols. (London: Routledge, 1989) for the domestic tradition of patriotism; and especially Hugh Cunningham, 'The Language of Patriotism, 1750–1914', *History Workshop Journal*, 12 (1981), 8–33.
51 J. A. Epstein, 'Feargus O'Connor and *The Northern Star*', *International Review of Social History*, 21 (1976), 69–80, 97.
52 *Chartist Circular*, 64 (19 December 1840).
53 Arblaster, *Rise and Decline of Western Liberalism*, p. 270.
54 Chris Waters, 'Morris's "Chants" and the Problems of Socialist Culture', in Boos and Silver, *Socialism and the Literary Artistry of William Morris*, p. 128.
55 Morris, *Letters*, II, p. 472.
56 *Ibid.*, p. 515.
57 Holzman, 'Propaganda, Passion and Literary Art', p. 372.
58 Paul Thompson, *Socialists, Liberals and Labour: The Struggle for London 1885–1914* (London: Routledge and Kegan Paul, 1967), p. 91.
59 Karl Marx and Friedrich Engels, *Writings on the Paris Commune*, edited by Hal Draper (New York: Monthly Review Press, 1971), pp. 74–75.
60 See Kristin Ross, *The Emergence of Social Space: Rimbaud and the Paris Commune* (London: Macmillan, 1988), p. 22.

61 Marx and Engels, *Writings on the Paris Commune*, p. 150.
62 Victor Shanin, 'Marxism and the Vernacular Revolutionary Traditions', in *Late Marx and the Russian Road: Marx and 'the peripheries of capitalism'* (London: Routledge and Kegan Paul, 1983), p. 255.
63 A. L. Morton, 'Britain and the Paris Commune', *Marxism Today*, 15: 3 (1971), 82–86.
64 Jack Lindsay, 'The Commune of Paris', p. 170, p. 173. Quite an interesting novel about the Commune was written by Eliza Lynn Linton, *The True History of Joshua Davidson, Christian and Communist*, written in 1872, and similar in some respects to Morris's evocation of the Commune thirteen years later. For a time Linton had been the wife of W. J. Linton, one of the old Chartists, and so her text provides one link between the generations of the working-class revolutionary movement. In this novel a young woman, Mary Princep, becomes part of and is sacrificed to the revolutionary movement, operating as an index of the Commune's republican purity, all as a foil to the allegorical narrative of Joshua Davidson, a Christian Socialist martyr. The novel went through three editions within three months of publication in 1872. For more on Linton, see Nancy Fix Anderson, *Woman Against Women in Victorian England: A Life of Eliza Lynn Linton* (Bloomington: Indiana University Press, 1987).
65 For a full discussion, see Kirk Willis, 'The Introduction and Critical Reception of Marxist Thought in Britain, 1850–1900', *The Historical Journal*, 20 (1977), 417–459.
66 Quoted in Yvonne Kapp, *Eleanor Marx: Family Life, 1855–1883* (London: Virago Press, 1979), I, p. 134.
67 Morton, 'Britain and the Commune', p. 85; Stanley Hutchins, 'The Communard Exiles in Britain', *Marxism Today*, 15 (1971): 183.
68 Hutchins, 'The Communard Exiles in Britain', p. 185.
69 Morris, *Letters*, II, p. 270.

CHAPTER 9

Urban utopias: socialism, religion and the city, 1880 to 1900

Lynne Hapgood

Linguistic liaisons and transformations lie at the heart of the struggle to explain and debate the nature of social structures at the end of the nineteenth century. At the same time that political activists, philanthropists and urban planners were changing the face of the concrete urban world, the questions they were asking were modifying public discourse by exposing its inadequacies in formulating relevant questions and in offering acceptable answers.

From the opening of the eighties there was a general sense that the thinking about social issues had overtaken the public discourse available to articulate it. The 'unintended irony' of the sociological writings of this period highlights the strains that were becoming apparent.[1] By the close of the 1880s, Charles Booth's *Life and Labour of the People: Poverty Series* had explicitly stated the need for an 'objective' language.[2] Yet his writings reveal how difficult this was to achieve. The record of his observations is constrained by the poverty of a language that described the poor as 'thriftless', 'loafers' and 'scroungers'. His recognition of this problem and his attempts to find a more objective terminology created a linguistic conflict that channelled him reluctantly towards 'quasi-socialism', a position which held little conviction for him politically or intellectually. The reality of the difficulties he faced are underlined by his evident relief when he describes the educated artisan class where the language at his disposal at last fits the observable social facts.[3]

Indirectly, these linguistic tensions constituted an attack on church authority. Although the church's authority on social matters had been steadily eroded since the mid-nineteenth century and at best was only one of a number of perspectives on social organization, the power of Christian discourse was still virtually unchallenged. The language of public life, of public institutions and of public behaviour was grounded in the ethics of Christian doctrine. What the social commentators of the day were calling into question was not just the adequacy of some hypothetically neutral discourse, but the adequacy of Christian interpretations of social structures.

The established church was anxious to maintain its power base in a society increasingly drifting towards secular notions of social analysis and latterly concerned with finding a scientific and objective mode of discourse. Influenced by a pervasive sense that society in the cities was breaking down and that the voice of civilization and morality was not being heard, it felt compelled to redefine its role. In this mood of urgency the Church committed itself to secularization.[4]

Once initiated, the process of secularization was to reach far beyond the development of 'practical Christianity' in social programmes which could demonstrate the church's concern with urban conditions. Some members of the church felt that secular action could only be fully expressed through a secular language. They believed they could divest Christian discourse of its symbolic weight and make it appropriate to the material world while still maintaining its distinctive nature as an expression of divine revelation. Yet the essential nature of Christian discourse makes its secularization linguistic nonsense. The central tenet of Christian doctrine – 'The Word was made Flesh' – provides an infrastructure for the metaphorical weight of Christian terminology. In other words Christian discourse is sacramental; an outward expression of inward meaning. In the eighties and nineties, those Christians most committed to social action enthusiastically set about dismantling their own discourse, deliberately attempting to unpick the material from the invisible, the ethical from the spiritual. Aware of the power of language as a tool of influence, they seemed unaware that a possible outcome of jettisoning the invisible, spiritual meaning while retaining the outward signifier might be a substantial and qualitative loss of meaning and of social influence.

Several factors combined to convince church social workers of the rightness of their approach. One was that several clearly articulated, secular alternatives to Christian discourse such as secularism, positivism, Marxism and Fabian socialism were competing to be the most effective means of articulating and explaining society. The terminology of Marxist versions of socialism was made accessible by the translation of *Das Kapital* into English in 1886 and the founding of three socialist societies in London in the early 1880s which all freely disseminated socialist literature. Their emergence was timely. The eighties turned out to be a politically tempestuous decade in which issues of poverty, unemployment and moral breakdown were responded to with anxiety and sometimes panic.[5] In their certain promise of swift and radical economic and social change, the ideologies of revolutionary socialism and its gradualist splinter, the Fabian Society, challenged the attraction of the Christian millenium.

Another factor in the secularization of Christian discourse was public criticism of the church for its lack of influence over the working classes. 'Reaching the working classes' became a popular call for action and exposed the perceived ineffectiveness of Christian discourse. The inability of the middle classes to understand the working classes was pervasively expressed in terms of the working class being 'dumb', or possessed only of a pre-language of inarticulate sounds.[6] If the church was to reach the working classes it was felt that a new language was needed, a language that would make possible common grounds for understanding between the classes.

The most powerful challenge to a Christian interpretation of society was not, therefore, on the streets or in the slums where there was considerable consensus about appropriate action, but on the battlefield of language. Committed Christians who were also social activists enthusiastically made more or less conscious partnerships with secular discourses in their attempts to secularize Christianity and, as they thought, influence social issues more effectively. Socialism played a particularly important part, assuming a significance in the public opinion of the 1880s far greater that the political power it was actually able to wield. Arguably, its most durable contribution to the debate was the permeation of Christian social ethics by its materialist world view. Socialism was perceived as providing the language to articulate the conclusions reached independently by social commentators and slum priests. They selected from it and adapted it for their purposes just as earlier the humanists and positivists had borrowed from a Christian vocabulary.[7] Christians, socialists and humanists became linked not only in social action but also in fascinating linguistic interchanges.

These interchanges or liaisons did not only pose a problem for Christian discourse. This further problem could be expressed as a displacement from the public domain of those metaphorical networks which articulate spiritual meanings. I would argue that this displacement left a void which, almost instantaneously, set up a compensatory drift towards symbolic, allegorical or utopian parallels.

While practising Christians sought secularization, a concerned middle-class audience was reluctant to jettison a spiritual dimension. This created a specific need to reconstruct metaphor to accommodate the spiritual meanings subordinated by secularization and to resolve the tensions between materialist imperatives and spiritual understanding.

That need was met by a complex web of fiction-making which attempted to sustain and realize a harmonious balance between secular and spiritual approaches to social problems. Journalism and realistic fiction, those intrinsically secular forms, became a means of achieving that balance. In doing so, they unconsciously undermined the secularization they overtly applauded, and set up the conditions for the creation of urban utopias. These utopias were almost exclusively set in London which, by the end of the 1890s had witnessed radical social changes and a multiplicity of responses to them. London became not only a topographical location beset by extraordinary social problems but an arena of debate where the concepts of conflicting value systems were materialized. London, always a unique phenomenon, assumed in the course of these twenty years consciously a kind of mythological status, a consciously amorphous, unknowable but vital identity that transcended its material, concrete existence and lent itself to visionary transformations.

Within this context, three major transformations of Christian discourse can be discerned. The first stems from an attempted integration of socialist and Christian objectives. Such a liaison already had a substantial history by the early 1890s. Mid-century Christian socialists had forged a link between the spiritual and ethical ideals of Christian theology and practical Christianity, or rather reaffirmed that social justice and concern was the natural expression of a Christian faith.

The Rev Stewart Headlam constructed a unique version of this integration. A familiar figure in the history of the late nineteenth century for his involvement in social issues, his own writings, which illuminate an extraordinary aspect of late Victorian optimism, remain largely unread. In his writings, Headlam explores beyond the humanitarian meeting point of socialist theory and Christian belief to investigate the possible reality of an evolution of discourse. While never questioning Christ and the significance of the Christian revelation, he suggested that that revelation might find different modes of expression from generation to generation. Socialism appeared to him to provide the latter-day language which could express the needs of the anxious, alienated late nineteenth-century citizen.

Headlam had found his niche in the church and his vocation when he founded the Guild of St Matthew in 1877 and established it as a meeting point for priests and committed laymen who were convinced about the crucial nature of the church's social role. It was through the Guild that Headlam met those church contemporaries who were to become notable as advocates of a socialist identity for the Church of England – men like the Reverend Percy Dearmer, the Reverend Thomas Hancock, the Reverend Conrad Noel and Canon Shuttleworth. Although the Guild did not include a political statement in its aims, much less a socialist statement, it was as Socialists that its members defined themselves. The perceived need to take up the challenge of secularism and a conviction of the social implications of the Incarnation and Holy Communion were fused into a doctrinal base for socialist activism. In its 'at once intensely religious and intensely political' ethos Headlam began to write the series of sermons and pamphlets in which he developed his theology.[8]

Other socialist theories were also in the air. Headlam enthusiastically supported those outlined by Henry George in his *Progress and Poverty* and helped to fund and organize a series of lectures during his first visit to England in 1884. Like many other Christians he became a Fabian in 1886 and served on the executive committee from 1890 to 1891, but his religious convictions made their theoretical and scientific approach to socialism uncomfortable for him. However, it was a feature of socialist groupings in the eighties that ideological boundaries were not always rigidly drawn. Frederic Harrison's comment that 'We are all socialists now' indicates how pervasive socialist ideas were at the time, but also how vague and ill-defined they had become.[9]

Stewart Headlam's political sympathies were strongly grounded in Christian doctrine, not in Marxist ideology. His fundamental aim was to unravel Christian thought and rescue it from centuries of institutionalization. The two doctrines he considered central to Christian thinking were expressed in church ritual through the two sacraments, baptism and Holy Communion, or Mass as it was called by the High Church. In these two sacraments he felt Christianity and socialism were inextricably bound together. As he was to say later:

'our Sacramentalism with our Socialism ... we are Socialists because we are Sacramentarians'.[10] The language of socialism, he believed, was in reality the Christian discourse for the end of the century.

When Headlam was first struggling to formulate and articulate this sacramental social theology, he concentrated first on the secularization of *ideas*. One of his earliest published collections of sermons, *The Service of Humanity*, explored this approach in the conventional mode of Christian exegesis.[11] His second concern, and the one most important for this discussion, was to test out the parallels between the imperatives of Christianity and those of socialism. As his ideas developed it is clear that he became increasingly convinced that socialism was not simply a political ideology that best served Christianity's secular purpose but that read correctly, the gospels and doctrines of Christianity *were* socialist texts. It is easy to see from the discussion of the sacraments of baptism and Holy Communion above, how he reached this position. A worker-Christ who emphasized equality, social responsibility and close social relationships above all else, could claim to be the father of socialism. He did not accept the reverse position. As he argued later in *The Socialists' Church* (1907), some socialists had exalted socialism into a form of religion and had mistakenly assumed it to be a reasoned and complete philosophy of life.[12]

From his earliest writings Headlam scattered socialist terminology apparently indiscriminately among conventional Christian terminology. While this practice partly suggests that in the early years he was emotionally but not intellectually clear about the connections, it is more likely that he hoped to shock his audience into rethinking the issues by juxtaposing the two discourses; to familiarize them with new vocabulary; to remove the threat from what many felt was a provocative and potentially destructive revolutionary philosophy. The variety of terminology would be bewildering if it were not accepted as being largely interchangeable: communism, communists, commune, communistic, socialism, socialists, socialistic, scientific socialists, Christian socialists, Christian democracy, democracy, are used with frequency and vigour. It is probably not helpful to demand too much precision since it is Headlam's attempt to draw contemporary socialist ideas into Christian discourse that is the important issue rather than the fitting of Christianity into the subtleties of political nuance. Within this collected series of sermons Headlam could state with a confidence grounded in a utopian discourse rather than in any actuality that: 'the Christian Church is distinctly and essentially democratic ... the Church is the true Commune [and that] ... it is a Socialistic Carpenter whom you are worshipping'.[13]

In 1884, Headlam published *The Laws of Eternal Life: Being Studies in the Church Catechism*. It was to be his most systematic attempt to give a contemporary expression of Christianity a socialist vocabulary. His aim was to root the theories of socialism into Christian theology and to articulate them in a new 'mixed discourse', and in so doing to unite the spiritual and secular sides of man's nature. At the same time, he was trying to combat the dualism set up by religion and propagated by social structures in the divisions of wealth and class. Since he took the major aspects of the catechism step by step, moving through the Creed, the Sacrament, the Ten Commandments and the Lord's Prayer, *The Laws of Eternal Life* is repetitive to read and the arguments inconsistent.

Basically, there are two main strands to his argument. The first radicalizes the image of Jesus as worker, revolutionary, rejector of the oppression of nations, of women, the weak and the sick, a lover of humankind. All Christ's words, actions, parables and the subsequent doctrines built on them by the church are measured against and interpreted through this secular reality. The second thread is the theological substructure. The acceptance of Christ's humanity confirms the Incarnation as proclaiming the uniqueness of man, and the class and time in which he entered history indicates the values he wished to propagate.

The Laws of Eternal Life was written at the high point of the Guild's membership and when Headlam was full of confidence for the future of the church and its role in society. In it he establishes a minimal vocabulary for the fusion of Christianity and socialism: for Baptism read Democracy; for Incarnation read Equality; for Holy Communion read Brotherhood; for Sacramentalism read Socialism; for Church read Commune; for Spiritual read Secular. These words echo like a drumbeat through all his writings, reaching their greatest clarity of exposition in *The Socialists' Church* in 1907. Bettany's comment that: 'When he had discovered the right words for his thoughts he was not afraid of repeating them, he did not go hunting about for synonyms', probably misrepresents Headlam's educative purpose in working out the ideas of Christianity for his contemporaries through a fresh, provocative and relevant vocabulary.[14] An insistence on a core vocabulary was very likely to be memorable.

Reading Headlam's writings today one has the sense not of a potential Christian revolution but an evolutionary cul-de-sac. His vision of a dynamic language that would resolve the duality of materialism and spirituality and embody past and present seems like a pedantic intellectual game. In 1918 – ten years after the publication of *The Socialists' Church* – he admitted that his vision of the future had failed: 'we have not succeeded in inducing Labour and Socialism to make of the Church a Brotherhood and use it as a great reforming instrument.'[15] Headlam's theological achievement was negligible; his practical achievements considerable (a judgment that would appear to validate materialism and reject the vision that informed his linguistic struggles as futile).[16] However, it is interesting to speculate how influential the work of The Guild of St Matthew's was on the development of socialism into the twentieth century, a powerful feature of which is its attachment to an ethical base.

Counterpointing Headlam's passionate but intellectual approach and its latter-day sense of a somewhat barren game, is a series of linguistic transformations. In the work of Father Jay, Christian doctrine is first communicated through a non-verbal secular language inferred from Christian practice within the set of relationships where the working class, the middle class and the divine intersect.[17]

In a radical social experiment, Father A. O. Jay, a High Church parish priest, sought to relocate the spiritual truths he believed were embodied in church language and ritual into the conventions and rituals of everyday living. The challenge was daunting. He worked in Shoreditch, one of the most notorious of London's slum areas, from 1886 to beyond the end of the century. As such he represents a number of priests of all denominations who worked selflessly and tirelessly in the slums dealing on a daily basis with the horrors of disease and the tragedies of poverty. Unlike most of his contemporaries though, he became well known for his unconventional methods and for his perceived success in bringing Christianity to the working classes.

Part of Jay's non-verbal language was his version of parish organization. He established a temporary 'church' in an old stable building and held informal services in the mode of daily social intercourse. There were no rules about dress or smoking; no formal procedures were followed; there was no sermon. The 'church' (or 'club') was simply an area for quiet conversation. However, Jay was a crucial part of the communication system: he offered himself, his physical presence and behaviour, as a counterpointing set of values to those informing slum life. In his own writings, intended for a middle-class audience, he claimed to use an apolitical radical discourse grounded in but not expressed through the language of Christianity.

The interest of Jay for my argument lies in the further trans-formations of him and his work which were constructed by contemporary journalism and fiction. Paradoxically, his attempt to construct a neo-Christian secular meaning was more successful in creating myths around the scope and nature of his success and around his own charismatic figure. These writings reveal the conflict between contemporary pragmatism and a contemporary need to sustain a vision of a spiritual future. They create utopias of a regenerated London, and transform a man who rejected what he considered as 'the great and visionary tendencies of our time' into a messianic interpreter of the 'old' in terms of the 'new'. Journalists were not slow to recognize the value of the material Jay's work offered. They created for the public a contemporary figurehead, a man capable of turning the 'abyss' of London into the Kingdom of God.

Jay first set in motion publicity for his parish with an appeal for funds to build a new church. But it was Frederick Greenwood's article in the *Daily Telegraph* of 1887 which first selected and wrote up the aspects of his ministry that were to reverberate through numerous articles for the next ten years.[18] On 1st October 1887, he had written about Shoreditch in 'London Fever Nests', pointing out the dangers of disease as vigorously as George Sims and Andrew Mearns before him. He followed this up on October 22nd with his account of Father Jay's work. No doubt the close juxtaposition of the articles went some way to creating a sympathetic and responsive support for a priest who offered some answer to readers' fears.

Greenwood writes in detail about the running of the club, listing all the facilities, rules, its history and its members' responses. Among these facts are mentioned the boxing ring, the freedom to smoke, and the upstairs church. He also singles out two anecdotes about thefts from the club. One in particular, told in Jay's own account, *The Story of Shoreditch*, about the theft and return of bagatelle balls, is amusingly expanded.

Greenwood also stresses Jay's own role and emphasizes the appropriateness of Jay's method in its lack of religious indoctrination, the interchange between club members and congregation and its informality. The article is long and loses no opportunity to make entertaining reading, but its purpose is fundamentally serious. Greenwood expresses enthusiasm and belief in Jay's effectiveness, but always within the context of well-informed, investigative journalism.

Another article about Jay published eight years later in *The New Budget* entitled 'The English Barbarian. His Haunts, His Homes, His Habits and His Heroes', shows the shift that has taken place in describing his work.[19] During those years, two of Jay's books had been published, gaining him wider publicity and making the details of his ministry more generally available. The article is notably couched almost entirely in the past tense, as if the problems of Shoreditch are now a thing of history to be considered as a curiosity. What is being described is a completed and successful mission.

In this article we see the beginning of a process of reclaiming secular activity for the realm of spiritual triumph. Firstly, Jay's personality is made the pivot to which facts and social commentary are subordinated, and much of the account is ostensibly the writing up of an informal conversation with Jay, where his down-to-earth pragmatism is emphasized. But there are significant additions which begin to build up a picture of Jay, not as a man who can allow other men to be themselves, but who is himself one of the men. We are told not only that there is a 'fully-equipped boxing-ring' but that 'The reverend gentleman himself often dons the gloves.'

However, a second strand of the article also portrays him as a supreme controller, whose unique qualities had transformed 'A spot which has been reckoned a very hell on earth...into a Christian Church.' How far Jay sanctioned this inflated interpretation, it is impossible to say. In a sense it was certainly what he and others desired, namely not eschatological prophecy, now fossilized and irrelevant, where men struggled from corrupted London to certain salvation, but the Kingdom of God created by transformed social relationships in temporal London. However, the use of metaphor here has the opposite effect since it actually reverses the process of secularization.

An article written as late as 1898 by Arthur Mee, when Jay was about to vanish from the public eye into oblivion, makes the apotheosis complete.[20] The first third of a long article entitled 'A Transformation in Slumland' belabours the horrors of Shoreditch *as it was*. Jay is interviewed as part of the article and the old familiar information about the club, the bagatelle balls, the boxing and the church over the stable is reiterated, but the emphasis on the personality of Jay has undergone a further stage of metamorphosis. His individuality is now subordinated to the abstract, the specific to the grand vision. Moving through metaphor towards parable, Mee compares the power of Christianity to the growth of a mustard seed in the language of St Matthew's Gospel. The introduction of electric lighting, the slum clearances and the consequent departure of some of Shoreditch's most depraved elements are all swept up into this metaphor as the article builds to its grand conclusion:

Never in the history of religion has there been a more signal triumph of right over wrong ... the crusade begun in a hayloft is more truly representative of greatness and power than the Stock Exchange of every capital in Europe. From such little causes spring the great events.

Here, the symbolic overlay of Christian discourse that Jay had done so much to jettison has been reconstructed to invest the parochial and secular base of Jay's ministry with an appropriate grandeur.

The image of Jay, 'the Saviour of Shoreditch', was potent enough to inspire writers of contemporary fiction. However, this second process of transformation is different since the novelist is less tied to the specifics of facts, time and place. Journalists universalized Jay's localized, marginal success by distracting the reader from those specifics and subsuming them into the symbolic. The novelist did not require such a strategy. The contemporary fascination with the slums, poverty and the secular forms of practical Christianity could be indulged. Any tension that arose between the writer's knowledge of the actual success of these approaches and their desire for that success, could be resolved by the narrative.

These texts work on the reader by becoming objects of desire. There is a collusion between reader and writer which allows utopian possibilities to flourish on the streets of London. Jay's function appears to lie in providing the images of secularization that could then be offered as models of success in secular terms but fictional context.

In *The Redemption of Edward Strahan* (1891), W. J. Dawson clearly drew on the Jay cult, although as a whole the novel is a medley of literary traditions, mingling plot elements of the morality tale and the quest within a framework of social realism.[21] The part of the novel immediately relevant to this discussion is concerned with Edward's stay in London. He goes to work with the 'worst' elements of the population in the 'worst' district of London, and his missionary activities are channelled through a warehouse which he transforms into a gymnasium. The incident that ties it specifically to Jay is Edward's recounting of the bagatelle ball incident, changed in the novel to billiard balls. Traditional religious elements are strong in both plot and characterization, with London being presented as a purgatory where Edward is doomed to expiate his sins. Here, then, the success of these activities is a version of personal redemption achieved outside formal church structures.

A more developed portrait occurs in *A Princess of the Gutter* by L. T. Meade.[22] Very similar in approach to the slum novels of the early eighties, it was not, in fact, published until 1895. Here Jay is barely disguised as Father Moore. The heroine, Joan Prinsep, having unexpectedly inherited a fortune but also a social obligation, takes herself off to the East End where she carries out her philanthropic intentions under his guidance.

The factual background of Jay's ministry is transferred unchanged to the novel. A physical description of Father Moore is not developed but his charisma is, as L. T. Meade describes how his very presence conveys power, urgency and authority leavened with sympathy and courage: 'His face was full of energy. He had dark eyes, which seemed to glow with a sort of inward fire.' (p. 86) Also consistent with Jay's contempt for half-hearted philanthropic action is Father Moore's demand that Joan choose between her old life and her new life. It is only when faced with his apparently impossible demands that Joan finds herself able to throw off doubts and fears and commit herself totally to the poor. Father Moore rejects her money if it is given without herself, and demands: 'If you give at all, give everything.'[23] Joan tells the reader that 'His strong soul bore me upwards on wings like an eagle', and in a moment of vision she sees in him the potentiality of every soul in Shoreditch.

Important as Father Moore is as a spiritual mentor, the weight of the novel revolves around the narrative of Joan's experiences; the experiences of a well-bred, well-educated woman in the East End. In Arthur Morrison's *A Child of the Jago*, Jay's persona Father Sturt, is not simply the moral fulcrum of the novel. Sturt has, in fact, a triple function. He has his own narrative – told directly by the author – of his struggles and his practices in the Jago. These are drawn directly from historical data and cover the now familiar facts. He also participates at many points of the other narratives – ordering, suggesting, alleviating, comforting. Most significantly, his physical presence, or even more magically his name, become emblems into which all his moral weight is gathered. The authority and Titan-like power with which he strides through the novel intensify and hallow the Jay myth while remaining closest to Jay's own desire for the community of the parish and the care of the parish priest.

Yet Morrison's fidelity to his material highlights the paradox at the centre of the novel. Morrison grew to like and respect Jay, claiming in his preface that he wished 'to show that Father Jay's method is the only one that is possible to employ in such a district', and dedicating the novel to him.[24] The narrative's statement of his power and the characters' apparent recognition of it to some extent sets up false expectations for the reader. As Wells points out in his review of *A Child of the Jago*, the narrative logic of the text works against its surface.[25] Dicky Perrott is the character in whom the potential is most obvious and whose fate Morrison traces most thoroughly. Yet despite his intelligence, his determination not to sink into the Jago horrors and his respect for Father Sturt, he dies at the end of the novel defeated by external circumstances set up by Jago life. In attempting to maintain a realism that is both truthful to the secular role of Father Sturt and to the environmental effects of the Jago, Morrison disguises but does not resolve the paradox between the desired ends of secular Christianity and the determining force of social structures.

If Jay had not existed I feel that it would have been socially necessary to invent him in order to fulfil the expectations already set up by philanthropic debate, journalistic outrage and political expediency. In a sense, this was the process that took place. Jay was more exciting than fiction because he existed, but he needed fiction to make the 'abyss' of London a nineteenth-century Kingdom of God. Through contemporary fiction he became the resolver of paradox. He could harrow hell and restore its inmates to their rightful position, yet his mode of action was secular and benign. It is only as a myth that he can survive today; a larger-than-life figure that stalks the streets of an imagined East End.

This dissolving of the boundaries between political and theological discourse in fiction creates intriguing versions of utopianism. The process can be investigated in a group of texts which I shall call 'social redemption' novels, that gave fictional form to the materialization of Christianity through the city and the secularization of

Christianity through humanist or socialist discourse. Their popularity and influence were widely acknowledged in their own time by theologians and critics alike, although opinions as to their value differed widely.[26]

In some ways these novels form an uncomfortable grouping, but they share several important common features. They all foreground issues of the relevance of Christianity to working-class concerns. They all see the perceived threats of secularism and atheism as due to the failure of the Church to reach this social group, and counter-attack by fashioning secular versions of Christianity. The narratives seek resolution of the spiritual/secular dilemma by universalizing from the experiences of a powerful hero-figure. They are all set in London, the focus and embodiment of contemporary religious and class conflict. Crucially, they were all seen as contributions to the contemporary debate. It is in these texts that we witness the final transformation I want to discuss – that of fictional texts as theological evidence or as theological texts in their own right.

The novels reveal a diversity of ways in which Christian discourse was used in fiction in an attempt to secularize it. I shall mention four that seem to me to be representative of the range of common themes. Mrs Humphrey Ward's *Robert Elsmere* (1888) is concerned with loss of faith and explores the reorientation of Christian ideas and Christian discourse in a new sense of urban community.[27] W. J. Dawson's *The Redemption of Edward Strahan* (1891), which has already been referred to, draws on traditional conventions of moral didacticism and slum realism but uses them as a framework for exploring the more contemporary problem of sustaining personal meaning outside the institutionalized church. Reverend James Adderley's *Stephen Remarx* (1893) finds a fictional parallel to the work of his fellow socialist, Stewart Headlam, in a quasi-Marxist articulation of religious commitment. Approaching the issue from a very different perspective, Robert Buchanan's *The Reverend Annabel Lee* (1898) constructs a counterpointing scientific utopia against a dystopic nightmare of Christianity as the religion which sanctifies pain and suffering.[28]

Novels such as these illustrate how writers were beginning to concern themselves with the instability of contemporary theology and morality, and saw their novels as restatements of them. They began to use their fictions, either wholly or partly, not only to explore social issues but to be specific instruments of influence. The latter part of the century revealed a conviction, for better or worse, that the religious novel was a quasi-political force in a new and potent way.

I would maintain that these novels had a peculiarly influential role in secularizing Christian discourse by transferring spiritual issues and theological debate from the theologians to the lay reader. Writers took advantage of fiction's ability to 'present through language a totally different vision of possible social formations'; they had the power to present fiction as fact, to imply the universal from the specific and to present a desired outcome as a realistic now.[29] These texts appeared to be attractive as secular/socialist alternatives to the gospels, religious commentary and political and social tracts probably because they bridged the gap between abstruse theological controversy, political action and the personal need for an expression of faith. Novels had the effect of individualizing religious opinion and freeing people from sectarian priests. They problematized institutionalized religion and, no doubt, fed as well as grew out of, the desire for the secularization of religion. Perhaps most importantly they were able to offer a version of that intersecting point where science, politics and religion crossed in a succession of hypotheses concerning the nature of man, God and society. Priests as well as writers chose fiction above the sermon, the debate or the philosophical tract as a more pervasive, immediate and appropriate way 'to reach the public'.[30]

However successful these novels were in their own day, they failed in their long-term objectives. They used realism as a device to secularize the narrative and show the power of religion in the context of poverty and the working classes but, in fact, offered utopias as the narrative outcome. In doing this they satisfied 'the warfare of conscience with theology' but sacrificed coherence of structure and discourse.[31] They created a concrete, temporal London in a period of actual historical crisis but relied on appeals to feeling in order to resolve the contradictions between different analyses of social ills. In responding to the public's desire for new answers, both Christian and socialist discourse were drawn into an alien fictional mode where their distinctive features became confused and weakened.

Socialism, as I have already noted, was thought by many to provide the language for describing daily reality, but as practical Christians drew on its source to explain and enrich their vision of this reality, whether in novels or in social and theological tracts, its own material definitiveness became leavened with metaphor. The social and economic concepts embodied in terms such as 'brotherhood', 'communism' and 'socialism' were transmuted into metaphysical terms which underpinned a moral landscape into which material facts such as 'labour', 'property' and 'capital' were transplanted. The fictional realizations of this semantic marriage in an experientially and aesthetically unsubstantiated discourse, compounded the theological and political confusions of the time. As Stephen Mayor concludes in *The Church and the Labour Movement*: 'It is difficult to attempt any summing-up of the relationship of religion to the progress of Socialism during this period (the 1890s) because of the repeated failure of all parties to the debate to define what they meant by the term.'[32]

However inconsistent and flawed they are as realistic novels, these texts focus on an important moment of flux in the struggle between spiritual and material conceptions of the world. They suggested a more comprehensive paradigm of the cause and resolution of man's sense of alienation. They did not pinpoint a moment of progress for Christianity, but rather a growing plurality of thought, facilitated by an increased public awareness of the languages of secularism and socialism, through which the same phenomenon – the suffering of the working classes in slum London – could be described.

This struggle for a satisfying public discourse at the end of the century grew out of a positive desire for change and an active determination to underpin the building of a new society. Yet the utopias it generated only demonstrate the weakness of that vision. As 1900 dawned, utopias were already giving way to dark dystopias. Specifically religious utopias seemed suddenly irrelevant. The balance had been shifted. The sediment of Christian discourse which remains today in our public discourse is merely a traditional and decorative framework for a materialist society.

NOTES

1 Charles Booth, *Labour and Life of the People: Poverty Series*, vols. 1 and 2 (London: Williams and Norgate, 1889), p. 30. The phrase is used here to convey the spirit of Booth's comment which goes far towards articulating the tension found in many of the quasi-sociological writings of the early 1880s between the available discourse and the perceived facts.

2 *Ibid.* Pages 15 to 19 contain Booth's argument for an objective language to describe social conditions.

3 *Ibid.* On page 51, Booth concludes his description of the class categories

by defining Class E – the artisan working class – as the class which 'holds its future in its own hands'.

4 See Owen Chadwick, *The Victorian Church* (1966; reprint London: Adam and Charles Black, 1971). Chadwick identifies the late eighties and early nineties as the point at which the gradual processes of secularization entered social consciousness. The Lambeth Conferences of this period also made this theme central to their agendas.

5 Helen M. Lynd's *England in the Eighteen Eighties* (London: Frank Cass, 1968) remains the best overview of the mood of the eighties.

6 The idea was not new. Elizabeth Gaskell had justified the material in her novel *Mary Barton* (1848) by claiming that she spoke for 'this dumb people'. The title of Andrew Mearns's pamphlet *The Bitter Cry of Outcast London* (London: James Clark, 1883) about the plight of the homeless gave the idea of a vernacular form which echoes through the journalism and social commentaries of the 1880s and 1890s.

7 See, for instance, the sacramental language used by Frederic Harrison in *The Meaning of History and Other Historical Pieces* (London: Macmillan, 1894).

8 Kenneth Leach, 'Stewart Headlam', in Maurice B. Reckitt (ed.), *For Christ and the People: Studies of Four Socialist Priests and Prophets of the Church of England between 1870 and 1930* (London: SPCK, 1968), p. 63.

9 Frederic Harrison, *Moral and Religious Socialism. A New Year's Address* (London: Reeves and Turner, 1891), p. 23.

10 *Church Reformer*, 9: 11 (November 1890), 244.

11 Stewart Headlam, *The Service of Humanity and Other Sermons* (London: John Hodges, 1882). The text discussed is the washing of Christ's feet by the disciples as a secular expression of a spiritual idea. The word 'secular' is reiterated as a marker of the central idea, but probably also to reclaim it from the secularists who were still very active at this time.

12 Stewart Headlam, *The Socialists' Church* (London: G. Allen, 1907), p. 48, p. 67.

13 Headlam, *The Service of Humanity*, p. 124, p. 72, p. 13.

14 F. G. Bettany, *Stewart Headlam: A Biography* (London: J. Murray, 1926), p. 229.

15 *Ibid.*, p. 144.

16 It is possible to argue that Christian discourse has had much greater success in integrating with the discourse of labour politics than Marx. See, for instance, Stanley Pierson, *British Socialists: The Journey From Fantasy to Politics* (Cambridge, Mass.: Harvard University Press, 1979), which traces the impact of Methodism.

17 Father A. O. Jay recorded his experiences as a parish priest in *Life in Darkest London* (London: Webster and Cable, 1891), and *A Story of Shoreditch* (London: Simpkin, Marshall and Co., 1896).

18 Frederick Greenwood (pseud. 'One of a Crowd'), 'A Shoreditch Club', *Daily Telegraph*, 22 October 1887, p. 2.

19 An American in London, 'The English Barbarian. His Haunts, His Homes, His Habits and His Heroes', *New Budget*, 22 August 1895, pp. 28–29.

20 Arthur Mee, 'The Transformation in Slumland: the remarkable story of a London Clergyman', *Temple Magazine*, 2: 181 (1898), 449–454.

21 W. J. Dawson, *The Redemption of Edward Strahan* (London: Hodder and Stoughton, 1891).

22 L. T. Meade, *A Princess of the Gutter* (London: Wells, Gardner, Darton, 1895), p. 86.

23 *Ibid.*, p. 92.

24 Arthur Morrison, *A Child of the Jago* (London: Methuen, 1896), Preface.

25 H. G. Wells, 'A Slum Novel', *Saturday Review*, 82: 28 November 1896, p. 573.

26 See for example the Rev S. Law Wilson, *The Theology of Modern Literature* (Edinburgh: T. and T. Clark, 1899), p. 8; Thomas G. Selby, *The Theology of Modern Fiction* (London: C. H. Kelley, 1890), p. 191; James Adderley, *In Slums and Society* (London: T. Fisher Unwin, 1916), p. 153.

27 Mrs Humphry Ward, *Robert Elsmere* (London: Smith, Elder, 1888).

28 Rev James Adderley, *Stephen Remarx: The Story of a Venture in Ethics* (London: Edward Arnold, 1893); Robert Buchanan, *The Reverend Annabel Lee* (London: C. Arthur Pearson, 1898).

29 A. P. Foulkes, *Literature and Propaganda* (London and New York: Methuen, 1983), p. 40.

30 Mrs Humphry Ward, *A Writer's Recollections* (London: W. Collins, 1918), p. 229.

31 Joseph L. Althoz, 'The Warfare of Conscience with Theology', in Joseph L. Althoz (ed.), *The Mind and Art of Victorian England* (Minneapolis: University of Minnesota Press, 1976), p. 59.

32 Stephen Mayor, *The Church and the Labour Movement* (London: Independent Press, 1967), p. 280.

CHAPTER 10

Vampires and the empire: fears and fictions of the 1890s

Alexandra Warwick

> And Empire after Empire, at their height
> Of sway, have felt this boding sense come on;
> Have felt their huge frames not constructed right,
> And drooped, and slowly died upon their throne.
>
> (Matthew Arnold, 'Revolutions')

The closing decades of the nineteenth century exhibit some significant manifestations of that modern myth – the vampire. The very existence of a modern myth is something of a curiosity as it appears to defy the kinds of explanations usually offered in terms of 'mankind's deepest fears' and the eternal and universal nature of those fears, and rather to imply a concentration of culturally specific horrors. As Chris Baldick writes of that other enduring monster, Frankenstein's creation:

Such a thing should not exist, according to the most influential accounts of what 'myth' is... Modern myths are marginalized by rational discourses, they do not command the same kind of assent as 'primitive' myths; their status bears, in short, the scars and handicaps imposed upon it by successive cultural transformations.[1]

The cultural transformations of the vampire that take place during the course of the nineteenth century are closely linked to several developing discourses of the period, principally gender, disease and the decline of the imperial (that is to say, British) race. These in turn are interlinked in the notion of degeneration that reaches a highly developed stage in the 1890s, providing the precursor to Edwardian legislation designed to protect the national stock. It is during this period that the myth of the vampire is consolidated; and while Bram Stoker's famous contribution cannot be understated (much of what we now accept as folklore on the subject is, in fact, of his invention – the prophylactic garlic, for example) there were several other texts which contributed further 'scars and handicaps' while still serving to substantiate important aspects of the myth in relation to the feared collapse of gender categories, the location of syphilitic infection in the female body and the health of the Empire. The high-water mark of British imperialism was celebrated by Queen Victoria's Diamond Jubilee in 1897, the same year that saw the publication of two significant vampire fictions: Florence Marryat's *The Blood of the Vampire*, and Stoker's *Dracula*; but the empire was already feeling, in Arnold's words, 'its huge frame not constructed right', a fact which was to become absolutely clear in the ensuing years of social tension, strikes and unemployment at home and uprisings in the colonies. The third text I intend to examine here is George MacDonald's *Lilith* (1895), and although the vampires of these texts are apparently quite different, perhaps inevitably, given the metamorphic nature of the vampire, they all exhibit important congruities through their definition by the rational discourses of 'race', gender and disease circulating at the *fin de siècle*.

One of the most important discourses is that of gender; it is conspicuous that apart from the Count himself, all the other vampires in Stoker's text are female. He is, in fact, the only male vampire to appear in these three novels. The categories of masculine and feminine are strongly defined in vampire fictions, but as Christopher Craft observes in his excellent essay on gender inversion in *Dracula*,[2] these are subject to continual re-allocation, gender does not constantly correspond with biological sex. Neither is the predominance of the female vampire a constant feature; in the texts of the early nineteenth century such as Polidori's *The Vampyre* (1819) and Rymer's *Varney the Vampire* (issued in serial form in the 1840s) the vampire is male and all the victims female. The aristocratic villains, Lord Ruthven and Sir Francis Varney are little more than versions of the rakish seducer; there seems to be no danger that their victims will themselves become vampires, they suffer either simple death or social disgrace. In the case of Varney, there would even seem to be some question as to whether he actually is 'undead', and not just a serial killer. The victims are the type of the vulnerable woman familiar from the Gothic novel and the seduction story – passive, beautiful and frequently, orphaned. The trope of infection – that those bitten become vampires – is largely absent at this point, but as the century progresses and the figure of the vampire acquires an immoral aspect in addition to its supernatural, it becomes one of the vital components of the myth; the relationship between gender and infection becomes central to the narratives, as it is the female body that is increasingly seen as the source of danger, and the disruption of gender identity as one of the effects of contagion.

One of the significant aspects of Polidori's story is the relationship between Lord Ruthven and Aubrey, the 'young gentleman' on whom the tale focuses. The former exercises on Aubrey the same mesmeric influence we see exerted by Dracula over Jonathan Harker. Aubrey and Harker are transfixed, apparently powerless to do anything but watch the actions of the monsters. Aubrey plainly takes pleasure in watching Ruthven and returns to him even after fairly conclusive proof of his part in Ianthe's death. Though there is no explicit mention of infection in Polidori's tale, Aubrey, like Harker, becomes ill as a result of his exposure to the vampire. It seems that the various 'illnesses' that are produced in vampire texts are contingent on the shifting of gender. Men are only directly attacked by women; but their contact with male vampires causes a different kind of infection. Both Aubrey's and Harker's illnesses, for example, significantly 'feminize' them: they become weak, pale, hysterical and ineffectual – impotent, in fact. Their illnesses correspond with the symptoms of vampire attacks that are manifested in women; Harker, for example, 'so thin and pale and weak-looking'[3] and Aubrey, 'he would often lie for days, incapable of being roused. He had become emaciated, his eyes had attained a glassy lustre.'[4] This is the equivalent of the contagious vampirism that only affects women, they become *like* women. Harker's illness is a source of shame, enclosed in a footnote to a letter and sealed in a diary, and we never discover what precipitates it. His curious and unexplained comment, 'If I be sane, then surely it is maddening to think that of all the foul things that lurk in this hateful place the Count is the least dreadful to me.'[5] provides some clues. As he then goes on to recount the assault on him by the female vampires we infer that it is they who are the most dreadful. In one of the clearest passages of gender inversion in the novel, they are the masculinized seducers, far from impotent with their hard, penetrating teeth and arched necks; and he is the coy maiden, peeping out from under his eyelashes. The threat that is offered by the de-feminized women is very different from that embodied by men. This is one of the 'dreadfulnesses' of vampirism; the revelation that gender categories are unstable, and a fear that sounded a profound echo in the culture of the 1890s, already shaken by such horrors as the trials of Oscar Wilde and the presence of the New Woman.

Though the feminizing of men appears in early nineteenth-century works, the masculinization of the women that takes place as a result of vampiric attentions is found only in the later texts. Polidori and Rymer rely on the victims' ignorance of the threat presented to them, Ruthven's attack on Ianthe and Varney's on the sleeping Flora Bannerworth do not implicate the women at all: they are 'innocent' victims. Whereas as the century progresses, the index of guilt rises steadily on the part of the victim, until *Dracula*, where apart from the transfixed responses of Mina, Lucy Westenra declares her wish to marry 'as many as want her'. This has usually been read as indicating a dangerous (masculine) sexual independence, but her desire seems to be more confused than this would suggest, as it embodies only a willingness to be possessed by those that want her, her wish is still shaped by passivity. There is a correlation too, between the guilty women and their punishments, both Carmilla and Lucy are staked in ritual fashion; Dracula is simply stabbed in the heart. They are wandering women, 'free lances' as Ralph Pullen describes the sexual (and vampiric) Harriet in *The Blood of the Vampire*:

She is not a girl whom men will marry, and so – we need go no further. Only, I should not be surprised if, notwithstanding her fortune and beauty, we should find Miss Harriet Brandt figuring before long, amongst the free lances of London.[6]

The choice of term is telling; the free lance is the independent phallus, not an attribute of the feminine woman. There is an interesting echo of the phrase in a letter published in *The Times* in December 1917, referring to the period of the turn of the century and signed simply 'M. D.':

Sexual freelances stalked through the land, vampires upon the nation's health, distributing and perpetuating among our young manhood diseases which institute a national calamity.

The link between the masculine woman, the vampire and syphilis is one which recurs frequently, and will be discussed further below. It would seem from this letter and from the fictional texts, that one of the manifestations of vampirism in women is freedom of movement, connected with the inability of men to restrain them. Van Helsing attempts to keep Lucy in her room, almost binding her with the garlic, and then after her death makes efforts to seal her inside the tomb. On coming close to Dracula's castle, Mina has to be restrained inside the holy circle. The wandering women, then, can only be stopped by the transparently phallic stake, wielded by a man. The orgasmic nature of Lucy's death at the hands of her fiancé (whose 'right' to kill her is recognized by the other vampire hunters) on what would have been her wedding night needs no further comment.

The characters of *Dracula* divide into a masculine and a feminine group, and even though Dracula is apparently the enemy, he exhibits closer bonds with the vampire hunters than with Lucy or Mina, or with the three women at the castle, who are seemingly relatives. Neither does he bite Renfield, the other man who is completely in his power. There is an ambivalence about the vampire hunters' attitude to the women; while seeming to regard them as innocent victims, their fear and profound distrust is made clear. The disturbance of gender definition causes the men to blame not the Count but the women, repeating Jonathan's remark that the Count is the 'least dreadful'.

Some of the spaces between Polidori's and Stoker's stories are bridged by Sheridan Le Fanu's *Carmilla* (1871). Here the threat from men to women that appears in the earlier works shifts through an intermediary stage where it is women who present a danger to other women, until by the 1890s it becomes woman's threat to man.[7] The text of *Carmilla* is burdened with clearly superfluous women: nursemaids and governesses; but the serious absence is of that essential woman, the mother. As with the female victims of all the other stories, their mothers are either dead at the beginning or shortly after, and fathers, or father figures such as Van Helsing carry sole parental authority. In *Carmilla* the struggle is between a league of women, Carmilla, her 'mother' and the mysterious black servant against the men, Laura's father, the general, the doctor and the Baron, over the body of Laura. Carmilla too is a wandering woman, she is able to elude the checks that Laura's father attempts to impose upon her, easily escaping from her locked bedroom, and one of the things she promises Laura is 'independence'.

There is also a significant development from Polidori, which is strongly carried through to *Dracula*; and that is the complicity of the victim with the attacker which is manifested in the inability to resist. Laura tells us: 'I used to wish to extricate myself; but my energies seemed to fail me ... I experienced a strange tumultuous excitement that was pleasurable, ever and anon, mingled with a vague sense of fear and disgust.'[8] This is common to both Jonathan – 'There was something about them that made me uneasy, some longing and at the same time some deadly fear' (p. 41) – and Mina Harker – 'I was bewildered, and, strangely enough, I did not want to hinder him.' (p. 321) The effect of this is to transfer responsibility to the victim; the suggestion that they are 'asking for it' is central to the vampire myth, Dracula makes it clear through Renfield that he has to be invited into a house, otherwise he cannot enter.

An interesting visual equivalent of this transfer of responsibility for sexual guilt from men to women is to be found in the comparison of two paintings; J. H. Fuseli's well known *The Nightmare* (1783), and Philip Burne-Jones's less famous *The Vampire* (1897). The nightmare in Fuseli's painting is located in the demon squatting on the woman's chest. She is sleeping or unconscious and the form of her legs and thighs is outlined by her nightdress. She appears to be suffering hysteria or suffocation, and this feeling of oppression is carried through in the crowded pictorial space and heavy curtains. The demon looks out at the viewer, and in the upright version its expression is less like guilt than gloating. The second picture is also clarified by its title, *The Vampire*: Burne-Jones represents a thin woman dressed in a white nightgown, again with her thigh contoured by the fabric. Her teeth are prominent in her open mouth, she crouches over the body of a man who is either dead or sexually exhausted, and in the same position as the woman in *The Nightmare*, while she repeats the posture of Fuseli's demon. The repetition is not limited to the positions of the man and woman; the setting is the same, with the parted curtains at the back, the heavy drape on the right, the raised bed that resembles a catafalque, the falling white bedclothes, even the small table with the curved legs in the left foreground. The point of comparison of these two pictures is that in the hundred years that separate them, the danger has been relocated; it is no longer the threat *to* women from outside dangers that occupies the popular imagination, but rather the threat *from* them, and more specifically the danger they represent to men. It is perhaps interesting that the original frontispiece of *Varney the Vampire* is a also a version of the *Nightmare* tableau, with Varney leaning over Flora who is uncomfortably draped over the bed.

The particular horror of all these pictures is the location of both of them within a domestic interior, the home, and in the inner sanctum of the bedroom. Burne-Jones' picture is a graphic representation of Freud's notion of the uncanny, the *unheimlich*,[9] whereby the known and familiar contains and can become in an instant the concealed and fearful. The literal translation of *unheimlich* as 'unhomely' underlines the uneasiness at the base of the Victorian cult of domesticity. The beautiful young woman too has accomplished the terrible switch to *unheimlich*ness. The state of undeadness, of being simultaneously alive and dead, seems a close correlative to the state of the *unheimlich*. Both are interstitial conditions, signified by the prefix 'un', and both indicate a return of the repressed which undermines security. Hélène Cixous in fact, in her commentary on Freud's essay 'The Uncanny', suggests that the concealed part of the *heimlich* is the knowledge of death, 'which should stay hidden, for if it is manifested to me it means I am dead: only the dead know the secret of death'.[10] Lucy exemplifies this in *Dracula*; she knows the secret of death, she is at once both the beautiful and feminine fiancée and the 'foul Thing', and capable of change in an instant, 'the sweetness was turned to adamantine, heartless cruelty, and the purity to voluptuous wantonness'. (p. 235) What is also clear from this quotation, is that it is not only the living/dead switch that is terrifying, but the switch from the pure woman to the sexual one.

The question of the visibility or otherwise of the vampire, of how it can be known, gains a particular currency in the late nineteenth century. It is derived in part from the taxonomy of witchcraft; looking for marks on the bodies of witches, the proof of their difference, hence their guilt and eligibility for extermination. The problem of whether the 'true self' is visible on the body is manifest in a number of contemporary discourses; the recent trials of Oscar Wilde in 1895 had raised anxieties that homosexuality actually constituted an identity, and worse, that these unspeakables were difficult to distinguish by sight from the 'normal' population. The burgeoning science of sexology embraced such questions, and in a related field Lombroso's work on identification of criminal types from purely external characteristics was also having some influence in Britain. Both these examples suggest in different ways the professionalizing of social investigation under medical auspices rapidly taking place in late Victorian Britain, and this is enacted in the vampire fictions of the period. It is the doctor who is called if there is any question of identification to be decided. The exception here is *Lilith*, because MacDonald is deliberately placing his book in a non-contemporary world, adhering to what he believes to be a timeless Christian economy of ideas. *Dracula* and *The Blood of the Vampire* are distinctly modern, Stoker particularly including new technology, like the wax cylinder dictaphone. The spiritual plays a very small part in *Carmilla* and *The Blood of the Vampire*, and though it is present in *Dracula* it is a confused and contradictory scheme that is collapsed into Van Helsing's professional medical knowledge. Vampirism is likened far more closely to disease than to possession, which might be the immediate religious comparison, and the disease that has already been observed as equivalent to vampirism is syphilis. Stoker's own probable death from tertiary syphilis is recorded by his biographer,[11] but even this putative personal connection is unnecessary in the analysis of the appearance of the disease in these texts; syphilophobia was common in the period. The notorious Contagious Diseases Acts, repealed finally in 1886, penalized the female prostitute for what was considered to be the debilitation of the British fighting forces. The enforcement of these acts relied totally on observation as no blood test for syphilis existed until Wasserman's in 1906. Firstly, the prostitute was identified by sight, only suspicion of her occupation was needed to require her attendance at a medical examination, where the disease was also identified by looking. Finally the woman was allowed to leave hospital if the doctor could be satisfied, again visually, that she was cured. Judith Walkowitz records some of the known devices for deceiving the inspectors,[12] underlining the ridiculous nature of this faith in being able to tell 'by looking'. In the fantasy of being able to tell the vampiric, diseased, bad woman from the healthy good one, Stoker and the other authors produce their own taxonomy – sharp teeth, red mouths, emaciation and pallor. Dr Phillips in *The Blood of the Vampire* states that he 'can tell at a glance' that Harriet has inherited her mother's (blood-thirsty) dispositions, and even her name, Brandt, suggests a mark or a scar. Stoker has an even more useful indicator, it is not only the specialist that can 'tell at a glance' but anyone, as Mina has a mark burnt into her forehead. 'Unclean! Unclean! Even the Almighty shuns my polluted flesh' (p. 331) she laments, emphasizing that the body rather than the soul is the infected part, and making treatment the province of the doctor rather than the priest. The authority of the doctor means professional control over the women, and the presence of doctors is certainly over-determined, one in Marryat's novel, two in *Dracula* and three in *Carmilla*. The doctors legitimate the actions that are carried out, so that the terrible treatment of Lucy's corpse becomes a medical procedure, akin to invasive surgery that violates in order to cure. They also legitimate the forms of knowledge circulated in the texts. Phillips, for example, is solely responsible for the accusations advanced against Harriet, he is never corroborated by any other real evidence, and having stated initially that he only 'knew of, rather than knew' Harriet's parents he ends by describing their activities as an eye witness, 'The mother was the most awful woman I have ever seen, and my experience of the sex in slums and back alleys has not been small',[13] and incidentally introducing ambiguity about his precise activities in these slums. We notice again the insistence on sight. He takes the gossip of the islanders and confers upon it the status of truth:

Neither is it the fault of a madman that his progenitors had lunacy in their blood, nor of a consumptive, that his were strumous. All the same the facts affect their lives and the lives of those with whom they come in contact. It is the curse of heredity ... she possesses the fatal attributes of the Vampire that affected her mother's birth ... that will make Harriet draw upon the health and strength of all with whom she may be intimately associated – that may render her love fatal to such as she may cling to. (p. 141)

He does this by identification of her symptoms, comparison with accepted medical conditions (his choice is interesting as lunacy and consumption are, with syphilis, the three most frequently quoted contributors to degeneration) and prognosis of the progress of the 'patient'. The terms of Phillips' diagnosis draw obvious parallels with syphilis, particularly his emphasis on the danger to those closest to her, the word intimacy readily suggesting the sexual transmission of the malady: Harriet's response when he eventually speaks to her supports this, 'And that is the truth, medically and scientifically – that I must not marry?' (p. 298) as does one of her later remarks, 'I am a social leper, full of contagion and death.' (p. 326) Her perception of herself as a *social* leper is telling, it is clear that she endangers the social group, her own fate is secondary. The metaphor of venereal disease is consolidated in both *Dracula* and *The Blood of the Vampire* by its origins 'abroad', in Eastern Europe and Jamaica respectively. The disease is conveyed to England by travellers of ambivalent status; Harriet is neither white nor black, Dracula is neither dead nor alive, and is positioned awkwardly between East and West in geographical origin. Disease is then transmitted to 'weak' members of the domestic community, therefore 'weakness' of any kind, physical, moral or spiritual places others in danger. The strengthening of moral and spiritual values is explicitly offered as a defence in *Lilith* and *Dracula*, it is the greater strength of character that differentiates Mina's fate from Lucy's, for example. The foreignness of vampirism is of primary significance in the national fears of degeneration exhibited in these vampire fictions. Max Nordau's *Degeneration* was published in English in 1895, but this was only the most notorious of a steady stream of texts propounding theories of cultural decline from the 1860s onwards. In a pamphlet called 'The Danger of Deterioration of the Race', published in 1866, for example we find this statement, 'wherever the blood of the community is extensively contaminated by this poison [syphilis], there likewise fears may be entertained respecting the future vigour of the race' (p. 34). The 'race', of course being the white, and specifically, the British, 'race'. Blood is a continuing synecdoche in these gloomy forecasts, along with a focus on urban dwellers, 'they are town dwellers, and thereby, a doomed "race". Without infusions of new blood in a few generations they die out.'[14] There is a picture here of the urban preying like vampires on the rural, and in using blood as a figure of speech, an evasion of the fact, what is really needed are new genes, and hence not blood, but semen. Links are conspicuously made with the decline of empire, 'We grieve over the fact that a third generation of Anglo-Indians attaining adult years is impossible; but it may be that we have the same non-continuance near home without our having ever given it a thought.'[15]

The undermining taking place here is physical and the frequently used metaphor, that of blood; the vampire fictions refract some of the implications by making the blood and body that of a woman. As Fothergill goes on to say, 'the deterioration, mental and bodily, of town populations is even more marked in the women than the men. They are idler, dirtier, more incontinent, and more indifferent to the opinions of others, than the men.'[16] The word 'incontinent' strongly suggests the lack of both social and sexual control. The concern with the health of the female population springs from the identification of women as child bearers. As forcefully as women were located as the source of degenerate stock, there was a countermovement of feminists that sought to position the blame, especially for syphilitic infection, on the shoulders of men. This struggle seems to take place over the body of the child. The fear of syphilis appears in many of the New Woman novels (such as Sarah Grand's *The Heavenly Twins*, 1893) in the figure of the syphilitic child, infected at birth by an unknowing mother, infected herself by her faithless husband and positioning them both, mother and child, as innocent victims.[17] The mother/child relationship is often picked up in the vampire fantasies to focus the monstrosity of the women; the children become the victims of their mothers' or other women's infection. Where Dracula concentrates his attention on fully grown adults, the women turn to children. The vampires at the castle are given a sack with a child in it, which they fall upon greedily. We are given the additional detail of its mother being eaten by wolves, mercifully, Harker thinks, as she no longer has a child, he assumes she no longer has a function. Lucy, too, after her transformation preys on small children: when the vampire hunters find her Stoker twice states that she has the child 'at her breast'. In a parody of breast feeding, Lucy drains blood from it, instead of allowing it to draw nourishment from her. There is another 'breast feeding' of a more shocking character when Dracula attacks Mina: 'Her white night-dress was smeared with blood, and a thin stream trickled down the man's bare breast which was shown by his torn open dress. The attitude of the two had a terrible resemblance to a child forcing a kitten's nose into a saucer of milk to compel it to drink.' (p. 315) The subtle inversions of gender that define the vampiric attacks are continued here: Dracula seems female with his breast and open dress, and through the elision of blood with milk. Blood serves as an index of relationships, as it becomes milk in these two incidents, it becomes semen when Lucy is receiving her transfusions: 'Arthur was saying that he felt since then as if they two had been really married ... None of us said a word of the other operations, and none of us ever shall.' (p. 193) The guilt felt is disproportionate to the action, and it drops into the wordless, the unspoken, as does so much else in this text. The equation of blood and semen underpins the discourse of degeneration, excessive sexual indulgence is variously thought to injure the health, exhaust the body, impair digestion, derange the brain and nervous system, induce depravity and destroy the marital relationship. What the female vampire is threatening to draw out of the man is not blood but semen (as in Burne-Jones's picture) and to no reproductive end; sex has replaced procreation. The mark of Mina's being saved is her return to a 'proper' female sexual role with the birth of her son.

Carmilla and Harriet Brandt both attack children, Laura is six at the time of Carmilla's first visitation, and it is emphasized several times that the breast is the place of the bite. Harriet hypnotizes Margaret Pullen's baby with her presence, and she says apparently innocently, 'What would I not give to have a baby of my own to do what I liked with?'[18] and later, we are told, 'cuddled the sleeping baby to her bosom, and laid her lips in a long kiss upon its little mouth' (p. 59) in an embrace that is clearly meant to disquiet the reader in its mimicry of motherly love which is, in fact, causing the slow death of the child. The most detailed conflation of vampire and infanticide is found in George MacDonald's *Lilith* (1895) a complex and frequently incoherent work that he called a 'fairytale for adults'. The whole text is submerged in a vampire aesthetic, everyone is either 'dead-alive' or 'living dead', the latter being the desirable state of spiritual transformation where death represents submission to the will of God.[19] The House of Death, administered by Adam, is the resting-place of all until the Day of Judgement but closely resembles a vampire's vault, cold, full of stone slabs supporting the bodies of the 'not-dead-but-sleeping'. (The marked predominance of this phrase on graves in the great Victorian necropolises may have suggested less comforting images after the publication of *Dracula*.) Though Mac-Donald never states explicitly that Lilith is a vampire, her character is clear; she is metamorphic, bats and snakes being among her manifestations. The description of her female self is familiar, when Vane, the narrator, finds her she is to all appearances dead, though actually alive. He describes her body, 'Its beautiful yet terrible teeth, unseemly disclosed by the retracted lips, gleamed ghastly through the dark',[20] and she bites, 'She drew down my face to hers, and her lips clung to my cheek. A sting of pain shot somewhere through me, and pulsed. I could not stir a hair's breadth. Gradually the pain ceased. A slumberous weariness, a dreamy pleasure stole over me, and then I knew nothing.' (p. 151). The sexual aggression of the female vampire, and the passivity of the male victim are familiar:

My will agonized, but in vain, to assert itself. I desisted and lay passive. Then I became aware of a soft hand on my face, pressing my head into the pillow, and of a heavy weight lying across me ... The princess was standing above me on the bed ... her mouth wore a look of satisfied passion; she wiped from it a streak of red. (p. 184)

The notion of woman's sexual disobedience gains mythic support in MacDonald's employment of the story of Lilith, Adam's first wife, whose transgression was to refuse to lie beneath Adam during intercourse, and MacDonald makes the implied accusation explicit, 'For her first thought was power; she counted it slavery to be one with me, and bear children for Him who gave her being.' (p. 204) The original Lilith then flees her husband and becomes a child-killer (significantly, female children are safe from her after twenty days, while boys are in danger until eight years old) and MacDonald retains and develops this, his Lilith not only kills babies but vamps them too. One mother tells of her child's death: 'when I saw the horrid mouth at my darling's little white neck' (p. 156) proving Lilith's sisterhood with Lucy, and Harriet whose first victim is the little Pullen baby. The murder of individual children is only part of Lilith's plan, however, as Lona asks:

'But what will become of her country if she kills all the babies?'
'She does not care about her country. She sends witches around to teach the women spells that keep babies away, and give them horrible things to eat. Some say she is in league with the Shadow to put an end to the race.' (p. 157)

Birth control and abortion are shown here as the work of the devil, and endangering the future of the nation. Through her double function as neutralizer of masculinity and killer of children she represents the racial suicide threatened by the independent sexual woman. Bulika is a rich and successful country, relying on the products of mining for its wealth but faced with the prospect of annihilation through the diminishing of the health, moral character and numbers of its population, precisely the spectre raised in the eugenic arguments of the *fin de siècle*. MacDonald's solution depends on the concept of the Christian family; redemption for women consists in their acceptance of motherhood, and their not 'asserting a right, which is a lie' over the children they produce. Adam states that 'even Lilith will be saved by her childbearing' (p. 205) and the ideal women in the novel are the suffering repentant Mara, the saintly Eve, and the child Lona, already de facto mother of a whole group of children. So the wife of Adam has split into the good and bad mothers, and the good mother into several more personae. The character of woman as snake is a collapsing of the elements of Eve's crime in the garden of Eden and the nature of Lilith. In pictorial versions of the fall, the snake is often represented with a woman's head and frequently with a woman's body. The misdemeanours of both Lilith and Eve are disobedience and independence. Lilith, in

MacDonald's novel is a snake-leech, and even more graphically dreadful is Arabella in Stoker's later work, *The Lair of the White Worm* (1911), who is described thus:

This [monster] is a woman, with all a woman's wisdom and wit, combined with the heartlessness of a cocotte and the want of principle of a suffragette. She has the reserved strength and impregnability of a diplodocus. We may be sure that in the fight that is before us there will no resemblance of fair play ... we have to protect ourselves and others against feminine nature.[21]

This is another character named Adam speaking, and again generalizing about all women, sliding easily from the specific monster to the monstrosity that is 'feminine nature'. Her monstrosity is explicit: sexual and political independence. The choice of the word 'impregnability' is curious too, suggesting defence against (male) attack and against pregnancy. He concludes by setting up the notion of fair play (men are at a loss against women because they won't 'play the game'). Arabella's undesirable qualities are revealed as more than just a lack of team spirit, however, as she is the locus of disease and death. Stoker's account of her dissolution is ghastly and transparently misogynistic:

Now the whole mass seemed to have become all at once corrupt. But that corruption was not all. It seemed to have attracted every natural organism which was in itself obnoxious. The whole surface of the fragments, once alive, was covered with insects, worms, and vermin of all kinds. The sight was horrible enough, but, with awful smell added, was simply unbearable. The worm's hole appeared to breathe forth death in its most repulsive forms. (p. 323)

The worm/woman's hole is where death lives, and not just ordinary death, but dreadful death from disease and corruption. *Worm* is largely only a revisiting of *Dracula*; the structure is the same, Lucy and Mina are echoed in Lilla and Mimi, in character as well as name. The pale, fair Lilla is dangerously susceptible to mesmeric men, and she dies through a form of psychic vampirism practised by Caswall and abetted by Arabella the worm in her human form. One significant addition is Oolanga, the 'black savage', who though in competition with Arabella also forms with her an equation of monstrosity. Oolanga combines a supernatural evil – voodoo – with a purely earthly dishonesty and greed for money. The text slides together recognizable imperialist assumptions about the inferior moral character of the black man and metaphysical fears of the black,

evil Other. In the same way Arabella is both socially unacceptable
– she behaves badly at tea parties – and the embodiment of a larger
evil. Blackness and femininity are the twin pillars of horror at the *fin
de siècle*.

The monstrosity of blackness is one of the final contributions of the
nineteenth century to the modern myth of the vampire. It is already
present in *Carmilla* where only one of the governesses sees this person,
'Then she described a hideous black woman, with a sort of coloured
turban on her head, who was gazing all the time from the carriage
window, nodding and grinning derisively towards the ladies, with
gleaming eyes and large white eye-balls, and her teeth set as if in
fury.'[22] She never reappears, or is explained but is profoundly
connected with the origins of Carmilla, she functions as a sign of
Carmilla's awful nature. The question of 'race' is foregrounded in
The Blood of the Vampire, and the notion of 'bad blood' flourishes both
metaphorically and literally. This is partly accomplished through the
collapsing together of several female figures in the novel. Harriet's
unnamed mother is a real blood sucker, she is said to dip her fingers
in the blood of the victims of Mr Brandt's torture, and she is
reputedly born of a woman bitten by a vampire bat. This real
mother, who is only reported in the text, is effectively replaced by the
Baroness Gobelli, who repeatedly claims Harriet as her own, 'the
daughter of the house'. Both mothers are presented as grotesque, fat,
greedy and cruel; Harriet's mother was 'obeah', a voodoo woman,
and Gobelli is a medium, though her powers seem much more akin
to obeah than spiritualism. Though Gobelli finally seems to be
nothing more sinister than a financial vampire, draining the cash
from the pockets of her credulous clients, Harriet carries the weight
of association with this woman and with her own mother, and adds
to it what the text suggests is a psychic vampirism. The 'bad blood'
in Harriet's case is emphatically black. She is the illegitimate
daughter of a white vivisector and torturer and a 'fat, flabby half-
caste', and she is frequently referred to as a quadroon, firmly placing
her in a racial hierarchy. Like Dracula, she comes from 'abroad' and
her money too is 'blood money' gained through the deaths of others.
Her miscegenation is compounded by her Catholicism, from which
the English women recoil in 'national Protestant horror'. Dr Phillips,
as well as presenting himself as the arbiter of truth, 'medical and
scientific', also pronounces on heredity, 'we medical men know the
consequences of heredity … she probably carries unknown dangers in

her train.'[23] What is significant is that Phillips suggests that all her 'terrible proclivities' are inherited from her mother, though her father is, by his account, an equally unpleasant creature. So bad blood is both black and female. The text suggests that her vampirism proceeds from a need to obliterate her black blood, by marriage into white society. Her offspring will be only an eighth part black, their children a sixteenth, after which we are told, 'regarded as Europeans', that is, white. She needs an infusion of blood from a white man (the equation of blood with semen is again obvious here) to redeem her, while they resist this through the fear of reversion, as Ralph Pullen says, 'She has black blood in her, her mother was a half-caste, so you see it would be impossible for a man in my position to think of marrying her. One might get a piebald son and heir!' (p. 261) The rulers of the empire must avoid contamination, but what is attractive to the men about Harriet is precisely what they know they should resist. Her colouring is in emphatic contrast to the pale and insipid looks of the English women, and there is a reciprocal animality in Harriet that Victorian readers would have no difficulty in reading as part of her terrible inherited proclivities, 'the touch of his cool hand on her heated palm seemed to rouse all the animal in Harriet's blood. Her hand, very slight and lissom, clung to his with a force of which he had not thought it capable.' (p. 109)[24]

The nature of Harriet's vampirism is of some ambiguity since it seems to shift between the psychic and the physical, corresponding to Todorov's idea of the element of hesitation in the fantastic, when events may or may not have supernatural explanations, but also to Marryat's own interest in spiritualism. One of her earlier books, published in 1891 and decisively titled *There Is No Death* dealt with this, and it seems to me that there is a close and complex intersection between spiritualism, mesmerism and vampirism in both her work and that of Stoker. Harriet does share many of the characteristics of other blood suckers – her superhuman strength, for example, is found in both Carmilla and Dracula. There are oblique references to the lesbianism of Carmilla too. Harriet's sick companion tells, in another echo of Fuseli's painting, of her feeling during the night: 'such a terrible oppression as though someone were sitting on my chest' (p. 37). Margaret Pullen refers directly to lesbianism – 'She had heard of cases, in which young unsophisticated girls had taken unaccountable affections for members of their own sex, and trusted that she was not going to form the subject for some such experience on Miss Brandt's part' (p. 38) – but what is clear from her responses is that it is she who is attracted to Harriet:

She had become fainter and fainter, as the girl leaned against her with her head upon her breast. Some sensation which she could not define, nor account for – some feeling which she had never experienced before – had come over her and made her head reel. (p. 28)

Thus, she exhibits the classic symptoms of attraction to the vampire and of the disruption of correct gender relations. The 'feeling that she had never experienced' is sexual attraction to Harriet. In her worldly dismissal of the affections of young girls she uses the word 'unaccountable', precisely the word she has previously used to describe her own feeling. Lesbianism becomes the undefinable, the thing of which no account can be given; it evades in the same way that Carmilla resists definition by patriarchal authority. Margaret's punishment for this guilty attachment is the death of her baby – she has been proved unfit to care for it. Despite Harriet's initial attacks on women and children, the Baroness astutely observes, 'I don't think that you'll confine your attentions to babies long' (p. 60), and this is the point of the novel: the real dangers are to the men. They are identified as servants of the empire: Margaret's husband is 'toiling out in India', and Ralph is an officer in the Indian Army. Harriet says when she is attempting to renounce Tony, 'I can never, never consent to sap your manhood and your brains, which do not belong to me but to the world.'(p. 306) Women belong to men, but men belong to the nation. Margaret's husband is safe from Harriet, simply because he never meets her, but the other two are seriously endangered. Phillips is placed beyond our concern, he is a 'bachelor of sixty' therefore not of the youth and strength that Lord Roseberry talked of:

An empire such as ours requires as its first condition an Imperial Race – a race vigorous and industrious and intrepid. Health of mind and body exalt a nation in the competition of the universe. The survival of the fittest is an absolute truth in the conditions of the modern world.[25]

What is threatened by Harriet is that which is threatened by Lilith and by Lucy Westenra, namely the body of the male and hence the body of the empire. The scenes of seduction in *Blood* are very close to those imagined by Stoker and MacDonald with their reversal of roles: 'Her hot breath fanned his cheek. "Kiss me!" she murmured in a dreamy voice ... He turned his face to Harriet's, and her full red lips met his own, in long drawn kiss that seemed to sap his vitality. As he raised his head again, he felt faint and sick.' (p. 110) However Ralph is saved, despite his sexual libertinism, and recuperated by a good English woman who is cool and reserved, but faithful. Pennell is not so fortunate. More 'manly looking', he is, perhaps, a more desirable target, he chooses to remain with Harriet, despite the warnings of Phillips, and he dies in her arms, sucked dry. Harriet takes an overdose of chloral, and dies too. The voluntary nature of her death is important, it is an acknowledgement of her own guilt and her danger to others. There is no need for her to be pursued and staked like Lucy, she sacrifices herself, as does Mina who makes her husband promise to kill her 'should the time come', and Lilith who begs Eve, 'persuade your husband to kill me'.

By 1900 the vampire's mythic status is unquestionable, and to the sketchy details of Polidori's blood-sucker have been added the specific fears of the period, centring on 'race', gender and disease. What we are offered in these vampire fictions of the 1890s is characteristic of the apocalyptic narratives of imperial Gothic, the simultaneous vision of collapse and salvation, the enactment of annihilation and the blueprint for its avoidance. The monster that is entertained here is the female vampire, the product of the disruption of perceived gender hierarchies, a horse-woman of the Victorian Apocalypse who threatens the end of the 'race' and the slow death of the British Empire on its throne.

NOTES

1 Chris Baldick, *In Frankenstein's Shadow* (Oxford: Clarendon Press, 1987), pp. 1–2.
2 Christopher Craft, 'Kiss Me With Those Red Lips: Gender and Inversion in Bram Stoker's *Dracula*', in Elaine Showalter (ed.), *Speaking of Gender* (New York and London: Routledge, 1989), pp. 216–242.
3 Bram Stoker, *Dracula* (Oxford: World's Classics, 1983), p. 56.
4 John Polidori, *The Vampyre*, ed. C. Haining (London: Gollancz, 1972), p. 45.
5 Stoker, *Dracula*, p. 40.
6 Florence Marryat, *The Blood of the Vampire* (London: Chatto and Windus, 1897), pp. 264–265.
7 It is perhaps interesting that Stoker chose to excise the lesbianism of *Carmilla* from his text. He had originally included a section in which Harker takes shelter in the tomb of a vampire countess.
8 Sheridan Le Fanu, *Carmilla* (Oxford: World's Classics, 1993), p. 264.

9 See 'The Uncanny', in James Strachey ed. and tr., *Standard Edition of the Complete Psychological Works of Sigmund Freud*, (24 vols., London: Hogarth Press, 1953–1974), vol. 17, pp. 217–252.

10 Hélène Cixous, 'Fiction and its Phantoms', *New Literary History*, 7: 3, (Spring 1976), 543.

11 David Farson, *The Man Who Wrote Dracula* (London: Michael Joseph, 1975), p. 233.

12 See Judith Walkowitz, *Prostitution and Victorian Society: Women, Class and the State* (Cambridge: Cambridge University Press, 1985).

13 Marryat, *Blood*, p. 137.

14 J. Fothergill, *The Town Dweller* (London: H. K. Lewis, 1889), p. 8.

15 James Cantlie, *Degeneration Amongst Londoners* (London: the Leadenhall Press, 1885), p. 45.

16 Fothergill, *Town Dweller*, p. 8.

17 The influence of popular conceptions of the New Woman on the construction of the female vampire seems to be a strong one; her independence, freedom of movement, her real or imagined sexual autonomy and her apparent challenge to the biological destiny of motherhood are all aspects which provoke immediate comparison. See also Sally Ledger's analysis of the New Woman novel in this volume.

18 Marryat, *Blood*, p. 49.

19 Or does so when entered into voluntarily. Sometimes, to paraphrase Freud, death is just death. The eschatology is not of the clearest.

20 George MacDonald, *Lilith* (London: Chatto and Windus, 1895), p. 131.

21 Bram Stoker, *The Lair of the White Worm* (London: Allen and Unwin, 1911), p. 206.

22 Le Fanu, *Carmilla*, p. 254.

23 Marryat, *Blood*, p. 125.

24 Unlikely strength is characteristic of the vampire, exhibited by both Carmilla and Dracula.

25 Quoted in Ronald Hyam, *Empire and Sexuality: The British Experience* (Manchester: Manchester University Press, 1990), p. 54.

Utopia, Limited: *nationalism, empire and parody in the comic operas of Gilbert and Sullivan*

Carolyn Williams

Gilbert and Sullivan's collaborative 'commitment to the foundation of a school of native English opera' involved a complex programme of reform: of current theatrical genres and practices, of several relatively distinct musical traditions, and of the theatre-going audience and its expectations.[1] In 1888, with a tone of boastful gusto, Gilbert wrote to Sullivan: 'We have the best theatre, the best composer, and (though I say it) the best librettist in England working together – we are world-known, and as much an institution as Westminster Abbey.'[2] The far-flung diffusion of their reputation that Gilbert imagines in this comment is quickly anchored and focused by the nostalgic monumentality of the Abbey; like the empire itself, their reputation is both worldwide and particularly English. And indeed, the comic appeal of the operas of W. S. Gilbert and Arthur Sullivan has always been linked strongly to their affectionate depiction of the peculiar styles of being – that is to say, of 'acting' – English. The establishment, rise, and fall of Gilbert and Sullivan opera as a national tradition has recently been treated in a provocative essay by David Cannadine.[3]

When turned upon the cultural politics of his own culture, however, Gilbert's reforming instincts were not always entirely affectionate. Compared to the grandiose mythic nationalism of Wagner or the passionately dramatic nationalism of Verdi, the nationalism of the Gilbert and Sullivan operas might at first seem excessively ironic; and indeed, I will argue in the following pages that the Gilbert and Sullivan œuvre exposes the 'aesthetic' formation of nationalism and patriotism. Though he has often been analyzed as 'the English Aristophanes', Gilbert has not yet been given credit enough for his biting, trenchant, often scathing political wit.[4] Perhaps because the libretti are so unruly, zany, chaotic, and ambivalent, critics often glance at the sharp edge of the satire only to reclaim it quickly as affectionate fun; and it is true that Gilbert's plots often attempt to patch up in the end what has been torn to shreds in the middle. His representations of 'England', of 'Great Britain', and of 'the English' also shore up, repair, and glorify what he parodies, teases, and attacks.

Beginning with a general discussion of the representation of national identity in the Gilbert and Sullivan operas, I will then turn to focus in some detail upon their little-known opera of 1893, *Utopia, Limited*. This odd and wonderful work should be better known, if for no other reason than that it casts an antic and somewhat hectic light on the cultural politics of the 1890s. In addition to the usual Gilbertian critique of the law and of other forms of professional-bureaucratic social management, this opera has other – and one might say larger – fish to fry, for it centres on a hilarious parody of the English attitudes involved in imperial domination and the capitalist driving force behind empire. *Utopia, Limited* is an anti-capitalist opera, whose critique of capitalism subtends the opera's treatment of all other issues. Fixated on the question of national identity – indeed, of 'corporate' identities of various kinds – the opera explores the ways in which visions of national identity are vexed by corporate capitalism and colonialism.

Utopia, Limited, or The Flowers of Progress takes the premise that the 'natives' of Utopia (which is represented as a South Sea island) have become 'Anglo-maniacs' who admire all things English and yearn to be 'thoroughly anglicized'. In order to effect this anglicization, the Utopian Princess Zara, returning from England (where she has 'taken a high degree at Girton'), brings with her the 'Flowers of Progress' – six representatives of the major institutions that have made Great Britain 'what she is'. These Flowers of Progress are imported so that they may conduct the process of reforming Utopia. Chief among those representatives is a company promoter, who recommends the reform of the island nation in accordance with the principle of limited liability – hence the title. Act II then considers the hilarious consequences of Utopia's 'anglicization' and 'com-panification'. As the one tiny island nation adopts the cultural peculiarities of the other, the opera experiments with a piquant version of Gilbertian topsy-turveydom: an allegory of empire and colonialism in which the imperial, ethnographic gaze is returned, reversed, and reflected by the subject people. The Utopians' grateful endorsement of English cultural institutions turns out to be the occasion for a complex and profound satire on those very institutions and the attitudes supporting them.

A light but nevertheless canny consideration of the paradoxes of national identity is present from the earliest days of the Gilbert and Sullivan collaboration.[5] The early operas reveal the theatricality of nationalism, while the later operas develop various forms of displacement, allegory, or topsy-turveydom with a particular focus on issues of national identity. The anthem 'He is an Englishman!' from *H. M. S. Pinafore* (1878), for example, dilates upon the arbitrariness of national identity. When the chorus of sailors sings: 'it's greatly to his credit / That he is an Englishman!...But in spite of all temptations/ To belong to other nations, / He remains an Englishman!' what they call attention to instead is precisely the accidental nature of this favoured state. The humour of the song rests in its complacent assumption that national identity is a matter of choice. The jingoistic xenophobia expressed in the anglicized (not to mention class-coded, cocknified) pronunciations of 'Roosian', 'Proosian', and 'Itali-an' was a staple of music-hall comedy of the time, and Sullivan's serious musical treatment of these ironic words refers to – and refigures – that musical as well as that political climate.[6] Gilbert and Sullivan lampoon contemporary jingoism, at the same time recognizing that a national attitude is constructed in large part through the oppositional relation to another culture.

In the same opera, Sir Joseph Porter gives to the sailors a song that is 'designed to encourage independence of thought and action in the lower branches of the service' (p. 97), but instead it seems merely to inculcate the performance of a national attitude. Given Sir Joseph's outspoken but thoroughly superficial devotion to democratic principles, it seems that this is a representation of class consciousness being deflected into national solidarity.[7] Accompanying Sir Joseph's glee ('A British tar is a soaring soul'), the sailors practise the poses required to indicate their independent, spirited defiance of 'a dictatorial word' or 'the tang of a tyrant tongue' (p. 99):

> His foot should stamp and his throat should growl,
> His hair should twirl and his face should scowl;
> His eyes should flash and his breast protrude,
> And this should be his customary attitude – [*pose*]

The stage direction makes clear the performative, theatrical quality of this 'attitude', as, in addition, its placement at the end of Act I (the same function that 'He is an Englishman!' serves for Act II) makes clear its thematic importance in the opera. In the same way as the grotesquely exaggerated 'Early English' poses adopted by the Duke, Colonel, and Major in *Patience* (1881) when they want to imitate the 'long-haired aesthetics':

> You hold yourself like this [*attitude*],
> You hold yourself like that [*attitude*],
> By hook and crook you try to look both angular and flat [*attitude*] –

the expressions of patriotic fervor in *Pinafore* are revealed to be equally aesthetic, posed, and 'put on' (p. 167, p. 189).

Indeed, in a sense the very superficiality of these representations of national culture is a large part of the point. Costumes, roles, and even languages may be easily put on and taken off; they are parts of the learned and performed national 'character'. When Sullivan is at his best, the music too participates in the characterization, as in the quoted (phoneticized) Japanese and grandly orchestrated 'Japanese' music of the 'March of the Mikado's troops' ('Miya sama, miya sama' (p. 329)). Bits and tags of languages other than English both recreate and satirize the patchwork 'culture' of a middlebrow cosmopolitanism that is both induced in and reflected by the reformed theatre audience, for example, in the hilarious *ensemble* at the end of Act I of *Iolanthe*, in which peers and fairies boisterously take turns demonstrating their command of French, Latin, and Greek 'remarks' (pp. 226–227). Like the schoolbook (or, more accurately, the tourist) Italian of *The Gondoliers*, all the 'shreds and patches' of other cultures in these operas both enact and parody the bluff English confidence of global access.

This emphasis on the arbitrary, relative, aesthetic and performative nature of national identity is often, especially in the later operas, elevated into a structural principle. The zany displacements of *The Mikado* (1885) illustrate a particular form of the topsy-turveydom for which Gilbert was known in many works: the creation of a fantastic world 'elsewhere' which audiences have usually easily identified as a burlesque of matters closer to home, in England.[8] The masquerade of 'Titipu' is slyly revealed throughout the opera in remarks that could only be made from an English point of view. The most flagrant is Ko-Ko's remark disclaiming all knowlege of Nanki-Poo's identity: 'It might have been on his pocket handkerchief, but Japanese don't use pocket-handkerchiefs! Ha! ha! ha!' (p. 336)

However, the opera begins with both tacit and overt acknowledgements that this is not 'really' Japan, but an aesthetic imitation of, or response to Japan. The opening stage direction has the gentlemen of Japan discovered '*in attitudes suggested by native drawings*', and of course they soon sing their admission that they figure 'On many a vase and jar – / On many a screen and fan' (p. 299). Instead of representing Japan, the opera represents, participates in, and at the same time parodies the current metropolitan craze for 'all one sees / That's Japanese' (as Bunthorne puts it in *Patience*).

But on the other hand, Gilbert's famously fastidious attention to detailed realism on the level of the spectacle worked to destabilize the reference to England.[9] The costumes for *The Mikado*, for example, were elaborately fashioned in Japanese prints by Liberty of London, and some (Katisha's robe, for example) were imported from Japan. There was much excited discussion of these fashions and their authenticity by reviewers.[10] Excruciating attention to detail was expended upon the stage set as well. It was supervised under consultation with the directors of a nearby tourist theme park, a fabricated Japanese setting which boasted real geisha girls serving tea in the traditional manner. *The Mikado*'s first night programme reads: 'The Management desires to acknowledge the valuable assistance afforded by the DIRECTORS and NATIVE INHABITANTS of the JAPANESE VILLAGE, KNIGHTSBRIDGE.'[11]

This sort of 'pop' japonism is a late growth of which the Crystal Palace is the best-known earlier flowering. Aestheticized late-century representations of 'other' lands, in other words, have a firm root in the mid-Victorian importation and exhibition of the products of 'foreign' cultures, especially the display of cultural artifacts resulting from imperial trade. This exhibition culture is a complex hybrid, expressing the volatile mixture of metropolitan curiosity and attraction with the urges to dominate, appropriate, and convert the foreign by containing and displaying it at home.[12] To the extent that Titipu provides an occasion for alluding to Japanese culture, it participates in the wide range of English cultural practices elaborating a sort of museum culture of 'foreign' tourism at home. But to the extent that Titipu is clearly a hybrid of England and a fantasied cultural other, it performs an exercise in cultural politics, questioning the substantive distinctions between cultures and examining the sort of cultural hybridity produced by their conjunction.

This studied and artfully constructed relation of national cultures actually did issue in some confusion later on. In the case of *The Mikado*, the confusion is perhaps best illustrated by the censorship of the opera in 1907 just before the state visit of Crown Prince Fushimi of Japan. Several members of parliament spoke out against this action on the part of the Lord Chamberlain, who reasoned that the opera might present an insult to Japanese national pride; and many who challenged his judgment alluded to the 'Gilbertianism' of this real-life situation. A distinguished Japanese journalist, asked to view and evaluate a performance of the opera, easily identified the representation as an utter fantasy, nothing like Japan, but despite his reassurances the ban continued for six weeks before being lifted by the Home Secretary.[13] An extreme example, nevertheless this story accurately illustrates how very unstable these reciprocal or reflexive representations of national character could be.

Gilbert's later works all court this sort of displacement and representational instability. As John Wolfson has pointed out, Gilbert increasingly chose a non-English setting: Venice and Barataria for *The Gondoliers* (1889); Sicily for *The Mountebanks* (with music by Alfred Cellier); 'Utopia' (which Wolfson identifies with Polynesia) for *Utopia, Limited* (1893); Denmark for *His Excellency* (with music by Frank Osmond Carr); and Germany for *The Grand Duke* (1896). Wolfson argues that these 'foreign' settings enable Gilbert's 'increasing concern with monarchy' to come to the fore. In an analysis of cancelled passages and songs, he shows that this abiding preoccupation of Gilbert's was allowed to become more explicit in the later operas.[14] But it seems to me that in addition to – and even more important than – Gilbert's sometimes fierce engagement with the satire of monarchy, we must look at his satirical consideration of national identity itself, within the late imperial and colonial context. For if the Gilbert and Sullivan operas seem to entertain the notion that national identity is something that may be 'put on' (like a costume) and 'taken-off' (like a burlesque parody), then at a certain point it must be stressed that it is precisely *English* national identity that travels far and wide. The sheer off-handedness of these topsy-turvy reversals indicates that 'England' easily goes everywhere; anyplace can suddenly turn out to be 'really' England. This situation resonates most profoundly in *Utopia, Limited*, where the wholesale allusion to the colonial encounter makes the point that this is exactly what the colonies are being asked to do, namely to 'put on' the accoutrements of another culture, in the name of 'civilization.'

At one point Gilbert planned that 'the piece may begin with a very short dialogue in Utopian'. Of course, he goes on, the 'Utopian' language will be 'mere gibberish'. Then an official would inform the Utopians that their language has been forbidden at court, and henceforth only English may be spoken.[15] This plan was abandoned. Instead of beginning with a representation of the sudden, violent imposition of English culture, Gilbert opens with the flagrantly absurd reversal of all colonial resistance: these 'natives' fervently desire and beg to be converted to English ways.[16] The scraps of Utopian that survive in the finished libretto suggest, at some points, the imitation of an unspecified African language and, at others, a parody of Wagnerian mytho-heroic sung declamation.[17] In the finished libretto, the allusion to colonial rule remains tacit, but it is, nevertheless, easily readable. Gilbert makes fun of the liberal, imperial Englishman's complacent confidence that his country's institutions provided a model for the rest of the world to follow, that a colonial people would feel nothing but excited gratitude accepting imperial domination. His decision to underplay (to say the least) the notion of colonial resistance (by portraying the natives excitedly yearning for anglicization) allows him to shift the explicit burden of the satire back toward England and her cultural institutions. But the global implications of the satire remain apparent. However, to understand the complexity of this interplay it is necessary to look in more detail at some features of the plot and staging.

As the curtain rises, Utopian maidens dispose themselves about the stage 'in lotus-eating fashion' (p. 507). Everyone eagerly awaits the return from England of Princess Zara, the eldest daughter of Utopian King Paramount. As if she were a cross between a secular missionary and the representative of a trading company, Zara is expected to bring to Utopia a full mastery of all things English, all the cultural practices that have made England 'the most powerful, the wisest country in the world' (p. 508). In a few months, as one maiden excitedly exclaims, 'Utopia may hope to be completely Anglicized!' When Zara arrives, she brings a delegation from England, the six so-called 'Flowers of Progress', each a representative of one of the cultural institutions that have made Great Britain great, each, in other words, a representative of progress, neatly divided into its departmentalized and bureaucratized functions. They are: Captain Fitzbattleaxe of the First Life Guards, a representative of the army; Sir Bailey Barre, Q. C. and M. P., a representative of the law; Lord

Figure 4 Utopian maidens 'lying lazily about the stage' in 'lotus-eating fashion'.

Dramaleigh, a Lord High Chamberlain, representing purity of court and stage; Mr Blushington, a county councillor, representing urban sanitation and the administration of the music halls; Mr Goldbury, a company promoter, representing corporate capitalism; and Captain Sir Edward Corcoran, R. N., a refugee from *H. M. S. Pinafore*, who represents the British Navy. The Utopian natives welcome these 'wanderers from a mighty State', and in jaunty and ridiculous doggerel, they beg those travelling paragons to 'teach us how to legislate' (p. 532). The Flowers then sing out various proposals for the reform of Utopia, each according to type (p. 537). The most important turns out to be Mr Goldbury, who proposes the 'companification' of Utopia. All the suggestions of the Flowers of Progress are adopted, and in Act II, Utopia has been transformed into a mock-England and a limited company. In the remaining pages of this chapter I will examine several crucial aspects of this transformation.

The cultural difference between Utopia and England is expressed in the scenic opposition between Act I, which takes place in a Utopian palm grove, and Act II, which takes place in the throne room of the Utopian palace after it has been 'completely anglicized'.[18] Moreover, the costume changes involved in signalling the conversion from Utopian to English culture were made as graphic as possible. The 'native Utopian dress' of the maidens, who lie about at the opening of Act I 'in lazy languor motionless', is coded for its loose and sexy freedom from restraint, at once suggesting exotic, 'Oriental' eroticism and 'natural' innocence (see Figure 4), while the Act I costume of King Paramount seems coded to represent a mythic yet playfully trivialized foreign barbarity (see Figure 5). In different ways, each gender-specific, these Act I costumes enact the simultaneous idealization (as 'natural', mytho-heroic) and denigration (as licentious, barbaric) of the cultural other. On the other hand, the English court dress of Act II refits the Utopians in elaborate clothing indicative of profession, rank, and status (for the men) and of up-to-the-minute fashionableness (for the women). The costumes in Act II were designed with care as meticulous (and produced at expense every bit as exorbitant) as the Japanese costumes of *The Mikado* – and to like purpose, for they served to exhibit the 'native dress' of English royalty, aristocracy, and the professions. Furthermore, Gilbert's dramatic emphasis on the restrictiveness of English dress participates in the opera's broad satire of Victorian propriety, especially its gendered dimensions.

Figure 5 Rutland Barrington as the original King Paramount, in 'native' Utopian
dress.

The initial humour of equating the precolonial with the scene of 'natural' innocence is a joke whose point only hits home when (and if) it deflates the prideful vantage of a 'cultured' metropolitan centre. Here, the lazy ease of the 'lotus-eating' Utopians contrasts immediately with the high Victorian 'gospel' of 'work' and 'progress'. Tennyson's poem 'The Lotus-Eaters' is one good place to see a certain conservative strain of 'utopian' thinking in nineteenth-century English culture, in which utopia itself is seen to be dystopic, and readers are returned to the messy and revalued 'real' world of struggles to survive, 'progress', and win glory.[19]

This easeful opening offers a vision of Utopia that will return, bitterly transposed, at the opera's close. Throughout the plot the Utopians' 'carelessness' is linked explicitly to their form of government; an absolute monarchy which, unbeknownst to the Utopian people, is really very 'limited' indeed. In England, explains a Utopian, 'every one has to think for himself. Here we have no need to think, because our monarch anticipates all our wants.' (p. 508) The parodic representation of the natives' guileless, childish trust in an absolute monarch, in other words, is paired with the equally parodic reference to its ostensible opposite; the attitude of the independent, individualistic, 'free' and liberal English citizen, an attitude which is jokingly credited with having made that nation 'what she is'. Gilbert's elaborate satire of monarchy, which is deeply entangled with all the issues I am discussing, will nevertheless be scantily treated here in favour of other aspects of the opera's cultural politics. Suffice it to say, at this point, that the establishment of a 'Limited Monarchy' at the end of the opera, instead of a 'Monarchy, Limited' is one gesture among many of turning away from Utopian 'carelessness' to the cares, struggles, and chaos of the *status quo* in 'real-life' England.

The graphic cultural difference signalled by the transformation from Utopian to English setting and costume is overstated, for the more profound point has to do with their confusion and conflation. After all, we have English actors and actresses acting like South Sea Island natives who then, in Act II, learn to act like the English. The question of any stable difference between 'home' and 'abroad', between national identity and the fantasy of a cultural other, is taken to the extremes of (anthropo)logical absurdity in *Utopia, Limited*. The ethnographic gaze is turned outward and then reflected, turned first toward the fantasy of otherness and then back toward the 'home' culture. Needless to say, all the usual epistemological questions are raised by this demonstration of cultural perspectivism. But the more spectacular questions are socially and culturally concrete: 'what must "we" look like to "them"?' and 'can "they" ever really learn to act like "us"?' These are two questions that subtend the cultural politics of representation in this ethnographic mirror. Like a dream, the theatrical spectacle represents both England and not-England at one and the same time, expressing a great deal of humorous complacency, a fair amount of satirical self-loathing, and perhaps not a little anxious discomfort.

The elaborately staged royal drawing-room early in Act II, after the 'anglicization' of Utopia has taken place, provides an illustration of the ethnographic gaze turned back upon English cultural practice. Every detail of the entrance of the royal household, the royal family and the court, as well as every detail of the presentation of the *debutantes* was followed 'practically as at Buckingham Palace'.[20] Rutland Barrington, who played King Paramount, reported that Gilbert hired a 'lady professor of deportment' to attend rehearsals and teach the actors precisely how to bow, the actresses how to handle their trains, and everyone exactly how and where to walk.[21] No expense was spared to satisfy Gilbert's intense interest in the accuracy of the spectacle, an interest which in the context of this argument must be called both sociological and auto-ethnographic. The total production costs ran to an astounding £7,200, of which more than £5,000 went for costumes, accessories, and 'hand-props'.[22] At the close of the ceremony, King Paramount interprets the scene in recitative: 'This ceremonial our wish displays / To copy all Great Britain's courtly ways.' (p. 547) However, this 'first South Pacific Drawing-Room' did represent one small innovation: the 'cheap and effective inspiration' of a 'cup of tea and...plate of mixed biscuits' (p. 552). According to all accounts, Gilbert's little dig at the reputed discomfort of the real-life drawing-room ceremony was soon adopted in all good humour by the real-life royal family as an 'improvement'. Thus did Savoy opera have its own small influence on the developing theatricality of royal pageantry.

As Reginald Allen points out, this scene prefigures a convention of later popular genres such as musical comedy and revue: namely the costume spectacle, in which the plot is suspended during a lengthy sequence of visual splendour, music, and dancing.[23] In this case, of course, we have not dancing, but the equally precise and regulated movement of court pageantry; and though the plot is temporarily suspended, the thematic development is all the while being enriched, for the spectacle raises complicated questions about the differences between 'us' and 'them'. The parody of court etiquette was one of Gilbert's favourite ways to raise such questions, but never had he hit so close to home as with the drawing-room scene in *Utopia, Limited*. In his 11 October 1893 review of the opera for the *World*, George Bernard Shaw wrote:

As to the 'Drawing-Room', with *debutantes*, cards, trains, and presentations all complete, and the little innovation of a cup of tea and a plate of cheap biscuits, I cannot vouch for its verisimilitude, as I have never, strange as it may appear, been present at a Drawing Room; but that is exactly why I enjoyed it, and why the majority of the Savoyards will share my appreciation of it.[24]

No doubt, as Shaw's comment suggests, a great deal of pleasure was derived by the largely middle-class audience from admission to this otherwise off-limits display of court behaviour. Here the ethnographic mirror reveals the division between 'us' and 'them' *within* the 'home' culture. Aristocrats and royalty are 'foreign' to most of the audience, and must be put on exhibition as cultural artifacts. Furthermore, as David Cannadine has argued, in the last decades of the nineteenth century, 'every great royal occasion was also an *imperial* occasion, designed to conceal and render acceptable the novelty of a mass society at home as well as a formal empire abroad.'[25]

The scene was 'played straight, not as a comic travesty of Queen Victoria's receptions'.[26] It is nevertheless important to keep in mind that these aristocrats and members of the royal household were being 'played' by South Sea Island 'natives' who were in the process of learning how to 'act' English. The metatheatrical implications are complex indeed; there is a continuous and complex humour in the conjunction here of auto-ethnography, spectacle, and the scene of cultural imperialism and colonial mimicry.[27] As King Paramount, dressed in his English regalia, anxiously puts it early in this scene: 'To a Monarch who has been accustomed to the uncontrolled use of his limbs, the costume of a British Field-Marshal is, perhaps, at first, a little cramping. Are you sure that this is all right? It's not a practical joke, is it?' (p. 544) If constriction, control, and regal or martial posturing are suggested here as metonymies of Englishness,

the native King cannot yet fully inhabit (much less appropriate or subvert) them, and the humour depends on this disjunction, this incomplete mastery.

King Paramount's anxiety throws the satire back toward the repressive restrictions of 'cultured' English behaviour, perhaps obscuring for the moment the rather more risky and politically charged yet persistent questions: can 'natives' ever truly learn how to 'act' English? And if they do, how would we distinguish 'ourselves' from 'them'? What if 'we' are tempted to act like 'them', to 'go native' or assimilate 'our' culture to 'theirs'? These questions are continuously in the air and continuously sublimated and deflected into the satire of English cultural and political institutions.

The best representation of these anxieties is staged in the scene of the cabinet council, a scene which is paired structurally and should be interpreted with the auto-ethnography of the drawing-room scene. Just before the drawing-room ceremony takes place, King Paramount calls together the Flowers of Progress and asks to be taught the proper procedures for an English cabinet council. Lord Dramaleigh, the Lord High Chamberlain, suddenly leads the Flowers to draw their chairs together in a long semi-circle, '*like Christy Minstrels*', as the stage direction makes clear (see Figure 6). The king, who takes the central position as interlocutor, again displays his nervousness: 'You are not making fun of us? This is in accordance with the practice at the Court of St James's?' to which Lord Dramaleigh, positioned as one of the corner-men, replies: 'Well, it is in accordance with the practice at the Court of St James's Hall.' (p. 545) This hilarious exchange, with its sudden parodic shift from high to low cultural reference, is a parody of minstrel dialogue. The metatheatrical analogy between the Court of St James's and St James's Hall, where the Christy Minstrels (and other minstrel acts) played in London, rewrites the overarching confusion between England and Utopia, this time briefly foregrounding the issue of 'race'.

Minstrel shows had been an extremely popular theatrical form in London since the late 1830s and 1840s and, by the 1890s, they had significantly influenced other forms of burlesque.[28] Like the native

---

Figure 6 The first South Pacific Drawing Room (above) and the Cabinet Council in the style of the Christy Minstrels (below).

English burlesque and music hall traditions, this first indigenous American genre of musical theatre included take-offs of other popular genres, comic skits, and female impersonation. But its dominant convention was blackface masquerade, in which white actors impersonated black male and female slaves, ex-slaves and urban 'swells'. In the context of the present argument, it is noteworthy that both minstrels and 'Ethiopian Delineators', one of their immediate precursor-forms, were often billed as a variety of the ethnographic exhibition. Though in the 1890s the theatrical depiction of slavery might be depoliticized to some extent by anachronism, the fact that even in the 1840s it was introduced as highly 'respectable' entertainment may be explained partly, I think, by virtue of this proto-ethnographic pretension.[29] The press advertisement for the inaugural appearance in London of *The Virginia Minstrels* in 1843 announced an 'exhibition' or 'a true copy of Ethiopian life' and promised a portrait of 'the sports and pastimes of the Southern slave race of America'.[30] Alternately burlesque and sentimental, slapstick and pathetic, these depictions were of course highly stereotyped and caricatured.

Within the context of our analysis of *Utopia, Limited*, this complex allusion to the American ex-colony and its own internalized cultural other, the black slave, creates a sort of imperialist *mise en abîme*. In addition, though the Flowers of Progress did not actually appear in blackface – in fact, *Utopia, Limited* is, instead, a sort of 'whiteface' masquerade – the allusion to blackface here takes its place alongside other forms of masquerade in the opera, as if 'race' could be put on and taken off as easily as costume, theatrical genre, or national identity. This number always brought down the house, and it was encored many times each night. In the performance diary kept by the stage manager of the Savoy, he records the number of each night's encores of the 'nigger song'.[31] Though this epithet did not have exactly the same resonance that it has within the cultural politics of the 1990s, Douglas Lorimer argues that attitudes of protective benevolence associated with abolitionism give way in middle and late century to a more strident racism associated with this term.[32] The metatheatricality of the scene, with its overarching analogy between the Court of St James's and St James's Hall, suggests that while the 'natives' are acting like the English court, the English delegation is acting out a displaced and highly conventionalized performance of 'native' theatre. At the same time, that metatheatricality manages the allusion, pitching it more overtly toward a set of theatrical conventions than to a set of racial stereotypes; this scene offers an impersonation of an impersonation, a burlesque of a burlesque. But it also serves to remind us of an important imperial premise: to be truly 'English' is to be white.

However, this premise is fleeting and subliminal in the opera, for once again the more profound implications of imperial domination are raised, only to be deflected into the satire of English institutions.

The King of Utopia dances a breakdown and sings 'alto in the approved style'.[33] Accompanying themselves on bones and tambourine, the cabinet minstrels sing, to the tune of 'Johnny, Get Your Gun', all about the transformation of Utopia, detailing each reform from the abolition of slums to the purification of court and 'native stage', the remodelling of the peerage 'on an intellectual basis', and the proper recognition of 'literary merit'. Gilbert's broad satire here imagines that the Utopians have easily managed to solve social problems that remain intractable in England, all the while believing that they are forming themselves exactly on England's model. The refrain, which is repeated three times in the course of the song, also bears repeating here:

It really is surprising
What a thorough Anglicizing
We have brought about – Utopia's quite another land;
In her enterprising movements,
She is England – with improvements,
Which we dutifully offer to our mother-land!' (p. 545)

With the reform of Utopia, the ethnographic reflection is fully moralized: now England must look to Utopia as the model society. While presenting herself as a model to other cultures, England has fallen short of her own cultural and political representations.

The reformed and anglicized Utopia of Act II is precisely Utopia, 'Limited'. For chief among the English institutions singled out for scathing indictment in the opera is the limited company. Of all the Flowers of Progress, Mr Goldbury turns out to have the central role, for he proclaims the gospel of corporate capitalism: 'Utopia's too big for one small head – / I'll float it as a Company Limited!' (p. 537) No one in Utopia, of course, even knows what that might be, so Mr Goldbury hastens to explain, in song:

> Some seven men form an Association
>   (If possible, all Peers and Baronets)
> They start off with a public declaration

To what extent they mean to pay their debts.
That's called their Capital: if they are wary
    They will not quote it at a sum immense.
The figure's immaterial – it may vary
    From eighteen million down to eighteenpence.
        I should put it rather low;
        The good sense of doing so
    Will be evident at once to any debtor.
        When it's left to you to say
        What amount you mean to pay
    Why, the lower you can put it at, the better.

They then proceed to trade with all who'll trust 'em,
Quite irrespective of their capital
    (It's shady, but it's sanctified by custom);
    Bank, Railway, Loan, or Panama Canal.
You can't embark on trading too tremendous –
    It's strictly fair, and based on common sense –
If you succeed your profits are stupendous –
    And if you fail, pop goes your eighteenpence.
        Make the money-spinner spin!
        For you only stand to win!
    And you'll never with dishonesty be twitted,
        For nobody can know,
        To a million or so,
    To what extent your capital's committed!

If you come to grief, and creditors are craving
    (For nothing that is planned by mortal head
Is certain in this Vale of Sorrow – saving
    That one's Liability is Limited), –
Do you suppose that signifies perdition?
    If so you're but a monetary dunce –
You merely file a Winding-Up Petition,
    And start another Company at once!
        Though a Rothschild you may be
        In your own capacity,
    As a Company you've come to utter sorrow –
        But the Liquidators say,
        'Never mind – you needn't pay,'
    So you start another Company tomorrow!   (pp. 537–539)

The privilege of limited liability, a mid-Victorian invention, is the crux of modern company law. In this song, Gilbert focuses on its provisions for disguising the accountability to risk of the company directors (and thus, of course, for passing that risk along to the shareholders). The beginning of the association is 'a public dec-

laration / To what extent they mean to pay their debts', which
Albert I. Borowitz calls 'one of the finest working definitions of
corporate capital, at least from the point of view of the creditors'.[34] As
Mr Goldbury's song makes clear, the limitation of liability allows for
trade on a vast scale, since 'you only stand to win'. And finally, the
process of liquidation or 'winding-up' allows for the closure of the
venture, again without strict accountability.

Perhaps Gilbert was moved to this satire by international events
such as the Panama Canal scandal (indicated in the song), which
broke earlier in 1893, or by national events such as the the Glasgow
Bank fraud case of 1878, both of which Borowitz suggests. On the
other hand, perhaps his sensitivity derives from his personal struggle
with Richard D'Oyly Carte to participate more fully in the financial
control of the Savoy Theatre, a legendary struggle expressed most
vividly in the notorious 'carpet quarrel' of 1890. Maybe, as Wolfson
claims, he was disgusted by D'Oyly Carte's scheme to 'float' a
renovation of his Royal English Opera House as the Palace Theatre
of Varieties.[35] He was, of course, trained in the law, although he spent
far more time in the travesty than in the practice of it. In any case,
there is plenty of evidence, including this opera, for his ability to
evaluate the implications of limited liability and of corporate
capitalism in general.

Utopia, Limited entertains the profound possibility that what it
really means to be 'anglicized completely' is to be incorporated and
protected for trade under the privilege of limited liability. On this
level, the premise of Gilbert's satire is simple: that this cultural
institution exists in order to assist England in evading her 'corporate'
responsibilities; that the state is already tantamount to a company
limited; that capitalism 'limits' the utopian potential of the nation.
Following Mr Goldbury's song, a long passage of recitative shows the
naïve, 'native' King of Utopia trying to come to grips with this new
concept of limited liability. Through its parodic reference to grand
opera, the recitative lends an air of ironized intensity to these lines:

> KING: Well, at first it strikes us as dishonest,
>   But if it's good enough for virtuous England –
>   The first commercial country in the world –
>   It's good enough for us...
>   And do I understand you that Great Britain
>   Upon this Joint Stock principle is governed?
> MR G: We haven't come to that, exactly – but

We're tending rapidly in that direction. (p. 539)

The king enthusiastically decides, then, that he will beat England at her own game. He will be the first sovereign in the history of the world to incorporate a whole country under 'the Joint Stock Company's Act of Sixty-Two!' The elaborate Act I finale ends with what Borowitz identifies as perhaps 'the only choral tribute to a corporation statute' in all of opera history.[36] The curtain falls as the chorus bursts into an ecstatic hymn to this 'mercantile pact': 'All hail, astonishing Fact! / All hail, invention new – / The Joint Stock Company Act – / The Act of Sixty-Two!' (pp. 540–541)

The Act of Sixty-Two was not exactly an 'invention new' in 1893. The principles of the joint stock company had existed since at least the mid-sixteenth century in England and had been prevalent as early as the eighteenth century. What is new in the nineteenth century is the principle of limited liability; but it was not instituted by the act of 1862, for that act only consolidated the provision for limited liability which had been made in 1856, with five subsequent statutes and elaborated procedures for winding-up.[37] The alliance of capitalism and the state especially was not new, for the granting of concessions and 'exclusive rights' of trading within certain areas to certain companies had been familiar practice for centuries, as had protests against such practices.[38] However, modern forms of finance and credit had accelerated the pace of capital accumulation, and these developments were inextricable from the rapid growth of the empire (and indeed, from the multinational capitalism of our 'post'-colonial present).

Gilbert seized upon the concept of limited liability as a topical link with which to forge together the ethnographic, colonial and national dimensions of the plot with the opera's anti-capitalist burden. The setting of the opera now alludes equally to the late-century addition to the empire of several islands in the South Pacific, and also to the notorious South Sea Bubble of 1720. This link is also clear from the hilarious consequences of 'companification' in Act II. The king's stereotypically evil and controlling advisors, turned entrepreneurs, have 'contracted to supply the entire nation with a complete English outfit' (p. 548). Here the change in costume, which already clearly signifies cultural colonization, is clearly linked to rapacious trading and monopolization. But when the Utopian capitalists send their bills for the 'complete English outfit', their customers refuse to pay, 'plead liability limited to a declared capital of eighteenpence, and apply to be dealt with under the Winding-Up Act, as in England' (p. 548). The capitalists are hoist with their own petard, for it turns out that every man, woman, and child in Utopia has incorporated as a limited company. Mr Goldbury has exploded the magic of the number seven and has transcended the notion of the 'association'; in this advanced state (not unlike our own), individuals may become corporate entities and be protected from full liability.[39] Perhaps Gilbert gestures here toward the limits of capitalist expansion. In any case, business in Utopia has been brought to a standstill, due to the universal application of the principle of limited liability.

This *reductio ad absurdam* is profoundly funny, for never in the history of rationalizations for the limitation of liability would it ever have been suggested that it could be a democratic principle. The whole point of the privilege is to endow powerful entrepreneurial initiatives with even more expansive power, to facilitate trading on an ever more extravagant scale, to detach the risk from individual persons by allowing both the capital accumulation and the liability to 'float' intangibly free from the personal finances of the members of an impersonal 'association'. In his song Mr Goldbury explained the importance of this detachment when it comes to winding-up: 'Though a Rothschild you may be / In your own capacity, / As a Company you've come to utter sorrow.' Gilbert had long been obsessed with the humour of this modern and artificial separation of 'capacities'. Earlier in his collaboration with Sullivan, he dilated upon various instances of the conflict or contradiction between various functions and roles assigned to one person.[40] Pooh-Bah, the 'Lord High Everything Else' in *The Mikado*, is perhaps the most famous example; another is the Lord High Chancellor in *Iolanthe*, who bewails his predicament of having to apply to himself for the hand of his own Ward in Chancery: 'I am here in two capacities, and they clash, my Lord, they clash!' (p. 239) This version of the humour of incorporation turns on the conflicts engendered by professional functionalism. Modern 'identity' is riven by these conflicts and becomes an uneasy amalgam of desires and professionally determined duties.

Late in his career, Gilbert turns the humour of this sort of contradictory 'incorporation' toward the political satire of capitalism. The Duke of Plaza-Toro in *The Gondoliers* represents this transition. A nobleman in 'straitened circumstances', he is incorporated as 'The Duke of Plaza-Toro, Limited'. Since his 'name' is all that remains to him of worth, he capitalizes on it, selling endorsements and fronting for some shady 'Companies bubble', who use his nobility to lend credence to the stocks they 'float' (p. 460, pp. 495–498). A 'company' is the topsy-turvy opposite of several 'capacities' at war within the same personal body, for it establishes a putative and impersonal 'body' of commerce by artificial association, for the purposes of producing capital. In structure like the 'legal fiction' advanced in *The Gondoliers* – where the two republican gondolieri act together in one capacity as king – the 'legal fiction' advanced in *Utopia Limited* – whereby 'some seven men form an association' and proceed to act as one body – carries with it a very different set of political implications. Within the logic of *Utopia, Limited*, capitalist incorporation is mechanical, artificial, absurd. Here the profound analogy that has been drawn between the company limited and the nation comes back to haunt: like a modern corporation, the nation itself is an 'association' of elements, not an 'identity'. Its fictionality – legal and otherwise – troubles the close of this work.

In the end, the anglicizing reforms of Utopia have been so successful that they have brought all the business of culture to a standstill. Gilbert seems to forget that the libretto had recently specified the universal extension of limited liability as the particular cause of business stagnation; and the ending of the opera focuses the alternative premise that all the Flowers of Progress have been utterly successful, and to no good end. Doctors are starving, for the county councillor's sanitary reforms have done away with sickness; lawyers are starving, for remodelled laws have eradicated crime and litigation; the army and navy have become so 'irresistible' that neighbouring nations have disarmed, and 'War's impossible'. In short, Utopia has been 'swamped by dull Prosperity' (p. 558). In a travesty of colonial resistance, the chorus of Utopians calls for the expulsion of 'those hated Flowers of Progress'.

But when the natives get restless, a further dose of anglification turns out to be the means of pacification. All of a sudden, Princess Zara remembers the most 'essential element' of all: government by party. As soon as this is introduced, one party will successively neutralize the attempted reforms of the other and 'there will be sickness in plenty, endless lawsuits, crowded jails, interminable confusion in the Army and Navy, and, in short, unexampled prosperity!' (p. 559)[41] Now the transformation of Utopia is complete; now she really will be like England. The hint of violent colonial repression is deflected, as usual, into the now-bitter satire of home institutions; but the meaning, prima facie, is that English culture is riddled with misery masquerading as prosperity, and that she communicates her own particular forms of misery 'abroad', in the name of progress. The dialogue closes on this note, with Gilbert's attempt to deflect the bitterness of his own satire through the humour of his anti-monarchical hobby-horse: King Paramount proclaims the institution of government by party and happily exclaims that 'henceforward Utopia will no longer be a Monarchy Limited, but, what is a great deal better, a Limited Monarchy!' (p. 559) Needless to say, the closing affirmation of a supposedly transvalued status quo is precipitous, forced, and bitter. The song that follows as the Act II finale, in the guise of a patriotic hymn to the greatness of Great Britain, raises directly some of the anxieties that have been tacit throughout the opera:

> There's a little group of isles beyond the wave –
>   So tiny, you might almost wonder where it is –
> That nation is the bravest of the brave,
>   And cowards are the rarest of all rarities.
> The proudest nations kneel at her command;
>   She terrifies all foreign-born rapscallions;
> And holds the peace of Europe in her hand
>   With half a score invincible battalions!
>
>> Such, at least, is the tale
>> Which is borne on the gale,
>>   From the island which dwells in the sea.
>> Let us hope, for her sake,
>> That she makes no mistake –
>>   That she's all she professes to be!
>
> Oh, may we copy all her maxims wise,
>   And imitate her virtues and her charities;
> And may we, by degrees, acclimatize
>   Her Parliamentary peculiarities!
> By doing so, we shall, in course of time,
>   Regenerate completely our entire land –
> Great Britain is that monarchy sublime,
>   To which some add (but others do not) Ireland.

The curtain falls, now, on a repeat of the refrain, 'Such at least is the tale', expressing clearly an anxiety about whether 'the nation' really *is* 'all she professes to be'.[42] But directly before the rousing sentimentalism of this hope (which attempts to cover the doubt) that she might live up to her own high standards of self-representation, an even greater anxiety is expressed in the parenthetical allusion to Ireland, and the fierce middle, late, and turn-of-the-century struggle for Home Rule. This anxiety strikes deep, not only because of its violent and painful topicality, but because it expresses profound doubt about the very identity of 'Great Britain'. What is the nation? What does it include and exclude? What is the proper relation to the colonies, not only those distant and exotic colonies which most easily lend themselves to 'careless' fantasy, but also those so close to home as to be a painful reminder of – indeed, (perhaps) a very part of – 'home' itself?

NOTES

1 Fredric Woodbridge Wilson, *An Introduction to the Gilbert and Sullivan Operas from the Collection of the Pierpont Morgan Library* (New York: The Pierpont Morgan Library in association with Dover Publications, Inc., 1989), p. 12. I am extremely grateful to Fredric Woodbridge Wilson for his expertise and his warm generosity in making available to me the resources of the Gilbert and Sullivan Collection at The Pierpont Morgan Library, New York.

2 Letter quoted in Wilson, *An Introduction*, p. 12.

3 David Cannadine, 'Gilbert and Sullivan: The Making and Unmaking of a British "Tradition"', in Roy Porter (ed.), *Myths of the English* (Cambridge: Polity Press in association with Blackwell, 1992), pp. 12–32. I will, however, be disagreeing in the following argument with Cannadine's assessment of 'the unabashed patriotism' of Gilbert and Sullivan. I do not find, as this chapter will make clear, 'that the Savoy operas were a paean of praise to national pride and to the established order' (Cannadine, p. 27, p. 19).

4 See Walter Sichel's 1911 essay from *The Fortnightly Review*, 'The English Aristophanes', in John Bush Jones (ed.), *W. S. Gilbert: A Century of Scholarship and Commentary* (New York: New York University Press, 1970), pp. 69–109; and Edith Hamilton's 1927 piece, 'W. S. Gilbert: A Mid-Victorian Aristophanes', also in Jones (ed.), *W. S. Gilbert*, pp. 11–134. James Ellis cites several earlier instances of this comparison in *The Comic Vision of W. S. Gilbert* (unpublished dissertation, State University of Iowa, 1964), pp. 82–83, n. 3. For recent discussions, see Max Keith Sutton, *W. S. Gilbert* (Boston: Twayne, 1975), pp. 88–94; and Alan Fischler, *Modified Rapture: Comedy in W. S. Gilbert's Savoy Operas* (Charlottesville, Virginia: The University Press of Virginia, 1991), pp. 103–106, 134–135.

5 See especially Jane W. Stedman (ed.), *Gilbert Before Sullivan: Six Comic Plays* (Chicago: University of Chicago Press, 1967).

6 *The Complete Plays of Gilbert and Sullivan* (New York: W. W. Norton and Co., 1976), p. 112. All citations to the libretti will refer to this edition, and will hereafter be cited in the main body of the text.

7 For an exploration of this dynamic, see E. J. Hobsbawm, *The Age of Empire, 1875–1914* (London: Weidenfeld and Nicholson, 1987), pp. 142–164.

8 Among the many treatments of Gilbert's topsy-turveydom, see Isaac Goldberg, 'W. S. Gilbert's Topsy-Turveydom', in Jones (ed.), *W. S. Gilbert*, pp. 135–146; Stedman, *Gilbert Before Sullivan*; and Sutton, *W. S. Gilbert*, pp. 91–92.

9 For Gilbert's devotion to the realism of the spectacle, see Jane W. Stedman, 'Gilbert's Stagecraft: Little Blocks of Wood', in *Gilbert and Sullivan*, ed. James Helyar (Lawrence, Kan.: University of Kansas Libraries, 1971), pp. 200–201.

10 Several excerpts from these reviews may be found in Reginald Allen, *The First Night Gilbert and Sullivan* (New York: The Heritage Press, 1958).

11 A facsimile of the first night programme may be seen in Allen, *The First Night Gilbert and Sullivan*, which is accompanied by a boxed set of reproductions of all the first night programmes.

12 For a related case study of this sort of projective exhibitionism, see Edward Said, 'The Empire at Work: Verdi's *Aida*', in his *Culture and Imperialism* (New York: Alfred A. Knopf, 1993), pp. 111–132. Sullivan's 1886 setting of Tennyson's *Ode for the Opening of the Colonial and Indian Exhibition* is also of interest in this connection.

13 For more details of this story, see Leslie Baily, *The Gilbert and Sullivan Book* (London: Cassell and Co., Ltd., 1952), pp. 390–392.

14 John Wolfson, *Final Curtain: The Last Gilbert and Sullivan Operas* (London: Chappell & Co., in association with Andre Deutsch, 1976) pp. 11–14.

15 W. S. Gilbert, plot book for *Utopia, Limited*, facing p. 6 (in the Gilbert and Sullivan Collection of The Pierpont Morgan Library, New York). Gilbert used the plot books to sketch out the plots of his operas in 'novelistic' fashion, before writing the libretti. The plot book at the Morgan Library would be the last one in the series for *Utopia, Limited*, since it was the one sent to Sullivan and contains his notations regarding the placement of musical numbers. My thanks to Fredric Woodbridge Wilson for this point.

16 Wolfson suggests that this scenario alludes to the recent annexation of a willing Fiji and Tonga: *Final Curtain*, p. 51. In fact Fiji asked for British protection in 1854 and was annexed in 1874; but Tonga remained independent until 1900. Thanks to Jonathan Strong for this point, and for his fine novel, *Secret Words* (Cambridge, Mass.: Zolanot Books, 1992), whose treatment of *Utopia, Limited* inspired my present argument.

17 John Wolfson makes the possible connection between one Utopian's

'raging gibberish' and the name of King Lobengula of Matabeleland, who had been sent a conciliatory deputation of First Life Guards a few years before *Utopia, Limited. Final Curtain*, p. 58, n.

18 Reproductions of hand-coloured photographs of the ravishing sets by Hawes Craven may be seen in Wolfson, *Final Curtain*, following p. 102. For contemporary comments on these sets 'of bewildering splendour', see Allen, *The First Night Gilbert and Sullivan*, pp. 378–379.

19 The large body of late nineteenth-century 'utopian' literature includes Morris's *News From Nowhere* (1890) and Bellamy's *Looking Backwards* (1888).

20 Allen, *First Night Gilbert and Sullivan*, p. 379.

21 *Ibid.*, p. 380.

22 *Ibid.*, p. 380.

23 *Ibid.*, p. 379.

24 George Bernard Shaw, *Music in London, 1890–1894, The Collected Works of George Bernard Shaw* (Ayot Street Lawrence edition) (New York: Wm. H. Wise and Co., 1931), vol. XXVIII, p. 66.

25 See David Cannadine, 'The Context, Performance, and Meaning of Ritual: The British Monarchy and the "Invention of Tradition", c. 1820–1977', in Eric Hobsbawm and Terence Ranger (eds.), *The Invention of Tradition* (Cambridge: Cambridge University Press, 1983), pp. 101–164, quoted passage on p. 124.

26 Allen, *First Night Gilbert and Sullivan*, p. 379.

27 The concept and dynamics of colonial mimicry are developed by Homi Bhabha in 'Of Mimicry and Man: The Ambivalence of Colonial Discourse', *October*, 28 (Spring 1984), 124–134; and 'The Other Question', *Screen*, 24 (November-December 1983), 18–36.

28 The best accounts of the adaptation of the minstrel act to its English setting are J. S. Bratton, 'English Ethiopians: British Audiences and Black-Face Acts, 1635–1865', *Yearbook of English Studies*, 11 (1981), 127–142; and Michael Pickering, 'White Skin, Black Masks: "Nigger" Minstrelsy in Victorian Britain', in J. S. Bratton (ed.), *Music Hall: Performance and Style* (Milton Keynes: Open University Press, 1986), pp. 70–91.

29 Additional (and other) explanations of the respectability of the minstrel shows are given in Bratton, 'English Ethiopians'; and Pickering, 'White Skin, Black Masks'.

30 William Torbert Leonard, *Masquerade in Black* (Metuchen, N. J.: The Scarecrow Press, 1986), p. 232.

31 Performance diary for *Utopia, Limited* in the Gilbert and Sullivan Collection at The Pierpont Morgan Library, New York.

32 Douglas Lorimer, *Colour, Class and the Victorians: English Attitudes to the Negro in the Mid-Nineteenth Century* (New York: Holmes and Meier Publishers, Inc., 1978), pp. 12, 16–20, 201–211.

33 Allen, *First Night Gilbert and Sullivan*, p. 379.

34 Albert I. Borowitz, 'Gilbert and Sullivan on Corporate Law', *American Bar Association Journal*, 59 (November 1973), 1278.

35 For an analysis of the Panama Canal scandal and the Glasgow Bank fraud case, see Borowitz, 'Gilbert and Sullivan on Corporate Law', pp. 1280–1281. For accounts of the 'carpet quarrel', see Isaac Goldberg, *The Story of Gilbert and Sullivan* (New York: Simon and Schuster, 1928), pp. 386–390, p. 404; and Baily, *The Gilbert and Sullivan Book*, pp. 323–342. For the story of the Royal English Opera House (later the Palace Theatre), see Wolfson, *Final Curtain*, pp. 23–24.

36 Borowitz, 'Gilbert and Sullivan on Corporate Law', p. 1278.

37 See Borowitz, 'Gilbert and Sullivan on Corporate Law', for the provisions of the 1856 and 1862 Acts. For the history of the joint stock company, see Fernand Braudel, *The Wheels of Commerce: Civilization and Capitalism*, vol. 2: Fifteenth to Eighteenth Century (New York: Harper and Row, 1982), pp. 433–455, especially 439–442.

38 Braudel, *Wheels of Commerce*, pp. 453–454.

39 I owe this point to Linda V. Troost, 'Economic Discourse in the Savoy Operas of W. S. Gilbert', in Kirk Combe and Brian Connery (eds.), *Theorizing Satire* (forthcoming).

40 Ellis briefly discusses Gilbert's interest in the comic device of 'multiplying a character's role or function', and he relates this interest to Gilbert's awareness of the workings of capital in an anecdote taken from Hesketh Pearson's biography of Gilbert: 'When the Savoy theatre was built by D'Oyly Carte ... and then leased by Gilbert, Sullivan, and Carte, Gilbert hinted that "as Carte the partner was paying one-third of the rent to Carte the proprietor, it was a sound investment for Carte the capitalist".' *The Comic Vision of W. S. Gilbert*, pp. 328–333; quoted passage on p. 333.

41 Zara's even more bitter final speech caused a flurry of objection in the press, and Gilbert cut it after the first night.

42 Sutton also calls attention to this anxiety as a response to 'imperial self-importance' in *W. S. Gilbert*, p. 116.

CHAPTER 12

Technologies of monstrosity: Bram Stoker's Dracula

Judith Halberstam

By way of an introduction to Bram Stoker's *Dracula*, I want to tell my own story about being consumed and drained by the vampire. Reading *Dracula* for the first time many years ago, I thought I noticed something about vampirism that had been strangely overlooked by critics and readers. Dracula, I thought, with his peculiar physique, his parasitical desires, his aversion to the cross and to all the trappings of Christianity, his blood-sucking attacks and his avaricious relation to money, resembled stereotypical anti-Semitic nineteenth-century representations of the Jew. Subsequent readings of the novel with attention to the connections in the narrative between blood and gold, 'race' and sex, sexuality and ethnicity, confirmed my sense that the anti-Semite's Jew and Stoker's vampire bore more than a family resemblance. The connection I had made began to haunt me; I uncovered biographical material and discovered that Stoker was good friends with, and inspired by, Richard Burton, the author of a tract reviving the blood libel against Jews in Damascus.[1] I read essays by Stoker in which he railed against degenerate writers for not being good Christians.[2] My conclusions seemed sound, the vampire and the Jew were related and monstrosity in the Gothic novel had much to do with the discourse of modern anti-Semitism.

Towards the end of my preliminary research, I came across a fantastic current news story which reported that the General Mills Cereal Company was being sued by the Anti-Defamation League because Count Chocula, the children's cereal character, was depicted on one of their cereal boxes wearing a Star of David.[3] While I felt that this incident vindicated my comparison between Jew and vampire, doubts began to creep in about stabilizing this relationship. By the time my doubts had been fully expressed and confirmed by other readers, I discovered that, rather than revealing a hidden agenda in Stoker's novel, I had unwittingly essentialized Jewishness. By equating Jew and vampire in a linear way, I had simply stabilized the relationship between the two as a mirroring, but I had left many questions unanswered, indeed unasked, about the production of monstrosity, whether it be monstrous 'race', monstrous class, monstrous sex.

Attempts to consume Dracula and vampirism within one interpretive model inevitably produce vampirism. They reproduce, in other words, the very model they claim to have discovered. So, an analysis of the vampire as perverse sexuality runs the risk of merely stabilizing the identity of perversity, its relation to a particular set of traits. The comparison between Jew and vampire still seems interesting and important to me but for different reasons. I am still fascinated by the occlusion of 'race' or ethnicity in critical interpretations of the novel, but now I am not simply attempting to bring those hidden facets to light. Instead, I want to ask how the Gothic novel, and Gothic monsters in particular, produce monstrosity as never unitary, but always as an aggregate of 'race', class and gender. I also want to suggest that the nineteenth-century discourse of anti-Semitism and the myth of the vampire share a kind of Gothic economy in their ability to condense many monstrous traits into one body. In the context of this novel, Dracula is otherness itself, a distilled version of all others produced by and within fictional texts, sexual science and psychopathology. He is monster and man, feminine and powerful, parasitical and wealthy; he is repulsive and fascinating, he exerts the consummate gaze but is scrutinized in all things, he lives forever but can be killed. Dracula is indeed not simply a monster, but a technology of monstrosity.

The otherness that Dracula embodies is not timeless or universal, not the opposite of some commonly understood meaning of 'the human', the others Dracula has absorbed and who live on in him take on the historically specific contours of 'race', class, gender and sexuality. They are the other side of a national identity that in the 1890s coincided with a hegemonic ideal of bourgeois Victorian womanhood. Mina and Lucy, the dark and the fair heroines of Stoker's novel, make Englishness a function of quiet femininity and maternal domesticity. Dracula, accordingly, threatens the stability and indeed the naturalness of this equation between middle-class womanhood and national pride by seducing both women with his particularly foreign sexuality.[4]

To claim that Dracula's sexuality is foreign, however, is already to obscure the specific construction of a native sexuality. Lucy, as many critics have noted, is violently punished for her desire for three men, and all three eventually participate in a ritual staking of her vampiric body. Mina represents a maternal sexuality as she nurtures and caters to the brave Englishmen who are fighting for her honour and her body. The foreign sexuality that confronts these women, then, depends upon a burgeoning definition of normal versus pathological sexual function which itself depends upon naturalizing the native. It is part of the power of *Dracula* that Stoker merges pathological sexuality with foreign aspect. The vampire Dracula, in other words, is a composite of otherness that manifests itself as the horror essential to dark, foreign and perverse bodies.

Dracula the text, like Dracula the monster, is multivalenced and generates a myriad of interpretive narratives: narratives which attempt to classify the threat of the vampire as sexual or psychological, as class-bound or gendered. The technology of the vampire's monstrosity, indeed, is intimately connected to the mode of the novel's production. *Dracula* is a veritable writing machine constructed out of diaries, letters, newspaper clippings and medical case notes. The process of compilation is similarly complex: Mina Harker, as secretary, makes a narrative of the various documents by chronologically ordering them and, where necessary, transcribing notes from a primitive dictaphone. There is a marked sexual energy to the reading and writing of all the contributions to the narrative. Reading, for instance, unites the men and Mina in a safe and mutual bond of disclosure and confidence. After Mina listens to Dr Seward's phonograph recording of his account of Lucy's death, she assures him: 'I have copied out the words on my typewriter, and none other need now hear your heart beat as I did.'[5] Seward, in his turn, reads Harker's diary and notes: 'after reading his account…I was prepared to meet a good specimen of manhood' (p. 237). Later, Seward passes by the Harkers' bedroom and on hearing 'the click of the typewriter' he concluded, 'they were hard at it' (p. 237). Writing and reading, on some level, appear to provide a safe textual alternative to the sexuality of the vampire. They also, of course, produce the vampire as the 'truth' of textual labour; he is a threat which must be diffused by discourse.[6]

The novel presents a body of work to which, it is important to note, only certain characters contribute. The narrative episodes are tape-recorded, transcribed, addended, edited and compiled by four characters – Jonathan Harker, Dr Seward, Mina Harker and Lucy Westenra. The control of the narrative by these characters suggests that the textual body, for Stoker, like the bodies of the women of England, must be protected from any corrupting or foreign influence. Van Helsing, Lord Godalming, Quincey Morris, Renfield and Dracula have only recorded voices in the narrative; at no time do we read their own accounts of events. Three of these men are foreigners; Van Helsing is Dutch, Quincey Morris is American and Dracula is East European. Lord Godalming, we assume, has English blood but as an aristocrat he is of a different class than the novel's narrators. Renfield has been classified as insane and his subjective existence is always a re-presentation by Dr Seward.

The activities of reading and writing, then, are crucial in this novel to the establishment of a kind of middle-class hegemony and they are annexed to the productions of sexual subjectivities. Sexuality, however, is revealed in the novel to be mass-produced rather than essential to certain kinds of bodies, a completely controlled production of a group of professionals – doctors, psychiatrists, lawyers. Writing, or at least the person who writes, must be controlled since it represents the deployment of knowledge and power; similarly, reading may need to be authorized and censored, as indeed it is later in the novel when Mina begins to fall under the vampire's influence. The vampire can read Mina's mind and so Mina is barred from reading the English group's plans. Dracula's reading and Mina's reading are here coded as corrupt and dangerous. Similarly, the English men censor Dracula's contaminated opinions out of the narrative. The vampire, indeed, has no voice, he is read and written by all the other characters in the novel. Dracula's silence in the novel (his only speeches are recorded conversations with Jonathan Harker) is pervasive and almost suffocating and it actually creates the vampire as fetish since, in so much of the narrative, writing takes on a kind of sexual function.

By examining Stoker's novel as a 'machine text' – a text that generates particular subjectivities – we can atomize the totality of the vampire's monstrosity, examine the exact nature of his parasitism and make an assault upon the naturalness of the sexuality of his enemies. By reading *Dracula* as a technology of monstrosity, I am claiming a kind of productivity for the text, a productivity which leads to numerous avenues of interpretation. But this does not mean that monstrosity in this novel is constantly in motion, for every now and then it settles into a distinct form, a proper shape, and in those moments Dracula's features are eminently readable and suggestive. Dracula is likened to 'mist', to a 'red cloud', a ghost or a shadow until he is invited into the home, at which point he becomes solid and fleshly. As flesh and blood, the vampire embodies a particular ethnicity and a peculiar sexuality.

Gothic anti-Semitism makes the Jew a monster with bad blood and it defines monstrosity as a mixture of bad blood, unstable gender identity, sexual and economic parasitism and degeneracy. In this section I want to flesh out my premise that the vampire as represented by Bram Stoker bears some relation to the anti-Semite's Jew. If this is so, it tells us nothing about Jews but everything about anti-Semitic discourse which seems able to transform all threat into the threat embodied by the Jew. The monster Jew produced by nineteenth-century anti-Semitism represents fears about 'race', class, gender, sexuality and empire: this figure is indeed gothicized or transformed into an all-purpose monster.

By making a connection between Stoker's Gothic fiction and late nineteenth-century anti-Semitism, I am not claiming a deliberate and unitary relation between fictional monster and real Jew, rather I am attempting to make an argument about the process of othering. Othering in Gothic fiction scavenges from many discursive fields and makes monsters out of bits and pieces of science and literature: the reason Gothic monsters are over-determined, which is to say open to numerous interpretations, is precisely that monsters transform the fragments of otherness into one body. That body is not female, not Jewish, not homosexual but it bears the marks of the constructions of femininity, 'race' and sexuality.[7]

Dracula, then, resembles the Jew of anti-Semitic discourse in several ways: appearance, his relation to money/gold, his parasitism, his degeneracy, his impermanency or lack of allegiance to a fatherland and his femininity. Dracula's physical aspect, his physiognomy, is a particularly clear cipher for the specificity of his ethnic monstrosity. When Jonathan Harker meets the Count on his visit to Castle Dracula in Transylvania he describes Dracula in terms of a 'very marked physiognomy': he notes an aquiline nose with 'peculiarly arched nostrils', massive eyebrows and 'bushy hair', a cruel mouth and 'peculiarly sharp white teeth', pale ears which were 'extremely pointed at the top' and a general aspect of 'extraordinary pallor' (p. 18). This description of Dracula, however, changes at various points in the novel. When he is spotted in London by Jonathan and Mina, Dracula is 'a tall thin man with a beaky nose and black moustache and pointed beard' (p. 180); similarly, the zoo keeper whose wolf disappears after a visit by Dracula to the zoological gardens, describes the Count as 'a tall thin chap with a 'ook nose and a pointed beard' (p. 145). Most descriptions include Dracula's hard, cold look and his red eyes.

Visually, the connection between Dracula and other fictional Jews is quite strong. For example, George Du Maurier's Svengali, the Jewish hypnotist, is depicted as 'a stick, haunting, long, lean, uncanny, black spider-cat' with brown teeth and matted hair, and, of course, incredibly piercing eyes. Fagin, the notorious villain of Charles Dickens's *Oliver Twist*, also has matted hair and a 'villainous-looking and repulsive face'. While Dracula's hands have 'hairs in the center of the palm' and long, pointed nails, Fagin's hand is 'a withered old claw'. Eduard Drumont, a French National Socialist who, during the 1880s, called for the expulsion of the Jews from France in his newspaper *Libre Parole*, noted the identifying characteristics of the Jew as 'the hooked nose, shifty eyes, protruding ears, elongated body, flat feet and moist hands'.[8] Faces and bodies, in fact, mark the 'other' as evil so that he could be recognized and ostracized. Furthermore, the face in the nineteenth century which supposedly expressed Jewishness, ('hooked nose, shifty eyes, etc.,') is also seen to express nineteenth-century criminality and degeneration within the pseudo-sciences of physiognomy and phrenology.[9] Degeneration and Jewishness, one could therefore conclude (or indeed ratify scientifically), were not far apart. Stoker draws upon the relation between degeneration and physiognomy as theorized by Cesare Lombroso and Max Nordau for his portrayal of Dracula.

Towards the end of *Dracula*, as the Dutch doctor-lawyer Van Helsing leads Harker, Lord Godalming, Dr Seward and the American Quincey Morris in the final pursuit of the vampire, a discussion of criminal types ensues between Van Helsing, Seward and Harker's wife Mina. Van Helsing defines Dracula as a criminal with 'a child-brain... predestinate to crime' (p. 361). As Van Helsing struggles to articulate his ideas in his broken English, he turns to Mina for help. Mina translates for him succinctly and she even adds sources for the theory Van Helsing has advanced: 'the Count is a criminal and of criminal type. Nordau and Lombroso would so classify him, and qua criminal he is of imperfectly formed mind' (p.

361). Since Mina, the provincial school-teacher, mentions Lombroso and Nordau, we may conclude that their ideas of criminality and degeneracy were familiar to an educated readership rather than specialized medical knowledge. As Mina points out, Lombroso would attribute Dracula's criminal disposition to 'an imperfectly formed mind', or, in other words, to what Van Helsing calls a 'child-brain'. Lombroso noted similarities between the physiognomies of 'criminals, savages and apes' and concluded that degenerates were a biological throwback to primitive man.[10]

Criminal anthropology, quite obviously, as it developed in the nineteenth century focused upon the visual aspects of pathology. The attempt to catalogue and demonstrate a propensity for degenerative behaviour by reading bodies and faces confirms that racial stereotyping demands that stereotypes be visualizable. And racial degeneracy, with its close ties to a social Darwinist conception of human development, also connects with sexual degeneracy. In describing the medicalization of sex, Michel Foucault describes a progressive logic in which 'perversion-hereditary-degenerescence'[11] became the basis of nineteenth-century scientific claims about the danger of undisciplined sexuality. Sexual perversions, within this chain, arise out of inherited physical weaknesses and they potentially lead to the decline of future generations. Furthermore, theorizing degenerescence or degeneration as the result of hereditary perversion takes, he claims, the 'coherent form of a state-directed racism' (p. 119).

Elsewhere, Foucault claims that 'modern antisemitism developed, in socialist milieus, out of the theory of degeneracy'. Surprisingly, this statement occurs during a discussion of vampire novels of the nineteenth century. Foucault is being interviewed by Alain Grosrichard, Guy Le Gaufey and Jacques-Alain Miller when the subject of vampires arises out of a discussion of the nobility and what Foucault calls 'the myth of blood'. In relating blood as symbolic object to the development of racial doctrines of degeneracy and heredity, Foucault suggests that the scientific ideology of 'race' was developed by the left rather than by right-wing fanatics. For example Lombroso, he points out, 'was a man of the Left'. Le Gaufey asks:

Couldn't one see a confirmation of what you are saying in the nineteenth century vogue for vampire novels, in which the aristocracy is always presented as the beast to be destroyed? The vampire is always the aristocrat and the savior a bourgeois...

FOUCAULT: In the eighteenth century, rumours were already circulating that debauched aristocrats abducted little children to slaughter them and regenerate themselves by bathing in their blood. The rumours even led to riots.

Le Gaufey again emphasizes that this theme develops as a bourgeois myth of that class's overthrow of the aristocracy. Foucault responds, 'Modern antisemitism began in that form'.[12]

I have described this discussion at length to show how one might begin to theorize the shift within the Gothic novel that transforms the threat of the aristocrat into the threat of the degenerate foreigner, the threat of money into the threat of blood. The bad blood of family, in other words, is replaced by the bad blood of 'race', and the scientific theory of degeneracy produces and explains this transition. While neither Le Gaufey nor Foucault attempts to determine what the role of the Gothic novel was in producing these new categories of identity, I have been arguing that Gothic fiction creates the narrative structure for all kinds of gothicizations across disciplinary and ideological boundaries. 'Gothic' describes a discursive strategy which produces monsters as a kind of temporary but influential response to social, political and sexual problems. And yet, Gothic, as I have noted, always goes both ways. So, even as Gothic style creates the monster, it calls attention to the plasticity or constructed nature of the monster and therefore calls into question all scientific and rational attempts to classify and quantify agents of disorder. Such agents, Gothic literature makes clear, are invented not discovered by science.

I am calling modern anti-Semitism 'gothic' because in its various forms – medical, political, psychological – it, too, unites and therefore produces the threat of capital and revolution, criminality and impotence, sexual power and gender ambiguity, money and mind, within an identifiable form, the body of the Jew. In *The Jew's Body*, Sander Gilman demonstrates how nineteenth-century anti-Semitism replaced religious anti-Judaism with this pseudo-scientific construction of the Jewish body as an essentially criminalized and pathologized body. He writes:

The very analysis of the nature of the Jewish body, in the broader culture or within the culture of medicine, has always been linked to establishing the difference (and dangerousness) of the Jew. This scientific vision of parallel and unequal 'races' is part of the polygenetic argument about the definition of 'race' within the scientific culture of the eighteenth century. In the nineteenth century it is more strongly linked to the idea that some 'races' are inherently weaker, 'degenerate', more at risk from diseases than others.[13]

In *Dracula*, vampires are precisely a 'race' and a family that weakens the stock of Englishness by passing on degeneracy and the disease of blood lust. Dracula as a monster/master parasite feeds upon English wealth and health. He sucks blood and drains resources, he always eats out. Jonathan Harker describes the horror of finding the vampire sated in his coffin after a good night's feed:

the cheeks were fuller, and the white skin seemed ruby-red underneath; the mouth was redder than ever, for on the lips were gouts of fresh blood, which trickled from the corners of the mouth and ran over the chin and neck. Even the deep, burning eyes seemed set amongst the swollen flesh, for the lids and pouches underneath were bloated. It seemed as if the whole awful creature were simply gorged with blood. He lay like a filthy leech, exhausted with his repletion (p. 54).

The health of the vampire, his full cheeks and glowing skin, of course, comes at the expense of the women and children he has vamped. Harker is disgusted not simply by the spectacle of the vampire but also by the thought that when the Count arrives in England he will want to 'satiate his lust for blood, and create a new and ever-widening circle of semi-demons to batten on the helpless' (p. 54). At this juncture, Harker picks up a shovel and attempts to beat the vampire-monster into pulp. The fear of a mob of parasites feeding upon the social body drives Harker to violence because the parasite represents the idle and dependent other, an organism that lives to feed and feeds to live.[14]

Dracula is surrounded by the smell or odour of awful decay as though, as Harker puts it, 'corruption had become itself corrupt' (p. 265). When Harker and his band of friends break into Carfax, Dracula's London home, they are all nauseated by a smell 'composed of all the ills of mortality and with the pungent, acrid smell of blood'(p. 265). Similarly, a worker, who delivered Dracula's coffins to Carfax, tells Seward: 'That 'ere 'ouse guvnor is the rummiest I ever was in. Blyme!... the place was that neglected that yer might 'ave smelled ole Jerusalem in it.' (p. 240) The worker is quite specific here, to him the smell is a Jewish smell. Like the diseases attributed to the Jews as a 'race', bodily odours, people assumed, just clung to them and marked them out as different and indeed repugnant objects of pollution.[15]

Parasitism was linked specifically to Jewishness in the 1890s via a number of discourses. In business practices in London's East End, Jews were vilified as 'middlemen' who lived off the physical labour of English working-class bodies.[16] Jews were also linked to the spread of syphilis: the Jewish body, in other words, was constructed as parasite, as the difference within, as unhealthy dependence, as a corruption of spirit that reveals itself upon the flesh. Obviously, the horror generated by the repugnant, disease-riddled body of the vampire bears great resemblance to the anti-Semite's 'Jewish body' described by Gilman as a construction of the nineteenth-century culture of medicine.

Dracula, as the prototype of the wanderer, the 'stranger in a strange land', exhibits the way that homelessness or rootlessness was seen to undermine nation. The threat posed by the wanderer within the novel, furthermore, is clearly identified by Stoker as a sexual threat. The nosferatu is not simply a standard reincarnation of Gothic's Wandering Jew, but rather an undead body, a body that will not rest until it has feasted upon the vital fluids of women and children, drained them of health and seduced them into a growing legion of parasites and perverts.

Dracula's racial markings are difficult to distinguish from his sexual markings. Critics, indeed, have repeatedly discussed vampire sexuality to the exclusion of 'race' or the vampire's foreignness as merely a function of his strange sexuality.[17] One critic, Sue Ellen Case has attempted to locate the vampire within the tangle of 'race' and sexuality. She is interested in the vampire in the nineteenth century as a lesbian vampire and as a markedly queer and outlawed body. She also connects the bloodlust of the vampire to the history of anti-Semitism and she opposes both lesbian and Jew within the vampiric form to a reproductive or maternal sexuality. Case describes the vampire as 'the double "she" in combination with the queer fanged creature ... The vampire is the queer in its lesbian mode.'[18]

Of course, vampiric sexuality as it appears in *Dracula* has also been described as homoerotic[19] and as heterosexual exogamy.[20] So which is it? Of course it is all of these and more; the vampire is not lesbian, homosexual or heterosexual, the vampire represents the productions of sexuality itself. The vampire, after all, creates more vampires by engaging in a sexual relation with his victims; and he reproduces vampires who share his specific sexual predilections. So the point really is not to figure out which so-called perverse sexuality Dracula or the vampire in general embodies, rather we should identify the mechanism by which the consuming monster who reproduces his own image comes to represent the construction of sexuality itself.

Vampire sexuality blends power and femininity within the same body and then marks that body as distinctly alien. Dracula is a perverse and multiple figure because he transforms pure and virginal women into seductresses, he produces sexuality through their willing bodies. Lucy's and Mina's transformations stress an urgent sexual appetite; the three women who ambush Harker in the Castle Dracula display similar voracity. Both Lucy and Dracula's women feed upon children: as 'nosferatu', buried and yet undead, Lucy walks the heath as the 'Bloofer Lady' who lures children to her and then sucks their blood. This act represents the exact reversal of a mother's nurturance. Crouching outside her tomb, Harker and his friends watch horrified as Lucy arrives fresh from the hunt. 'With a careless motion,' notes Seward, 'she flung to the ground, callous as a devil, the child that up to now she had clutched strenuously to her breast, growling over it as a dog growls over a bone.' (p. 223) Lucy is now no longer recognizable as the virginal English woman who had been engaged to marry Lord Godalming, and the group take a certain sexual delight in staking her body, decapitating her and stuffing her mouth with garlic.[21]

When Mina Harker falls under Dracula's spell, he inverts her maternal impulse and the woman who, by day, nurtures all the men around her, by night, drinks blood from the bosom of the King Vampire himself: 'Her white nightdress was smeared with blood and a thin stream trickled down the man's bare breast which was shown by his torn-open dress.' (p. 298) Apart from the obvious reversal of Mina's maternal role, this powerful image feminizes Dracula in relation to his sexuality. It is eminently notable, then, that male not female vampires reproduce; Lucy and the three female vampires in Transylvania feed from children but do not create vampire children. Dracula alone reproduces his form.

Dracula, of course, also produces male sexuality in this novel as a composite of virility, good blood and the desire to reproduce one's own kind. Male sexuality in this respect is a vampiric sexuality (and here I diverge from Case's claim for vampirism as specifically lesbianism). As critics have noted, the birth of an heir at the novel's conclusion, a baby boy named after all the men who fought for his mother's virtue, signifies a culmination of the transfusion scene when all the men give blood to Lucy's depleted body. Dracula has drunk from Lucy and Mina has drunk from Dracula so paternity by implication is shared and multiple. Little Quincey's many fathers are the happy alternative to the threat of many mothers, all the Bloofer Ladies who might descend upon children at night and suck from them instead of suckling them. Men not women within this system reproduce; the female body is rendered non-productive by its sexuality and the vampire body is distinguished from the English male bodies by its femininity.

Blood circulates throughout vampiric sexuality as a substitute or metaphor for other bodily fluids (milk, semen), and once again the leap between bad blood and perverse sexuality, as Case points out, is not hard to make. Dracula's sexuality makes sexuality itself a construction within a signifying chain of class, 'race' and gender. Gothic sexuality, furthermore, manifests as a kind of technology, a productive force which transforms the blood of the native into the lust of the other and an economy which unites the threat of the foreign and perverse within a single monstrous body.

A Gothic economy may be described in terms of a thrifty metaphoricity; one which, rather than simply scapegoating, constructs a monster out of the traits which ideologies of 'race', class, gender, sexuality and capital want to disavow. A Gothic economy also complies with what we might call the logic of capitalism, a logic which rationalizes even the most supernatural of images into material images of capitalism itself. To take a remarkable image from *Dracula* as an example, readers may recall the scene in Transylvania at Castle Dracula when Jonathan Harker, searching for a way out, stumbles upon a pile of gold:

The only thing I found was a great heap of gold in one corner – gold of all kinds, Roman, and British, and Austrian, and Hungarian, and Greek and Turkish money, covered with a film of dust, as though it had lain long in the ground. None of it that I noticed was less than three hundred years old. There were also chains and ornaments, some jewelled, but all of them old and stained. (p. 49)

This image of the dusty and unused gold, coins from many nations and old, unworn jewels, immediately connects Dracula to the old money of a corrupt class, to a kind of piracy of nations and to the worst excesses of the aristocracy. Dracula lets his plundered wealth rot, he does not circulate his capital, he only takes but never spends. Of course this is exactly the method of his vampirism: Dracula drains but it is the band of Englishmen and Van Helsing who must restore. I call this an instance of a Gothic economy because the pile of gold both makes Dracula monstrous in his relation to money and produces an image of monstrous anti-capitalism, one distinctly associated with vampirism. Money, the novel suggests, should be used and circulated and vampirism somehow interferes with the natural ebb and flow of currency, just as it literally intervenes in the ebbing and flowing of blood.

Marx himself emphasized the Gothic nature of capitalism, its investment in Gothic economies of signification, by deploying the metaphor of the vampire to characterize the capitalist. In *The First International* Marx writes: 'British industry ... vampire-like, could but live by sucking blood, and children's blood too.' The modern world for Marx is peopled with the undead; it is indeed a Gothic world haunted by spectres, and ruled by the mystical nature of capital. He writes in the *Grundrisse*:

Capital posits the permanence of value (to a certain degree) by incarnating itself in fleeting commodities and taking on their form, but at the same time changing them just as constantly; ... But capital obtains this ability only by constantly sucking in living labour as its soul, vampire-like.[22]

While it is fascinating to note the coincidence here between Marx's description of capital and the power of the vampire, it is not enough to say that Marx uses Gothic metaphors. Marx, in fact, is describing an economic system, capitalism, which is positively Gothic in its ability to transform matter into commodity, commodity into value and value into capitalism.

Vampirism, Franco Moretti claims, is 'an excellent example of the identity of fear and desire'.[23] He, too, points to the radical ambivalence embodied within the Gothic novel and to the economy of methaphoricity within Gothic monstrosity. For Moretti, Frankenstein's monster and Dracula are 'totalizing' monsters who embody the worker and capital respectively. Dracula is gold brought to life and animated within monopoly capitalism. He is, as we have discussed, dead labour as described by Marx. While Moretti finds Dracula's metaphoric force to be inextricably bound to capital, he acknowledges that desire unravels and then confuses the neat analogy. The vampire represents money, old and new, but he also releases a sexual response that threatens bourgeois culture precisely from below.

Like Frankenstein's monster, Dracula's designs upon civilization are read by his enemies as the desire to father a new race. Harker fears that Dracula will 'create a new and ever-widening circle of semi-demons to batten on the helpless' (p. 54). More than simply an economic threat, then, Dracula's attack seems to come from all sides, from above and below; he is money, he is vermin, he is the triumph of capital and the threat of revolution. Harker and his cronies create in Dracula an image of aristocratic tyranny, of corrupt power and privilege, of foreign threat in order to characterize their own cause as just, patriotic and even revolutionary.

In one interaction between Harker's band of men and the vampire, the Gothic economy that Dracula embodies is forcefully literalized. Having broken into Dracula's house the men are surprised by Dracula's return. In the interaction that follows, the vampire is turned into the criminal or interloper in his own home. Harker slashes at him with a knife: 'A second less and the blade had shorn through his heart. As it was, the point just cut the cloth of his coat, making a wide gap whence a bundle of banknotes and a stream of gold fell out.'(pp. 323-4) Dracula is then driven back and forced out of the window by Harker, who holds up a crucifix, but not before 'he swept under Harker's arm' in order to grasp 'a handful of the money from the floor'. Dracula now makes his escape: 'Amid the crash and glitter of the falling glass, he tumbled into the flagged area below. Through the sound of the shivering glass I could hear the "ting" of the gold, as some of the sovereigns fell on the flagging.' (p. 324)

This incident is overdetermined to say the least. The creature who lives on a diet of blood, bleeds gold when wounded; at a time of critical danger, the vampire grovels upon the floor for money, and then his departure is tracked by the 'ting' of the coins that he drops during his flight. Obviously, the metaphoric import of this incident is to make literal the connection between blood and money, and to identify Harker's band with a different and more mediated relation to gold. Harker and his cronies *use* money and they use it to protect their women and their country: Dracula hoards gold and he uses it only to attack and seduce.

But there is still more at stake in this scene. A Gothic economy, I suggested, may be identified by the thriftiness of metaphor and so the image of the vampire bleeding gold connects not only to Dracula's abuses of capital, his avarice with money and his excessive sexuality, it also identifies Dracula within the racial chain of signification that, as I have shown, links vampirism to anti-Semitic representations of Jewishness. The scene vividly resonates with Shylock's famous speech in *The Merchant of Venice*:

I am a Jew. Hath not a Jew eyes? hath not a Jew hands, organs, dimensions, senses, affections, passions? fed with the same food, hurt with the same weapons, subject to the same diseases ... if you prick us do we not bleed? if you tickle us do we not laugh? if you poison us do we not die? and if you wrong us shall we not revenge? (Act III, sc. i)

Bram Stoker was stage manager for the 250 performances of *The Merchant of Venice* in which Henry Irving, his employer, played Shylock and so it is not so strange to find echoes of Shakespeare's quintessential outsider in Stoker's Dracula. But, Stoker epitomizes the differences between Dracula and his persecutors in the very terms that Shylock claims as common ground. Dracula's eyes and hands, his senses and passions are patently alien; he does not eat the same food, he is not hurt by the same weapons or infected by the same diseases, and when he is wounded or 'pricked', he does not bleed, he sheds gold. In the character of Dracula, Stoker has inverted the Jew's defence into a damning testimony of otherness.[24] We might interpret Moretti's claim that the vampire is 'a totalizing monster' in light of the Gothic economy which allows Dracula to literalize an anti-capitalist, an exemplary consumer and the anti-Semite's Jew. With regard to the latter category, Dracula is foreignness itself. Like the Jew, his function within a Gothic economy is to be all difference to all people; his horror cannot and must not be pinned down exactly.

Marx's equation of vampire and capital and Moretti's analysis of Dracula and gold must be questioned in terms of the metaphoricity of the monster. As Moretti rightly points out, in the literature of terror 'the metaphor is no longer a metaphor: it is a character as real as the others.' (p. 106) Gothic, indeed, charts the transformation of metaphor into body, of fear into form, of narrative into currency. Dracula is (rather than represents) gold, his body bleeds gold, it stinks of corruption, and it circulates within many discourses as a currency of monstrosity. The vampire's sexuality and his power, his erotic and economic attraction are Gothic in their ability to transform multiple modes of signification into one image, one body, one monster, a totality of horror.

The technology of *Dracula* gothicizes certain bodies by making monstrosity an essential component of a 'race', a class, a gender or some hybrid of all of these. I have tried to show that gothicization, while it emerges in its most multiple and overt form in the Gothic novel, is a generic feature of many nineteenth-century human sciences and ideologies. Gothic economies produce monstrous capitalist practice, Gothic anti-Semitism fixes all difference in the body of the Jew, and Gothic fiction produces monstrosity as a technology of sexuality, identity and narrative. I have also tried to make the case for the productivity of the Gothic fiction. Rather than simply demonizing and making monstrous a unitary other, the Gothic is constantly in motion. The appeal of the Gothic text, then, partly lies in its uncanny power to reveal the mechanisms of monster production. The monster, in its otherworldly form, its supernatural shape, wears the traces of its own construction. Like the bolt through the neck of Frankenstein's monster in the modern horror film, the technology of monstrosity is written upon the body. And the artificiality of the monster denaturalizes, in turn, the humanness of his enemies.[25]

Dracula, in particular, concerns itself with modes of production and consumption, with the proximity of the normal and the pathological, the native and the foreign. Even though by the end of the novel the vampire is finally staked, the monster is driven out of England and laid to rest, even though monogamous heterosexuality appears to triumph in the birth of Quincey Harker, the boy is as much the son of Dracula as he is of the 'little band of men' (p. 400) after whom he is named. Blood has been mixed, after all; and like the 'mass of material' which tells the story of the vampire but contains 'hardly one authentic document', Quincey is hardly the authentic reproduction of his parents. Monster, in fact, merges with man by the novel's end, and the boy reincarnates the dead American, Quincey Morris, and the dead vampire, Dracula, as if to ensure that, from now on, Englishness, rather than a purity of heritage and lineage, or a symbol for national power, will become nothing more than a lost moment in Gothic history.

NOTES

1 Sir Richard Burton, *The Jew, the Gypsy and El Islam*, ed., with a preface and notes, by W. H. Wilkins (London: Hutchinson and Co., 1898). In *The Devil Drives: A Life of Sir Richard Burton* (New York: W. W. Norton and Co., 1967), a generally sympathetic biography of Burton, Fawn Brodie notes that Burton backed up his accusations against the Jewish

population of Damascus with no historical evidence whatsoever; he simply 'listed a score or so of such murders attributed to Jews from 1010 to 1840'! (p. 266) Burton was unable to find a publisher for his book because the subject matter was considered too inflammatory and libellous. When the book did finally appear (posthumously) in 1898, thanks to the efforts of Burton's biographer and friend W. H. Wilkins, an appendix entitled 'Human Sacrifice amongst the Sephardim or Eastern Jews' had been edited out. In addition to editing Burton's work, Wilkins was very involved in the debate about Jewish immigration to England in the 1890s. See W. H. Wilkins, 'The Immigration of Destitute Foreigners', *National Review*, XVI (1890–91), 114–24; W. H. Wilkins, 'Immigration Troubles of the United States', *Nineteenth Century*, XXX (1891), 583–95; W. H. Wilkins, 'The Italian Aspect' in Arnold White ed., *The Destitute Alien in Great Britain* (London: n.p., 1892), pp. 146–67; W. H. Wilkins, *The Alien Invasion* (London: n.p., 1892).

2 See Bram Stoker, 'The Censorship of Fiction', *Nineteenth Century* 47 (September 1908), 485. Degenerate writers, he claims, have 'in their selfish greed tried to deprave where others had striven to elevate. In the language of the pulpit, they have "crucified Christ afresh".'

3 'General Mills Puts Bite on Dracula's Neckpiece', (AP), *Minneapolis Star and Tribune* (17 October 1987): 5B. The caption notes that the offensive picture of Dracula on the cereal box came from Bela Lugosi's 1931 portrayal of him in *The House of Dracula*. General Mills responded to the protest by saying that 'it had no intention of being anti-Semitic and would redesign the covers immediately.'

4 In an excellent essay on the way in which 'foreignness merges with monstrosity' in *Dracula*, John Stevenson claims that the threat of the vampire is the threat of exogamy; a threat of interracial competition. See 'A Vampire in the Mirror: The Sexuality of *Dracula*', *PMLA* 103: 2 (March 1988), 139–149.

5 Bram Stoker, *Dracula* (1897) (New York: Bantam Books, 1981), p. 235. All further references appear in the text.

6 A wonderfully clever and witty discussion of the technology and modernity of *Dracula* and its participation in the production of mass culture can be found in Jennifer Wicke's 'Vampiric Typewriting: *Dracula* and its Media' in *ELH*, 59: 1 (Summer 1992), 467–93. Wicke claims that the vampire Dracula 'comprises the techniques of consumption'. I am much indebted, as is obvious, to her reading.

7 In 'The Other Question: Difference, Discrimination and the Discourse of Colonialism', Homi Bhabha describes the way that colonial discourse creates stereotypes as fetishes. This equation between stereotype and fetish allows Bhabha to discuss colonialism as a discipline, or, in other words, a 'non-repressive form of knowledge' which can sustain opposing views and contradictions. I find Bhabha's formulation to be very helpful in thinking through the productive nature of othering and the way

othering always also constructs selves. See Bhabha in *Literature, Politics, Theory*, ed. Francis Barker (London: Methuen, 1986).

8 As quoted in George L. Mosse, *Toward the Final Solution: A History of European Racism* (New York: Howard Fertig, 1978), p. 156.

9 See Sander L. Gilman, 'Sexology, Psychoanalysis, and Degeneration: From a Theory of Race to a Race to Theory' in *Degeneration: The Dark Side of Progress* (New York: Columbia University Press, 1985). Gilman writes: 'Nineteenth-century science tried to explain the special quality of the Jew, as perceived by the dominant European society, in terms of a medicalization of the Jew.' (p. 87)

10 Cesare Lombroso, Introduction to Gina Lombroso Ferrero, *Criminal Man According to the Classifications of Cesare Lombroso* (New York and London: G. P. Pitman's Sons, 1911), p. xv.

11 Michel Foucault, *The History of Sexuality*, vol. 1, tr. Robert Hurley (New York: Vintage, 1980), p. 118.

12 Michel Foucault, 'The Confession of the Flesh' in *Power/Knowledge: Selected Interviews and Other Writings 1972–1977*, ed. Colin Gordon, tr. Colin Gordon, Leo Marshall, John Mepham and Kate Soper (New York: Pantheon Books, 1980), pp. 222–224.

13 Sander Gilman, *The Jew's Body* (New York and London: Routledge, 1991), p. 39.

14 In an anti-Semitic tract called *England Under the Jews*, Joseph Banister, a journalist, voiced some of the most paranoid fears directed against an immigrant Jewish population, a population steadily growing in the 1880s and 1890s due to an exodus from eastern Europe. Banister feared that the Jews would spread 'blood and skin diseases' among the general population and he likened them to 'rodents, reptiles and insects'. Banister, whose book went through several editions, made pointed reference to Jews as parasites calling them 'Yiddish bloodsuckers'. Joseph Banister, *England Under the Jews* (3rd edn, London: n.p., 1907) as quoted in Holmes, *Anti-Semitism in British Society 1876–1939* (New York: Holmes and Meier Publishers Inc., 1979), pp. 39–42.

15 These beliefs are linked to what is commonly known as the blood libel and have a long history in England. See C. Roth (ed.), *The Ritual Murder Libel and the Jew* (London: n.p., 1935).

16 See for example Henry Arthur Jones, 'Middlemen and Parasites', *The New Review* 8 (June 1893), 645–54; and 'The Dread of the Jew' in *Spectator* 83 (9 September 1899), 338–9, where the author discusses contemporary references to Jews as 'a parasitical race with no ideals beyond the precious metals'.

17 On vampire sexuality see Carol A. Senf, '*Dracula*: Stoker's Response to the New Woman' in *Victorian Studies* 26 (1982). Also Stephanie Demetrakopoulos, 'Feminism, Sex Role Exchanges, and Other Subliminal Fantasies in Bram Stoker's *Dracula*', *Frontiers: A Journal of Women's Studies* 2 (1977); Phyllis Roth, 'Suddenly Sexual Women in

Bram Stoker's *Dracula'*, *Literature and Psychology* 17: 3 (1977); Judith Wasserman, 'Women and Vampires: *Dracula* as a Victorian Novel', *Midwest Quarterly* 18 (1977).

18 Sue Ellen Case, 'Tracking the Vampire', *Differences*, 3: 2 (Summer 1991), 9.

19 Christopher Craft, '"Kiss Me With Those Red Lips": Gender and Inversion in Bram Stoker's *Dracula'* in *Speaking of Gender*, ed. Elaine Showalter (New York: Routledge, 1989).

20 See John Allen Stevenson, 'A Vampire in the Mirror: The Sexuality of *Dracula'*, *PMLA*, 103: 2 (March 1988), 139–149.

21 It is worth noting a resemblance between the Bloofer lady and the terms of the blood libel against the Jews.

22 Karl Marx, *Grundrisse: Foundations of the critique of Political Economy*, tr. Martin Nicolaus (Harmondsworth: Penguin 1973), p. 646.

23 Franco Moretti, *Signs Taken For Wonders: Essays on the Sociology of Literary Forms*, tr. Susan Fischer, David Forgacs and David Miller (London: Verso Editions and New Left Books, 1983), p. 100.

24 The 'pound of flesh' scene in *The Merchant of Venice* also connects suggestively with Stoker's *Dracula*. Shylock, after all, is denied his pound of flesh by Portia's stipulation that 'in the cutting it, if thou dost shed / One drop of Christian blood, thy lands and goods / Are (by the laws of Venice) confiscate / Unto the state of Venice.' (Act IV, sc. i, ll. 305–8).

25 In the recent film by Francis Ford Coppola, *Bram Stoker's Dracula*, it must be observed that this Dracula was precisely not Stoker's, not the nineteenth-century vampire, because Coppola turned this equation of humanness and monstrosity around. While I am claiming that Dracula's monstrosity challenges the naturalness of the 'human', Coppola tried to illustrate how Dracula's 'humanity' (his ability to love and to grieve) always outweighs his monstrous propensities.

CHAPTER 13

Postmodernism, a Chance to reread?

Scott McCracken

'You understand?' he asked.

'Perfectly,' I said, 'You are an expert in the psychological wilderness. This is like one of those Redskin stories where the noble savages carry off a girl and an honest backswoodman with his incomparable knowledge follows the track and reads the signs of her fate in a footprint here, a broken twig there, a trinket dropped by the way. I have always liked such stories. Go on.'

Marlow smiled indulgently at my jesting. 'It is not exactly a story for boys,' he said.

(Joseph Conrad, *Chance*)[1]

If Joseph Conrad's *Chance* is not exactly a story for boys, then neither is it, as it was advertised, a story for women. Instead, the novel is difficult to categorize on a number of levels. It has an anomalous position within Conrad's work. Critics who have favoured Conrad's style as part of the beginnings of high modernism have seen the novel's popular elements as evidence of his decline. Its content differs markedly from Marlow's earlier tales like *Heart of Darkness* and *Lord Jim*. In contrast to the way women are excluded or marginalized in those texts, *Chance* contains three New Woman characters, Flora de Barral, Mrs Fyne and the (unnamed) governess. The plot revolves around the transactions and crises of finance capital and international trade as well as the politics of personal identity. In terms of form, the narrative is unusually (even by Conrad's standards) discontinuous and disruptive and the authority of the veteran narrator is constantly questioned. These elements raise many of the questions involved in the current modernism/postmodernism debate. The title itself indicates some of the confusions that arise in defining the differences between the two terms. 'Chance' might, at once, suggest the ephemerality which defines an aspect of the modernist aesthetic,[2] but the concept of chance is also depthless in the sense that often defines postmodernism:[3] it has no place for grand narrative and seems to wreck any hermeneutic project on the rocks of indeterminacy.

In this chapter I ask how useful the concept of postmodernism is for the rereading of a text like *Chance* which is rooted in the cultural politics of the *fin de siècle*. The concept of postmodernism is notoriously undefined. Currently it signifies neither a clear period nor an aesthetic, nor yet a philosophical position. Instead confusingly, it can be any of these things insofar as the concept represents the possibilities that emerge out of the cultural contradictions of modernism. For example, one of the definitions of postmodernism has been the end of a clear divide between high and low culture.[4] This puts a novel like *Chance*, which never fitted well into the critical debates around modernism, into a new and interesting position. Other definitions have emphasized fragmentation, suggesting that issues like gender can be better addressed from the perspectives of postmodernism; but it also raises questions of periodization. How valid are classifications like modernism and postmodernism as periodizing categories? In rereading *Chance*, I intend to take these issues in reverse order and to look first at the question of periodization in the postmodernism debate, secondly at the question of fragmentation and difference, and thirdly at the relationship between high and low culture. Finally, I suggest how the novel's climax can be read as bringing together these aspects of the modernism/postmodernism debate in a way that demonstrates some of the problems of contemporary historical criticism in relation to the *fin de siècle*.

The first question, then, is that of periodization.[5] In his discussion of post-Fordism, the sociologist Bob Jessop writes of the problematical status of the prefix 'post': a discussion which is useful in relation to the concept of postmodernism. Admitting that it would be more prudent not to write about post-Fordism at all, he makes it clear that any prerequisite for serious analysis must 'go beyond noting that it occurs after Fordism and show how it relates to specific developmental tendencies and crises of Fordism'.[6] This exemplary argumentative rigour has not always been present amongst theorists of postmodernism. Lyotard, whose philosophical work, *The Postmodern Condition* did much to begin the postmodernism debate, argues against a strict form of periodization: 'A work can only become modern if it is first postmodern. Postmodernism thus understood is not modernism at its end but in its nascent state, and this state is constant.'[7] Modernity here is understood as flux or ephemerality and modernism as an attempt, always too late, to capture and define that flux. Meaghan Morris has explained Lyotard's formulation eloquently:

Postmodernism, then, is the original modern gesture and it is only a terminal phase of modernism insofar as it terminates modernism's various phases. That is to say, the 'postmodern' in Lyotard's argument here corresponds to the action of criticism proper to the avant-garde, while the 'modern' corresponds to the institutionalization (celebration and destruction) of the results.[8]

Thus for Lyotard, the modernist aesthetic needs to reinvent itself constantly. It must always have hindsight, always be 'post'. These criteria open up the opportunity to understand *Chance* as a reflection on the already (by 1912) institutionalized character of Conrad's own style, its high modernist characteristics. The novel transgresses the established form of the earlier work, incorporating popular elements like romance and 'love-interest' which were kept under careful aesthetic control in a novel like *Lord Jim*. The problem with Lyotard's formulation is that although it does undoubtedly reopen the debate about modernism – asking us to redefine it – it leaves that debate stranded in the realm of aesthetics. We are no nearer to an understanding of the historical specificity of the cultural politics of the *fin de siècle*, or why they might be clearer at the end of the twentieth century.

An alternative approach to the modernism/postmodernism debate is that practised by Marxist cultural critics like David Harvey and Fredric Jameson.[9] In Jameson's dialectic, postmodernism is the 'cultural logic of late capitalism', a formulation that understands postmodernism by classifying the characteristics of modernism (parody, depth, a division of high and low culture) and sees postmodernism as the logical outcome of the previous epoch's cultural contradictions. For Harvey, modernism and postmodernism reflect the socio-economic epochs of Fordism and post-Fordism respectively. To read *Chance* within the neo-Lukácsian models of Jameson or Harvey, the novel needs to be understood within a particular cultural epoch in the context of the development of capitalism. While Jameson maintains an element of dialectical criticism, Harvey gives a less mediated account of the relationship between modernism and developments in political economy:

the vast expansion of foreign trade and investment after 1850 put the major capitalist powers on the path to globalism ... Not only was the relative space revolutionized through innovations in transport and communications, but what that space contained was also fundamentally re-ordered. The map of domination of the world's spaces changed out of all recognition between 1850 and 1914.[10]

Harvey sees 1910 as a key moment when the (above) changes in geopolitics and the global political economy give rise to literary modernism, and if we wanted to seize on *Chance*'s content in order to insert it into his schema, linking political economy to literary modernism, we might look no further than Flora's father, 'The Great de Barral', who is prosecuted and sent to prison for fraud while she is still a child. De Barral's frauds can only be perpetrated because of the type of world Harvey describes as developing at the end of the nineteenth century. They rely on the simple mass market device of newspaper advertisements which promise an exceptional return on small investments. The advertisements work by evoking the puritan value of thrift, an ethic which, by the *fin de siècle*, seemed increasingly anachronistic. Thrift in the burgeoning consumer society of *fin-de-siècle* London becomes an image or simulacrum of saving. The accumulation of wealth becomes instantaneous, no longer related to work. Instead the process of labour and earning is excised by the promise of instant gratification. Marlow's knowledge of de Barral is refracted through this new world, so that it is not knowledge in the traditional sense. He denies the frame narrator's suggestion that he had 'studied' him:

I have not studied de Barral, but that is how I understand him so far as he could be understood through the din of the crash; the wailing and gnashing of teeth, the newspaper contents bills: 'The Thrift Frauds. Cross-examination of the accused. Extra special' – blazing fiercely; the charitable appeals for the victims, the grave tones of the dailies rumbling with compassion as if they were the national bowels. (p. 85)

The prism of the mass media disrupts any sense of certain, subjective knowledge, and at the same time their plural codes fragment the public sphere. Harvey argues that it was only in the new, *fin-de-siècle* context of 'rationalized and totally organized external and public space, that interior and very private senses of time and space could properly flourish'.[11] These interior and private spaces are the subject of novels like *Lord Jim* and *Victory*, which concentrate on the loneliness of masculine consciousness in the face of a chaotic and asocial modernity; but in *Chance*, Marlow's sense of private space for the self is far less secure. There is nothing new in that for Conrad's male characters, but Marlow's position is unusual in the way the questionable legitimacy of his perspective is foregrounded. He tells the tale to an anonymous frame narrator, but to one who is unusually present and interventionist, and this dialogic is further complicated by the overlapping and uncompleted narratives that comprise Marlow's reconstruction of events. Often the 'I' that signifies Marlow's subject position loses its authority, and crucially its masculine authority, in the intersubjective context. The chapter 'On the Pavement' is archetypal in its use of the urban street to signify the nineteenth-century understanding of modernity. In the thorough-fare, speaking to the woman who is ostensibly the novel's central character, Flora de Barral, Marlow's 'I' is displaced when he responds to the public feminine.[12] At first Flora is kept distanced and controlled by the double inverted commas of her speech within Marlow's narration:

[FLORA]: 'I didn't want him to know.'
[MARLOW]: 'I approved heartily. Quite right. Much better. Let him ever remain under his misapprehension which was so much more flattering for him.' (p. 236)

Here Marlow's knowledge that Flora came close to attempting suicide puts him in a position of power. The fact that her fiancé, Captain Anthony, is a man who does not know merely reinforces Marlow's authority. In the next part of the dialogue however, Marlow's subjectivity is split when he himself breaks out into speech:

[FLORA]: '... you would never mention – never – that – that – you had seen me over there.'
[MARLOW]: 'My dear young lady,' I cried, horror-struck at the supposition. 'Why should I? What makes you think I should dream of...' (p. 236)

Marlow's split subjectivity is positioned half in the dialogic conversation with Flora, and half justifying that context in dialogue with the frame narrator. In the context of the ephemera of modern culture, Flora embodies the threat that culture poses to Marlow's authority. Her father later groans when he hears that she met Captain Anthony 'on a road' (p. 364) and later accuses her of being no better than a prostitute: 'You are [unfortunate] as much as if you had gone on the streets.'(p. 384) On the street himself, Marlow is revealed as a fragmented, even a schizophrenic subject. This undermines his long disquisitions about the essential nature of woman, which become sardonic performances for the frame narrator, and Marlow as self-reflexive narrator is aware that they say more about his own fears and anxieties about women than anything else. The difficulty of representation that Flora provokes also complicates Marlow's gender position, both allowing him to vent his misogyny on a 'minx', while, paradoxically his own authority is diminished by his new doubleness, and the minx-like carping of his disrupted narrative. Marlow's unstable identity lacks the potential for ideal fullness imagined (if never achieved) for Conrad's masculine subjects in his earlier romances. He is challenged as a 'knowing' voice both by mass culture – for example, by the presence of the city 'mob' outside de Barral's courtroom (when events have to be explained to him by a journalist friend) – and by the presence of Flora herself.

Marlow's position in *Chance* raises the question of how far some of the characteristics of postmodernism can be differentiated from an earlier modernist epoch. The 'persistent opposition' between the modernist and the postmodernist aesthetic is described by Meaghan Morris as 'between *modernism* as a problematic of self-reference, purism, ontological preoccupation and concern with media specificity, and *post-modernism* (avant-gardism) as an insistence on problems of reference'. Morris resists this definition as:

one which still rests on an art/world dichotomy, assuming as it does both that it is possible for some art to talk about art while other art talks about the world, and that the loquacity is in either case intrinsic to the artwork concerned regardless of how, when and by whom it is read.[13]

This argument restates the difficulties of a cultural criticism that can site a cultural artifact in its social and historical context, and still be aware that siting is itself effected through discourse. This is missed by the broad brush-strokes of an historical critic like Harvey. Consequently, he fails to examine the complexity and differential nature of the new divisions between the private and the public spheres. As feminist critics of Harvey and Jameson have argued, it is the new sense of differential identities which are lived and *represented* in such new spaces, that complicates an historical account of modernism and postmodernism.[14] Harvey would be happier consigning such complexity to the anarchy of postmodernism. In *Chance* it exists already.

In order to introduce difference into the Marxist grand narrative from modernism to postmodernism it is necessary to turn to a feminist who works in cultural studies, Angela McRobbie. McRobbie remarks that the experience of fragmentation is common to modernism and postmodernism, but that

[t]he more important issue might be who gets to express their fragmentation, and who is able to put into words or images or sounds the language of their private broken subjectivities. In this sense who can contest, who can represent and who gets listened to? In this sense fragmentation can be linked with the politics of empowerment, with finding a way of mounting a challenge. A unity of sorts emanates from the tumult of fragmented voices. But for Jameson [in *The Cultural Logic of Late Capitalism*] (and for white middle-class masculinity?) it means disempowerment, silence or schizophrenic 'cries and whispers'.[15]

I take the general issue of empowerment to be correct here, but the vague conception of 'a unity of sorts' is not really enough to replace a Marxism which McRobbie sees to be in 'eclipse or decline'. If the concept of postmodernism has allowed Marxists to evade 'the *logic* of cultural studies' and that logic is 'the problematizing of the relations between culture and the economy and between culture and politics,'[16] then the solution must surely be a Marxism that does the work again, but in a way that includes the full dimensions of those problematic relations. Determinism is not the necessary outcome of introducing economics or of a Marxist framework, as the cultural analyses of Antonio Gramsci and Raymond Williams make clear.[17] In his discussion of Fordism and post-Fordism, Bob Jessop stresses that general categories need not prescribe political outcomes. For example, the 'Fordist compromise between capital and labour', was operated by social democratic and labour parties in north-west Europe, but by conservative parties elsewhere.[18] Students of culture need to be similarly wary of prescriptive generalizations about culture. Jessop is also at pains to distinguish between structural and strategic moments: 'Structure is the legacy of a complex historical process and often embodies major structural contradictions, strategy could well be short-term or ephemeral.'[19] Fordism, in effect, turns out to be a very broad categorization, describing a general tendency, but not defining in any detail economic structures or distinguishing them from economic strategies. Jessop concludes that: 'Fordist mode of regulation, if such there is or was, had proved so varied that its consequences for societalization also vary massively'.[20] It is an analysis that demonstrates the problems involved in tying together the features of Fordism and the cultural phenomenon of modernism. Equally he argues that the 'post-Fordist "mode of societalization" is especially uncertain because, in contrast to the postwar dominance of the American model, there is now strong competition between Japanese, West German and American models'.[21] The conclusion is that it is too soon to talk about a generalized post-Fordist mode of societalization. The proper task for the moment is to examine the changing social relations, particularly those of class, 'race' and gender and the social and political problems that emerge from Fordism's crisis.[22]

Jessop's lack of 'substantive results', provides a superb Gramscian example of a cautious approach to social, political and economic change. Above all, it keeps alive a sense of politics and possibility in an analysis which paves the way for an examination of not, in Harvey's subtitle 'the origins of cultural change', but the contradictions and dynamics of cultural process. Following Jessop's Gramscian methodology it might be suggested that the 1890s need to be understood as a complex combination of related crises in the fields of gender, 'race' and class relations which are specific to the fragmentation of the cultural dominants of the nineteenth century, and must be (but cannot be easily) compared with the postmodernism of the 1990s. In order to explore how the questions of difference and fragmentation can be viewed in the context of an historical criticism, I now intend to look at the cultural politics of gender difference in *Chance*, central to which is McRobbie's question: who is empowered?

Chance is a novel which, as I have mentioned, has its roots in the 1890s. Conrad first mentions a short story called 'Dynamite' in 1898.[23] The tale, about a shipload of explosives appears not to differ appreciably from Conrad's other sea tales of the same period; but in 1899, a letter mentions a short story, 'the one about a Captain's wife', which suggests a feminine subject outside the usual concerns of the sea tales.[24] As I have argued elsewhere,[25] while the feminine appears alien to Conrad's subject matter, it is possible to argue that Conrad's own evasion and mystification on the subject of women is not so much a sign of unconcern as blindness or absence which signifies the centrality of gender in his writing. The gendered subjectivity of Conrad's masculine heroes can be related back to the new feminine subjects of the New Woman writers, to which the individuated Jim or Marlow can be seen as a response. It is this dialogic that makes *Chance* such a fascinating text. No fewer than three New Women emerge from its pages, and it is their textual presence which disrupts the speech act – from man to man – of Marlow's narration; a speech act which in previous novels has striven for near total self-sufficiency, even if it has not been achieved.[26]

Flora acts to disrupt ironic distance in the novel, and this disruption works on at least two different levels. Firstly, there is the delegitimation of Marlow's narration, so that he becomes self-mocking in the face of femininity; almost a pastiche of his former self. Secondly, there is the wider social context of Flora's social positioning, one which threshes out the ethereal world of women and makes it more concrete *and*, consequently, more threatening. Significantly, this takes the narrative beyond the closed masculine world of Conrad's ship. Marlow first encounters Flora in the context of Mrs Fyne's circle of feminist disciples. In a suitably carnivalesque inversion Mrs Fyne is described as 'masculine', while her husband is described as a 'feminist'. The figure of the mannish 'brain woman' was a common one at the time and was used to represent the dangers of women de-sexing themselves.[27] Marlow uses the popular 1890s image of role-reversal to describe himself as feminine in contrast to Mr Fyne's feminist masculinity. Marlow is feminine but anti-women, Charles Fyne is masculine but pro-women. The transgression of the fixed borderlines of gender roles and political positions creates a perverse comedy, allowing Marlow to play the part of wry commentator on the bizarre series of events that lead up to Flora's elopement with Captain Anthony, Mrs Fyne's brother. Marlow inserts himself in Flora de Barral's narrative – he claims reluctantly, although the narrative depends upon his gossipy 'old-womanish' desire for information – through a 'chance' encounter with her as she is about to commit suicide. She is, again comically, prevented from achieving her aim through fear that a small dog will follow her over the cliff. Once implicated, he uses his position to analyze her. Like many of the New Woman characters of the 1890s[28], Flora 'requires' analysis because she does not fit easily into dominant nineteenth-century modes of representing the feminine. As a single woman – one of the 'odd women' in Gissing's famous phrase[29] – she occupies no simple category, but the space in which previous categorizations no longer seem to work. Although her nervous disposition would have been recognized by contemporary sexologists like Havelock Ellis,[30] she does not fit well into her original position as Mrs Fyne's disciple. She emerges from the topsy-turvy world of the Fyne family into Marlow's gaze to act out the role of heroine in a traditional heterosexual romance; but Flora's elopement is a parody of the Fynes' marriage, against the wishes of Mrs Fyne's patriarchal father (who is modelled on Coventry Patmore, the very inventor of 'the angel in the house'[31]). The Fynes disapprove of her marriage and, as we shall see, she is escaping not from, but to her father.

In an historical reading in the context of the modernism/postmodernism debate, the construction of Flora's disruptive femininity cannot be separated from the history of the women's movement of the late nineteenth and early twentieth century.[32] If the New Woman novelists represented this change, then Flora is an example of how a different textual strategy registers the impact of that movement on gender relations, and of how that recognition does not necessarily mean women's empowerment. The form of her representation constructs her in relation to Marlow, and while Marlow is, clearly, forced into a more self-reflexive mode, he is allowed to maintain his central role as the only narrator who can fit every part of the narrative together. If we return to Jessop's distinction between structure and strategy we might say that, while *Chance* recognizes a structural change or crisis in gender relations, it only represents one strategic, textual response to that crisis. In recognising Flora's representation as a product of the gender relations of the *fin de siècle*, we recognize that the crisis is historically specific, but in recognizing her representation as a strategy we must also note that the *fin de siècle* had a cultural politics in which different arguments were trying to make themselves heard. And if modernism grew out of a cultural politics then postmodernism equally provides a new context, a new cultural politics from within which we reread the texts of the *fin de siècle*. The problematic of postmodernism includes the history of the post-war women's movement, and its influence in terms of feminist criticism means that male critics are reading for gender; but this is not to say that feminism is the dominant form of reading in the 1990s. Meaghan Morris has warned of the dangers of assuming that the postmodern condition (in the Lyotardian sense of a crisis of grand narratives) is a good thing for women and other politically marginalized groups.[33] Rather, feminist criticism has provided new strategies for rereading in the context of the late twentieth-century crisis in gender relations.

A comparison between the history of gender relations and that of imperialism can demonstrate what I meant earlier by looking at different but 'related crises' in their historical specificity. The absence of the colonial subject in *Chance*, is an example of how the text can recognize the New Woman but still exclude other voices. In contrast to the way a 'racial' other is (mis)represented in *Heart of Darkness* or *The Nigger of the 'Narcissus'*, there is no subject position as such for the colonial other in *Chance*. This absence masks, more than is usual in Conrad's narratives, the centrality of the history of imperialism in the function of the ship, the *Ferndale*, which links up the global outposts of the British Empire. As has been argued by Gillian Rose, arguments for the cultural logic of postmodernism also ignore the contrary tendencies of anti-colonial movements.[34] These remain absent in Harvey's text, except as part of a collective, undifferentiated, global working class. This tends to presume a unipolar world which conflates dominance with logic. It may look rational from an economistic point of view, but it only makes Harvey's cultural politics seem mechanistic.[35] Part of the problematic of postmodernism has been the strong influence of postcolonial criticism, for example the work of Edward Said or Gayatri Spivak, which has meant that silences and misrepresentations within modernism have been reread in terms of the history of imperialism.[36] In *Chance*, there is no doubt that part of the romance of the tale is the fact that it is a 'shipboard romance' and therefore contains in its popular appeal part of the powerful evocation of the empire that marked the cultural politics of the *fin de siècle*. Postcolonial critical strategies have opened up modernist texts, but the very concept of new strategies indicates once again the need to pay attention to the historical specificity of a text's production and reception. I now intend to look in more detail at the context of *Chance*'s production and reception in relation to one of the claims for a distinctively postmodernist epoch: that there has been a shift from the division within modernism between high, elite culture and low or mass culture. This requires a short excursus on the writing of the novel.

Despite Leavis's typically idiosyncratic judgement and widespread praise for the ambitious nature of the narrative, *Chance* is more often seen as tipping the scales towards its author's decline.[37] The novel was written and rewritten over a period of sixteen years. Conrad began writing it in 1898, it was serialized in the *New York Herald* in 1912 and only published in book form in 1914, a year in which the outbreak of the First World War brought to an end the turn-of-the-century epoch. It is sometimes held, somewhat mechanically, that this long gestation period accounts for its overlapping narratives.[38] What is clear is that in his correspondence Conrad writes about *Chance* as his big project to which some of his other, better known, novels, like *The Secret Agent* and *Under Western Eyes*, were supposed to be subsidiary. These other narratives grew and were published as diversions from the main work; and one of the factors that led Conrad to see them as such was their lack of commercial success. As his debt to his literary agent, J. M. Pinker grew, Conrad became increasingly concerned with the idea and the material necessity of popularity.

In this sense Conrad's relationship with the mass market was felt personally. At times, Conrad's position comes to that of a piece worker, where several thousand words, or the promise that he will complete so much of *Chance*, accompanies a plea to Pinker for a cheque for ten pounds. This personal history, which is often forgotten when Conrad is inserted unproblematically into the canon of English literature, throws up an unexpected comparison between Conrad's position and that of the Eastern European immigrants who were exploited as sweated labour in the East End. It is a comparison which is reinforced by a later dispute between Conrad and Pinker (which ended their friendship), when Pinker accused Conrad of not speaking comprehensible English. There can be no doubt that the comparison would have been odious to Conrad himself; but it demonstrates the marginal position of Jozef Teodor Konrad Korzeniowski in English culture. The desire for popularity was about acceptance in more ways than one. In this context, *Chance* came to represent a number of different goals. In a letter written on 15 February 1907, Conrad puns on the title, speculating that it 'is going to bring a real turn of luck';[39] and perhaps responding to various pressures, social and financial, the idea of 'striking a blow for popularity' enters into a letter of 6 May of the same year where the novel is discussed.[40]

At the same time, Conrad, responding to different pressures, rebelled against commercialism, complaining that he was not a 'sausage-machine' (it is not clear whether he saw the machine as Polish, producing sausages for an English market).[41] While he was in no position to turn down *Chance*'s serialization in the *New York Herald*, Conrad's attitude towards the novel was contradictory. He consistently played up its commercial possibilities to Pinker, while downplaying its literary worth to other writers and critics, like

Galsworthy; and this contradictoriness in the correspondence can be related to a contradiction within modernism itself between popularity and literary merit. At times, *Chance* becomes a metaphor for the resolution of all Conrad's problems, material, mental and artistic.

There is a clear link between the overt concern for gender in *Chance* and its reputation as a 'down-market' Conradian novel. Apart from the very early reference, quoted above, to a story about a Captain's wife, there is little indication in the correspondence of the novel's content. The pre-publication publicity in the *New York Herald* however, stressed the novel's romantic elements. An interview with Conrad was printed in which he stated: 'it gives me the keenest pleasure when I find that woman kind appreciates my work, and in writing the story for the *NYH* I aimed at treating my subject in a way which would interest women. That's all.'[42] The serial was shrewdly advertised as a shipboard romance: in the words of the interview, 'it deals with the life of a seaman and a woman, and it is while they are on board ship that, if I may say so, the situations develop that, I think, will appeal strongly to my readers'.[43] The 1914 edition had a picture of a woman on the book jacket, and this was expected to boost sales.

Some critics have seen the book's subsequent genuine popularity, which did indeed ensure financial security for Conrad, as a bad case of judging a book by its cover. Marlow's grumpy misogyny is taken to demonstrate the text's anti-feminist tenor. So it is, perhaps, unfair that some of the same critics have also condemned the novel for its romantic elements. Cedric Watts is paradigmatic in this respect: '[t]he garrulous commentary seems to drain and dissipate the symbolic potential of events; and, above all, the conventionally romantic materials of the novel are eventually endorsed instead of being challenged and astringently ironised.'[44] This type of criticism endorses a view that sees Conrad's decline as at one with his 'descent' into romanticism: a descent that is traced back to the romantic second half of *Lord Jim*. It gives a version of Conrad's work which operates along a clear binary divide: on the one hand, the Conrad of symbolism, impressionism and a hard, spare form of writing; on the other, the Conrad of romantic adventure, love-stories and loose, 'garrulous' narration. It is a divide which is equally clearly gendered, in the way Huyssen describes in his essay 'Mass Culture as Woman: Modernism's Other':

the nightmare of being devoured by mass culture through co-option, commodification, and the "wrong" kind of success is the constant fear of the modernist artist, who tries to stake out his territory by fortifying the boundaries between genuine art and inauthentic mass culture. Again, the problem is not the desire to differentiate between forms of high art and depraved forms of mass culture and its co-options. The problem is rather the persistent gendering as feminine of that which is devalued.[45]

Conrad's contradictory engagement with the popular is equated with his incorporation of romance. The mass-market is seen as part of a degraded world which is feminized. Modernism, by contrast is legitimized and valued through its association with the figure of the masculine artist.

Perceived through the problematic of postmodernism this divide might be theorized in a different way. The key question here must be whether the high-low divide in modernism is a valid critical judgement, or whether it has been imposed by 'modernist' criticism. Lyotard's aesthetic analysis suggests that a text like *Chance* can indeed be read as the postmodern in modernism. A more historical account might suggest that the modernist conception of literary value needs to be more rigorously historicized in the late twentieth century because of the way that valuation has changed. One formalist approach might be to differentiate modernist form in *Chance* from its more popular elements. This formal method might then allow an historical account of this binary opposition.

As we have seen, in *Chance* Marlow becomes the teller of other people's tales, a process which admits an overt dialogic, and which disrupts his authority. In some ways this is a surprising development. Because of his experiences at sea, Conrad's own writer's myth relied perhaps more heavily than most modernist artists on personal experience; but, in fact, the voice of authentic experience is not lost in *Chance*, rather it is passed onto the younger Powell, whose innocence and solitude (his only relationship on earth appears to be with an aged aunt) leave him, as yet, untouched by the world's degrading influences. This preserves an aesthetic ideal from Conrad's earlier texts, which manifests itself in Powell's subjective apprehensions. If we wanted to see the kernel of *Chance* in 'Dynamite', the short story of the 1890s, we might trace the following passage back to that text:[46]

Wisps of mist floated like trails of luminous dust, and in the dazzled reflections of water and vapour, the shores and the murky, semi-transparent darkness of shadows cast mysteriously from below. Powell, who had sailed out of London all his young sailor's life, told me that it was then, in a moment of entranced vision an hour or so after sunrise, that the river revealed to him for all time, like a fair face often seen before, which is suddenly perceived to be the expression of an inner and unsuspected beauty, of that something unique and only its own which arouses a passion of wonder and fidelity and an unappeasable memory of its charm. (pp. 276–7)

There are echoes here in the description of the water of the impressionist writing of *The Nigger of the 'Narcissus'*; although, even here, Powell's impressions are retold by Marlow, and therefore contextualized as of a particular experience, time and place. There is preserved in the first sentence a sense of natural mystery which serves to project Powell's masculine subjectivity against a canvas of otherness. The shadow-like quality of the shore, 'cast mysteriously from below' inverts the realist metaphor of the relationship between land – solid, material, safe – and river, sea, water – fluid, abstract, uncertain – to make the land the reflection of some unseen reality. The effect is to throw all signifiers into a free-floating realm so that there is no clear subject-object relation between Powell and the mysterious source of the shadows. In this sentence Powell himself is in danger of losing his identity and becoming insubstantial. His position only solidifies in the second sentence, where the distant nature of the river is transformed into the image of 'a fair face'. The key to this transformation is control along gender lines. As 'a fair face', the river is feminized, so that, in a single stroke, the subject-object hierarchy is re-established. It is only then that the final dialectic of the passage can be performed: the transformation of the controlled feminine, that is a masculine aesthetic into a transcendent sublime. Its uniqueness and self-sufficiency, 'only its own', are able to arouse 'a passion of wonder', which goes beyond the subjective apprehension of beauty.

If the point for a late twentieth-century rereading is that, given our saturation in mass culture, the sublime always be read as a symptom of that culture, then it might be argued that the sublime in *Chance* is equally contextualized by Marlow's narration. This brings with it a more jaundiced and knowing apprehension which, while it might recognize Powell's experience, could also argue that Powell's wonder is simply the sentimentality of romantic youth. It is here that the three 'postmodern' questions I have chosen to look at – periodization, difference and the high-low culture divide – come together. Marlow's relationship to the young Powell marks out two old positions in Conrad's writing, which correspond to that of father and son. In *Lord Jim* this relationship allows Marlow's authority to go unquestioned. Jim provides him with an opportunity to reflect upon his own self-development; but in *Chance*, an unrepresented social world that informs the (apparently) private bond impedes in the form of the three New Women. The principle female character, Flora de Barral, is as central to the narrative as young Powell is peripheral; and her textual centrality is all the more surprising when we consider the insubstantial nature of Conrad's usual heroines. Where Powell still occupies the position of Jim, the Marlow of *Chance* is a response to a commercialized social world which, although it is characterized as feminine, represents far more than that. We might compare the relationship between Bloom and Stephen in *Ulysses*; but if we do, then we must also recognize that this commercial world is not that of the late twentieth century. It still contains a place for the young masculine modernist, Powell, Stephen and the young Conrad himself, who are trying to live in and against that environment. The late twentieth century has eroded the ground of that form of hegemonic, masculine modernism, though not male power itself. The result for historical criticism is that the cultural politics of the *fin de siècle* now appear in forms that allow us to move outside the canon of male modernists and even to explore the way in which the canon itself may contain elements that contradict its own elitism. In order to explore this further and to conclude this discussion I intend to look at the novel's dramatic (some would say melodramatic) climax as a moment which brings together the considerations of the postmodern problematic.

The climax takes place on board the *Ferndale*, bringing together Flora, her father and the young Powell, in whom we might see embodied disruptive femininity, the commercial or mass culture of the *fin de siècle*, and masculinist modernism respectively. Flora's personal history emerges gradually in the novel after her first encounter with Marlow, and it goes some way towards explaining her disruptive presence, making the link between her femininity and commercial culture.[47] Her childhood has been shaped by two factors: the early death of her mother, which leaves her at the mercy of a ferocious, vindictive and sexually voracious governess; and the activities of her distant father, who is at first too involved in his numerous dubious financial schemes to spend much time with her. It is Flora's relationship with her father which makes the vital link in the novel between her problematic femininity and an unknowable and immaterial world of finance. Her elopement is perverse because, as I have already mentioned, she is running to, not from, her father. When she finally retrieves Mr de Barral he turns out not to be what she is looking for. He is as much a parody of Dickens's patriarch Mr Dombey as the more obvious Mr Merdle.

Flora and her father join Captain Anthony's ship, the *Ferndale* together, and together they disrupt the previous relationship between captain and crew in a way which links back to the question of the family. In Conrad's novels, the ship is often an escape for men who cannot cope with the pressures of domestic life with women, but who attempt to recreate a masculine domesticity on board ship. The *Ferndale*'s chief mate, who recommends a good mother rather than the problem of a wife, is an example of this, and Captain Anthony himself feels that he no longer has any real connection with his family ashore. The ship provides a safe space and an opportunity to engage in imperial adventures, and thus threats, particularly 'racial' threats, to its harmony are often the central dynamic of Conrad's earlier tales.[48] There is no embodied 'racial' threat to the *Ferndale*, but the differentiated characters of Flora and her father present a complex view of the binary opposition between social and asocial worlds. Powell's presence on board keeps alive the unblemished tradition of the honourable seafarer, untouched by shore life.

Normally in Conrad's work the domestic space of the ship is represented as various hierarchical areas of personal privacy. The new interior spaces of the late nineteenth century are carefully ordered in contrast to the confused and mystifying public sphere which is the shore. There is, of course, an historical irony in this, because it is the ship itself which is carving out the infrastructure for a global culture; but it is within this context that the ordering of the ship as forms of individual consciousness becomes important, taking us back to McRobbie's question about who is empowered in a fragmented world. The space occupied by the crew is private in relation to the shore, but the captain's space is more private than that of the crew. (Conrad examines the dimensions and dilemmas of the captain's privacy in 'The Secret Sharer' and 'The Shadow Line', where a gendered private space breaks down with the collapse of the Captain into a split or schizophrenic sense of self.)

The intervention of Flora and her father in the society of the ship follows the pattern marked out above in relation to Huyssen's account of mass culture as woman. Flora's position as a New Woman can be seen to follow her father as the logical outcome of the commercial culture he represents. De Barral's financial schemes disrupt the nineteenth-century divide between the public and the private by reducing the thrift and hard work that characterized the ideology of the Victorian middle-class family to the status of images: Chapter 3 is called 'Thrift – And The Child'.[49] It is this new, fragmented and degraded public sphere that allows women to intervene. Flora is then a monster, created by de Barral's practices and by his neglect; but, once created, she becomes the outrider of commercial culture, not only as a disruptive influence in herself, but also by allowing her father on board ship. The ship, surrounded by the commercial uncertainty which is the sea, might now be seen as a metaphor for the modernist text itself. To de Barral it seems no less a prison than the one from which he has just been released; and, indeed, his analysis is in part correct. The strategy of putting him on the ship is a form of forcible privatization, an attempt to limit his destructive role; or, in aesthetic terms, an attempt to contain and control the threat of mass culture.

In fact, the attempt looks likely to fail because the presence of Flora and her father maps out a new space on board ship. Captain Anthony's first act after his marriage is to refurbish the captain's quarters and to inform his chief mate that he will no longer be dining with him. His next, and more disturbing move, for the chief mate at least, is when he leaves the captain's usual cabin on the starboard side to his wife and starts to sleep in a cabin on the port side. This means that when Powell tries to wake the captain because of an imminent collision which would blow up the dynamite-laden ship, he stamps on the wrong side, causing Flora not Anthony to arrive on deck. The disordering of the ship's space implies an inversion of the social hierarchy – a ship of fools perhaps – and a loss of command which has its corollary in Anthony's lack of sexual mastery over his wife: the steward sarcastically asks Powell, 'Wife! Call her a wife, do you?' (p. 390)

It is this situation which sets the scene for the climax which must try and resolve the social, sexual and aesthetic contradictions the text represents. Frustrated by his inability to escape the ship or take up a new position as a financier, de Barral attempts to end a marriage, which he does not recognize anyway, by poisoning Captain Anthony. He is prevented by the young Powell, who, we are told, by *chance*, sees the attempt to administer the poison through a skylight that looks into the captain's quarters. His revelation leads Anthony to announce that he is giving up on Flora and her father; but de Barral's plot is foiled when Flora rejects her father and announces a passionate attachment to Anthony, suggesting for the first time that he represents more than just a refuge for de Barral. This acts as a spur to Anthony which not even de Barral's suicide, using the same poisoned glass, can impede: 'No! No! I am not going to stumble now over that corpse'(p. 435) mutters the captain, as he resolves not to tell his wife her father is dead until the morning in case it damps down her desire.

This climax replaces what I take to be the original anti-climax of the original short story 'Dynamite', which is the near collision on Powell's first voyage. Flora helps him light the flare and they save the ship together. This would imply that the whole de Barral side of the narrative is developed out of the presence of a woman on board ship. Starting from the idea of women invading a carefully ordered masculine world, Conrad develops a text which opposes that world to the chaos beyond. In the pursuit of the popular, however, the two worlds become more and more interrelated, and the text becomes more and more complex, incorporating a fascinating and entertaining series of interactions, so that, at times, Marlow seems to lose control of the narrative altogether.

Powell's privileged view into the disorder at the heart of the *Ferndale* has, of course, nothing to do with 'chance'. It represents an attempt to assert a modernist perspective which will put the popular narrative back into its box. His intervention achieves a reordering of the ship along sexual and social lines: Flora turns away from her father towards her husband, the death of de Barral relieves some of the tensions he has created on board ship. But this is only a partially successful resolution from the perspective of 'modernist' criticism, not least because the narrative is unfinished and requires Marlow's attendance at a wedding between Flora and Powell to complete it, a step with which he appears uncomfortable. (p. 447)

To conclude, it is clear that many of the forms and much of the content associated with postmodernism are present in *Chance*. This is not just because the text is seen anew from the standpoint of a late twentieth-century rereading. The issues of mass culture, feminist politics and the history of imperialism were already present. Postmodernism is the broad and often overrated term which describes the new agenda for cultural criticism in the 1990s. If we are to make use of its opportunities we need to hold on to two older issues in criticism: history and politics. The historical aspect must stress the conditions of production and reception of a particular text. This means that some form of periodization is valuable, although, clearly, modernism and postmodernism are very general terms. The point of an historical method should not be to produce a strict set of categories for the modernist or postmodernist work of art, but to define particular cultural configurations as the conditions of possibility for a particular place and time. The second key aspect, the politics of culture, means allowing for difference and conflict within a given period, so that large-scale generalizations cannot be allowed to subsume the role of culture as a site of contestation. One aspect of postmodernism which is generally recognized as positive is the new interest in differential forms of historical subjectivity, but as the instance of *Chance* shows, recognizing these forms is not the same as empowering new, oppositional identities (although equally this does not mean that recognition is simply a new form of dominance). Postmodernism's interest in mass culture is perhaps one of its most exciting elements, because struggles over cultural value have long been at the centre of radical politics. An 'anomalous' novel like *Chance* demonstrates the contradictions in the definition of work as modernist, transgresses the strictly kept limits of such definitions. Marlow is parodied, the ship invaded, impressionism is displaced by melodrama and romance, and elitist art is debased by selling itself to the mass market. Ultimately, however, the binary opposition of high art and mass culture is not lost in *Chance*; instead it remains the pivot around which a more popular text can be written. The material result was that Conrad was assured financial security, but the novel was felt to occupy an ambivalent position in the modernist canon.

I started by saying that postmodernism is not clearly defined as an aesthetic, a philosophy or as a cultural epoch, but that it can be all these things. As a term its great strength has been its broadness, its ability to encompass questions that have previously been considered outside the provenance of literary criticism. However, if postmodernism has expanded the area of study in cultural criticism, the chances it gives us will only be useful insofar as we have a cultural politics to provide the critical edge.

NOTES

I would like to thank Sally Ledger, Brian Longhurst and Andrew Roberts for commenting on drafts of this paper.

1 Joseph Conrad, *Chance* (Oxford: Oxford University Press, 1988), p. 311. All subsequent references to the novel will be cited in the text.
2 Jürgen Habermas, 'Modernity's Consciousness of Time', in *The Philosophical Discourse of Modernity*, tr. Frederick Lawrence (Cambridge, Mass.: MIT Press, 1987), pp. 1–22.
3 Fredric Jameson, *Postmodernism, or, The Cultural Logic of Late Capitalism* (London: Verso, 1991), p. 9.
4 Jameson, *Postmodernism*, pp. 2–3.
5 For a more general discussion of periodization and the *fin de siècle* see the introduction to this volume.
6 Bob Jessop, 'Fordism and post-Fordism: A Critical Reformulation', *Pathways to Industrialization and Regional Development* (London: Routledge, 1992), p. 60.
7 Jean François Lyotard, *The Postmodern Condition: A Report on Knowledge*, tr. Geoff Bennington and Brian Massumi (Manchester: Manchester University Press, 1984), p. 79.
8 Meaghan Morris, 'Postmodernity and Lyotard's Sublime', in *The Pirate's Fiancée: Feminism, Reading, Postmodernism* (London: Verso, 1988), p. 234.
9 Jameson, *Postmodernism*; David Harvey, *The Condition of Postmodernity* (Oxford: Basil Blackwell, 1990).
10 Harvey, *Condition of Postmodernity*, p. 264.
11 *Ibid.*, p. 270.
12 See Elizabeth Wilson, 'The Invisible Flâneur', *New Left Review* 191 (January/February 1992), 90–110, for an argument that 'the *flâneur* represented not the triumph of masculine power, but its attenuation', (p. 109).
13 Morris, 'Postmodernity and Lyotard's Sublime', pp. 236–7.
14 Doreen Massey, 'Flexible Sexism', *Environment and Planning D: Society and Space*, 9 (1991), 31–57; Angela McRobbie 'New Times in Cultural Studies', *New Formations* 13 (Spring 1991), 1–17; Meaghan Morris, 'The Man in the Mirror: David Harvey's "Condition" of Postmodernity', *Cultural Theory and Cultural Change* (London: Sage, 1992), pp. 253–79; Gillian Rose, review of David Harvey, *The Condition of Postmodernity* in *The Journal of Historical Geography*, 17: 2 (1991), 118–121.
15 McRobbie, 'New Times', p. 5.
16 *Ibid.*, p. 6.
17 Antonio Gramsci, *Cultural Writings* (London: Lawrence and Wishart, 1985); Raymond Williams, *Marxism and Literature* (Oxford: Oxford University Press, 1977).

18 Jessop, 'Fordism and Post-Fordism', p. 52.

19 *Ibid.*, p. 52.

20 *Ibid.*, p. 58.

21 *Ibid.*, p. 65.

22 *Ibid.*, pp. 67–8.

23 Joseph Conrad to Edward Garnett, 28 May 1898, in Frederick R. Karl and Laurence Davies (eds.) *The Collected Letters of Joseph Conrad* (Cambridge: Cambridge University Press, 1986), vol. 2 (1898–1902), pp. 62–3.

24 Conrad to David Meldrun, 14 February 1899, *Collected Letters*, vol. 2.

25 Scott McCracken, 'A Hard and Absolute Condition of Existence: Reading Masculinity in *Lord Jim*', Andrew Michael Roberts (ed.), *Conrad and Gender* (Amsterdam: Rodopi Press, 1993), pp. 17–38.

26 For a discussion of how Marlow's own gender distinctions constantly 'undo' themselves see Andrew Michael Roberts 'Secret Agents and Secret Objects: Action, Passivity and Gender in Conrad's *Chance*', in Andrew Michael Roberts (ed.), *Conrad and Gender*, pp. 89–104.

27 Ellen Key, *The Woman Movement* (New York and London: Knicker-bocker Press, 1912), p. 73.

28 New Woman writers included George Egerton (Maria Chavelita Dunne), Sarah Grand and Mona Caird.

29 George Gissing's *The Odd Women* (1893) (London: Virago 1980), well represents men's contradictory feelings about *fin-de-siècle* feminism.

30 Havelock Ellis, *Man and Woman: A Study of Human Secondary Sexual Characteristics* (1894; reprint London: Walter Scott, 1904), p. 350.

31 E. E. Duncan, 'Some Sources of *Chance*', *Review of English Studies*, 20 (1969), 468–71.

32 For an account of *fin-de-siècle* feminism see Chapter 2: Sally Ledger, 'The New Woman and the Crisis of Victorianism'.

33 Morris, 'Postmodernity and Lyotard's Sublime', p. 222.

34 Rose, review of *The Condition of Postmodernity*, p. 118.

35 This is despite Harvey's recent reply to his critics where he acknowledges the influence of feminist and postcolonial critics on his conception of postmodernism. 'Postmodern Morality Plays', *Antipode* 24: 4 (1992), 300–326.

36 See Edward Said, *Culture and Imperialism* (London: Chatto and Windus, 1993); Gayatri Chakravorty Spivak, *In Other Worlds* (London: Rout-ledge, 1988).

37 Albert J. Guerard, *Conrad the Novelist* (Cambridge, Mass.: Harvard University Press, 1966), pp. 254–72; Fredric Jameson, *The Political Unconscious* (London: Methuen, 1981), p. 221; Thomas Moser, *Joseph Conrad: Achievement and Decline* (Cambridge, Mass.: Harvard University Press, 1957), pp. 163–172.

38 Martin Ray, Introduction to *Chance* (Oxford: Oxford University Press, 1988), p. xiii.

39 Conrad, *Collected Letters*, vol. 3: 1903–1907 (Cambridge: Cambridge University Press, 1988), p. 411.

40 *Ibid.*, p. 435.

41 Conrad to J. B. Pinker (17(?) February 1908), *Collected Letters*, vol. 4: 1908–1911 (Cambridge: Cambridge University Press, 1990), p. 44.

42 Conrad to the *New York Herald* Sunday magazine (late 1911) in *Collected Letters*, vol. 4, pp. 531–32.

43 Conrad, *Collected Letters*, vol. 4, p. 531 n. 3.

44 Cedric Watts, *Joseph Conrad: A Literary Life* (London: Macmillan, 1989), p. 121.

45 Andreas Huyssen, *After the Great Divide: Modernism, Mass Culture, Postmodernism* (Bloomington and Indianapolis: Indiana University Press, 1986), p. 53.

46 No copy exists of the original short story, leaving the way clear for me to speculate as to its contents.

47 Rachel Bowlby's *Just Looking* (London: Methuen, 1985) gives a fascinating account of women's position in the new consumer culture of the *fin de siècle*.

48 McCracken, 'A Hard and Absolute Condition of Existence', pp. 19–25.

49 The best historical account of the Victorian middle-class family is Leonore Davidoff and Catherine Hall, *Family Fortunes: Men and Women of the English Middle-Class 1780–1850* (London: Hutchinson, 1987).

CHAPTER 14

Is market society the fin of history?

Regenia Gagnier

In 1989, Irving Kristol's *The National Interest* devoted a volume to Francis Fukuyama's article 'The End of History?' and commentary on it. Fukuyama, former analyst at the Rand Corporation and then deputy director of the State Department's policy planning staff, offered the 'Hegelian' argument that with the 'triumph of Western economic and political liberalism' we are witnessing 'the end of history as such...the end point of mankind's ideological evolution and the universalization of Western liberal democracy as the final form of human government'.[1] Citing the 'spectacular abundance of advanced liberal economies and the infinitely diverse consumer culture made possible by them' (p. 8), Fukuyama announced that political liberalism is following economic liberalism 'with seeming inevitability' (p. 10) and that class and 'race' antagonism are merely 'historical legacies of premodern conditions', already on the way out. Only in his last paragraph, when describing the way that passions under market economies give way to interests, which are subsumed under bureaucratic rationality, does Fukuyama sentimentally express a nostalgia for history as such:

The end of history will be a very sad time. The struggle for recognition, the willingness to risk one's life for a purely abstract goal, the worldwide ideological struggle that called forth daring, courage, imagination, and idealism, will be replaced by economic calculation, the endless solving of technical problems, environmental concerns, and the satisfaction of sophisticated consumer demands. (p. 18)

By contrast, the economist Samuel Bowles addressed a working group in Moscow in 1991, when Russia was still enamoured of markets.[2] Warning against simplistic formulations of alternatives between command and market economies, Bowles invoked Smith, Mill and Marx as examples of economists sensitive to the peculiarities of objects of exchange, for example, the natural limits to the supply of land or the unusual status of labour as a commodity embodied in human beings. Using Albert Hirschman's now familiar terms of 'voice' and 'exit',[3] Bowles argued that democratic values require the ability to process and communicate complex information, to make collective decisions, and the capacity to feel empathy and solidarity with others; abilities and capacities of 'voice' that were not fostered by the market, or economic, right of 'exit'.

Here I will sketch a brief history of Fukuyama's and Bowles's positions, which may be described, respectively, as the belief that the unconstrained development of markets and technology will provide the values most conducive to the social good (the 'capitalism equals democracy' position), and the belief that the values of the market are insufficient to produce the social good (the 'capitalism does not equal democracy' position). I shall briefly describe the co-development of classical political economy and high Victorian imaginative literature within this continuing contest for the values of democratic market society. In these, intersubjective, communal, and objective social relations took precedence over the subjectivism, formalism, and psychologism associated with the *fin-de-siècle* economics and aesthetics that are my main subject. Understanding the road that economics and aesthetics took at the end of the nineteenth century is crucial to our understanding of the possibilities of democratic market society today.

The most unreserved faith in the market to provide the social good goes back not to the early political economists, who typically understood the structural flaws of *laissez-faire*, but to the early technophiles just postdating the proverbial 'take-off' period. In the Ur-Systems Analyst Charles Babbage's *On the Economy of Machinery and Manufacture* (1832), the universe itself is one large system of potentially free markets, of the freedom 'every man has, to use his capital, his labour, and his talents, in the manner most conducive to his interests'.[4] Within this universal system, Britain's role is to export machinery and commodities. Babbage is confident that British industry will not be threatened by its competitors insofar as the success of British industry is predicated on the British system of government. He writes that 'These great advantages cannot exist under less free governments. These circumstances ... give such a decided superiority to our people, that no injurious rivalry, either in the construction of machinery or the manufacture of commodities,

can reasonably be anticipated.' (p. 364) Babbage's view of progress
is that English people will use time saved by machines in gratifying
some other wants; and that each new machine will add new luxuries
that will then become socially necessary to our happiness (p. 335).
Within this technological advance, workers must be subjectively as
flexible as the flow of commodities. Babbage asks whether machines
should be made so perfect as to supplant workers suddenly or rather
be slowly improved to force them out of employment gradually. He
concludes that workers should be forced out immediately, so that
they will have no choice but to retrain, and additionally recommends
that workers in one family diversify their labour, so that parents and
children will not be thrown out of work simultaneously and so plunge
the entire family into destitution (p. 336). Thus for Babbage the
human population will be forced to progress at the rate of technology.
Babbage does not anticipate Marx's view that one's labour might be
relevant to one's sense of identity. Rather, he anticipates postmodern
theory in that identity is as fluid and exchangeable as other
commodities.

If Babbage is optimistic about the flexibility of human subjectivity,
Andrew Ure in *The Philosophy of Manufactures* (1835) thought the
human component of the market system should be subordinated to its
function by any means necessary. Ure propounds 'the great doctrine
... that when capital enlists science in her service, the refractory hand
of labour will always be taught docility',[5] and he treats workers'
failure to conform to the needs of production as infractions of natural
law. Of workers stopping when they need to, he writes: 'Of the
amount of the injury resulting from the violation of the rules of
automatic labour, [the worker] can hardly ever be a proper judge;
just as mankind at large can never fully estimate the evils consequent
upon an infraction of God's moral law.' (p. 279)

In passages that I give my students to contrast with Dickens's *Hard
Times* or with autobiographical accounts of workers who were
children in the textile industry, Ure describes how the factory system
improves women and children:

The children seemed to be always cheerful and alert, taking pleasure in the
light play of their muscles, enjoying the mobility natural to their age. The
scene of industry, so far from exciting sad emotions in my mind, was always
exhilarating. It was delightful to observe the nimbleness with which they
pieced the broken ends... As to exhaustion by the [ten-hour] day's work,
they evinced no trace of it on emerging from the mill in the evening; for they

immediately began to skip about any neighbouring play-ground, and to commence their little amusements with the same alacrity as boys issuing from a school. (p. 301)

In a series of examples of 'model' factories, Ure writes of the women who run the power-looms who are beautified by their work: 'Their light labour and erect posture in tending the looms, and the habit which many of them have of exercising their arms and shoulders, as if with dumb-bells... opens their chest[s], and gives them generally a graceful carriage... and... not a little of the Grecian style of beauty.' (p. 350) He has pages on the health and beauty ('symmetry of form') of female spinners, and of the stove-girls hanging calico print in 140-plus degrees fahrenheit: 'Some are very fine-looking girls, and all appear to be in perfect health. They work barefooted, and have often leisure to sit. Mr. R states that they are as healthy as any girls in the establishment, and that when any of them happen to catch cold, they are very soon cured by going into the stove again.' (pp. 392–393)

Most of the great political economists did not share Babbage and Ure's unreserved faith that market values alone would result in desirable human outcomes. Although the rhetoric of supply-side economics often invoked Adam Smith's 'Invisible Hand' in Book IV of *The Wealth of Nations* (1776), the single most cited passage of Smith in the massive scholarly literature is that in Book V, in which he contrasts the brutalizing and divisive effects of the division of labour, the source of national wealth, with the simple but pleasant equality of barbarous societies. Here it should be remarked that with all its manichaean functions, 'civilization' is a technical term in historical political economy, whose meaning is characterized by technological superiority based on the division of labour. Its counterpart 'barbarism' meant, alternatively, little or no industrial technology but often complex capabilities at the individual level. Thus, using 'barbarism' to critique the brutality of 'civilization' in the passage referred to, Smith concluded that the elite few who do benefit from 'civilization' may not contribute any benefits to society at large.[6]

Smith, of course, believed that the 'moral sentiments' of empathy and sympathy were as innate to humankind as the political economic virtues of self-interest and the desire for wealth.[7] Indeed 'sympathy' played the important role in early political economy of allowing interpersonal comparisons of utility – a possibility that economics after 1870, as we shall see, largely rejected. On balance, Smith believed that under global market conditions unless steps were taken to prevent it, the large mass of humankind might well acquire great material benefits on the one hand, but, on the other, decline in its ability to exercise those faculties and propensities such as reason, imagination, and sympathy, on which ethics – or the justification of our behaviour toward one another – depended. Granting that Smith predated democracy as we know it, the compatibility of his views on the limits of the market to set democratic values and Bowles speaking to Muscovites in 1991 is noteworthy.

Smith was particularly concerned about the low status of liberal education in market society.[8] J. S. Mill himself argued that education under capitalism would tend to promote hedonistic and self-interested citizens and eventually drive out 'moral sentiments' like sympathy and altruism. In the final two books of his *Principles of Political Economy* (1848), he unequivocally condemns the abstract goal of expanding growth, arguing that economic man's competitive struggle for accumulation and self-interest are merely part of one stage (the industrial stage) toward progress, and are by no means the end. He is worth quoting at length, but instead I will cite his well-known conclusion: 'It is only in the backward countries of the world that increased production is still an important object: in those most advanced, what is economically needed is a better distribution.'[9] Here and elsewhere, the United States is Mill's chief illustration of failure to progress beyond accumulation. He expresses his distaste for its national materialism with a characteristic disapproval of growth in the reproductive sphere as well (Mill was an obsessive defender of family planning): 'They have the six points of Chartism, and they have no poverty: and all that these advantages seem to have done for them is that the life of the whole of one sex is devoted to dollar-hunting, and of the other to breeding dollar-hunters.' (p. 496) He concludes that he does not share political economy's fear of the stationary state that will follow upon international competition, and, like Smith, questions whether industrial technology (that defined civilization for technophiles like Babbage and Ure) in fact contributed to the greater happiness of the greatest number. It is the only passage in Mill that Marx ever praised:

Hitherto it is questionable if all the mechanical inventions yet made have lightened the day's toil of any human being. They have enabled a greater population to live the same life of drudgery and imprisonment, and an increased number of manufacturers and others to make fortunes. They have increased the comforts of the middle classes. But they have not yet begun to effect those great changes in human destiny, which it is in their nature and in their futurity to accomplish. (p. 498)

Thus Mill, like Smith, had no faith that either technological growth or market activity alone would result in progress.

Mill does, however, outline a progressive programme. Once women are liberated to participate freely in market relations and thus be self-supporting, and the poor are educated to take their governance into their own hands, wage-labour itself ought to ease in favour of workers' control of markets (what today we would call market socialism). This is not the place to develop Mill's views on social progress, but in brief he agreed with socialist critics that current institutions of private property did not conform to the principle that justified it, which was to guarantee to individuals the fruits of their own labour and abstinence, and in Book II ('Distribution') of the *Principles* and in his very late, posthumously published, writings on socialism, he considered at length the perversions of capitalism under current conditions and the possibility of socialism. Throughout these deliberations, Mill was constant on two points. First, that although the laws of production partook of the character of physical truths, distribution was a matter of human institutions only. It was, therefore, subject to change and, it was hoped, improvement in the direction of equality.

The second point on which Mill was firm was that in order to be successful, socialism required a high standard of moral and intellectual education in all members of the community and that this education would not be available under capitalism: 'Only a communistic Association can effectually train mankind for communism.'[10] He predicted that, despite its democratic promise, the United States would not progress beyond dollar hunting and that its democratic institutions and educational goals would fail due to its unchecked pursuit of individual and national profit. He also predicted that communist revolutions would fail when their populations were uneducated, because the relinquishing of self-interest in favour of the social good was a matter of cultivation. For a society of both liberty and equality, rational economic man needed a level of comfort sufficiently high to be educated, and the kind of education that a society based upon self-interest could not provide.

The examination of the scope and limits of market values that was

internal to classical political economy was also the main preoccupation of high Victorian literature. The material of the political
economists was the productive relations between the three perceived
economic classes of their time (landowners, workers, and capitalist
entrepreneurs) and their commodified objects of exchange (land,
labour, and capital), resulting in rent, wages, and profits in domestic
and colonial markets. At the core of high Victorian fiction are
representations of the relations between stable (or lazy) landed
gentry, energetic (or cruel) entrepreneurs and docile and dependent
(or angry and seditious) labourers. As Marx said, 'capital is not a
thing, but a social relation between persons... property in money,
means of subsistence, machinery, and other means of production do
not yet stamp a man as a capitalist if there be wanting the correlative
– the wage-worker'.[11] Victorian fiction went even further in its study
of social relations than political economy or its critics had done in
representing the so-called 'private sector' – the sphere of 'women's'
work (from housework and childcare to, notoriously, prostitution)
traditionally excluded from economic notions of value. As Ruskin in
Unto This Last (1862) and Olive Schreiner in *Woman and Labour*
(1911) argued at length, the imputation of value to women's labour
at home would have changed the entire course of political economy
as well as the definition and fate of economic man: see our own
contemporary feminist economists.[12]

The science of political economy took a decisive turn after 1870
with the 'marginal' and later 'ordinal' revolutions, which grounded
their analyses solely in the perspective of consumers and consumption, relegating labour to the status of one commodity among
others, and refusing to make interpersonal comparisons of utility
between, for example, luxuries and necessities, needs and wants, rich
and poor. Under the new political economy, now simply called
'economics' – as if politics, classes, or power had nothing to do with
one's initial endowments, capacities or choices – Mill's notions of
progress gave way to a reversion to Babbage and Ure's mechanistic
belief in markets and technologies, only now in the psychological
terms of diminishing marginal utility. This law posited a definite (if
subjective) relationship between the quantities of goods possessed
and the extra satisfaction to be derived from additional amounts of
them. It allowed the economist to explain the market behaviour of
buyers faced with an array of prices, their responses to changes in
price, the gains to be made from exchange, and the optimal allocation

of a given stock of resources among alternative uses. Economics became a quasi-mathematical discipline in which the important issues were not Marx's 'social relations among persons' but the individual pursuit of preference among scarce resources. In Smith, Ricardo and Mill rational economic man pursued his self-interest but contributed to the wealth and, especially in Smith, Mill, and Marx, the progress of the world. With the marginal revolution, rationality comes to mean simply an individual's ordering of preference among desirable goods, a purely formal definition. The point of ordinalism was that utilities need only be ranked, not measured. Marginalism meant that relevant factors could be equated at the margin without concern for the total or average values of those quantities. Thus a great, perceived virtue of the revolution was that it enabled mathematicization of economics without measurement of most economic variables. It no longer seemed necessary for economists to make comparisons between the utilities of different persons or social groups (for example, economic classes).

Although the underlying assumptions of neoclassical economics (rationality, maximization, efficiency and neutrality) have been attacked by a variety of opponents (most notably Marxists, Institutionalists, development economists, and most recently feminists), they have constituted the dominant economic model until our own day, receiving popular consent under Reaganomics and Thatcherism in the 1980s. These assumptions include the belief (1) that interpersonal comparisons are impossible, (2) that tastes are exogenous and unchanging, (3) that economic actors are selfish, and (4) that what they choose is the basis of economics.

Historically, a corollary of the new theory was that with the satisfaction of every lower want a want of a higher order was created, so that scarcity would be the inevitable condition of humankind, and choosing between scarce commodities would be the species's primary occupation. Thus for Carl Menger in *The Principles of Economics* (1871), civilization means the proliferation of higher order goods and insatiable wants.[13] There is no memory here of Smith's barbarism that brings contentment, but only contempt for societies with low levels of desire. If the political economists often used the distinction between 'civilization' and 'barbarism' in order to criticize civilization from the perspective of the excesses of industrialism, with the marginal revolution the critical force of the distinction was lost. Modern economic man, man-as-consumer, would henceforth be

known by the insatiability of his desires and the indolent races of
savages need only be inspired by envy to desire his desires, imitate his
wants, to be on the road to his progress and his civilization. In *The
Theory of Political Economy* (1871), Stanley Jevons asked, 'whether
the creating of wants be not the likeliest way to produce industry in
a people? If Irish peasants were accustomed to eat beef and wear
shoes, would they not be more industrious?'[14] Under neoclassical
economics, economic man's insatiability was human nature itself. His
mode, capitalist consumer society, was no longer one stage of progress
but its culmination and end (as in Fukuyama). Modern economic
man must choose from a universe of goods on display, and his
'status', his level of civilization (his 'tastes'), will be revealed by his
choices or preferences. The terms are the terms of twentieth-century
economics – rational choice, revealed preference – and so are the
methods: methodological individualism, subjectivism, behaviourism.
These are also the terms of late Victorian aesthetics.[15]

In his suggestive book *Conditions for Criticism*, Ian Small
argues that for the aesthetes of the 1870s and 1880s, the subjective
experience of art replaced the role of art that had prevailed
throughout most of the nineteenth century.[16] Ruskinian or Millian
theories of the centrality of art for society were replaced, largely
through academic aesthetics, with quantifying theories of aesthetic
pleasure. As aesthetics was brought under the discipline of psychology, the quality of the aesthetic experience was determined by
the quantity of pleasure it yielded. Subjective 'impression', 'pleasure' and 'relativity' are key terms in the associationist psychology
underlying late Victorian aesthetics, as they are in late-Victorian
economics.[17] Furthermore, in Spencer as in Jevons, the pleasure of
art is of the highest order in the scale of human wants.

To illustrate the extent to which the convergence of economics and
aesthetics occurred in the *fin de siècle*, I shall use two anti-institutional
aesthetes: Walter Pater and Oscar Wilde. Yet virtually all the middle
to late-Victorian aesthetes (as opposed to academic aestheticians)
were only too conscious of their own implication within consumer, or
commodity, culture: from Rossetti's ambivalent ruminations on the
jock's responsibility for the prostitute in 'Jenny'; Ruskin's revulsion
after *The Stones of Venice* at Victorian Gothic architecture; Morris's
anguish at the price of The Firm's furniture and textiles; to Wilde's
notorious self-advertisement. Economic man and aesthetic man
converge in Pater's discriminating consumer of the art object; the

specularity of Arthur Symons's and J. A. Symonds's respectively hetero- and homoerotic poetic objectifications; the characters who people Wilde's spectacular stages; and Conrad's corporate colonizer Kurtz. They are all insatiable. Indeed Wilde captured the essence of modern economic man when he named the cigarette the perfect type of a perfect pleasure because it left one unsatisfied. For this reason, of course, the cigarette is the perfect commodity.

Pater begins the 1873 preface to *The Renaissance: Studies in Art and Poetry* with the denial of absolute value and the demand for quantification, 'discriminating between what is more and less'. In his first chapter, Jevons insists that economics is mathematical 'simply because it deals with quantities ... with things greater or less'.[18] If one were to substitute 'value' for 'beauty' and 'economics' for 'art and poetry', Pater's text could read like Jevons's of two years earlier:

Many attempts have been made by writers on art and poetry to define beauty in the abstract, to express it in the most general terms, to find some universal formula for it ... Such discussions help us very little ... Beauty, like all other qualities presented to human experience, is relative; and the definition of it becomes unmeaning and useless in proportion to its abstractness.[19]

In the same passage where he pronounced economics to be a quantifying science, Jevons also pronounced it to be a 'calculus of pleasure and pain' within one individual subject. Rejecting Arnold's critical and objectivist aim 'to see the object as in itself it really is', in the second paragraph of the preface Pater claims that the first step of aesthetic criticism is 'to know one's own impression as it really is' (p. xix):

What is this song or picture, this engaging personality presented in life or in a book, to *me*? What effect does it really produce on me? Does it give me pleasure? and if so, what sort or degree of pleasure? ... The aesthetic critic regards all the objects with which he has to do ... as powers or forces producing pleasurable sensations, each of a more or less peculiar or unique kind.' (p. xx)

This science of pleasure, or aesthetics, 'becomes complete in proportion as our susceptibility to these impressions [of pleasure] increases in depth and variety' (p. xx).

The conclusion to *The Renaissance* provides images of an external world in flux, which some have associated with consumer society ('at first sight experience seems to bury us under a flood of external objects' (p. 187)), and an inner life subjective to the point of solipsism. As in Jevons, there are no intersubjective comparisons:

Experience, already reduced to a group of impressions is ringed round for each one of us by that thick wall of personality through which no real voice has ever pierced on its way to us... Every one of those impressions is the impression of the individual in his isolation, each mind keeping as a solitary prisoner its own dream of a world. (p. 188)

Yet as if in mockery of the wealth of impressions, the time for enjoyment is scarce: had we but world enough and *time*. In his influential *Essay on the Nature and Significance of Economic Science* (1935), Lionel Robbins described the centrality of time to modern economic theory thus:

Here we are, sentient creatures with bundles of desires and aspirations, with masses of instinctive tendencies all urging us in different ways to action. But the time in which these tendencies can be expressed is limited. The external world does not offer full opportunities for their complete achievement. Life is short. Nature is niggardly... The disposition of [economic man's] time and his resources has a relationship to his system of wants. It has an economic aspect.[20]

Pater concludes the conclusion with mortal thoughts of how 'on this short day of frost and sun' one must not 'sleep before evening'; of 'the splendour of our experience and of its awful brevity'; of how 'theories or ideas or systems which require of us the sacrifice of any part of this experience in consideration of some interest into which we cannot enter' have 'no real claim upon us' (p. 189); concluding this litany of scarcity and self-interest with 'we are all under sentence of death but with a sort of indefinite reprieve'. Now one of the worldly philosophers, in Robert Heilbroner's phrase, indeed perhaps the most sensuous of his generation, Pater advises us to 'get as many pulsations as possible into the given time' (p. 190). In 'Aesthetic Poetry' (1889), he, in fact, defined the aesthetic economy of his contemporaries as 'the desire of beauty quickened by the sense of death'.[21]

Pater's 1889 essay, 'Style', suggests how scarcity amid abundance leads to a preoccupation with form in aesthetic matters, as it led to formalism in twentieth-century economics. Here Pater's return to *ascesis* (which means for him 'self-restraint, a skilful economy of means'), a term that is central to *Marius the Epicurean* (1885) and his later work on the Greeks, calls up the discipline that would make modernists such as Pound write of stylistics after Flaubert as a 'science'. Pater begins with a rejection of the 'false economy' of contemporary distinctions between verse and prose.[22] He defines all literary art as 'the representation of fact as connected with soul, of a specific personality, in its preferences, its volition and power' (p. 106). Thus literary art is *subjective*, involving *choices* (preferences) and *desire* (volition). Choice comes in the form of ascesis (self-restraint), a skilful economy of means, which is a formal property of works of art. Pater deplores 'the narcotic force of [literary ornament] upon the negligent intelligence to which any *diversion*, literally, is welcome' (p. 111), and makes masculine leanness (youth's asceticism) a charac-teristic to be prized: 'Surplusage. [The artist] will dread that, as the runner on his muscles.' (p. 111)[23] Flaubert is Pater's type of the ascetic artist, or economizing aesthete, whose 'idea of a natural economy' (choice) amid surplus becomes the formal principle of literary modernism: the discriminating artist or critic's economy (Pound's *mot juste*) that distinguished him from the 'negligent' public that 'welcomes' diversion, ornament, the 'flood' of commodities of consumer society: 'the one word for the one thing, the one thought, amid the multitude of words, terms that just might do: the problem of style was there!' (p. 117) Flaubert's referent is not objective but subjective. The word is chosen not by reference to the external world but by Flaubert's introspection, the inventory of his subjective needs. Flaubert managed his economy, that is, by ranking his preferences: 'The first condition of [style, "the word's adjustment to its meaning"] must be, of course, to know yourself, to have ascertained your own sense exactly.' (p. 118) Upon the discerning artist *and* the discerning critic 'a flood of random sounds, colours, incidents, is ever penetrating from the world without' (p. 118). 'The mind sensitive to "form"' selects from these in conformity with 'That other world it sees so steadily within', and 'it is just there, just at those doubtful points' between external objects and inner needs and desires 'that the function of style, as tact or taste, intervenes' (p. 118). This is Flaubert's formal aesthetic of taste, tact or choice.

Pater's Flaubert represents rational aesthetic man, who sounds much like rational economic man: 'The style, the manner, would be the man, not in his unreasoned and really uncharacteristic caprices, involuntary or affected, but in absolutely sincere apprehension of what is most real to him.' (p. 121) The style is the man. In true behaviourist fashion, we know him by the choices he makes. Truth is Beauty; Beauty, Truth.

The Portrait of Mr W. H., 'The Soul of Man Under Socialism', 'The Critic as Artist', 'Pen, Pencil and Poison', and much of Wilde's criticism all testify to his concern with taste, tact, style, subjectivism, and individualism. According to Wilde, human individuals have unique temperaments and tastes that should be allowed to flourish according to the laws of their own being. Like the connoisseur Des Esseintes consuming the exotica of the world outside the West, Wilde was sensitive to the revelation of personality through choice and preference. Chapter 11 of *The Picture of Dorian Gray* (1891) is a textbook psychology of *fin-de-siècle* economic man. Chapter 10 concludes with Dorian's discovery of a fascinating book, a story of an insatiable young Parisian 'who spent his life trying to realize ... all the passions and modes of thought that belonged to every century except his own'.[24] For years, we are told in chapter 11, Dorian could not free himself from its power of suggestion: 'The more he knew, the more he desired to know. He had mad hungers that grew more ravenous as he fed them.' (p. 142) He cultivates 'a new Hedonism' that, *à la* Pater, 'was never to accept any theory or system that involved the sacrifice of any mode of passionate experience' (p. 13). Scarcity is again assured by mortality: one must 'concentrate oneself upon the moments of a life that is itself but a moment' (p. 144). For years, Dorian 'searches for sensations that would be at once new and delightful' (p. 145). His conspicuous consumption, variously referred to as 'collecting' and 'accumulating', like Des Esseintes's, includes the products of 'all parts of the world' (p. 147): perfumes, music, embroideries, tapestries, ecclesiastical vestments, and finally up to the highest order of pleasure, not the crude material goods themselves but rather 'the wonderful stories' of the goods, or the rarefied pleasure of literature itself.

Yet while the desire for escalating orders of goods is itself insatiable, each good reaches its point of diminishing marginal utility: 'Yet, after some time, [Dorian] wearied of them [all]' (p. 147), and he experiences 'that terrible *taedium vitae* that comes on those to whom life denies nothing' (p. 157). In the midst of this cycle of excess and ennui, Dorian finds himself in a society that prefers form to substance. The narrator describes market society as the society of spectacle, style or form over substance: 'Civilized society is never very ready to believe anything to the detriment of those who are both rich and fascinating' says the narrator, 'it feels instinctively that manners are of more importance than morals, and, in its opinion, the highest respectability is of much less value than the possession of a good chef' (p. 154). The very lack of substance, for those who can afford the multiplication of pleasure, is liberating. 'Form' or 'insincerity' is 'merely a method by which we can multiply our personalities ... man was a being with myriad lives and myriad sensations, a complex multiform creature' (p. 155). The chapter reaches a climax with a fantastic crescendo of insatiables: 'Pietro Riario ... whose beauty was equalled only by his debauchery ... who gilded a boy that he might serve at the feast as Ganymede ... Ezzelin, whose melancholy could be cured only by the spectacle of death, and who had a passion for red blood as other men have for red wine ... Giambattista Cibo ... into whose torpid veins the blood of three lads was infused' (pp. 157–58), and so forth until the famous concluding sentence, 'There were moments when [Dorian] looked on evil simply as a mode through which he could realize his conception of the beautiful.'

The consequence of Dorian's insatiability, escalation of wants, and formal equivalencing of all desires is, of course, his portrait, where the shame of his consumption is permanently and absolutely recorded. At this price he is given a beauty without limit, the scarcest commodity in a mortal world, and that is his sole source of value to others, like Basil, who commodify and consume him in turn.

Wilde's *Salomé* (1894) is perhaps the most dramatic representation we have of the world of neoclassical economics, including the assertion of personal preference over social values and of subjective isolation over social life. From the first lines of the play the characters are isolated within their subjective desires, without common standards or values. The young Syrian cannot hear the page; the Pharisees and Sadducees contest among themselves the existence of angels, the Nubian and Cappadocian, the existence of gods; the Cappadocian thinks it a terrible crime to strangle a king, yet the soldier finds kings 'like other folk ... having but one neck'.[25] Herodias's page and the young Syrian are lost in their respective love lyrics, while their interlocutors, the soldiers, are concerned only with Herod. Tigellinus finds the Stoics ridiculous. The Jews do not agree among themselves. The Syrian and Herod are obsessed with Salomé, Salomé with Iokanaan. Salomé and Iokanaan are simply the most isolated in their respective desires, with Iokanaan desiring all to seek out the Son of Man and Salomé desiring the prophet's body, his hair, and his mouth.

Nothing has value for its own sake, but is made or marred by the quality of desire it evokes. Salomé rejects Herod's wine, his fruits, and his offer to sit at the throne, for she is not thirsty, hungry, or tired. He offers her jewels and 'great treasures above all price' (p. 425) in exchange for the head she desires, but she has a surfeit of these. Herod himself is currently experiencing the diminishing marginal utility of his wife Herodias, and he therefore desires the more novel pleasures of her daughter, the princess of Judea. Moreover, the desires on display in the play are, as they say in economics, transitive and complete. As Salomé says, 'I am athirst for thy beauty; I am hungry for thy body; and neither wine nor apples can appease my desire... Neither the floods nor the great waters can quench my passion.' (p. 428) As the kingdom crumbles, Herod retires to contemplate himself in mirrors, and the soldiers advance to kill her, Salomé's only response is to ask, 'But what matter? What matter? I have kissed thy mouth.' (p. 429)

Critics of neoclassical economics frequently point out that the satisfaction of preferences does not equal the maximization of utility or the maximization of welfare. Neoclassical economics is concerned with the individual consumer getting the goods, not distributing them rationally or even using them. Salomé gets Iokanaan in the long run, but only in the form of a dead head with bloody lips, and the kingdom is destroyed in the process.

In fact (and I shall get fairly technical for a moment) *Salomé* illustrates the formal theory of rational choice. The play, that is, presents the world that rational choice theorists take to be the real world. The theory of rational choice gives agents the aim of maximally satisfying their preferences. Agents are assumed to be able to order comprehensively all states of affairs open to them according to their preferences, and are then instructed to choose those states of affairs which they most prefer. Critics of the theory have claimed that there is no unified interpretation of what 'preferences' are, such that it is always rational to satisfy them.[26] In *Salomé*, for instance, preferences include: (a) dispositions or habits to choose one thing over another (for example, the preferences of the Jews, Nazarenes and soldiers); (b) desires ranked by their strength or intensity (Salomé's); (c) informed desires (Herodias's, her page's); (d) desires ranked by higher order desires (Iokanaan's); (e) value judgments of the relative worth of options (Herod's); (f) bare 'likings' ranked by intensity (for fruit or wine or jewels); and (g) whims, impulses, or yens, similarly ranked (an outsider's view of Salomé's caprice with regard to Iokanaan's head).

As previously mentioned, the formal theory of rational choice demands that agents' preferences be ranked in a complete transitive ordering, for example, Salomé's overriding preference for Iokanaan's head. Indeed one critic of choice theory has concluded that transitivity and completeness requirements are unconditionally valid only for fanatics and monomaniacs who value only one thing.[27]

Formal rational choice theory also maintains a 'sunk-cost rule' and a principle that 'tastes are exogenous'. The former says that it is irrational to consider sunk costs in choosing among future plans, thus working against the values of commitment and tradition and endorsing the perspective of speculators, opportunists and casual lovers. Herodias leaves her husband for the novel pleasures of Herod, and Herod, when the play opens, is bored with Herodias and eyeing Salomé. In the second case, of exogenous tastes, choice theory never questions the content of preferences or tastes, nor indicates with respect to maximization when 'enough' can be 'too much'; nor does it sufficiently draw attention to trade-offs when trading. Salomé's, the young Syrian's, Herod's, the Jews', and Nazarenes' tastes are given. It is a world without critique, or self-critique, or even dialogue. It is the world of neoclassical economics, but it is, in fact, a very un-Wildean world.

The reason this world is unWildean is because, in the majority of his works, Wilde is critical not just of the *status quo ante* but also of the construction of taste or preference, including the constraints upon the formation of taste and preference.[28] Although Wilde was tempted by the individualism, subjectivism, anarchy, even the consumerism central to *fin-de-siècle* aesthetics and economics, I would argue that he never entirely abandoned his commitment to the more substantive values of the earlier Victorians.

Nor, in fact, did Pater. While emphasizing the subjective and formal aspects of aesthetics at both moments of production and consumption, Pater, finally, was unwilling to perform Jevons's reduction. He shockingly concludes the essay on 'Style' with the subordination of rational aesthetic man to a 'greater', romantic, aesthetic reminiscent of Marx or Ruskin. He compares good art to music in its formal excellence but then retreats in favour of substantive value. This value entails a shift from methodological individualism to concern for the social good:

Good art, but not necessarily great art; the distinction between great art and good art depending immediately, as regards literature at all events, not on its form, but on the matter ... It is on the quality of the matter it informs or controls, its compass, its variety, its alliance to great ends, or the depth of the note of revolt, or the largeness of hope in it, that the greatness of literary art depends, as *The Divine Comedy, Paradise Lost, Les Misérables, The English Bible*, are great art. Given the conditions I have tried to explain as constituting good art; – then, if it be devoted further to the increase of men's happiness, to the redemption of the oppressed, or the enlargement of our sympathies with each other, or to such presentment of new or old truth about ourselves and our relation to the world as may ennoble and fortify us in our sojourn here ... it will be also great art; if ... it has something of the soul of humanity in it.[29]

As with his contemporary Alfred Marshall, most subsequent readers of Pater retained his formalism and ignored his ethics. Yet 'the soul of humanity', like Wilde's 'Soul of Man Under Socialism', is greater than a partial (economic or aesthetic) man. Even the ascetic aestheticist Pater would not, like neoclassical economists, entirely abandon it to the dustbin of history.

Pater and Wilde's incomplete satisfaction with the values of Dorian, Salomé and Flaubert returns us to the values of market society. One of the few late-Victorian economists who defended making interpersonal comparisons, F. Y. Edgeworth in *Mathematical Psychics* (1881) argued, against Mill, that in calculating the amount of utility economically possible in a given society we had to weigh 'the comfort of a limited number' against 'numbers with limited comfort'. He opted for the comfort of a limited number on the principle that the capacity for pleasure evolves. Thus men have more capacity for pleasure than women, Europeans have more capacity for pleasure than non-Europeans, so the greatest happiness, mathematically speaking, will be achieved by allocating it *not* to the greatest number (with their relatively low capacities) but to the most highly evolved. As Edgeworth says, 'In the general advance, the most advanced should advance most.' 'In fact', he writes in mixed Darwinian metaphor, 'the happiness of some of the lower classes may be sacrificed to that of the higher classes ... Contemplating the combined movements we seem to see the vast composite flexible organism, the play and the work of whose members are continually readjusted, by degrees advancing up the line of evolution; the parts about the front advancing most, the members of the other extremity more slowly moving on and largely dying off.'[30] I could cite similar biological models justifying world trade policy between North and South in the 1980s.[31]

But I want to conclude with a different recent example of belief in markets to take us to the end of history; that expressed in W. W. Rostow's *Stages of Economic Growth: A Non-Communist Manifesto* (1960). Rostow's book begins with a graph charting the nations of the world through the take-off, maturity, and high mass consumption trajectories that by 1960 dominated economic thought. Given the seeming inevitability of the trajectory *to* high mass consumption, Rostow concluded with the question, 'what is next?' In good neoclassical fashion, what he predicted for the United States in 1960 was the declining utility of wealth itself. As the consumption of durable goods slowed down, Americans seemed to want not more commodities or even more income, but, as Mill had feared, more babies. They preferred the extra baby to the extra unit of consumption. Would the rest of the world, the economist speculated, 'follow the Americans and reimpose the strenuous life by raising the birth-rate?' Would other societies turn to war? Outer space? Huntin', fishin' or shootin' in the suburbs? While thus worrying that 'man' may not find sufficient outlet for the expression of his 'energies, talents, and instinct to reach for immortality', Rostow notes parenthetically that this worry will probably not be shared by women. It is unlikely, he says, 'that women will recognize the reality of the problem; for the raising of children in a society where personal service is virtually gone is a quite ample human agenda, durable consumers' goods or no. The problem of [the end of history] is a man's problem, at least until the children have grown up.'[32]

Such was the end of history in 1960 – women still excluded from its march, busy with the children, while men wondered what to do next. Then came the 1980s, when many economists abandoned the notion of declining marginal utility of income: there was no amount of wealth that sufficed for the comfort of Edgeworth's 'limited number', and that limited number displayed its insatiability, its highly evolved capacity for pleasure, but not in the sense that the Victorians meant. For both classical and neoclassical Victorian economists equally shared the *Buddenbrooks* model (after Mann's novel of that name – the novel most cited by economic theorists from 1902 when it was published to 1980). In *Buddenbrooks*, the first generation sought money; the second, born to money, sought civic position; the third, born to comfort and status, sought the life of music. Victorian economists believed that with maturity, society would increasingly develop appreciation of the *highest* order of goods, what Jevons called 'the pleasure derived from the beauties of nature and art'.[33] American society and American economists in the 1980s did not subscribe to this hierarchy of goods as they pursued markets in everything from music to education, babies to blood. But with the end of history in universal markets, the women and workers who are pauperized and disenfranchised by the globalization of markets and new machines are still outside. In 1949, George Orwell feared that the image of the future would be a boot stamping on a human face forever. If we are prepared to say that Marxism is dead, and that Smith's sympathy and Mill's progressivism are discredited, are we also prepared to make the image of our future the stage of *Salomé* or the picture of Dorian Gray; Fukuyama's 'infinitely diverse consumer culture' or Pater's 'flood of external objects'; or just 'each mind keeping as a solitary prisoner its own dream of a world'?

NOTES

1 Francis Fukuyama, 'The End of History?', *The National Interest* (Summer 1989), 3–4. All subsequent references to this text will be cited in the main body of the chapter.

2 Samuel Bowles, 'What Markets Can and Cannot Do', *Challenge* (July-August 1991), 11–16.

3 Albert Hirschman, *Exit, Voice, and Loyalty* (Cambridge, Mass.: Harvard University Press, 1970).

4 Charles Babbage, *On the Economy of Machinery and Manufacture* (1832) (New York: Kelley, 1963), p. 370. All subsequent references to this text will be cited in the main body of the chapter.

5 Andrew Ure, *The Philosophy of Manufactures* (1835) (London: Frank Cass, 1967), p. 368. All subsequent references to this text will be cited in the main body of the chapter.

6 Adam Smith, *An Inquiry into the Nature and Causes of the Wealth of Nations* (1776) (New York: Modern Library, 1965), pp. 734–736.

7 Adam Smith, *The Theory of Moral Sentiments* (1759) (London: George Bell, 1907).

8 Adam Smith, *Lectures on Jurisprudence* (1762–66) (Oxford: Oxford University Press, 1977).

9 John Stuart Mill, *The Principles of Political Economy* (1848) (London:

Routledge, n.d.), pp. 496–497. All subsequent references to this text will be cited in the main body of the chapter.

10 John Stuart Mill, *On Socialism* (1869) (New York: Prometheus, 1987), p. 131.

11 Karl Marx, *Capital* (1867) (New York: International Publishers, 1967), vol. 1, p. 766.

12 John Ruskin, *Unto This Last and Other Writings* (1862) (London: Penguin, 1985); Olive Schreiner, *Woman and Labour* (London: T. Fisher Unwin, 1911); Marianne A. Ferber and Julie A. Nelson, *Beyond Economic Man: Feminist Theory and Economics* (Chicago: University of Chicago Press, 1993); Myra Strober, 'Feminist Economics and the Improvement of Women's Economic Condition', paper prepared for the Annual Meetings of the Allied Social Sciences, Anaheim, CA, 5–7 January 1993; Marilyn Waring, *If Women Counted: A New Feminist Economics* (San Francisco: Harper and Row, 1988).

13 Carl Menger, *Principles of Economics* (1871) (Glencoe, Illinois: Free Press, 1950).

14 Stanley Jevons, *The Theory of Political Economy* (1871) (London: Macmillan, 1888), p. 182.

15 I have described the transition from classical political economy to neoclassical economics, and the corresponding shift from high to late Victorian aesthetics, in detail in 'On the Insatiability of Human Wants: Economic and Aesthetic Man', *Victorian Studies* (Winter 1993).

16 Ian Small, *Conditions For Criticism: Authority, Knowledge, and Literature in the Late Nineteenth Century* (Oxford: Clarendon, 1991).

17 Margaret Schabas, in her *A World Ruled by Number: W. S. Jevons and the Rise of Mathematical Economics* (Princeton: Princeton University Press, 1990), observes repeatedly that with Jevons economics was brought under the science of psychology.

18 Jevons, *Political Economy*, p. 3.

19 Walter Pater, *The Renaissance: Studies in Art and Poetry* (Berkeley: University of California Press, 1980), p. xix. All subsequent references to this text will be cited in the main body of the chapter.

20 Lionel Robbins in Daniel M. Hausman (ed.), *The Philosophy of Economics* (Cambridge: Cambridge University Press, 1984), p. 114.

21 Walter Pater, *Selected Writings* (New York: Signet, 1974), p. 198.

22 Pater, *Selected Writings*, p. 103. All subsequent references to this text will appear in the main body of the chapter.

23 For impressive treatments of the masculinity, or gender implications, of Pater's science of style, see James Eli Adams, 'Gentleman, Dandy, Priest: Manliness and Social Authority in Pater's Aestheticism', *ELH*, 59 (1992), 441–466; and Herbert Sussman's 'Masculinity Transformed: Appropriation in Walter Pater's Early Writing' in his forthcoming book on masculinities in Carlyle, Browning, and the Pre-Raphaelite Brotherhood.

24 Oscar Wilde, *The Picture of Dorian Gray* (New York: New American Library, 1983), p. 138. All subsequent references to this text will be cited in the main body of the chapter.

25 Oscar Wilde, *Salome*, in *The Portable Oscar Wilde*, ed. Richard Aldington (New York: Penguin, 1978), p. 396. All subsequent references to this text will appear in the main body of the chapter.

26 See Elizabeth Anderson, 'Some Problems in the Normative Theory of Rational Choice with Consequences for Empirical Research' (MSS, University of Michigan, Ann Arbor 1990); Neva R. Goodwin, *Social Economics: An Alternative Theory, Vol. 1: Building Anew on Marshall's Principles* (New York: St Martin's, 1991).

27 Anderson, 'Rational Choice', p. 9.

28 See Regenia Gagnier, *Idylls of the Marketplace: Oscar Wilde and the Victorian Public* (Stanford: Stanford University Press, 1986; and Hampshire, UK: Scolar, 1986); and 'A Critique of Practical Aesthetics', in *Aesthetics and Ideology*, ed. George Levine (New Brunswick: Rutgers University Press, 1994).

29 Walter Pater, *Selected Writings*, p. 123.

30 Francis Ysidro Edgeworth, *Mathematical Psychics* (London: C. Kegan Paul, 1881), p. 68, p. 71.

31 See Arjo Klamer, D. N. McCloskey, Robert M. Solow (eds.), *The Consequences of Economic Rhetoric* (New York: Cambridge University Press, 1988), p. 212.

32 W. W. Rostow, *Stages of Economic Growth: A Non-Communist Manifesto* (Cambridge: Cambridge University Press, 1960), p. 91.

33 Jevons, *Theory of Political Economy*, p. 43.

Select bibliography

PRIMARY TEXTS FROM THE *FIN DE SIÈCLE*

Adderley, Rev James. *Stephen Remarx: The Story of a Venture in Ethics.* London: Edward Arnold, 1893.

Allen, Grant. *The Woman Who Did.* London: John Lane, 1895.

Allen, Grant. 'Plain Words on the Woman Question'. *Fortnightly Review*, 46 (1889): 455–456.

American in London. 'The English Barbarian: His Haunts, His Homes, His Habits, His Heroes'. *New Budget* (August 1895): 28–29.

Aveling, Edward, and Marx, Eleanor. *Shelley's Socialism: Two Lectures.* Manchester: Lesley Preger, 1947.

Blatchford, Robert. *Merrie England.* 1895; reprint London: Clarion Press, 1908.

Booth, Charles. *Labour and Life of the People: Poverty Series.* Volumes 1 and 2. London: Williams and Norgate, 1889.

Booth, William. *In Darkest England and the Way Out.* London: International Headquarters, Salvation Army, 1890.

Bradfield, Thomas. 'A Dominant Note of Some Recent Fiction'. *Westminster Review*, 142 (1894): 543–549.

Buchanan, Robert. *The Reverend Annabel Lee.* London: C. Arthur Pearson, 1898.

Burton, Richard. *The Jew, the Gypsy and El Islam.* London: Hutchinson and Co., 1898.

Buxton-Forman, H. *The Books of William Morris Described.* London: Frank Hollings, 1897.

Caine, Hall. *The Christian: A Story.* London: William Heinemann, 1897.

Caird, Mona. *The Daughters of Danaus.* London: Bliss, Sands and Foster, 1894.

Cantlie, James. *Degeneration Amongst Londoners.* London: Field and Tuer, the Leadenhall Press, 1885.

Carpenter, Edward. *Love's Coming of Age.* 1896; reprint New York and London: Mitchell Kennerley, 1911.

Clapperton, Jane Hume. *Margaret Dunmore; or, A Socialist Home.* London: Swan, Sonnenschein and Lowrey, 1888.

Conrad, Joseph. *Chance.* 1913; reprint Oxford: Oxford University Press, 1988. Edited with an introduction by Martin Ray.

Conrad, Joseph. *The Collected Letters of Joseph Conrad,* vol. 2: 1898–1902. Frederick R. Karl and Laurence Davies (eds.). Cambridge: Cambridge University Press, 1986.

Conrad, Joseph. *Collected Letters,* vol. 3: 1903–1907. Frederick R. Karl and Laurence Davies (eds.). Cambridge: Cambridge University Press, 1988.

Conrad, Joseph. *Collected Letters,* vol. 4: 1908–1911. Frederick R. Karl and Laurence Davies (eds.). Cambridge: Cambridge University Press, 1990.

Corelli, Marie. *The Sorrows of Satan.* London: Methuen, 1895.

Davidson, John. *The Testament of an Empire Builder.* London: Grant Richards, 1901.

Dawson, W. J. *The Redemption of Edward Strahan.* London: Hodder and Stoughton, 1891.

Dawson, W. J. *The Makers of English Fiction.* London: Hodder and Stoughton, 1905.

'Death of a Decadent'. *Woman's Signal,* 3 (May 1895): 289.

Dowie, Menie Muriel. *Gallia.* London: Methuen, 1895.

Edgeworth, Charles. *Mathematical Psychics.* London: C. Kegan Paul, 1881.

Egerton, George. *Keynotes* (1893) and *Discords* (1894). Introduced by Martha Vicinus. London: Virago, 1983.

Ellis, Havelock. *Man and Woman: A Study of Human Secondary Sexual Characteristics.* 1894; reprint London: Walter Scott, 1904.

Ellis, Havelock and Symonds, John Addington. *Sexual Inversion.* London: Wilson and Macmillan, 1897.

Garrett Fawcett, Millicent. Review of *The Woman Who Did.* *Contemporary Review,* 47 (1895): 630.

Garrett Fawcett, Millicent. *Woman's Suffrage.* London: T. C. and E. C. Jack, 1912.

George, Henry. *Progress and Poverty.* London: Kegan Paul, Trench and Co., 1882.

Gilbert, W. S. *The Bab Ballads.* James Ellis (ed.). Cambridge, Mass.: Harvard, The Belknap Press, 1970.

Gilbert, W. S. *The Complete Plays of Gilbert and Sullivan.* New York: W. W. Norton and Company, 1976.

Gladstone, W. E. '*Robert Elsmere* and the Battle of Belief'. *Nineteenth Century,* 23 (May 1888): 766–788.

Grand, Sarah. *The Heavenly Twins.* 3 vols. London: William Heinemann, 1893.

Grand, Sarah. 'The New Aspect of the Woman Question'. *North American Review,* 158 (1894): 271–273.

Grand, Sarah. 'The Woman's Question'. *Humanitarian,* 8 (1896): 160–169.

Greenwood, Frederick. 'A Shoreditch Club'. *Daily Telegraph* (22 October 1887): 2.

Haggard, H. Rider. *King Solomon's Mines*. London: Longman, Green and Co., 1885.

Haggard, H. Rider. *She*. London: Longman, Green and Co., 1887.

Harper, Charles G. *Revolted Woman: Past, Present and to Come*. London: Elkin Matthews, 1894.

Harrison, Frederic. *The Meaning of History and Other Historical Pieces*. London: Macmillan, 1894.

Headlam, Stewart. *The Service of Humanity and Other Sermons*. London: John Hodges, 1882.

Headlam, Stewart. *The Sure Foundation*. London: F. Verinder, 1883.

Headlam, Stewart. *The Laws of Eternal Life*. London: F. Verinder, 1888.

Headlam, Stewart. *The Socialists' Church*. London: G. Allen, 1907.

Hichens, Robert. *The Green Carnation*. 1894; reprint London: Icon Books, 1961.

Housman, A. E. *A. E. Housman, Collected Poems and Selected Prose*. Ed. Christopher Ricks. Harmondsworth: Penguin, 1988.

Howells, W. D. *et al. In After Days: Thoughts on the Future Life*. New York and London: Harper and Brothers, 1910.

Hyndman, H. M. *The Historical Basis of Socialism in England*. London: Kegan Paul, 1883.

Jay, Father A. O. *Life in Darkest London*. London: Webster and Cable, 1891.

Jay, Father A. O. *The Social Problem: its Possible Solution*. London: Simpkin, Marshall and Co., 1893.

Jay, Father A. O. *A Story of Shoreditch*. London: Simpkin, Marshall and Co., 1896.

Key, Ellen. *The Woman Movement*. New York and London: Knickerbocker Press, 1912.

Krafft-Ebing, R. von. *Psychopathia Sexualis with Especial Reference to Contrary Sexual Instinct: A Medico-Legal Study*. Tr. Charles Chaddock. 1892; reprint Philadelphia: F. A. Davis and Co., 1893.

Linton, Eliza Lynn. *The True History of Joshua Davidson, Christian and Communist*. 1872; reprint New York: Garland Publishing, 1975.

Linton, Eliza Lynn. 'The Partisans of the Wild Woman'. *Nineteenth Century*, 31 (1892): 455–464.

Lissagaray, Prosper-Oliver. *History of the Paris Commune*. 1876; reprint London: New Park Publications, 1976.

Lombroso, Cesare. Introduction to Gina Lombroso Ferrero, *Criminal Man According to the Classification of Cesare Lombroso*. New York and London: G. Pitman's Sons, 1911.

Mann, Thomas. *Buddenbrooks*. 1902; reprint New York: Vintage, 1992.

Marholm Hansson, Laura. *Studies in the Psychology of Woman*. Trans. Georgia A. Etchinson. Chicago and New York: Herbert S. Stone, 1899.

Marshall, Alfred. *The Principles of Economics*. 1890; reprint London: Macmillan, 1920.

Meade, L. T. *A Princess of the Gutter*. London: Wells, Gardner, Darton, 1895.

Mearns, Rev Andrew. *The Bitter Cry of Outcast London*. London: James Clark, 1883.

Mee, Arthur. 'The Transformation in Slumland: the remarkable story of a London Clergyman'. *Temple Magazine*, 2: 181 (1898): 449–454.

Meredith, George. *Modern Love*. London: Rupert Hart-Davis, 1948.

Morris, William, Bax, E. Belfort, and Dave, Victor. *The Socialist Platform – No 4: A Short Account of the Commune of Paris*. London: Socialist League Office, 1885.

Morris, William. *Collected Letters*. Edited by Norman Kelvin. Volume II: 1885–1888. New Jersey: Princeton University Press, 1987.

Morris, William. *The Pilgrims of Hope*. 1886; reprint London: Lawrence and Wishart, 1968.

Morrison, Arthur. *A Child of the Jago*. London: Methuen, 1896.

Pater, Walter. *Selected Writings*. New York: Signet, 1974.

Pater, Walter. *The Renaissance: Studies in Art and Poetry*. Berkeley: University of California Press, 1980.

Pearson, Karl. *The Ethic of Freethought*. London: T. Fisher Unwin, 1888.

Pearson, Karl. 'Woman and Labour'. *Fortnightly Review*, 29 (May 1894): 561–572.

Schreber, Daniel. *Memoirs of My Nervous Illness*. Tr. and ed. Ida Macalpine and Richard Hunter. London: Wm Dawson and Sons, 1955.

Schreiner, Olive. *The Story of an African Farm*. London: Chapman and Hall, 1883.

Schreiner, Olive. *Dreams*. London: T. Fisher Unwin, 1890.

Schreiner, Olive. *Dream Life and Real Life*. London: T. Fisher Unwin, 1893.

Schreiner, Olive. *Trooper Peter Halket of Mashonaland*. London: T. Fisher Unwin, 1897.

Schreiner, Olive. *Woman and Labour*. London: T. Fisher Unwin, 1911.

Schreiner, Olive. *Thoughts on South Africa*. London: T. Fisher Unwin, 1923.

Schreiner, Olive. *From Man to Man: or Perhaps Only...* London: T. Fisher Unwin, 1926.

Schreiner, Olive. 'The Woman's Rose'. *Dream Life and Real Life*. 1892; reprint Chicago: Academy Chicago, 1981.

Schreiner, Olive. 'The Policy in Favour of Protection –'. *Dream Life and Real Life*. 1892; reprint Chicago: Academy Chicago, 1981.

Schreiner, Olive. 'The Buddhist Priest's Wife' (1892). Carol Barash (ed.). *An Olive Schreiner Reader*. London: Pandora Press, 1987.

Schreiner, Olive. 'The Child's Day' (1887). Carol Barash (ed.). *An Olive Schreiner Reader*. London: Pandora Press, 1987.

Schreiner, Olive. 'The Woman Question' (1899). Carol Barash (ed.). *An Olive Schreiner Reader*. London: Pandora Press, 1987.

Shaw, George Bernard. *Music in London, 1890–1894*. Volume 28 of *The Collected Works of George Bernard Shaw*. Ayot Street Lawrence Edition; New York: William H. Wise and Company, 1931.

Sims, George. *How the Poor Live and Terrible London*. London: Chatto and Windus, 1889.

Spencer, Herbert. *Principles of Ethics.* 2 vols. London: Williams and Norgate, 1892–1893.

Stevenson, Robert Louis. *The Strange Case of Doctor Jekyll and Mr Hyde.* New York: Bantam, 1985.

Stoker, Bram. *Dracula.* 1897; reprint Oxford: Oxford University Press, 1989.

Stoker, Bram. *Dracula's Guest.* 1914; reprint London: Arrow Books, 1975.

Stoker, Bram. *A Glimpse of America: A Lecture Given at the London Institute, 28th December 1885.* London: Sampson Low, Marston and Co., 1886.

Stoker, Bram. *Personal Reminiscences of Henry Irving.* 2 vols. New York: Macmillan and Co., 1906.

Symonds, John Addington. *The Memoirs of John Addington Symonds.* Ed. Phyllis Grosskurth. New York: Random, 1984.

Ward, Mrs Humphry. *A Writer's Recollections.* London: W. Collins, 1918.

Wells, H. G. 'A Slum Novel'. *Saturday Review*, 82 (28 November 1896): 573.

Wilde, Oscar. *The Picture of Dorian Gray.* 1891; reprint Harmondsworth: Penguin, 1985.

Wilde, Oscar. *Salome* (1894), in Richard Aldington (ed.), *The Portable Oscar Wilde.* New York: Penguin, 1978.

Wilde, Oscar. *The First Collected Edition of the Works of Oscar Wilde, 1908–1922.* Robert Ross (ed.). London: Methuen and Co., 1908 and London: Dawsons of Pall Mall, 1969.

Wilde, Oscar. *The Selected Letters of Oscar Wilde.* Ed. Rupert Hart-Davis. Oxford and New York: Oxford University Press, 1979.

Wilde, Oscar. *More Letters of Oscar Wilde.* Ed. Rupert Hart-Davis. Oxford: Oxford University Press, 1987.

Wilson, Rev S. Law. *The Theology of Modern Fiction.* Edinburgh: T. and T. Clark, 1899.

Yeats, W. B. *Autobiographies.* London: Macmillan, 1955.

Yeats, W. B. *Essays and Introductions.* London: Macmillan, 1974.

Yeats, W. B. *Collected Poems.* London: Macmillan, 1981.

Yeats, W. B. *Letters to the New Island.* London: Macmillan, 1989.

Yeats, W. B., and Kinsella, Thomas. *Davis, Mangan, Ferguson? Tradition and the Irish Writer.* Dublin: Dolmen Press, 1970.

TEXTS RELATING TO THE *FIN DE SIÈCLE*

Adams, James Eli. 'Gentleman, Dandy, Priest: Manliness and Social Authority in Pater's Aestheticism'. *ELH*, 59 (1992): 441–466.

Adams, James Eli. 'Pater's Muscular Aestheticism', in Donald E. Hall (ed.), *Muscular Christianity: Reading and Writing the (Male) Social Body.* Cambridge: Cambridge University Press, forthcoming.

Adderley, Rev James. *In Slums and Society.* London: T. Fisher Unwin, 1916.

Allen, Reginald. *The First Night Gilbert and Sullivan.* New York: Heritage Press, 1958.

Ardis, Ann L. *New Women, New Novels: Feminism and Early Modernism*. New Brunswick and London: Rutgers University Press, 1990.

Baily, Leslie. *The Gilbert and Sullivan Book*. London: Cassell and Co. Ltd., 1952.

Banta, Martha. *Henry James and The Occult: The Great Extension*. Bloomington: Indiana University Press, 1972.

Bartlett, Neil. *Who Was That Man? A Present for Mr Oscar Wilde*. London: Serpent's Tail, 1988.

Beckson, Karl (ed.). *Oscar Wilde: The Critical Heritage*. London and New York: Oxford University Press, 1970.

Bettany, F. G. *Stewart Headlam: A Biography*. London: J. Murray, 1926.

Bjorhovde, Gerd. *Rebellious Structures: Women Writers and the Crisis of the Novel*. Oslo: Norwegian University Press, 1987.

Boos, Florence and Silver, Carole G. (eds.). *Socialism and the Literary Artistry of William Morris*. Columbia and Missouri: University of Missouri Press, 1990.

Borowitz, Albert I. 'Gilbert and Sullivan on Corporate Law.' *American Bar Association Journal*, 59 (November 1973): 1276–1281.

Boumelha, Penny. *Thomas Hardy and Women*. Brighton: Harvester Press, 1982.

Bowlby, Rachel. *Just Looking*. London: Methuen, 1985.

Brandon, Ruth. *The New Women and the Old Men*. London: Secker and Warburg, 1990.

Brantlinger, Patrick. *Rule of Darkness: British Literature and Imperialism, 1830–1914*. Ithaca, N.Y.: Cornell University Press, 1988.

Brown, Malcolm. *The Politics of Irish Literature from Thomas Davis to W. B. Yeats*. London: George Allen and Unwin Ltd., 1972.

Buerger, Janet E. *The Last Decade: The Emergence of Art Photography in the 1890s*. New York: International Museum of Photography, 1984.

Cameron, Sharon. *Thinking in Henry James*. Chicago: University of Chicago Press, 1989.

Cannadine, David. 'Gilbert and Sullivan: The Making and Un-Making of a British "Tradition"', in Roy Porter (ed.), *Myths of the English*. Cambridge: Polity Press, 1992, pp. 12–32.

Cannadine, David. 'The Context, Performance and Meaning of Ritual: The British Monarchy and the "Invention of Tradition", c. 1820–1977', in Eric Hobsbawm and Terence Ranger (eds.), *The Invention of Tradition*. Cambridge: Cambridge University Press, 1983.

Carter, Margaret (ed.). *Dracula: The Vampire and the Critics*. Ann Arbor and London: U.M.I. Research Press, 1988.

Case, Sue Ellen. 'Tracking the Vampire', *Differences*, 3: 2 (Summer 1991).

Chamberlain, Edward J. and Gilman, Sander L. *Degeneration: The Dark Side of Progress*. New York: Columbia University Press, 1985.

Chapman, E. M. *English Literature and Religion: 1800–1900*. London: Constable, 1910.

Chauncey, George. 'From Sexual Inversion to Homosexuality.' *Salmagundi*, 58–59 (1982–1983): 114–46.

Chrisman, Laura. 'Allegory, Feminist Thought and the Dreams of Olive Schreiner', in Tony Brown (ed.), *Edward Carpenter and Late-Victorian Radicalism*. London: Frank Cass, 1990.

Chrisman, Laura. 'Colonialism and Feminism in Olive Schreiner's 1890s Fiction'. *English in Africa*, 20: 1 (May 1993).

Claeys, Gregory. *Citizens and Saints: Politics and Anti-Politics in Early British Socialism*. Cambridge: Cambridge University Press, 1989.

Cohen, Ed. 'Writing Gone Wilde: Homoerotic Desire in the Closet of Representation.' *PMLA*, 102: 5 (October 1987): 801–13.

Cohen, Ed. 'Foucauldian Necrologies: "Gay" "Politics"? Politically Gay?' *Textual Practice*, 2: 1 (Spring 1988).

Cohen, Ed. 'Legislating the Norm: From Sodomy to Gross Indecency'. *South Atlantic Quarterly*, 88: 1 (Winter 1989): 181–218.

Cohen, Ed. *Talk on the Wilde Side*. London and New York: Routledge, 1993.

Colls, Robert and Dodd, Philip (eds.). *Englishness: Politics and Culture 1880–1920*. London and Sydney: Croom Helm, 1987.

Cominos, Peter. 'Late Victorian Respectability and the Social System.' *International Review of Social History*, 8 (1963): 18–48 and 216–50.

Craft, Christopher. '"Kiss Me With Those Red Lips": Gender and Inversion in Bram Stoker's *Dracula*', in Elaine Showalter (ed.), *Speaking of Gender*. New York and London: Routledge, 1989, pp. 216–242.

Davin, Anna. 'Imperialism and Motherhood'. *History Workshop*, 5 (Spring 1978).

Davis, Tracy C. 'The Savoy Chorus'. *Theatre Notebook*, 44 (1990): 26–38.

Dijkstra, Bram. *Idols of Perversity: Fantasies of Feminine Evil in the Fin de Siècle*. New York: Oxford University Press, 1986.

Dowling, Linda. 'The Decadent and the New Woman in the 1890s'. *Nineteenth-Century Fiction*, 33 (1979): 434–453.

Dowling, Linda. *Language and Decadence in the Victorian Fin de Siècle*. Princeton: Princeton University Press, 1986.

Duncan, E. E. 'Some Sources of *Chance*'. *Review of English Studies*, 20 (1969): 468–71.

Ellmann, Richard (ed.). *Edwardians and Late Victorians*. New York: Columbia University Press, 1960.

Ellmann, Richard. *Oscar Wilde*. Harmondsworth: Penguin, 1988.

Faber, Richard. *The Vision and the Need: Late-Victorian Imperialist Aims*. London: Faber and Faber, 1966.

Fletcher, Ian. *Decadence and the 1890s*. London: Edward Arnold, 1979.

Foster, R. F. 'Anglo-Irish Literature, Gaelic Nationalism and Irish Politics in the 1890s', in *Ireland After the Union: proceedings of the second joint meeting of the Royal Irish Academy and the British Academy, London, 1986*. Oxford: Oxford University Press, 1989.

Foster, R. F. 'Protestant Magic: W. B. Yeats and the Spell of Irish History'. *Proceedings of the British Academy*, LXXV (1989): 243–266.

Gagnier, Regenia. *Idylls of the Marketplace: Oscar Wilde and the Victorian Public*. Stanford: Stanford University Press, 1986; Hampshire, UK: Scolar, 1986.

Gilbert, Sandra and Gubar, Susan. *No Man's Land. The Place of the Woman Writer in the Twentieth Century*, vol. 2: 'Sexchanges'. London: Yale University Press, 1989.

Glut, Donald. *The Dracula Book*. Metuchen, N.J.: The Scarecrow Press, 1975.

Goldberg, Isaac. *The Story of Gilbert and Sullivan*. New York: Simon and Schuster, 1928.

Goode, John. 'Margaret Harkness and the Socialist Novel', in Gustave Klaus (ed.), *The Socialist Novel in Britain*. Brighton: Harvester Press, 1982.

Graves, Richard Perceval. *A. E. Housman, The Scholar-Poet*. Oxford: Oxford University Press, 1981.

Grosskurth, Phyllis. *Havelock Ellis*. London: Allen Lane, 1980.

Grosskurth, Phyllis. *John Addington Symonds*. London: Longmans, 1964.

Guerard, Albert J. *Conrad the Novelist*. Cambridge, Mass.: Harvard University Press, 1966.

Halliday, R. J. 'Social Darwinism: A Definition.' *Victorian Studies*, 14 (1971).

Harfe, Simon. *Fin de Siècle: The Illustrators of the '90s*. London: Barrie and Jenkins, 1992.

Harris, Frank. *Oscar Wilde*. 1916; reprint New York: Dorset Press, 1989.

Harris, Ruth. *Murders and Madness: Medicine, Law and Society in the Fin de Siècle*. Oxford: Clarendon, 1989.

Heaney, Seamus. 'A tale of two islands: reflections on the Irish Literary Revival'. *Irish Studies*, 1 (1980): 1–20.

Helyar, James (ed). *Gilbert and Sullivan (Papers Presented at the International Conference)*. Lawrence, Kan.: University of Kansas Libraries, 1971.

Herbert, Christopher. *Culture and Anomie: Ethnographic Imagination in the Nineteenth Century*. Chicago: University of Chicago Press, 1991.

Hobsbawm, Eric. *Industry and Empire*. Harmondsworth: Penguin, 1969.

Hobsbawm, Eric. *The Age of Empire: 1875–1914*. London: Weidenfeld and Nicolson, 1987.

Holland, Laurence Bedwell. *The Expense of Vision: Essays in the Craft of Henry James*. Princeton: Princeton University Press, 1964.

Holmes, Colin. *Anti-Semitism in British Society, 1876–1939*. New York: Holmes and Meier Publishers Inc., 1979.

Holzman, Michael. 'Propaganda, Passion and Literary Art in William Morris's *The Pilgrims of Hope*'. *Texas Studies in Literature and Language*, 24 (1982): 372–393.

Huberman, Jeffrey H. *Late-Victorian Farce*. Ann Arbor, Michigan: UMI Research Press, 1986.

Hutchins, Stanley. 'The Communard Exiles in Britain'. *Marxism Today*, 15 (1971): 90–92.

Hyam, Ronald. *Empire and Sexuality: The British Experience*. Manchester: Manchester University Press, 1990.

Jackson, Holbrook. *The Eighteen Nineties*. 1913; reprint London: The Cresset Library, 1988.

James, Henry. *The Art of the Novel*. New York: Charles Scribner's Sons, 1934.

James, Henry. *Henry James: Letters*, vol. 4: 1895–1916. Leon Edel (ed.). Cambridge, Mass.: Harvard University Press, 1984.

Jones, Greta. *Social Darwinism and English Thought: The Interaction Between Biological and Social Theory*. Brighton: Harvester Press, 1980.

Jones, John Bush (ed.). *W. S. Gilbert: A Century of Scholarship and Commentary*. New York: New York University Press, 1970.

Kapp, Yvonne. *Eleanor Marx: Family Life, 1855–1883*. London: Virago, 1979.

Kelly, John. 'The Fall of Parnell and the Rise of Irish Literature: An Investigation'. *Anglo-Irish Studies*, 11 (1976): 1–23.

Kelly, John and Domville, Eric (eds.). *The Collected Letters of W. B. Yeats*, vol. 1: 1865–1895. Oxford: Oxford University Press, 1986.

Kennedy, Hurbert. *Ulrichs*. Boston: Alyson, 1988.

Kern, Stephen. *The Culture of Time and Space 1880–1918*. Cambridge, Mass.: Harvard University Press, 1983.

Leatherdale, Clive. *Dracula: The Novel and the Legend*. Wellingborough, Northamptonshire: The Aquarian Press, 1985.

Lynd, Helen Merrell. *England in the Eighteen-Eighties*. London: Frank Cass, 1968.

McCracken, Scott. 'Writing the Body: Edward Carpenter, George Gissing and Late Nineteenth-Century Realism', in *Prose Studies*, 13: 1 (May 1990): 178–200.

McCracken, Scott. 'A Hard and Absolute Condition of Existence: Reading Masculinity in *Lord Jim*', in Andrew Michael Roberts (ed.), *Conrad and Gender*. Amsterdam: Rodopi, 1993, pp. 17–38.

Mackail, J. W. *The Life of William Morris*. London: Longman's, 1932.

Marsh, Jan. *Back to the Land: The Pastoral Impulse in England, from 1880 to 1914*. London: Quartet, 1982.

Matthiessen, F. O. (ed.). *The James Family*. New York: Vintage, 1980.

Morris, May. *William Morris: Artist, Writer, Socialist. Volume the Second: Morris as a Socialist*. Oxford: Basil Blackwell, 1936.

Morton, A. L. 'Britain and the Paris Commune'. *Marxism Today*, 15: 3, (1971): 82–86.

Moser, Thomas. *Joseph Conrad: Achievement and Decline*. Cambridge, Mass.: Harvard University Press, 1957.

Munich, Adrienne. '"Capture the Heart of a Queen": Gilbert and Sullivan's Rites of Conquest'. *The Centennial Review*, 28 (1984): 23–44.

Munich, Adrienne. 'Queen Victoria, Empire, and Excess'. *Tulsa Studies in Women's Literature*, 6 (1987): 265–281.

North, Michael. *The Political Aesthetic of Yeats, Eliot and Pound*. Cambridge: Cambridge University Press, 1991.

O'Brien, Conor Cruise. 'Passion and Cunning: An Essay on the Politics of W. B. Yeats', in A. Norman Jeffares and K. G. W. Cross (eds.), *In Excited Reverie: A Centenary Tribute to William Butler Yeats 1865–1939*. London: Macmillan, 1965.

O'Day, Alan. *The English Face of Irish Nationalism: Parnellite Involvement in British Politics, 1880–1886*. Dublin: Gill and Macmillan, 1977.

Owen, Alex. *The Darkened Room: Women, Power and Spiritualism in Late Victorian England*. London: Virago, 1989.

Page, Norman. *A. E. Housman, A Critical Biography*. Basingstoke: Macmillan, 1983.

Pick, Daniel. *Faces of Degeneration*. Cambridge: Cambridge University Press, 1989.

Przybylowicz, Donna. Review of Paul B. Armstrong, *The Phenomenology of Henry James. Henry James Review*, 7: 1 (Autumn 1985): 49.

Regan, Stephen. '"Oil and Blood": Yeats's Return to the Nineties'. *Yeats Annual* 7. London: Macmillan, 1990.

Roberts, Andrew Michael (ed.). *Conrad and Gender*. Amsterdam: Rodopi, 1993.

Roth, Phyllis. 'Suddenly Sexual Women in Bram Stoker's *Dracula*'. *Literature and Psychology*, 17: 3 (1977): 113–121.

Rowbotham, Sheila, and Weeks, Jeffrey. *Socialism and the New Life*. London: Pluto Press, 1977.

Rowell, George. *Theatre in the Age of Irving*. Totowa, N.J.: Rowman and Littlefield, 1981.

Rubinstein, David. *Before the Suffragettes*. Brighton: Harvester Press, 1986.

Said, Edward. *Yeats and Decolonization*. Derry: Field Day, 1988.

Semmel, Bernard. *Imperialism and Social Reform: English Social-Imperial Thought, 1895–1914*. London: Allen and Unwin, 1960.

Senf, Carol A. '*Dracula*; Stoker's response to the New Woman'. *Victorian Studies*, 26 (1982).

Senf, Carol A. *The Vampire in Nineteenth Century English Literature*. Bowling Green State: Popular Press, 1988.

Showalter, Elaine. *Sexual Anarchy: Gender and Culture at the Fin de Siècle*. New York: Viking, 1990; and London: Bloomsbury, 1991.

Smith-Rosenberg, Caroll. 'Discourses of Sexuality and Subjectivity: the New Woman 1870–1936', in Martin Duberman, Martha Vicinus and George Chauncey (eds.), *Hidden From History: Reclaiming the Gay and Lesbian Past*. Harmondsworth: Penguin 1991.

Stedman, Jane W. 'From Dame to Woman: W. S. Gilbert and Theatrical Transvestism'. *Victorian Studies*, 4 (1970): 27–46.

Stedman, Jane W. 'Gilbert's Stagecraft: Little Blocks of Wood', in James Helyar (ed.), *Gilbert and Sullivan*. Lawrence, Kan.: University of Kansas Libraries, 1971.

Stephens, John Russell. *The Profession of the Playwright: British Theatre 1800–1900*. Cambridge: Cambridge University Press, 1992.

Stevenson, John Allen. 'A Vampire in the Mirror: The Sexuality of *Dracula*'. *PMLA*, 103: 2 (March 1988): 139–149.

Stokes, John. *In the Nineties*. Hemel Hempstead: Harvester Wheatsheaf, 1989.

Stokes, John. *Fin de Siècle, Fin du Globe: Fears and Fantasies of the Late Nineteenth Century*. Basingstoke: Macmillan, 1992.

Sussman, Herbert. 'Masculinity Transformed: Appropriation in Walter Pater's Early Writing'. Chapter in book ms.

Sutton, Max Keith. *W. S. Gilbert*. Boston: Twayne, 1975.

Teich, Mikulas and Porter, Roy. *Fin de Siècle and its Legacy*. Cambridge: Cambridge University Press, 1990.

Thomas, Keith. 'The Double Standard'. *Journal of the History of Ideas*, 20: 2 (April 1959): 195–216.

Thompson, Edward. *William Morris: Romantic to Revolutionary*. London: Lawrence and Wishart, 1955.

Thompson, Edward. *William Morris: Romantic to Revolutionary*. 2nd edn; London: Merlin Press, 1976.

Thornton, R. K. R. *The Decadent Dilemma*. London: Edward Arnold, 1983.

Tsuzuki, C. H. M. *Hyndman and British Socialism*. Oxford: Oxford University Press, 1961.

Vicinus, Martha. *Independent Women: Work and Community for Single Women 1850–1920*. London: Virago, 1985.

Walkowitz, Judith R. *City of Dreadful Delight: Narratives of Sexual Danger in Late-Victorian London*. Chicago: University of Chicago Press, 1992.

Watson, G. J. *Irish Identity and the Literary Revival*. London: Croom Helm, 1978.

Watts, Cedric. *Joseph Conrad: A Literary Life*. London: Macmillan, 1989.

Weissman, Judith. 'Bram Stoker: Semidemons and Secretaries' in *Half Savage and Hardy and Free*. Middleton, Connecticut: Wesleyan University Press, 1987.

Weissman, Judith. 'Women and Vampires: *Dracula* as a Victorian Novel'. *Midwest Quarterly*, 18: 4 (Summer 1977).

Willis, Kirk. 'The Introduction and Critical Reception of Marxist Thought in Britain, 1850–1900'. *The Historical Journal*, 20 (1977): 417–459.

Wilson, Fredric Woodbridge. *An Introduction to the Gilbert and Sullivan Operas from the Collection of the Pierpont Morgan Library*. New York: The Pierpont Morgan Library in association with Dover Publications, Inc., 1989.

Wolfson, John. *Final Curtain: The Last Gilbert and Sullivan Operas*. London: Chappell and Co. in association with Andre Deutsch, 1976.

Index